T0360403

Investment in Startups
— and —
Small Business Financing

*To view the complete list of the published volumes in the series, please visit:
www.worldscientific.com/series/wssf

World Scientific Series
in FINANCE vol. 17

Investment in Startups
———— and ————
Small Business Financing

Editors

Farhad Taghizadeh-Hesary
Tokai University, Japan

Naoyuki Yoshino
Keio University, Japan

Chul Ju Kim
Asian Development Bank Institute, Japan

Peter J Morgan
Asian Development Bank Institute, Japan

Daehee Yoon
Korea Credit Guarantee Fund, South Korea

World Scientific

NEW JERSEY · LONDON · SINGAPORE · BEIJING · SHANGHAI · HONG KONG · TAIPEI · CHENNAI · TOKYO

Published by

World Scientific Publishing Co. Pte. Ltd.

5 Toh Tuck Link, Singapore 596224

USA office: 27 Warren Street, Suite 401-402, Hackensack, NJ 07601

UK office: 57 Shelton Street, Covent Garden, London WC2H 9HE

British Library Cataloguing-in-Publication Data
A catalogue record for this book is available from the British Library.

World Scientific Series in Finance — Vol. 17
INVESTMENT IN STARTUPS AND SMALL BUSINESS FINANCING

Copyright © 2021 by Asian Development Bank Institute (ADBI)

ISBN 978-981-123-581-8 (hardcover)
ISBN 978-981-123-582-5 (ebook for institutions)
ISBN 978-981-123-583-2 (ebook for individuals)

For any available supplementary material, please visit
https://www.worldscientific.com/worldscibooks/10.1142/12246#t=suppl

Desk Editor: Sandhya Venkatesh

Typeset by Stallion Press
Email: enquiries@stallionpress.com

Printed in Singapore

About the Editors

Farhad Taghizadeh-Hesary is an Associate Professor of economics at Tokai University in Japan and a Visiting Professor at Keio University in Tokyo, Japan. He is a grantee of the Excellent Young Researcher (LEADER) status from the Ministry of Education of Japan (MEXT). He taught as an Assistant Professor at Keio University and Waseda University, Tokyo, Japan. He was a Visiting Professor/Visiting Scholar at the University of Tokyo, Griffith University (Australia), University of Tasmania (Australia), and The Institute of Energy Economics of Japan (IEEJ). He is currently serving as Editor of *Cognet Business & Management* and Associate Editor/Board Member of *Energy Efficiency, Singapore Economic Review, Global Finance Journal,* and *Frontiers in Energy Research.* He has guest-edited special issues for prestigious journals, including *Energy Policy, Energy Economics, Finance Research Letters* and *Journal of Environmental Management.* His research credits include authoring more than 150 academic journal papers and book chapters and editing 10 books published by renowned publishers, including Springer, Routledge, and World Scientific. He holds a PhD in economics from Keio University with a scholarship from the Government of Japan (MEXT).

Naoyuki Yoshino is Professor Emeritus of Keio University in Tokyo, Japan, and Director of Financial Research Center (FSA Institute, Government of Japan). He obtained a PhD from Johns Hopkins University in 1979, where his thesis supervisor was Sir Alan Walters (UK Prime Minister Margaret Thatcher's Economic Adviser). He worked as Assistant Professor at the State University of New York at Buffalo, Visiting scholar at MIT (United States), Visiting Scholar at the Central Bank of Japan,

Visiting Professor at the University of New South Wales (Australia), Fondation Nationale des Sciences Politiques (France). He received Honorary Doctorates from the University of Gothenburg (Sweden) and Martin Luther University of Halle-Wittenberg (Germany). He was also conferred the Fukuzawa award from Keio University for his contribution to research. He was the Dean & CEO of the Asian Development Bank Institute (ADBI) in Tokyo (2014–2020).

A national of the Republic of Korea, **Chul Ju Kim** has been a key policy maker for the Government of the Republic of Korea, dealing with a wide range of policy issues in areas of macroeconomic, financial, industrial, and social sectors for more than 30 years. Before joining ADBI as Deputy Dean in 2017, he was a secretary to the country's President for economic and financial affairs, one of the key positions in the Republic of Korea's bureaucracy. He has assumed various important positions at the Korean Ministry of Economy and Finance, including deputy minister for planning and coordination, director general of the Economic Policy Bureau, and director general of the Public Policy Bureau. He also has extensive experience in international development, having worked at the World Bank and the Asian Development Bank. He holds a BA in economics from Seoul National University, Republic of Korea, and an MS in finance from Georgia State University, United States.

Peter J. Morgan is Senior Consulting Economist and Vice Chair of Research at the Asian Development Bank Institute (ADBI), and has been with ADBI since 2008. He has 23 years experience in the financial sector in Asia, most recently serving in Hong Kong, China as Chief Asia Economist for HSBC, responsible for macroeconomic analysis and forecasting for Asia. Previously, he served as Chief Japan Economist for HSBC, and earlier held similar positions at Merrill Lynch, Barclays de Zoete Wedd, and Jardine Fleming. Prior to entering the financial industry, he was a consultant for Meta Systems Inc in Cambridge, MA, in energy and environmental analysis, and at International Business Information KK in Tokyo, in financial sector consulting. He earned his MA and PhD degrees in economics from Yale University. His research interests are in macroeconomic policy and financial sector regulation, reform, financial development, financial inclusion, fintech, financial literacy, and financial education.

Daehee Yoon is currently the Chairman & CEO of Korea Credit Guarantee Fund (KODIT). He has over 40 years' experience in the economic sector as a government official. He was a Senior Presidential Secretary for Economic Affairs and served as Minister of the Office for Government Policy Coordination of the Republic of Korea. After his career as Minister, he moved to Gachon University in the Republic of Korea where he taught economics as a Chair Professor until he was appointed as the Chairman & CEO of KODIT. He holds a BA degree in economics from the Seoul National University, an MA degree in economics from the University of Kansas, and a PhD in economics from the Kyung Hee University.

Introduction: Investment in Startups and Small Business Financing

Farhad Taghizadeh-Hesary*, Naoyuki Yoshino[†],
Chul Ju Kim[‡], Peter J. Morgan[§] and Daehee Yoon[¶]

*Tokai University, Japan
[†]Keio University, Japan
[‡]Asian Development Bank Institute, Japan
[§]Asian Development Bank Institute, Japan
[¶]Korea Credit Guarantee Fund, Republic of Korea

Successful startup businesses can play a significant role in economic growth and job creation. They also contribute to economic dynamism by spurring innovation and injecting competition. Startups are known to introduce new products and services that can create new value in the economy. If startups can survive and become giants, they can have significant roles in job creation. It is notable that most startups exit within their first ten years and most surviving young businesses do not grow but remain small (Yoshino and Taghizadeh-Hesary, 2019a).

However, a small fraction of young firms exhibit very high growth and contribute substantially to job creation. These high-growth firms such as unicorns (startups valued at over US$1 billion) make up for nearly all of the job losses associated with shrinking and exiting firms in their cohort. The implication is that each entering cohort of startups makes a long-lasting contribution to net job creation (Decker *et al.*, 2014). Honda, Sony, Toyota, Samsung, and LG are examples of small startup businesses having grown to big companies in Japan and the Republic of Korea.

Nevertheless, not all startups necessarily will become giants and unicorns, but many startups will thrive nonetheless as small or medium-sized enterprises (SMEs) producing novel technologies or high-quality products, and thereby gain trust of customers.

Startups face several obstacles to their development. Accessing capital is a crucial constraint on the development of startups. Most startups have difficulties in getting the funds they need because of their lack of performance track record, making it difficult for lenders or investors to assess their risk. Besides, they are in the early stages of development and face a very high possibility of failure, which significantly raises financing and investment risk.

Venture capital has been developed in the US and other Western countries and has recently emerged in Asia, mainly in the People's Republic of China and India; however, generally venture capital is not so popular in Asia. Banks are the primary source of financing dominating the financial markets in most Asian countries.

In addition to the widespread difficulties faced by startups and SMEs in fundraising from banks, the recent Basel capital accord has made this environment even harsher. Basel III introduced new rules — liquidity frameworks and leverage ratio frameworks — to strengthen banks' risk management while also adopting strengthened capital requirements. These new measures may prevent banks from providing long-term credit to enterprises and limit financing options for startups and SMEs (Yoshino and Taghizadeh-Hesary, 2015).

Given the lack of venture capital and the risk-averse environment in most Asian countries, and considering that banks are often not interested in or not allowed to finance risky businesses and startups, new innovative forms of raising money are needed. One such example is hometown investment trust (HIT) funds that have emerged in Japan as a new form of community-based funding mechanism. HIT funds help the project owners, or the small businesses collect funds from many small investors — similar to "crowdfunding." For example, startups in solar energy or wind power can collect necessary funds from those interested in environmental issues. Each investor contributes a small amount of money (e.g., US$100 or 200 or so) to the project. If they are successful, the principal and dividend will be returned to the investors (Yoshino and Taghizadeh-Hesary, 2019b).

To increase the flow of funds to the startup sector, it is vital to develop a scheme to reduce the information asymmetry between the borrower and the lender or investors, decrease the risk of investment, and increase the rate of return. This will make it easier to lend or invest in startups, and as a result startups can enjoy much improved access to funds. Establishing a technology appraisal system is crucial to assess technology in knowledge-based startups through a techno-economic feasibility study. Not all technologies and startup businesses are worthwhile targets for financing and investment. Therefore, it is essential to assess the level of technology, uniqueness, feasibility, competitiveness, marketability, and several other factors.

For small businesses with financial background and transaction records, various government and donor initiatives have emerged in developed and developing economies to establish credit guarantee schemes (CGSs) to reduce supply-demand gap in the SMEs financing (Yoshino and Taghizadeh-Hesary, 2019c). CGSs have been used in many countries and in various forms over the decades to increase the flow of funds to targeted sectors and segments of the economy, including SMEs. A CGS makes lending more attractive by absorbing or sharing the risks associated with it. A CGS can also increase the amount of funds available to enterprises beyond their collateral limits because the guarantee itself is a form of collateral.

In order to have a financially sustainable CGS, an optimal credit guarantee ratio needs to be set. The credit guarantee ratio is the portion of the loans guaranteed by the CGS. This ratio should be at such a level that it achieves the government's goal of minimizing banks' nonperforming loans to SMEs and realizing the government policy objective of supporting SMEs by reducing information asymmetry. To avoid moral hazard and ensure the stability of lending to SMEs, it is crucial for governments to set the optimal credit guarantee ratio based on macroeconomic conditions and differentiate it for each bank or each group of banks based on their soundness (Yoshino and Taghizadeh-Hesary, 2019d).

On the other hand, to avoid moral hazard, the credit guarantee fee should be also different for sound and unsound SMEs. The credit guarantee fee is the cost that the SMEs need to pay to the credit guarantee corporation for the guarantee coverage. Besides, the credit guarantee fee needs to vary depending on the macroeconomic situation (higher in the economic boom and lower in the recession) (Taghizadeh-Hesary *et al.*, 2020).

During economic recessions and crises like the current era of the COVID-19 pandemic, where the vulnerable sectors such as SMEs are suffering more, governments could and should use the CGS as a policy measure to the extent possible. Governments need to increase the credit guarantee ratio and/or reduce the credit guarantee fee to support SMEs in recovering their losses for survival. This support needs to be continued till the world economy passes the crisis.

Investment in Startups and Small Business Financing provides 12 studies on new methods for bringing private investment (loans or equity) to startups and easing small businesses' access to finance (debt and capital). This book is the outcome of the joint call for papers of the Asian Development Bank Institute and the Korea Credit Guarantee Fund (KODIT) and the conference on investments in startups and small business financing organized on 29–30 January 2020, in Tokyo.

The contributors are senior-level policy experts and researchers from governments, think tanks, academia, and international organizations. The chapters have been authored in a policy-oriented way to be understandable to readers with different backgrounds. It is our hope that this book is a valuable source for governments for adopting the right policies to develop SMEs and startup businesses as well as valuable for researchers in economics, business, and finance.

The chapters are categorized into three parts.

Part I is on the regulatory and policy framework of funding startup businesses and SMEs, and consists of two chapters

Wisuttisak, in Chapter 1, provides a comparative study on the regulatory frameworks for the promotion of startup businesses and SMEs in Japan, the Republic of Korea, Malaysia, and Thailand. The chapter shows different regulatory frameworks that governments in these countries have adopted and the unique challenges they face in stimulating startups and SMEs' finance.

In Chapter 2, Kumar Singh assesses India's startup action plan to provide policy and regulatory changes for a thriving startup ecosystem. Careful consideration of pertinent issues from the policy and regulatory perspective is required for a successful startup revolution. This chapter explores the initiatives that the Government of India has taken and identifies the gaps that require attention from different stakeholders. The chapter also investigates the major challenges and potential solutions arising from the Indian experience of initiatives in the startup revolution.

Part II is on the schemes for fostering investments in startups, and consists of six chapters

In Chapter 3, Kim and Jeon study the case of the Korea Credit Guarantee Fund (KODIT) to show the measures needed to enhance startup financing effectiveness. Recently, in response to the Government of the Republic of Korea's focus on vitalizing the startup ecosystem, startup financing has been gaining further importance. This chapter proposes practical ways to support startup financing by exploring the cases of financing programs managed by KODIT, including Startup NEST, First Penguin guarantee, guarantee with investment option, and Iguarantee. The authors also provide policy recommendations for developing Asian countries to improve startup financing through public programs based on the KODIT experiences.

In Chapter 4, Subramanian and Taghizadeh-Hesary highlight the importance of techno-economic feasibility study in startup financing. The techno-economic feasibility study is an effective method to safeguard against such risks leading to startup failures and the wastage of valuable investment resources. The chapter explores the significance and essence of the techno-economic feasibility study in stepping up the startups' growth and advancement prospects. The study findings provide useful insights into the value of techno-economic feasibility methods and policy implications in advancing startup financing.

In Chapter 5, Eghbalnia analyzes the role of soft infrastructure in fostering startup businesses with difficulties in accessing finance, focusing on a case study in Iran. There are essential soft factors that can establish a strong drive for succeeding and creating high commitment cultures among founders, investors, and employees, and shaping vibrant cultures of survival, growth, and success in firms. The chapter provides an evaluation of such factors in fostering the startups' finance.

In Chapter 6, Vandenberg, Hampel-Milagrosa, and Helble evaluate access to funding for tech startups in four sectors — greentech, agritech, edtech, and healthtech — that are linked directly to the Sustainable Development Goals. Focusing on four countries, Cambodia, India, Thailand, and Viet Nam, the chapter provides insights from interviews with startups, incubators, and other players. They find that tech startups rely on an array of funding sources, while venture capital is not a common source. Besides, greentech and agritech startups produce products that require long-term support through the design, testing, prototyping, and certification stages. Such "patient capital" is in short supply. On the positive side, enterprises in development-oriented sectors can seek funds from impact investors[1] and international development (aid) agencies.

In Chapter 7, David, Gopalan, and Ramachandran assess India's startup environment and funding activity. India has the third-largest startup ecosystem globally with an estimated 26,000 startups, 26 unicorns, and US$36 billion in consolidated investments over 2017–2019. The ecosystem has expanded rapidly, mainly through private investments, including seed, angel, venture capital, private equity, technical support from incubators/accelerators, and public policy. The government has tried to create a conducive environment through its flagship Startup India initiative. Despite the progress made so far, however, Indian startups face enormous challenges. These challenges are evaluated, and policy recommendations are provided, in this chapter.

In Chapter 8, Lee addresses the efficiency of financing mechanisms and tools for SMEs implemented in Kazakhstan through the national SME

---

[1] Impact investment refers to investments made into companies, projects, and funds with the intention to generate a measurable, beneficial social or environmental impact alongside a financial return.

development institute Entrepreneurship Development Fund (Damu). This study considers the data on Damu financing provided to SMEs and their relationship to SMEs' overall contribution to the country's GDP during 2005–2019. The chapter analyzes how Damu has promoted startup business in Kazakhstan; whether such activities have contributed to the country's economic development. If so, through what factors; and whether Damu is overall financially efficient as an organization. How Damu has promoted start-up businesses, and the factors by which micro-financing affects economic development in Kazakhstan.

Part III is on the solutions for easing small businesses' access to finance, and consists of four chapters

In Chapter 9, Chang and Kock highlight CGS's role in filling the SMEs' finance gap compared to four very diverse CGS experiences, namely Germany, Italy, Japan, and the Republic of Korea. These four CGSs had contributed to the economies' dynamic growth, which had been severely decimated in World War II and the Korean war. This chapter also takes stock of the existing CGSs in various Asian countries and seeks to draw valuable lessons for policy implementation from the four CGSs mentioned above.

In Chapter 10, Thaker et al. introduce the potential of Islamic banking and finance for small businesses. Islamic banking and finance is a broad framework that has great potential for supporting development finance, particularly related to small businesses, given their fundamental criteria emphasizing generating positive societal impact. The main objectives covered by this chapter are: (i) to identify and unpack innovative financing opportunities within Islamic banking and financial instruments such as Mudharabah (profit-sharing), Musharakah (profit–loss sharing), Murabahah (sale with cost plus profit margin, Ijarah [Islamic leasing]), and Salam (forward sale) as potential solutions for addressing small businesses' funding gaps; and (ii) to initiate the development of systematic principles for the utilization of such instruments in financing small businesses.

In Chapter 11, Im and Yoon discuss the role of financial technology (FinTech) in improving SMEs' financial access. Towards this aim, the chapter proposes a new infrastructure that enables one to make real-time evaluation of SMEs' current business activities using big data. It also introduces a non-face-to-face service online platform adopted by the KODIT that reduces SMEs' physical difficulties accessing finance and enables 24-hour, 365-day financial service.

In Chapter 12, Kim, Ham, and Cha elaborate on credit guarantee institutions' role in the Fourth Industrial Revolution to contribute to SMEs' development and inclusive growth. The emergence of the Fourth Industrial Revolution and the need for inclusive growth and other environmental changes require further innovation in the CGSs. This chapter reviews KODIT activities and performance to play a new part in this changing environment. The case presented in this chapter provides practical policy implications for the facilitation of SME financing in Asia.

References

Decker, R., J. Haltiwanger, R. Jarmin, and J. Miranda. 2014. The role of entrepreneurship in US job creation and economic dynamism. *Journal of Economic Perspectives*, 28(3): 3–24.

Taghizadeh-Hesary, F., N. Yoshino, L. Fukuda, and E. Rasoulinezhad. 2020. A model for calculating optimal credit guarantee fee for small and medium-sized enterprises. *Economic Modelling,* https://doi.org/10.1016/j.econmod.2020.03.003.

Yoshino, N. and F. Taghizadeh-Hesary. 2015. Analysis of credit risk for small and medium-sized enterprises: Evidence from Asia. *Asian Development Review*, 32(2): 18–37.

Yoshino, N. and F. Taghizadeh-Hesary. 2019a. Application of distributed ledger technologies to improve funding in the startup ecosystem. *Fintech for Asian SMEs*. N. Nemoto, and N. Yoshino Eds. Tokyo: Asian Development Bank Institute.

Yoshino, N. and F. Taghizadeh-Hesary. 2019b. Role of hometown investment trust funds and spillover taxes in unlocking private-sector investment into green projects. *Handbook of Green Finance: Energy Security and Sustainable Development*. J. Sachs, W.T. Woo, N. Yoshino, and F. Taghizadeh-Hesary Eds. Tokyo: Springer.

Yoshino, N. and F. Taghizadeh-Hesary. 2019c. *Unlocking SME Finance in Asia: The Role of Credit Rating and Credit Guarantee Schemes.* Editors: N. Yoshino and F. Taghizadeh-Hesary, ADBI-OECD. London: Routledge.

Yoshino, N. and F. Taghizadeh-Hesary. 2019d. Optimal credit guarantee ratio for small and medium-sized enterprises' financing: Evidence from Asia. *Economic Analysis and Policy*, 62: 342–356.

Contents

Part I

Regulatory and Policy Framework

Chapter 1

Comparative Study on Regulatory Frameworks for Promotion of Startup Businesses and SMEs in Japan, Republic of Korea, Malaysia, and Thailand

Pornchai Wisuttisak

Faculty of law, Chiang Mai University 239 HuayKaew Road,
Muang District, Chiang Mai, Thailand
pornchai.w@cmu.ac.th

Abstract

The vital factors which can facilitate the development of Startups and Small and Medium-Sized Enterprises (SMEs) in markets are the appropriate regulatory and policy frameworks. However, there is a difference in the frameworks which may contribute to different levels of development of startups and SMEs in different countries. This chapter thus focuses on the comparative study of the frameworks of selected countries to display their possible challenges in those countries. The chapter shows that governments in Japan, Republic of Korea, Malaysia, and Thailand adopt different regulatory frameworks which help stimulate the creation of startups and SMEs. It provides comparisons of the frameworks in those four countries, and also presents that there are challenges from these regulatory frameworks for startups and SMEs developing there.

Keywords: Regulation, policy, SMEs, Japan, Republic of Korea, Thailand, Malaysia

1. Introduction

The startups and small and medium-sized enterprises (SMEs) are important drivers for economic and innovation developments. Countries pay attention to formulate and adopt regulatory frameworks, which provided incentives and encouragement to the proliferation of startups and SMEs in. There are also various programs for startups and SMEs that can stimulate overall economic developments. Startups and SMEs are the majority of businesses and can provide significant value-added to economic development (OECD, 2019). Startups and SMEs with the small scale of businesses play an essential role in interacting with communities and creating innovative products and services for customers in a market economy. This is because, with the digitization of the economy, startups and SMEs are the agents of changes from the current market toward a new structure of the market. Governments in countries have to make sure that laws and regulatory frameworks can support the creation of startups and SMEs. Most countries thus adopt their own regulation and policies to encourage startups and SMEs.

This chapter aims to provide comparative studies of regulatory frameworks for SMEs and startups in some major Asian countries. The comparative study would suggest possible development for regulatory frameworks for promotion of startups and SMEs. The chapter focuses on Japan and Republic of Korea, which are high-income countries with high level of development of SMEs and startup, and Malaysia and Thailand, which are upper-middle-income countries with the aim of enhancing their SMEs and startups. In these four countries, the governments have adopted regulations and policies which help encourage their startups and SMEs with the view to improve overall economic productivity and innovation. However, while there are some similarities in their regulatory frameworks for supporting startups and SMEs, there are also some differences. The difference and similarities become the core content of this chapter by focusing on the comparative study of the regulatory frameworks. The comparative study generates an understanding of these regulatory frameworks for startups and SMEs in the four countries. The study also displays different stages of development and challenges from these regulatory frameworks for startups and SMEs. Thus, this chapter adds to academic literature relating to regulations on startups and SMEs in Asia. The chapter also provides recommendations for possible reform on regulatory frameworks in order to promote startups and SMEs.

After the introduction, the second part discusses general ideas on regulation and policies supporting startups and SMEs. The third part of the chapter describes the regulatory and policy frameworks for startups and SMEs' promotion in the four countries. The fourth part discusses the comparative perspectives of the regulatory and policy frameworks in these countries, while the fifth part examines some challenges posed by the regulatory and policy frameworks. The last part concludes the chapter with policy implications for the development of regulatory frameworks for startups and SMEs in the four Asian countries of Japan, Republic of Korea, Malaysia, and Thailand.

2. Regulatory Frameworks Supporting Startups and SMEs

Before discussing regulatory frameworks for startups and SMEs, it is essential to note the definition of startups and SMEs. This chapter defines startups and SMEs as *non-subsidiary, independent firms which employ fewer than 300 employees with the business turnover not exceeding US 50 million* The definition is based on regulations from Japan, Republic of Korea, EU, US, Malaysia, Thailand, and Republic of Korea (MSS Korea, 2019; OECD, 2005; SME Agency Japan, 2019; SMEcorp Malaysia, 2019; Thailand, 2018). In addition, it may be argued that a startup is different from SMEs to the extent that the startup is still an initial stage of business, which can be considered as the temporary business created to search for a repeatable and enlargeable business model (Blank, 2010). However, this chapter considers that startups are under the scope of SMEs' definition as a startup is a small business with an aim to sustain market competition by offering new products or services. In this sense, the startup is not different from small businesses with a similar objective to succeed in the market economy. Thus, in this chapter, the startup as an initial small business is classified under the scope of SMEs.

Startups and SMEs are the vital economic drivers, delivering efficiency and productivity in Asian countries (Yoshino *et al.*, 2019; Yoshino and Taghizadeh-Hesary, 2019; Aboojafari *et al.*, 2019). SMEs are accounted as more than 96% of all Asian businesses and they contribute to significant private-sector jobs in Asia. In OECD economies (Yoshino and Taghizadeh-Hesary, 2019), startups and SMEs are the primary source of job creation and represent in the business sectors almost the totality of the businesses (OECD, 2019). Startups and SMEs are vehicles for entrepreneurship, giving employment and social stability, innovation and market competition (Thurik, 2004). In general, SMEs contribute to more than one-third of GDP in developing countries and account for 52% employment (OECD, 2018). According to the International Labour Organization's World Employment and Social Outlook, globally startups and SMEs, from 2003 through 2016, account for 79 million to 156 million full-time employees (ILO, 2018). The increase led to the improvement in countries level of economic development and the change of economic structure by the reduction of poverty (ILO, 2018). Governments in countries have to craft effective regulatory and policy frameworks for supporting startups and SMEs. The frameworks are in terms of; special assistance for establishment of startups and SMEs, tax exemption and incentives, specific laws and regulation permitting governmental support, training and information for startups and SMEs, initial grants, research grants, financial support, and investment matching. Governments, with their aim to increase startups and SMEs, adopt regulatory frameworks for promoting establishment of startups and SME. Governments also shape their regulatory frameworks as to assure that the regulatory frameworks are not barriers for startups and SMEs to begin their business journey in markets. Governments may provide knowledge center and training on how the startups and SMEs can proceed with the regulatory process in order to obtain initial registration for their businesses (OECD, 2020).

Besides, tax exemption and incentives are a vital part of regulatory and policy frameworks for facilitating startups and SMEs. All businesses pay great attention to tax compliance because tax is the vital legal cost for their businesses. Startups and SMEs must make sure that in doing their businesses, they are tax compliant and able to pay taxes. Countries to build up startups and SMEs may provide essay tax compliant schemes or tax exemption so as to encourage startups and SMEs (Kamleitner, 2012). In EU, tax is used as an incentive for SMEs by the way of preferential tax rates and reduction of tax liability (Bergner *et al.*, 2017). The incentive is to support the creation and operation of SMEs. OECD and EU countries have also adopted tax incentives for venture capital and to foster the investment of SMEs and startups. The objective of the tax incentive under the venture capital is to make sure that there is sufficient capital directed to startups and SMEs (European Commission, 2017).

Passage of specific laws and regulations relating to startups and SMEs is also a vital mechanism for supporting startups and SMEs. Various countries have passed specific laws and regulations in order to establish specific government agencies for SMEs and use legal text suggesting the promotion of SMEs. In their report, Binh et al (Binh *et al.*, 2017) show that various countries adopted specific laws in order to build up regulatory frameworks for promoting startups and SMEs. Specific laws are assigned as the underlying mechanisms for ensuring that SMEs have special preference and support from government. The laws and regulations to some extent direct government agencies to formulate economic policies which facilitate startups and SMEs' development. In some cases, the specific laws and regulations link with the government budgets to feed-in grants for startups and SMEs.

Startups and SMEs can also have special financial access in terms of seed funding, startup grants, special loans, venture capital, and loan guarantees. The access to financial support is to encourage their initial set up or research for innovation (OECD, 2012). The example from US is that the office of small business administration cooperates with various organizations to offer grants to SMEs (US SBA, 2020). In some cases, the grant can lead to venture capital deals between startup SMEs and large corporates. In EU, grants and income subsidies are provided for startups and SMEs to stimulate entrepreneurial activity (OECD, 2014).

The financial access and support are the key elements because startups and SMEs in many cases lack finance for maintaining their businesses. Governments tend to issue various regulations and policies which require financial institutions to provide loan schemes for startups and SMEs. To some extent, governments regulate SMEs' credit guarantee system which can be a vital financial support to startups and SMEs because in most of the cases startups and SMEs lack collateral assets for loan guarantees resulting in difficulties in raising money for their businesses (OECD, 2014; Yoshino and Taghizadeh-Hesary, 2015).

To avoid asymmetric information distribution, governments provide training and consultation courses for startups and SMEs. Startups and SMEs' lack of business information can lead to inability to keep up with the changing markets (Yoshino and Taghizadeh-Hesary, 2016). Government provided training and consultative courses are to ensure that startups and SMEs can at least obtain business knowledge to equally compete with large corporates in markets. Startups and SMEs are reluctant to invest in training themselves because some training requires higher costs and some training courses do not answer specific needs of SMEs (Jayawarna, 2007). Additionally, startups and SMEs in pursuing their businesses are no different from large corporates in having to understand accounting and tax report, human resource management, financial management of costs and benefits, IT, and other know-hows of specific business sectors. Governments in this regard become supporters that provide training and consultative schemes for business sustainability of startups and SMEs (Farvaque *et al.*, 2009).

Governments in most countries utilize variety of regulations and policies that can be combined as a supportive framework for startups and SMEs. However, with increasing attention to research and innovation, governments tend to gear up their support to startups and SMEs with the agendas to tap into the new research frontier and commercialization of innovation (Bellavitis *et al.*, 2017). Governments, while adhering with the variety of regulations and policies supporting SMEs, ensure that the regulations and policies stimulate innovation and research from the startups and SMEs. In some cases, the governments play vital roles to bridge startups, research from academic institutions, and venture capitals to develop new businesses (Croce *et al.*, 2014). Startups and SMEs are incentivized to innovate new products and services to meet market demand, and equip their business to achieve technological advancement (Intarakumnerd and Goto, 2016). The regulatory frameworks provide support to startups and SMEs' development, but the recent trend has been to have the framework pay more attention to supporting the startup businesses and technological innovation.

3. Regulatory Frameworks for Startups and SMEs' Promotion in Japan, Republic of Korea, Malaysia, and Thailand

This section aims to explore the regulatory frameworks for startups and SMEs' promotion in Japan, Republic of Korea, Malaysia and Thailand.

3.1 *Regulatory Frameworks for Startups and SMEs' Promotion in Japan*

The consideration over SMEs' development in Japan started in 1945, when the government adopted Basic tools for SMEs Policies (SMEA Japan, 2020). In 1948, the government established the Small and Medium Enterprise Agency as the leading agency having a duty to initiate SMEs' policy and support SMEs' developments (SMEA Japan, 2020). The agency initiated various policies for SMEs which encourage SMEs' development in Japan. The government also adopted the specific law for SMEs, namely "Small and Medium-Sized Enterprise Cooperatives Act" (Act No. 181 of June 1, 1949). The purpose of the act is to support SMEs to secure business opportunity and to maintain fair economic activities for improvement of the Japanese economy. The government also initiated the tax reform which facilitates simple bookkeeping and merits of a tax return. The reform on the tax system contributed to the improvement of financial accounting and the strengthening of SMEs' financial systems (SMEA Japan, 2020). The Japanese economy, during 1955–1972, experienced significant booms with the increase of SMEs, which played an important role in stimulating economic growth during the period (Sato, 1989). Government, by adoption of economic regulations and plans, supported the increase of SMEs under the consideration that SMEs are important to achieve economic efficiency and productivity (Matsushima, 2001). In 1963, the Japanese government issued the Small and Medium-sized Enterprise Basic Act (No. 154 of 1963) with the objective to create (Article 1):

> *comprehensive manner measures for small and medium enterprises by establishing the basic principles, basic policies and other basic matters relating to measures for SMEs and clarifying the responsibilities, etc. of the State and of local public entities, so as to contribute to the sound development of the national economy and improvement in the quality of life of the people.*

By relying on legal texts from the SMEs Basic Act 1963, the government planned and implemented promotional measures, supportive financial schemes, and consultative programs for SMEs. The government later amended the SMEs Basic Act 1963 in 1999 to ensure that the legal underlining can keep up with the rapid changes of startup SMEs. The 1999 Amendment (Article 1) led to essential changes of supportive government schemes by the inclusion of:

> —*Promoting business innovation and startups, and promoting creative business activity among SMEs;*
> —*Strengthening the business fundamentals of SMEs by facilitating the acquisition of business resources by SMEs and improving the fairness of transactions involving SMEs, etc.;*
> —*Smoothing adaptation to changes in the economic or social environments by promoting the business stability and facilitating the business conversion of SMEs in response to such changes, etc.;*
> —*Facilitating the financing of SMEs and enhancing the equity capital of SMEs.*

By the adoption of the SMEs Basic Act 1963 and the amendment in 1999, it is seen that the Japanese government focused attention on supporting SMEs and the government kept up on regulatory changes so as to make sure that regulations serve the promotion of SMEs. The importance of the 1999 amendment is that the government initially recognized it necessary to move SMEs' schemes toward startups under the flexible regulatory and policy frameworks. Nevertheless, Japan has not only stipulated specific laws and regulations to support startups and SMEs, it also provided policies as a tool to promote startups and SMEs. The current supportive frameworks for startups and SMEs in Japan are according to the following Table 1;

In addition to the existing support listed in Table 1, the Japanese government started the startup called "J-Startup," directed to attract and

Table 1:   Regulatory Framework for Startups and SMEs in Japan

Major SME Regulations and Policies	Supporting Schemes
Management Support	• Startups and ventures • Business innovation • New collaboration • Business revitalization • Employment and human resources • Globalization • Trade practices and public procurement • Business stability • Mutual aid system • Small and medium manufacturers • Technological innovation, IT, and energy efficiency • Intellectual property • SME Assistance Centers
Financial Support	• Safety-net guarantee program • Safety-net loans
Fiscal Support	• Taxation advice and support • Accounting • Advice on Companies Act • Advice on Business succession
Commerce and Regional Support	• Revitalization of commerce • Improve Regional industries • Collaboration between agriculture, commerce, and industry • Knowledge sharing by "Meet and Experience Regional Attractiveness" campaign

Source: SMEA Japan (2020).

incubate internationally competitive and winning startups to stay in Japan (METI Japan, 2020b). The J-startup also encourages private sector to support the establishment of startups and SMEs by allowing the corporates to take part in the venture businesses with a startup. The venture business is estimated to be around US$1 billion by 2023 (METI Japan, 2020b). These businesses are set by the cooperative mechanisms between government and the private sector for startups and SMEs. Examples of the joint support to startups and SMEs in Japan are listed in Table 2:

The policy support also includes the facilitated visa option for overseas persons who are classified as startups. The policy is to build up the attractiveness of overseas startup establishments in Japan (MEIT Japan, 2020). Thus overall, the government has implemented a variety of effective regulations and policy frameworks which can nurture developments of startups and SMEs in Japan.

Table 2:   Government and Private Cooperative Support Under J-Startup

Support by the Private Sector	Support by the Government
✓ Providing business space and granting fee with preferential treatment (office space, vacant space within factory, training facilities, and show rooms, etc.) ✓ Working together in doing experimental studies with robots, products and parts, and infrastructure network providing the test environment and analysis equipment ✓ Providing acceleration programs and granting preferential treatment in manufacturing support programs ✓ Providing advice by specialists and human resources with know-hows ✓ Referring startups to its customers and related companies	• Allowing startups to use the official logo of J-Startup (branding as a certified company) • Publicizing through a dedicated website and domestic and overseas media outlets • Welcoming startups on overseas missions led by ministers and other government officials • Assisting in exhibiting at large-scale overseas and domestic events • Granting preferential treatment in support measures such as subsidies, and simplifying procedures • Providing business matching (individual connections to executives of large firms, ministries, and agencies) • Utilization of a regulatory sandbox system • Handling requests related to regulations

Source: METI Japan (2020a).

3.2 Regulatory Frameworks for Startups and SMEs' Promotion in Republic of Korea

After the war, during 1960s–1970s the government of Republic of Korea set initiative policy to stimulate SMEs' development by five-year economic development plans (Sung *et al.*, 2016). However, the government focused on creating heavy industries and directed the policy support mainly to large-scale businesses and manufacturing (Dollar and Sokoloff, 1990). The government later considered that the SMEs were the main elements for economic growth as the SMEs manufacturing and businesses exceeded the economic contribution from the large manufacturing enterprises (Sung *et al.*, 2016). In 1980s, the government changed its primary policy of supporting large-scale businesses and became more SMEs friendly. The government implemented massive reform policies with the efforts to building up SMEs in the marketplace. The SMEs policy was emphasized by the article 123 of the Korean constitution which stipulates that *the state should protect and promote SMEs.*

By adhering to the legal requirements in the constitution, the governments passed various laws, regulations, and policies which promote and protect SMEs. In 1996, the government established the Small and Medium Business Administration (SMBA) to be a principle agency working on SMEs' promotion (MSS Korea, 2020a). In the strengthening of the institutional support by the SMBA, the government also issued many laws which are of regulatory significance for the SMEs' promotion. The list of various laws passed to support the SMEs are in the following Table 3.

The list of laws issued by the government to facilitate SMEs in the Republic of Korea's represents the real efforts of the government to provide a legal climate, stimulating SMEs' development. Along with the list of various laws above, *the Framework act on small and medium enterprises 2007* is considered as the specific and primary law for SMEs' promotion. Section 1 of the act provides primary purpose of the law to provide basic matters concerning the direction-setting for SMEs and measures for promoting SMEs' growth as well as facilitating the development of the national economy of the Republic of Korea. Based on the

Table 3: Laws Passed to Support the SMEs in Republic of Korea

1. Framework act on small and medium enterprises 2007 (latest amendment 2016)	2. Special act to support small urban manufacturers 2014 (latest amendment 2015)
3. Act on facilitation of the purchase of small and medium enterprise-manufactured products and support for the development of their markets 2009 (latest amendment 2015)	4. Small and medium enterprise cooperatives act 2007 (latest amendment 2015)
5. Act on special cases concerning the regulation of the special economic zones for specialized regional development 2004 (latest amendment 2016)	6. Small and medium enterprises promotion act 2009 (latest amendment 2015)
7. Act on the protection of and support for microenterprises 2015	8. Special act to support human resources of small and medium enterprises 2003 (latest amendment 2016)
9. Act on special measures for the promotion of venture businesses 1997 (latest amendment 2015)	10. Special act on the development of traditional markets and shopping districts 2006 (latest amendment 2013)
11. Korea Technology Finance Corporation Act 2012	12. Support for small and medium enterprise establishment act 2007 (latest amendment 2014)
13. Act to support female-owned businesses 1999 (latest amendment 2013)	14. Regional credit guarantee foundation act 1999 (latest amendment 2017)
15. Act on the promotion of collaborative cooperation between large enterprises and small–medium enterprises 2006 (latest amendment 2013)	16. Act to Support Protection of Technologies of Small and Medium Enterprises 2017
17. Act on the promotion of technology innovation of small and medium enterprises 2001 (latest amendment 2015)	18. Act on Special Cases Concerning Support for Techno-parks 2015
19. Promotion of disabled persons' enterprise activities act 2005 (latest amendment 2012)	

Source: MSS Korea (2020b).

framework act, the government must ensure the increase of SMEs and assist SMEs in the market.

Besides the legal support by the various laws, the government also provides policies that promote and facilitate SMEs. Examples are tax incentives, credit guarantee, and special loan for SMEs (Deliotte, 2019). According to the Republic of Korea's Ministry of SMEs and Startups, the current elements of policies for SMEs' promotion are in Figure 1.

What can be seen from the Republic of Korea is that the government has prepared legal instruments and policy support for startups and SMEs, and continues to focus on creating innovative startups and SMEs. In addition to the available laws and policies for SMEs, the government ensures that the startups can connect with joint venture investment and the research from universities (Han, 2019). This helps boost the use of research and innovation from universities through startups combined with venture investments. Overall, the Republic of Korea has various regulatory and policy frameworks in place for startups and SMEs' promotion. The focus of the government's supportive frameworks for startups and SMEs is for the facilitation toward innovation for the Republic of Korea economy.

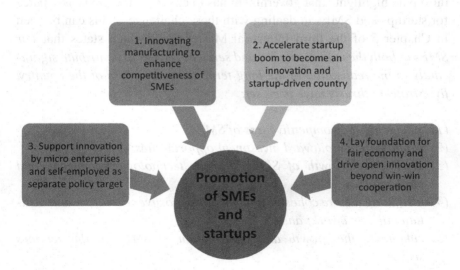

Figure 1:   Ministry of SMEs and Startups: Policy Direction of the Year 2020
Source: MSS Korea (2020c).

3.3 *Regulatory Frameworks for Startups and SMEs Promotion in Malaysia*

Similar to Japan and the Republic of Korea, Malaysia has embarked on the establishment of regulatory frameworks, supportive of startups and SMEs. The Malaysian government has founded the special agency for SMEs — "Small and Medium Industries Development Corporation" (SMIDEC) in 1996. The SMIDEC was under the government direction to create and facilitate the increase of startups and SMEs in Malaysia. The government gave priority to the development of SMEs by stipulating supportive plans for SMEs in the Second Industrial Master Plan 1996–2005 (Chin and Lim, 2018). The second master plan stipulated support policies for SMEs such as access to markets; increasing technology capabilities; enhancing the adoption of ICT; and increasing access to finance (Chin and Lim, 2018). The third Industrial Master Plan 2006–2020 also includes the significant policies for startups and SMEs' promotion. The third plan has identified six key challenges faced by SMEs, which are: innovation and technology adoption; human capital development; access to financing; market access; legal and regulatory environment; and infrastructure. The third plan highlights that government has to ensure that there is assistance for startups and SMEs in dealing with these challenges. This can be seen in Chapter 5 of the third Industrial Master Plan, which states that *For SMEs in both the manufacturing and services sectors to contribute significantly to the realisation of the long-term competitiveness of the country, five strategic thrusts have been set:*

(1) enhancing the competitiveness of SMEs;
(2) capitalising on outward investment opportunities;
(3) driving the growth of SMEs through technology, knowledge and innovation;
(4) instituting a more cohesive policy and supportive regulatory and institutional framework; and
(5) enhancing the growth and contribution of SMEs in the services sector.

Based on the masterplan, 15 government ministries and more than 60 agencies have to cooperate in supporting the development of startups and SMEs. The plan greatly controls all government agencies and provides public recognition on how government will pursue their policy toward startups and SMEs. SMIDEC, which was later renamed as SME Corporation Malaysia (SME Corp) in 2009, drives the plan for SMEs' promotion. The SME Corp states its policy to promote startups and SMEs in terms of: capacity building, market access, financial support and guarantee, branding development, technology change, *Bumiputera*, credit rating, and awards for SMEs (SME Corp, 2020b). In addition, the SME Corp and government agencies adopted various policies to follow the RMKe-11, which is the strategic government policy to foster SMEs' development. The strategic details of the RMKe-11 are presented in the following Table 4.

In addition, the Malaysian government has also set their policies for the transformation of ICT and innovation of startups and SMEs. The Malaysian government has not only supported local startups and SMEs to

Table 4: Malaysia Rancangan Malaysia Kesebelas-11 (RMKe-11) (The Eleventh Malaysia Plan) for SMEs' Promotion

Strategic Thrusts	Related Measures
Enhancing inclusiveness towards an equitable society	(i) Provide financing and training for households to venture into entrepreneurship (ii) Increase productivity of farmers, fishermen, and small holders through adoption of modern technology (iii) Encourage adoption of ICT to enhance market access by micro enterprises (iv) Enhance integrated entrepreneurship programs, which include integrated entrepreneurship development packages from startups to market product placement
Accelerating human capital development for an advanced nation	(i) Improving labor market efficiency to accelerate economic growth by improving labor productivity and management of foreign workers (ii) Transforming businesses to meet industry demand
Strengthening infrastructure to support economic expansion	(i) Unleashing growth of logistics and enhancing trade facilitation (ii) Encouraging sustainable energy use to support growth

Source: SME Corp (2020a).

develop but also encourages overseas startups to be established in Malaysia. This policy helps build up a vibrant startup landscape where innovative startups can flourish and grow in a sustainable manner. The Malaysia Digital Economy Corporation Sdn. Bhd. (MDEC) by the government support issued various policies for facilitating the overseas startups to establish their businesses in Malaysia. The policies include fast-track and special visa for startups, tax exemption and allowance, and facilitated process of registrations (MDEC Malaysia, 2020).

3.4 *Regulatory Frameworks for Startups and SMEs' Promotion in Thailand*

In the initial stage of the development during 1940s–1960s, Thailand adopted laws and policies to stimulate the increase in the agricultural sector and small businesses. During 1970s–1990s, the government shifted its economic policies to become an export-led country (Jansen, 2001). The export-led policies provided the expansion of SMEs and propelled the rapid growth of manufactured export (Nidhiprabha, 2017). However, the policies specific to SMEs' promotion had not been issued and government focused on supporting entrepreneurs aiming to export products. The Thailand economy was later faced with economic crisis with the collapse of businesses during 1997–1998. As a result of this crisis, the government, with realization of the importance of SMEs in economic development, enacted the Small and Medium Enterprises Promotion Act B.E. 2543 (2000) and established the Office of Small and Medium Enterprises Promotion (OSMEP) as the main agency to promote SMEs (OSMEP, 2017). The SMEs Act became an important legal mechanism driving SMEs' development. The Act Section 34 stipulated the SME funds to support the OSMEP and lend to SMEs for increasing their effectiveness and capabilities. The fund is also to be used for fostering joint venture investment in relation to the development and promotion of SMEs. By the SMEs Act Section 6, the OSMEP has to prepare appropriate "Action Plan on Small and Medium Enterprises Promotion" and propose the same to the National Board of SMEs promotion, with the Prime Minister as Chairperson. The board, led by the Prime Minister, adopted policies, promoting SMEs' development in Thailand (OSMEP, 2017). Most of the SMEs promotion plans will be harmonized with national economic development plans. The promotion plan links with the plan for economic development at regional and local levels in Thailand. Since the adoption of the specific laws for SMEs' promotion and the establishment of OSMEP, SMEs have been booming, attracting both local and international investors. Figure 2 outlines the implementation of SMEs promotion policies along with related policies for economic reform and development.

The current 4th SME Promotion Master Plan adopted by the National board of SMEs points out important promotion schemes for SMEs, such as the elevation of IT to SMEs; open access to capitals and funds; support entrepreneurship; revision of laws supporting SMEs; promote SMEs clusters; and creation of value-added startups (OSMEP, 2016). The plan provides greater support to SMEs with increasing consideration to innovative startups. In addition to the plan, government has established SMEs

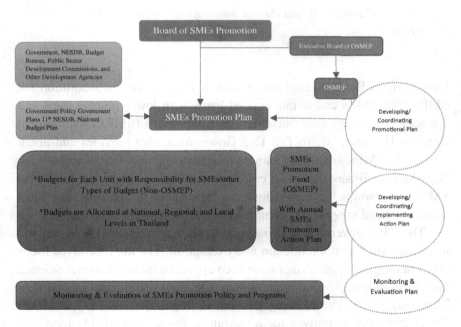

Figure 2:   The Implementation of SME Promotion Master Plan

Source: OSMEP (2016).

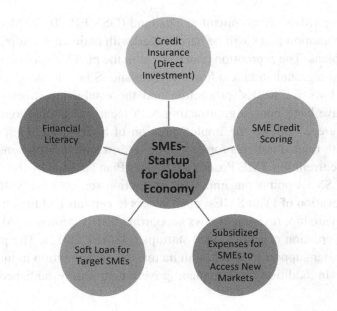

Figure 3:   Project Plan for Boosting SME 4.0 in Thailand

Source: OSMEP (2016).

Development Bank of Thailand, which is major financial institution for SMEs. The SMEs can obtain special loans with lower interest rates and can acquire business assistance from the SMEs Bank (SMEs Development Bank of Thailand, 2020). The Thai Government also provides additional support to SMEs, including loan credit guarantee and Tax Incentives for New Startup Businesses. The credit guarantee is a support available to SMEs and startups for requesting loans from banks in Thailand. The additional financial support to startup SMEs are presented in Figure 3.

The Thai government also supports startups and SMEs by the tax incentives such as tax reduction and exemption. The tax incentives focus on technological startups that have been approved by the National Science and Technology Development Agency (NSTDA) (Revenue Department Thailand, 2020). The Ministry of Finance regulation No. 337 2018(BE 2561) gives tax incentives for a startup in the sectors of: (1) food and agriculture, (2) energy saving, (3) biotechnology business, (4) medical and public health, (5) tourism, service, and creative economy, (5) advanced materials, (6) textile and decorations, (7) automotive and parts, and (8) electronic, computer, software, and information service. Overall, Thailand has developed regulatory and policy frameworks to foster SMEs and refocused its frameworks on new technological startups and SMEs.

4. Comparative Perspectives and Challenges

Based on the discussion about the regulatory and policy frameworks for startups and SMEs in the four abovementioned countries, this part of the chapter aims to compare the frameworks so as to present the similarities and differences in the frameworks of the four countries. This section also discusses the challenges for the regulatory frameworks for supporting startups and SMEs in the four countries.

4.1 *Comparative Perspectives*

Overall, the four countries have a vital concern in adopting regulatory and policy frameworks for supporting startups and SMEs. The trend followed in the four countries has been that the initial frameworks pay attention to the promotion of SMEs, and the countries later adapted the framework toward startups with value-added from technological advancement. While having various similarities in the frameworks for SMEs' promotion, there are some differences in the frameworks and implementation. A brief comparison of the frameworks in the four countries is presented in Table 5.

From Table 5 below, on the comparative perspective of the frameworks, the four countries have advanced their regulatory and policy frameworks for startups and SMEs' promotion. However, by ranking perspective, Thailand seems to be the country lacking behind Japan, Republic of Korea, and Malaysia. From the view of attracting overseas startups, Republic of Korea and Malaysia have effective regulatory and policy frameworks, government schemes to attract overseas startups. Republic of Korea and Malaysia have harmonized regulation on immigration for attracting international startups to establish their businesses in their countries. While, Thailand has not adopted easing of regulations on

Table 5:   Comparative Perspectives on Regulatory Frameworks for Startups and SMEs' Promotion

Frameworks for Startups and SMEs' Promotion	Countries
1. Specific laws and policies for Startups and SMEs' Promotion	**Japan, Republic of Korea, Thailand** issued specific laws for promotion of startups and SMEs **Malaysia** resorted to government policy and cooperation as a mechanism to build up startups
2. Government grant for startups and SMEs	**All four countries** provide government grants for startups
3. Financial Support for startups and SMEs	**All four countries** have established financial schemes which help support startups and SMEs — Special loans and Credit guarantees
4. Taxes Incentives	**All four countries** have issued Tax regulation incentives for startups and SMEs (Business taxes exemption or other taxes benefit)
5. Overseas Startup Incentives	**Republic of Korea and Malaysia** provide effective government schemes to attract overseas startups **Japan** has some specific incentives for overseas startups **Thailand** lacks harmonized schemes and incentives for the overseas startups — Issue in immigration laws and foreign investment regulation
6. Private joint venture under government support and crowd funding	**Japan, Republic of Korea, Malaysia** provide reliable programs for joint ventures — The established corporation can cooperate with the startups **All four countries** have set policies for crowdfunding **Thailand,** while having an initial policy to support joint ventures, lacks effectiveness
7. Government program for ICT Advocacy and Consultancy	**Japan, Republic of Korea, Malaysia** provide platforms and training courses for Startup ICT transformation **Thailand,** while having a training program, lacks appropriate policy driver for Startup ICT transformation
8. Nurture to sustain market uncertainty	**Republic of Korea has** adopted various regulations supporting the sustainability of startups and SMEs to survive in the market **Japan and Malaysia**, at the middle ground, have some certain programs but do not have program continuity for startups and SMEs to sustain market uncertainty **Thailand** has applied initiation policy, but lacks continuity to nurture the startups and SMEs

Source: Author.

immigration for the overseas startups. With regards to frameworks to make sure that startup SMEs can sustain the market changes, Republic of Korea seems to provide various regulations supporting the sustainability of startups and SMEs to survive in the market. In contrast, Thailand tends to have an approach to support the startups and SMEs in their establishment, but lacks continuity in nurturing startups and SMEs to sustain in markets.

4.2 Challenges from Regulatory and Policy Frameworks

The four countries studied in this chapter adopted regulatory and policy frameworks that are important to the promotion of startups and SMEs. Nevertheless, there are challenges in terms of regulation and policies. The challenges include the following:

Startups and SMEs in the criteria of government support: The development of startups and SMEs vitally relies on regulatory frameworks. Nevertheless, any government intervention to the market economy like policy assistance to startups and SMEs can also create a concern for the growth of the startups and SMEs. The more support to startup and SMEs can lead to the inefficiency in the startup and SMEs. Government subsidies and support to startups and SMEs may not merely contribute to development (Eshima, 2003). The startups and SMEs may also prove to be inefficient to receive funding and support from the government. Besides, with the adherence to specific criteria classifying of startups and SMEs for government assistance, the startups and SMEs would prefer to be under specific criteria in order to continue receiving support such as tax incentive, low-interest rate loan, and funding benefits. This creates the situation of *Bonzinisation* where startups and SMEs do not aim to grow so as to continue receiving government support. In implementing regulatory and policy frameworks for startups and SMEs, it is essential to ensure that governments evaluate the frameworks and stimulate the startups and SMEs' efficiency rather than continuing to support them without significant results (Nakagawa, 2012; Jones and Kim, 2014). This chapter notes that regulatory and policy support is still essential and beneficial to startups and SMEs. However, there must be a practical assessment of the efficiency increase among startups and SMEs.

Financial support with complexity: Governments in the four countries have issued policies for giving financial support to startupd and SMEs, but such policies may not reach their objectives to support startups and SMEs. It is because the government's financial support can only be gained following complicated information and requirements (Uchida, Udell, and Yamori, 2012). Startups and SMEs may choose not to request support when considering working through the complicated requirements from lending institutions. Startups and SMEs have to make sure that they prepare required documents, show sufficient collateral, have a good relationship with the financial institution, and have a sound financial record (Haron *et al.*, 2013). Thus, the financial support is recommended to come with simplifying the process in order to effectively assist the necessities of startups and SMEs. The simplified process will improve lending-infrastructure for optimal financial assistance (Kumar and Rao, 2015).

Moreover, financial support may not only come from the government but from the crowd funding from collective help. The example is the *Hometown Investment Trust (HIT) funds,* which can be a significant source of finance for startups and SMEs (Yoshino, 2013). The HIT provides new crediting methods for financial loans, and it gives opportunities for startups and SMEs to obtain financial assistance from their community (Yoshino, 2013). In view of the HIT and similar help, the government does not have to provide direct loan or financial support to startups and SMEs, but simply let the community to collectively help startups and SMEs.

Policy credibility and certainty: While the governments in the four countries has adopted effective regulatory and policy frameworks for startups and SMEs, they may find it difficult to ensure the credibility and certainty of policies when the market economy comes under disruptive changes. Compared to large firms, SMEs have to be very adaptive for market change in order to serve consumer expectation which connects SMEs' revenue and profitability (Yeow *et al.*, 2018). The regulatory frameworks which support the SMEs may create the difficulty for SMEs to transform themselves with the changing world. This will be a complicated task for governments, in keeping up their regulation and policies aligned with the changing world. The situation mostly happens in developing countries. An example case is of the startup brewery beer businesses in Thailand. While these new startups aim to introduce new brewery to consumers, the Thai regulations do not allow startups to brew beer and sell beer to consumers (Ongdee, 2017). This is due to the outdated laws which provide opportunities to only large businesses to brew and sell beer in Thailand (Ongdee, 2017). The possible regulatory frameworks that enable startups to test markets is by regulatory sandbox. The regulatory sandbox allows the government to support the startup businesses and permits the startups to test their innovative businesses in the market without concern for laws and regulations (Im, 2020). By the sandbox, governments refrain from regulatory intervention and relying on market mechanisms. The example is the adoption of regulatory sandbox for startups in Republic of Korea. The government passed a law allowing regulatory sandbox for startups and SMEs in the information and communication technology sector (Ji-young, 2019). The startups and SMEs would be able to obtain a regulatory wavier for a set amount of time in order to test out their innovative products, services, and business models in the market (Im, 2020; Ji-young, 2019).

Government-led policy for startups and SMEs: While playing a vital role in promoting startups and SMEs, governments also serve predominant roles in shaping up the startups and SMEs. The government policy and direction tend to be forms of command and control. Some startups and SMEs have to follow the regulatory frameworks in order to obtain tax incentives, and other support mechanisms. There is a lack of bottom-up approach in drafting regulatory frameworks for the promotion of startups and SMEs. In some cases, government command and control can be considered as the intervention and distortion of markets. The command and control may stimulate the startups and SMEs in some economic sectors but will leave some sectors behind. Governments to some extent pay more attention to 'successful' approaches of regulatory frameworks for SMEs' promotion but neglect the reality of their original aim to facilitate all SMEs' growth in their countries (Xavier, 2016). It is accepted that the government has to formulate its regulatory frameworks by gearing up toward startups and SMEs that create innovation for businesses. However, the government may lack consideration of the business sectors such as retail and agriculture, which are rudimentary to economic sustainability. Most recent regulations and policies gear up toward high-tech startups and put the real business sectors under a shadow. It is vital to make sure that the government sets its regulatory frameworks for startups and SMEs in a harmonized manner in order to create overall sustainable businesses and economy.

In some cases, regulations and policies have to ensure that startups and SMEs can fail. It is because startups and SMEs initially only test the markets. They have a higher rate of failure. The regulations and policies must allow assisting them to pass any failure condition. The example is the bankruptcy laws, which must be agile to support startups and SMEs working through their failure stages. These agile regulations and policies can encourage the startups and SMEs to test their innovative products and services. The outcome will be that there will be an increase in successful businesses out of various failed businesses.

Shortage of evaluation on regulatory outcomes: Governments adopt various regulatory frameworks to support startups and SMEs. Nevertheless, there is a lack of evaluation on the regulation and policy outcomes aiming to promote startups and SMEs. The established regulations and policies for SMEs promotion may create a positive impact on startups and SMEs. Regulations and policies can create a negative impact on SMEs, as well. It is a difficult task to specify a direct impact of a specific regulation and policy for SMEs' development. The governments mainly pronounce the availability of the regulatory frameworks supporting SMEs but refrain from showing how the regulatory frameworks can nurture or hamper the startups and SMEs. Thus, governments must evaluate their regulations and policies to ensure they adhere to economic efficiency norms.

Lack of international or regional arrangement: Regulatory frameworks for startups and SMEs in the four countries are mostly constrained within their jurisdiction and tend to follow a similar regulatory and policy setting. The four countries have applied similar regulations and policies, but do not show the uniqueness of the regulatory frameworks. However, the governments may have to reconsider the regulatory frameworks to make sure that they work well and are distinct from others. There is also a lack of international and regional cooperation on regulations and policies to promote startups and SMEs. The four countries seem to adapt their regulatory frameworks to compete in attaining SMEs' development. Nevertheless, policy cooperation is vital to regional development. The four countries may have to reconsider cooperation for regional SME promotion to contribute to regional connectivity and regional development in the long term.

5. Conclusion

Regulatory and policy frameworks are crucial to the development of startups and SMEs. The frameworks, in general, come with preferential assistance for startups and SMEs, such as tax incentives, specific regulations, training courses, initial funds, and investment matching. The frameworks contribute to the increase and success of SMEs. This chapter explores the regulatory and policy frameworks for startups and SMEs in Japan, Republic of Korea, Malaysia, and Thailand. The four countries have developed regulatory frameworks in place for assisting the growth of startups and SMEs. The recent development of the frameworks is that countries pay attention to value-added and innovative startups. The chapter presents the difference in the elements and the effectiveness of implementation to promote startups and SMEs. The chapter also examines some challenges over the regulatory and policy frameworks which affect the startups and SMEs. The challenges include complicated criteria of government support and finance, policy creditability, government centralized policy, shortage of assessment on policy outcome, and lack of regional cooperation on policy.

The policy implication is that governments in the four countries would have to focus on the evaluation of the current frameworks for startups and SMEs' promotion, with consideration of simplified process in requesting support and of the effective determinant to facilitate the growth of startup and SMEs. The governments also have to ensure that their frameworks come from the need of the SMEs community. The international and regional cooperation on SMEs regulations and policies will facilitate the connectivity of regional startups and SMEs among the four countries.

References

Aboojafari, R., A. Daliri, F. Taghizadeh-Hesary, M. Mokhtari, and M. Ekhitiari. 2019. Role of Credit guarantee scheme in the development of small and medium-sized enterprises: With emphasis on knowledge-based enterprises. In N. Yoshino and F. Taghizadeh-Hesary (Eds.), *Unlocking SME Finance in Asia: Roles of Credit Rating and Credit Guarantee Schemes.* Abingdon, OX: Routledge.

Bellavitis, C., I. Filatotchev, D.S. Kamuriwo, and T. Vanacker. 2017. Entrepreneurial finance: New frontiers of research and practice. *Venture Capital,* 19(1–2): 1–16. doi:10.1080/13691066.2016.1259733.

Bergner, S.M., R. Bräutigam, M.T. Evers, and C. Spengel. 2017. *The Use of SME Tax Incentives in the European Union.* Retrieved from http://ftp.zew.de/pub/zew-docs/dp/dp17006.pdf.

Binh, L.D., N.K. Dung, and T.D. Trong. 2017. *SME Laws in Selected Countries and Implication for Vietnam.* Retrieved from https://www.economica.vn/Portals/0/Documents/SME%20Laws%20-%20Intl%20Practices%20and%20Implication%20to%20VN.pdf.

Blank, S. 2010. *What's a Startup? First Principles.* Retrieved from https://steve-blank.com/2010/01/25/whats-a-startup-first-principles/.

Castillo, V., A. Maffioli, A.P. Monsalvo, S. Rojo, and R. Stucchi. 2011. *Can SME Policies Improve Firm Performance? Evidence from an Impact Evaluation in Argentina.* Retrieved from https://papers.ssrn.com/sol3/papers.cfm?abstract_id=1848984#.

Chin, Y.-W. and E.-S. Lim. 2018. *SME Policies and Performance in Malaysia.* Retrieved from https://www.iseas.edu.sg/images/pdf/ISEAS_EWP_2018-3_ChinLim.pdf.

Croce, A., L. Grilli, and S. Murtinu. 2014. Venture capital enters academia: A look at university-managed funds. *The Journal of Technology Transfer,* 39, 688–715. doi:10.1007/s10961-013-9317-8.

Deliotte. 2019. *International Tax Korea Highlight 2019.* Retrieved from https://www2.deloitte.com/content/dam/Deloitte/global/Documents/Tax/dttltax-koreahighlights-2019.pdf (Accessed on October 5, 2020).

Dollar, D. and K. Sokoloff. 1990. Patterns of productivity growth in Republic of Korean manufacturing industries, 1963–1979. *Journal of Development Economics,* 33(2): 309–327. doi: https://doi.org/10.1016/0304-3878(90)90026-8.

Eshima, Y. 2003. Impact of public policy on innovative SMEs in Japan. *Journal of Small Business Management,* 41(1): 85–93. doi:10.1111/1540-627X.00068.

European Commission. 2017. *Effectiveness of Tax Incentives for Venture Capital and Business Angels to Foster the Investment of SMEs and Startups.* Retrieved from https://ec.europa.eu/taxation_customs/sites/taxation/files/final_report_2017_taxud_venture-capital_business-angels.pdf.

Farvaque, N., E. Voss, M. Lefebvre, and K. Schütze. 2009. *Guide for Training in SMEs.* Retrieved from https://ec.europa.eu/social/BlobServlet?docId=3074&langId=en.

Han, J.-w. 2019. Promotion of technology-based startups: TIPS policy of Korea. *Asian Journal of Innovation & Policy*, 8(3). Retrieved from https://web.a.ebscohost.com/abstract?direct=true&profile=ehost&scope=site&authtype=crawler&jrnl=22871608&AN=140969240&h=eEndMxkrYnGBTDTXeLa0xwl924SCihSbVWxw97uMSrGgZGtOuCqKZl0WDYfSFnXCLUtsH-BF8oRKXJKSOaDuikQ%3d%3d&crl=c&resultNs=AdminWebAuth&resultLocal=ErrCrlNotAuth&crlhashurl=login.aspx%3fdirect%3dtrue%26profile%3dehost%26scope%3dsite%26authtype%3dcrawler%26jrnl%3d22871608%26AN%3d140969240.

Haron, H., S.B. Said, K. Jayaraman, and I. Ismail. 2013. Factors influencing small medium enterprises (SMES) in obtaining loan. *International Journal of Business and Social Science*, 4(15): 18. Retrieved from http://www.ijbssnet.com/journals/Vol_4_No_15_Special_Issue_November_2013/25.pdf.

ILO. 2018. *World Employment and Social Outlook.* Retrieved from https://www.ilo.org/wcmsp5/groups/public/---dgreports/---dcomm/---publ/documents/publication/wcms_615594.pdf.

Im, H. 2020. *Comments and Suggestions on Regulatory and Policy Frameworks for Promotion on Startup and SMEs in Japan, Republic of Korea, Malaysia and Thailand.* Paper presented at the ADBI-KODIT Conference on Investment in Startups and Small Business Financing, ADBI, Tokyo.

Intarakumnerd, P. and A. Goto. 2016. *Technology and Innovation Policies for Small and Medium-Sized Enterprises in East Asia.* Retrieved from https://www.adb.org/sites/default/files/publication/186199/adbi-wp578.pdf.

Jansen, K. 2001. Thailand: The making of a miracle? *Development and Change*, 32(2): 343–370. doi:10.1111/1467-7660.00208.

Jayawarna, D. 2007. Training commitment and performance in manufacturing SMEs: Incidence, intensity and approaches. *Journal of Small Business and Enterprise Development*, 14(2): 321–338. doi:10.1108/14626000710746736.

Ji-young, S. 2019. [News Focus] Korea's finance 'regulatory sandbox' experiment takes effect in April. *The Korea Herald.* Retrieved from http://www.koreaherald.com/view.php?ud=20190328000331.

Kamleitner, B. 2012. Tax compliance of small business owners: A review. *International Journal of Entrepreneurial Behavior & Research*, 18(3): 330–351. doi:10.1108/13552551211227710.

Kumar, S. and P. Rao. 2015. A conceptual framework for identifying financing preferences of SMEs. *Small Enterprise Research*, 22(1): 99–112. doi:10.108 0/13215906.2015.1036504.

Matsushima, S. 2001. Creation and development of small and medium enterprise policies in post-war japan. *Entreprises et histoire*, 28(2): 10–19. doi:10.3917/ eh.028.0010.

MDEC Malaysia. 2020. *Malaysia Tech Entrpreneure Program*. Retrieved from https://www.mtep.my/.

MEIT Japan. 2020. *What is the "Startup Visa"?* Retrieved from https://www. meti.go.jp/english/policy/economy/startup_nbp/startup_visa.html.

METI Japan. 2020a. *About J-Startup summary*. Retrieved from https://www.j-startup.go.jp/en/about/

METI Japan. 2020b. *J-Startup*. Retrieved from https://www.meti.go.jp/english/ press/2018_06/0611_003_00.html.

MSS Korea. 2019. *Scope of SME*. Retrieved from https://www.mss.go.kr/site/ eng/02/10205000000002019050902.jsp.

MSS Korea. 2020a. *History of Ministry of SMEs and Startup*. Retrieved from https://www.mss.go.kr/site/eng/01/10103000000002016111504.jsp.

MSS Korea. 2020b. *Korean SMEs: Law*. Retrieved from https://www.mss.go.kr/ (Accessed on October 5, 2020).

MSS Korea. 2020c. *Policy Direction of the Year*. Retrieved from https://www. mss.go.kr/site/eng/03/10301000000002016111504.jsp.

Nakagawa, R. 2012. The policy approach in promoting small and medium sized enterprises in Japan. *International Business & Economics Research Journal (IBER)*, 11, 1087. doi:10.19030/iber.v11i10.7254.

Nidhiprabha, B. 2017. The rise and fall of Thailand's export-oriented industries*. *Asian Economic Papers*, 16(3). Retrieved from https://www.mitpressjour-nals.org/doi/pdf/10.1162/asep_a_00556.

OECD. 2005. *Small and Medium Enterprises (SMEs)*. Retrieved from https:// stats.oecd.org/glossary/detail.asp?ID=3123.

OECD. 2012. *OECD Science, Technology and Industry Outlook*. Retrieved from https://www.oecd.org/sti/sti-outlook-2012-highlights.pdf.

OECD. 2014. *Policy Brief on Access to Business Startup Finance for Inclusive Entrepreneurship Entrepreneurial Activities in Europe*. Retrieved from https:// www.oecd.org/cfe/leed/Finacing%20inclusive%20entrepreneurship%20 policy%20brief%20EN.pdf.

OECD. 2018. *Strengthening SMEs and Entrepreneurship for Productivity and Inclusive Growth*. Retrieved from https://www.oecd.org/cfe/smes/ministerial/documents/2018-SME-Ministerial-Conference-Key-Issues.pdf.

OECD. 2019. *OECD SME and Entrepreneurship Outlook 2019*.

OECD. 2020. *Starting a Business*. Retrieved from https://data.oecd.org/entrepreneur/starting-a-business.htm.

Ongdee, S. 2017. Time to POP CAP on Thai craft beer industry. *The Nation Thailand*. Retrieved from https://www.nationthailand.com/opinion/30305063.

OSMEP. 2016. *Role of OSMEP Thailand*.

OSMEP. 2017. *Role of OSMEP*.

Randall, S. Jones, and M. Kim. 2014. *Promoting the Financing of SMEs and Start-ups in Korea*. Retrieved from https://www.oecd-ilibrary.org/docserver/5jxx054bdlvh-en.pdf?expires=1579945557&id=id&accname=guest&checksum=FAED1F184D7B57B5986C7BC5ED37C6DE.

Tax Mechanism and Support for startup. 2020.

Sato, Y. 1989. Small business in japan: A historical perspective. *Small Business Economics*, 1(2): 121–128. Retrieved from www.jstor.org/stable/40228503.

SME Agency Japan. 2019. *2019 White Paper on Small and Medium Enterprises in Japan/2019 White Paper on Small Enterprises in Japan (Summary)*. Retrieved from https://www.chusho.meti.go.jp/sme_english/whitepaper/whitepaper.html.

SME Bank Thailand. 2020. *The SME Bank Information*. Retrieved from https://www.smebank.co.th/ (Accessed on October 5, 2020).

SME Corp. 2020a. RMKe-11. Retrieved from http://www.smecorp.gov.my/index.php/en/policies/2015-12-21-09-26-24/rmke-11.

SME Corp. 2020b. *Welcome to SME Corporation Malaysia*. Retrieved from https://www.smecorp.gov.my/index.php/en/.

SMEA Japan. 2020. *Japan's SME Policies in Relation to the Country's Economic Development*. Retrieved from https://www.chusho.meti.go.jp/sme_english/outline/01/01_01.html.

SMEcorp Malaysia. 2019. *SME Definition*. Retrieved from http://www.smecorp.gov.my/ (Accessed on October 5, 2020).

Sung, C.-Y., K.-C. Kim, and S. In. 2016. Small and medium-sized enterprises policy in Korea from the 1960s to the 2000s and beyond. *Small Enterprise Research*, 23(3): 262–275. doi:10.1080/13215906.2016.1269665.

Thailand, O. 2018. *SMEs Definition*. Retrieved from https://www.sme.go.th/upload/mod_download/%E0%B8%99%E0%B8%B4%E0%B8%A2%E0%B8%B2%E0%B8%A1%20SMEs.pdf.

Thurik, R. 2004. Entrepreneurship, small business and economic growth. *Journal of Small Business and Enterprise Development*, 11(1), 140–149. doi:10.1108/14626000410519173.

Uchida, H., G.F. Udell, and N. Yamori. 2012. Loan officers and relationship lending to SMEs. *Journal of Financial Intermediation*, 21(1): 97–122. doi:https://doi.org/10.1016/j.jfi.2011.06.002.

US SBA. 2020. *Grants*. Retrieved from https://www.sba.gov/funding-programs/grants.

Xavier, S.R. 2016. Malaysia's startup ecosystem: A work in progress.

Yeow, A., C. Chan, T. Yen, and G. Pan. 2018. Agility in responding to disruptive digital innovation: Case study of an SME. *Information Systems Journal*. doi:10.1111/isj.12215.

Yoshino, N. 2013. Background of Hometown Investment Trust Funds. In N. Yoshino and S. Kaji (Eds.), *Hometown Investment Trust Funds: A Stable Way to Supply Risk Capital*. Tokyo: Springer.

Yoshino, N. and F. Taghizadeh-Hesary. 2015. Analysis of credit ratings for small and medium-sized enterprises: Evidence from Asia. *Asian Development Review*, 32(2): 18–37. doi:10.1162/ADEV_a_00050.

Yoshino, N. and F. Taghizadeh-Hesary. 2016. *Major Challenges Facing Small and Medium-sized Enterprises in Asia and Solutions for Mitigating Them*. Retrieved from https://papers.ssrn.com/sol3/papers.cfm?abstract_id=2766242.

Yoshino, N., F. Taghizadeh-Hesary, P. Charoensivakorn, and B. Niraula. 2019. Credit risk analysis of small and medium-sized enterprises based on thai data. In N. Yoshino and F. Taghizadeh-Hesary (Eds.), *Unlocking SME Finance in Asia Roles of Credit Rating and Credit Guarantee Schemes*: Routledge.

Yoshino, N. and F. Taghizadeh-Hesary. 2019. Role of SMEs in Asia and the Financing Challenges They Face. In N. Yoshino and F. Taghizadeh-Hesary (Eds.), Unlocking SME Finance in Asia: Roles of Credit Rating and Credit Guarantee Schemes. Abingdon, OX: Routledge.

Chapter 2

Policy and Regulatory Changes for a Successful Startup Revolution: Experiences from the Startup Action Plan in India

Vijay Kumar Singh

*School of Law, University of Petroleum and
Energy Studies in Dehradun, India
vrsingh.vk@gmail.com; vksingh@ddn.upes.ac.in*

I see startups, technology and innovation as exciting and effective instruments for India's transformation.

— Narendra Modi, Prime Minister of India

Abstract

In January 2016, the Government of India launched the Startup India initiative, which has transformed the way in which the markets, potential entrepreneurs, and investors view startups. This transformation included a slew of policy measures intended to promote a startup culture and allow younger population members to take risks with their ideas and become "job creators" rather than "job seekers." India's demographic dividend required a suitable channelization of human resources. The

Startup Action Plan (SAP) of 2016 proposed to address three key areas for empowering potential startups: (i) handholding and simplification; (ii) funding support and incentives; and (iii) incubation and industry–academia partnership. Emerging as the third-largest startup ecosystem of the world, India has potential for enormous growth. There have been several policies at all levels of government, industry, and academia to promote a startup culture. However, it is important to examine these initiatives and determine whether they move beyond the subsidy/tax holiday mindset and work on the root corrections necessary for a robust startup ecosystem. There are several issues that require consideration from the policy and regulatory perspective for a successful startup revolution. This chapter explores these initiatives that the Government of India has taken and identifies the gaps that require attention from stakeholders. The chapter also investigates the major challenges and potential solutions arising from the Indian experience of initiatives in the startup revolution.

Keywords: Startup, legal compliance, financing, investors, global partnerships, entrepreneurship, incubation

1. Introduction

Entrepreneurial initiatives, as a factor of production, are central to the economic development of any country (Tripathi, 1971). Traditionally, the majority of the population in India followed the *Varna* system (*Brahmin* — the priest, *Kshatriya* — the warrior, *Vaishya* — the trader, and *Shudra* — the artisan). The Vaishya community was generally associated with commercial activities. The concept of the Hindu undivided family (HUF) as a business entity is unique to India, where family members are coparceners with the eldest member of the family as the decision maker, called *Karta*. The colonial rule in India and the influences of industrialization in Europe changed the social and economic dynamics of commerce, making inroads into the *Varna* system and enabling the permeation of non-business classes into commercial activities (Tripathi, 1971).

India has mainly been an agricultural (including animal husbandry, fishing, and forestry) economy. In the 1850s, the textile industries of cotton and jute, and subsequently tea, coal, and paper, sowed the seeds of the modern factory system (Medhora, 1965). The literature on the history of industry in India has highlighted divergent perspectives ranging from social and economic to political factors influencing the entrepreneurial spirit (Ray, 1994). While discussing startups, one should not forget the rural artisans, self-entrepreneurs like potters, blacksmiths, weavers, cobblers, stone workers, carpenters, engravers, and so on. However, policy making has generally overlooked them, clubbing them together with non-farm workers (Solanki, 2008).

The brunt of colonial rule introduced a socialistic pattern of governance in India, and the Indian government opted for a planned economy balancing social and industrial development. The regulations became tighter and sometimes onerous for private enterprises, which led to decelerated growth, inefficiencies, and corruption (Jang *et al.*, 2013). Tight controls and skewness toward public enterprises guided the industrial policy resolutions (Burange and Yamini, 2011). While progressive liberalization was apparent following the industrial policy of 1956, significant reform came in 1991 when the government decided to take a series of measures to unshackle the industrial economy from unnecessary bureaucratic control. These measures, among others, aimed to reform the trade policy, foreign exchange policy, industrial licensing policy, competition policy, and so on.

Professor Redlich (1948) reported a tripartite division of entrepreneurial function, that is, capitalist (provider of funds), manager (to manage the nuts and bolts), and entrepreneur in a narrow sense of the term, specifically planner, innovator, and ultimate decision maker (startup owner) (Hoselitz, 1952). Broadly, it is possible to categorize entrepreneurs into "imitative" (who follow the beaten track) and "innovative" (who adopt new and improved business methods) groups. Startups focus on these innovative entrepreneurs and their ability to come up with a replicable and scalable business model (Blank, 2013).

The "startup" ecosystem emerged globally in the United States (US), in what people popularly refer to as Silicon Valley, mainly constituting information technology (IT) companies such as Google, Apple, HP, Oracle, Cisco, Facebook, Twitter, and so on. Silicon Valley has the highest concentration of startups in the world (Ester, 2017). India makes its own contribution to this success through its software engineers who found an abode in Silicon Valley in the 1970s and 1980s. However, it is paradoxical to note that India could not arrest this "brain drain" due to a lack of policies promoting "innovator entrepreneurs." Albeit, this trend has changed in the last decade with the vitality of the globalizing cities in India and the prospects that they offer (Chacko, 2007). India is one of the largest consumer markets in the world currently.

One of the significant steps that the Government of India (GOI) took was to launch, in January 2016, the Startup Action Plan (SAP), popularly known as the "Startup India" initiative. The SAP transformed the way in which the markets, potential entrepreneurs, and investors view startups. This transformation included a slew of policy measures intending to promote a startup culture and allow younger population members to take risks with their ideas and become "job creators" rather than "job seekers." India's demographic dividend required a suitable channelization of human resources with a focus on handling issues of unemployment and creating first-generation entrepreneurs (Venkatapathy, 1989).

Defining the stages of startups' growth could be tricky, as various startup experts have suggested different numbers of stages ranging from three to six (McGowan, 2017). In India, it is possible to divide the startup life cycle into four major stages as Idea Validation, Seed Funding, Growth/Scaling up Stage, and Maturity Stage (Department of Industrial Policy and Promotion (DIPP) 2018). However, there are no strict boundaries between these stages, and often there is a twilight zone between them.

Table 1 shows the startup in different stages in India.

Alphalogic Techsys, a Pune-based software consulting firm, was the first to float its IPO, which enabled it to raise growth capital from a group of investors instead of selected VCs. The SEBI, the Indian securities regulator, has relaxed the listing norms, providing an exclusive institutional trading platform (ITP), now called the "Innovators Growth Platform"

Table 1: Startup in Different Stages in India (as on 17 December 2019)

Ideation	Validation	Early Traction	Scaling	Total
19,407	22,871	20,361	6,668	69,307

Source: www.startupindia.gov.in.

(IGP). The SEBI has further provided norms whereby, after a year of being on the IGP, startups may move to the main stock exchanges by expanding their shareholder base to 200 (the minimum required for going public). They further require a profitability/net-worth track record of three years or at least 75% of their shareholding as qualified institutional investors.

2. Startup Action Plan (SAP) of 2016

The Government of India launched the SAP, which addressed various aspects of the startup ecosystem and provided innovative entrepreneurs with a launch pad and support system, in 2016. The driving objective behind the action plan was to fast-track the spread of the startup movement from the digital/technology sector to a wide array of sectors, including the social sector, manufacturing, agriculture, education, and healthcare, and from existing Tier-1 cities (like Delhi, Mumbai, Bengaluru, etc.) to Tier-2 (Agra, Lucknow, Nagpur, etc.) and Tier-3 cities, including semi-urban and rural areas (Kothari, 2016). The SAP contains 19 points bifurcated into three key areas for empowering potential startups: (i) handholding and simplification; (ii) funding support and incentives; and (iii) incubation and industry–academia partnership (StartupIndia, 2016).

Definition of "Startup"

According to the notification that the Government of India issued (19 February 2019, originally issued on 11 April 2018), when an enterprise meets the following conditions, it will treat it as a startup:

(i) It has been incorporated/registered for not more than 10 years (previously seven years, except in the biotechnology sector according to the notification dated 11 April 2018) in any of the following forms:
   a. A private limited company under the Companies Act, 2013 (including one-person companies);
   b. A partnership firm under the Partnership Act, 1932;
   c. A Limited Liability Partnership (LLP) under the LLP Act, 2008.

(ii) Its turnover has not exceeded INR 100 crore (previously INR 25 crores) for any of the financial years since incorporation/ registration.

(iii) It is working toward the innovation, development, or improvement of products or processes or services or it is a scalable business model with high potential for employment generation and wealth creation.

However, "an entity formed by splitting up or reconstruction of an existing business shall not be considered a 'startup'. An entity shall also cease to be a startup on completion of 10 years from the date of its incorporation/registration or if its turnover for any previous year exceeds INR 100 crore."

The above definition lays down a clear parameter on the basis of the age of the entity, its turnover, and its objective, which necessarily focuses on innovation, employment generation, and wealth creation. An entity that meets the aforesaid criteria needs to apply for recognition as such from the Department for Promotion of Industry and Internal Trade (DPIIT).

One of the major challenges for startups has been legal compliance. Addressing this issue, the government provided the following points, emphasizing an "ecosystem without the trappings of a system."

Compliance Regime Based on Self-Certification

India has worked extensively on its EODB ranking, which is evident from the consistent improvement in the latest rankings from 142nd in 2014 to 63rd in 2020. One of the important parameters for the EODB ranking has been the "ease of starting a business," and for this parameter there has been an improvement from 158th in 2014 to 136th in 2020 (World Bank, 2020). For startups, India has relaxed the compliance regime further, especially in the two areas of compliance relating to labor laws and the environment. For five applicable pieces of labor legislation, startups just have to provide self-certification and there will be no inspection for 3 years, unless some complaint arises in this regard. For environmental law compliance, startups are allowed to give "self-certification" in 36 of the newly introduced "white category industries." These categories are in industrial sectors with a pollution index score of up to 20 and are practically non-polluting (Korreck, 2019). This self-certification mechanism offers great relief to startups.

Startup India Hub and Mobile App and the Startup India Portal

Finding a mentor and resolving teething troubles have been a considerable challenge for startups. The SAP addressed this issue by creating the "Startup India" hub, working on a hub-and-spoke model and bringing different stakeholders of the startup ecosystem into one platform. To this effect, the government created an online portal (https://www.startupindia.gov.in) and a mobile app. These act as an official networking portal connecting more than 70,000 startups, 65 investors, 480 mentors, 95 accelerators, 470 incubators, and 38 government bodies (as of 25 December 2019). There are about 3.5 lakh users of this portal.

Fast-Tracking Patent Examination at Lower Costs and Legal Support

Startups operate on their innovation strength; hence, the protection of the idea/brand in the form of a patent, trademark, or design is crucial. The recognition of these intellectual property rights (IPRs) facilitates commercialization for startups and opens up funding opportunities (Conti *et al.*, 2013). In this regard, the SAP came up with the scheme for Startup Intellectual Property Protection (SIPP) with the aim of facilitating the filing of IPRs. The Controller General of Patents, Designs, and Trademarks (CGPDTM) is the nodal agency to steer this policy. The CGPDTM has a panel of more than 4,000 facilitators who help startups in obtaining IPRs at rebated rates. These applications also receive fast-tracking by virtue of coming from startups. The government has extended the scheme, which initially operated for a year, to 3 years until March 2020.

Relaxed Norms of Public Procurement for Startups

A new startup cannot compete with established players, especially in cases of public procurement, wherein two of the major qualification criteria are based on "prior experience" and "prior turnover." To promote startups in the manufacturing sector in India, the government has relaxed the requirements of prior experience, prior turnover, and earnest money deposit (EMD) in cases of startups without compromising on the quality standards and technical parameters. The Government e Marketplace (GeM) also facilitates startups, and Startup India is integrated with the Central Portal for Public Procurement (CPPP).

Faster Exit for Startups

Fear of failure and associated problems with insolvency operate as a dampener for new-age entrepreneurs. Among the major problems are the lock-in of capital, unusual delays in resolution, and ultimate erosion of capital. To improve this situation, the new insolvency law of India, namely the Insolvency and Bankruptcy Code 2016 (IBC), provides a fast-track mechanism for insolvency resolution of startups, which takes 135 (90 + 45) days instead of 270 days in the normal channel for startups (other than a startup organized as a partnership firm, as insolvency regulations applicable to partnership firms are not included).

2.1 *Funding Support and Incentives*

Scalability is one of the major characteristics of the startup revolution. In Silicon Valley, "think big" is the focus of innovation. Its conventional business model is all about scale, reaching large markets, and the ambition to create a social impact (Ester, 2017). Scalability requires funding support; however, it is extremely difficult to convince someone to invest in startups, which by nature are not impervious, and there is a question of survival in most cases. The good news for India is that an expert committee on venture capital (VC) opined that "India has the potential to build about 2,500 highly scalable businesses in the next 10 years, and given the probability of entrepreneurial success that means 10,000 Startups will need to be spawned to get 2,500 large-scale businesses" (Press Information Bureau (PIB), 2016). This necessitated the creation of a special ecosystem for funding support and incentives for private investors (Shrivastava and Garg, 2017). The SAP addressed these concerns in the following ways.

Providing Funding Support through a Fund of Funds for Startups (FFS)

This is an initiative in which, with a corpus of INR 10,000 crores, the GOI has created a Fund of Funds for Startups (FFS). The Small Industries Development Bank of India (SIDBI) manages the fund, and it supports different alternative investment funds (AIFs) registered with the Securities and Exchange Board of India (SEBI). AIFs extend funding support to startups (twice the SIDBI's contribution). The SIDBI identifies experienced professionals (fund managers) in the venture funding ecosystem through its Venture Capital Investment Committee. "SIDBI has committed Rs. 3123.20 crore to 49 SEBI registered AIFs. These funds have raised a corpus fund of INR 27,478 crore. INR 483.46 crore have been drawn from Fund of Funds for Startups. Further, the AIFs have invested a total of Rs. 1,625.73 crore into 247 startups" (PIB, 2019b).

Credit Guarantee

The GOI formulated the Credit Guarantee Scheme for Startups (CGSS) with a corpus contribution of INR 2,000 crores. This will enable startups to raise loans without any collateral for their business purposes. A startup with DIPP recognition is eligible for a credit guarantee up to INR 500 lakhs through member lending institutions (MLIs) per case, inclusive of the term loan, working capital, or any other instrument (PIB, 2017). The National Credit Guarantee Trustee Company (NCGTC) has the trusteeship management of this scheme.

Tax Exemptions

Tax incentives/exemptions are one of the major driving forces for startups. The SAP envisaged the following main tax benefits:

a. *Tax Exemption on Capital Gains*: Under Section 54EE of the Income Tax (IT) Act, startups are exempt from capital gains tax on capital invested through a fund that the government has notified. The existing section 54GB of the IT Act is also available to startups now; this provides exemption from tax on long-term capital gains on the sale of a residential property to HUFs and individuals if they invest such gains in startups for a period of 5 years.

b. *Tax Exemption/Holiday for Startups for 3 Years*: Startups incorporated after 1 April 2016 can avail themselves of a tax rebate of 100% on their profits for a total period of 3 years within a block of 7 years (Section 80 of the IT Act).

c. *Tax Exemption on Investments above Fair Market Value (FMV)*: Investments not registered as a venture capital fund (VCF) or incubators above the FMV are exempt for eligible startups.

d. *Angel Investors*: A robust financial ecosystem to support startup initiatives is crucial. The emergence of high net-worth individuals (HNIs) as Angel investors contributes substantially to this ecosystem. Tax exemptions for Angel investors provide significant encouragement.

Industry–Academia Partnerships and Incubation

"A pivotal component for growth of Startups is regular communication and collaboration within the Startup community, both national as well as international. An effective Startup ecosystem can't be created by the Startups alone. It is dependent on active participation of academia, investors, industry and other stakeholders" (Action Plan, 2016). To this effect, the SAP provides the following eight action points:

- Organizing Startup Fests for Showcasing Innovation and Providing a Collaboration Platform.
- Launch of the Atal Innovation Mission (AIM) with the Self-Employment and Talent Utilization (SETU) Program.
- Harnessing Private Sector Expertise for Incubator Setup.
- Building Innovation Centers at National Institutes.
- Setting up Research Parks.
- Promoting Startups in the Biotechnology Sector.
- Launching Innovation-Focused Programs for Students.
- Annual Incubator Grand Challenge.

The objective of the aforesaid points is to create a culture of first-generation entrepreneurship. Awareness and the availability of training programs and mentors, competitions and roadshows, and incubation facilities play an important role in creating a startup culture.

Building a Startup Infrastructure and Culture

The SAP envisages the organization of startup fests, both national and international, to showcase innovation and provide collaboration platforms for new entrepreneurs. Incubator grand challenges motivate new players to participate and test their ideas and passion for innovation, leading to business ideas. These platforms also allow the harnessing of private-sector expertise. The national institutes of learning, that is, the National Institute of Technology (NIT), the Indian Institute of Management (IIM), and the Indian Institute of Technology (IIT), have become involved by establishing centers of innovation and entrepreneurship through government funding with an objective of setting up and scaling up technology business incubators (TBIs) at these NITs/IITs/IIMs. With an objective of promoting industry–academia collaboration through joint research projects and consulting assignments, the SAP anticipated the setting up of seven new research parks in the IIT.

Atal Innovation Mission (AIM)

The AIM is an initiative that promotes the establishment of Atal Incubation Centers (AICs) for nurturing innovative startup businesses in their quest to become scalable and sustainable entities in subject specific areas, such as manufacturing, energy, transport, health, agriculture, education, water and sanitation, and so on. The AIM will provide a grant-in-aid of up to INR 10 crore for a maximum period of 5 years to cover the capital and operational expenditures involved in launching an AIC. Entities such as higher education institutions, groups of individuals, individuals, R&D institutes, the corporate sector, AIFs registered with the SEBI, and business accelerators are eligible to apply. The objective of AICs is to "create world class incubation facilities across various parts of India with suitable physical infrastructure in terms of capital equipment and operating facilities, coupled with the availability of sectoral experts for mentoring the startups, business planning support, access to seed capital, industry partners, training and other relevant components required for encouraging innovative startups." To create an environment of scientific temperament, innovation, and creativity among Indian students, the government has established Atal Tinkering Labs in schools. NITI Aayog, the planning body of the GOI, oversees this initiative. There are also schemes like the National Initiative for Developing and Harnessing Innovations (NIDHI) and Million Minds Augmenting National Aspiration and Knowledge (MANAK).

An analysis of the SAP shows a clear focus of the government on building a startup culture in the country and facilitating the entrepreneurship revolution. This is a highly necessary requirement for unemployed youths, who traditionally have looked toward the job market, especially government jobs, to find useful/fruitful engagement. The success of the SAP would be a significant cultural transition (Paltasingh, 2012).

2.2 *Regulatory Ecosystem*

The Department for Promotion of Industry and Internal Trade (DPIIT), previously known as the Department of Industrial Policy and Promotion (DIPP), is the nodal agency for dealing with matters related to startups in India (https://dipp.gov.in). The DPIIT comes under the Ministry of Commerce and Industry, the Government of India, which also deals with issues relating to industrial policies and foreign direct investment (FDI). To obtain the benefits of "startups" under the Startup India initiative, as outlined above, recognition from DPIIT is necessary. Startups meeting the definition criteria of startups may apply for recognition in the prescribed format. The government charges no fees for this recognition.

The Inter-Ministerial Board set up by DPIIT undertakes the validation of startups for granting tax-related benefits. The Board comprises the following three members (initially there were eight members):

- Joint Secretary, DPIIT, Convenor
- Member Representative, Department of Biotechnology
- Member Representative, Department of Science and Technology

To review the progress of the Startup India program on a regular basis, the government put in place the Monitoring Committee, comprising high officials from different concerned ministries, to review continuously the progress and implementation of various measures for the growth of the startup ecosystem (PIB, 2019c). The Government of India has further established the structure of the National Startup Advisory Council (NSAC) to help create an environment of absorption of innovation in industry and taken measures to foster a culture of entrepreneurship. The Minister of Commerce and Industry will chair the NSAC (PIB, 2020).

The National Institution for Transforming India (NITI) is the new *avatar* of the erstwhile Planning Commission (*Yojana Aayog*), which came into existence on 1 January 2015 as the government's premier think tank. Reflecting the changed dynamics of the new India, NITI aims to "foster cooperative federalism through structured support initiatives and mechanisms with the States on a continuous basis, recognizing that strong States make a strong Nation" (PIB, 2015). NITI Aayog drives the Atal Innovation Mission and indirectly supports the SAP through its initiatives; for example, NITI Aayog launched "Pitch to MOVE — a mobility pitch competition that aims to provide budding entrepreneurs of India a unique opportunity to pitch their business ideas to a distinguished jury" (PIB, 2018).

3. Complementary Framework and Schemes

Startups begin with a small venture, scaling up to a bigger enterprise in due course. As a legacy of Gandhian philosophy and the focus on the socialistic pattern of administration, the small-scale sector has been an important agenda item for all political parties, policy makers, and intelligentsia since independence in India. The special push for this sector has had the multiple objectives of regional dispersal of industries, employment generation, and providing a "seedbed for Entrepreneurship" (Uddin, 1989; Singh, 2010). There are several complementary frameworks that accelerate the startup revolution.

Micro, Small, and Medium Enterprises (MSMEs)

Due to their nature of permeability into local areas, providing large employment opportunities at a low capital cost, small-scale industries (SSIs) play a crucial role in economic development. They also help in reducing regional imbalances by creating opportunities for industrialization of rural and backward areas, assuring more equitable distribution of the national income and wealth. Due to their focus on socioeconomic development, SSIs have featured consistently in the industrial policies of India (Reddy, 2008). Subsequent to an amendment of the GOI (Allocation of Business) Rules 1961, two ministries, specifically the Ministry of Small-Scale Industries and the Ministry of Agro and Rural Industries, merged to create the Ministry of Micro, Small, and Medium Enterprises (M/o MSMEs) in May 2007. The M/o MSMEs now creates an ecosystem through policies, projects, programs, and schemes to assist MSMEs in scaling up with the support of state governments, which have the primary responsibility for MSMEs.

The definition of MSMEs concerns their investment threshold (there is now a proposition to change this to define them solely on a turnover basis): Table 2 provides classification of MSMEs in India. The last column contains the latest definition effective 1st July 2020.

Table 2: Classification of MSMEs

Enterprise	Manufacturing Sector on the Basis of Investment in Plant and Machinery	Service Sector on the Basis of Investment in Equipment	New Classification Criteria Proposed on the Basis of Annual Turnover Only*
Micro	Not more than INR 25 lakh	Not more than INR 10 lakh	Not more than INR 5 crore
Small	INR 25 lakh to INR 5 crore	INR 10 lakh to INR 2 crore	INR 5 to INR 75 crore
Medium	INR 5 crore to INR 10 crore	INR 2 crore to INR 5 crore	INR 75 crore to INR 250 crore

*Revised Composite Criteria: Investment in Plant & Machinery/equipment and Annual Turnover, w.e.f. 1st July 2020
Source: DCMSME (2018).

The National Small Industries Corporation Limited (NSIC), working under the Ministry of MSMEs, has set up six livelihood business incubators under the "Scheme for Promotion of Innovation, Entrepreneurship & Agro Industry" (ASPIRE). These rapid incubation centers provide facilities for hands-on training and education on working projects and offer support to prospective entrepreneurs and startup companies to start product manufacturing.

Make in India Program

In September 2014, the GOI launched the "Make in India" program with the objectives to

- inspire confidence in India's capabilities among potential partners abroad, the Indian business community and citizens at large;
- provide a framework for a vast amount of technical information on 25 industry sectors; and
- reach out to a vast local and global audience via social media and constantly keep them updated about opportunities, reforms, etc.

The DPIIT is also the nodal point to run this program; however, a dedicated investor facilitation cell (IFC) assists investors in seeking regulatory approval and provides handholding services through the pre-investment and execution phases, as well as after-care support. While there may be criticism of the success of this program (Green, 2014), it is undeniable that the EODB rankings have significantly improved for India, reflecting the positive perception of foreign investors in Indian markets. Standup India and then Startup India followed the Make in India initiative. The government launched the *Standup India* scheme with the objective of supporting disadvantaged groups, in particular the scheduled castes/tribes (SC/ST) and/or female entrepreneurs with bank loans from INR 1 Lakh to INR 1 crore for setting up a greenfield enterprise (a startup).

There is also an umbrella program, called Digital India, which the GOI launched in 2015, involving multiple government ministries and departments. The objective of this program is to realize the full potential of digitization in all walks of life. The Department (now Ministry) of Electronics and Information Technology (D/MeitY) coordinates this program. There are nine growth areas in this program, namely the Universal Access to Mobile Connectivity, Broadband Highways, Public Internet Access Program, Reforming Government through Technology, e-Governance: e-Kranti — Electronic Delivery of Services, Electronics Manufacturing, Information for All, IT for Jobs, and Early Harvest Programs. Startups have a natural home in the digital sector, and this initiative complements the startup revolution well.

Skill India Program

While the demographic dividend is a plus factor for any country, it takes no time to turn negative if youths are not skillful enough for employment. With the objective of enhancing youth employability through skill development, the government formed a dedicated Ministry for Skill Development and Entrepreneurship (MSDE) in July 2015. The National Skill Development Corporation (NSDC) under the guidance of the MSDE has introduced an initiative that allows aspirant candidates to register for skill training/learning and employment opportunities through the online portal. The Skill India Mission under the National Policy on Skill Development and Entrepreneurship 2015 created sector skill councils (SSCs), which the NSDC monitors. It has identified forty priority sectors based on a skill gap analysis, for example, the food industry, healthcare, telecoms, banking and finance, and so on. It runs National Skill Qualification Framework recognized courses that meet the requirements and standards of the industry in these sectors. These courses focus on the practical delivery of work and thus startups can obtain skilled resources that they may employ in different sectors (MSDE, 2009).

National Schemes

Inspired by the initiatives and push from the Prime Minister himself, various ministries and departments of the GOI are complementing the startup revolution by way of more than a hundred schemes. These schemes may encourage entrepreneurs to test a startup idea for scalability. Some example of these schemes are:

- The Ministry of Electronics and Information Technology — Support for International Patent Protection in Electronics and Information Technology (SIP-EIT).
- The Khadi and Village Industries Commission under the Ministry of MSME — Scheme of Funds for Regeneration of Traditional Industries (SFURTI).
- The National Minorities Development and Finance Corporation (NMDFC) — Virasat — A Credit Scheme for Craftpersons.

A review of the aforesaid initiatives from the GOI shows how the central government has geared up the overall machinery to make Startup India successful. For example, the Startup *Yatra* (journey) initiative involves a mobile van traveling throughout the states recording ideas from budding entrepreneurs and offering them the chance of incubation. However, the success of GOI schemes like "Startup India" lies in its adaptability and in the enthusiasm of the state governments.

MUDRA Loans

To provide business finance for micro-business units, including startups, the GOI has established the Micro-Units Development and Refinance Agency (MUDRA). Micro or small businesses operating in the manufacturing, trading, and services sectors (including startups) are eligible for loans in the following three categories:

- *Sishu* (*infant*): loans up to INR 50,000
- *Kishor* (*adolescent*): loans up to INR 5 lakhs
- *Tarun* (*young*): loans up to INR 10 lakhs

International Linkages

India has also entered into global partnerships to make the startup ecosystems of India and its partners closer and to facilitate joint innovation, which it refers to as "international bridges." It has entered into such global partnerships with Finland, the Netherlands, the United Kingdom, the Russian Federation, the United States, Portugal, Japan, Sweden, Israel, Singapore, and the Republic of Korea. For example, it conceptualized the India–Korea Startup Hub as part of a joint statement signed between the Korea Trade-Investment Promotion Agency (KOTRA) and Invest India on 9 July 2018. The hub's objective was "to enable collaborations between startups, investors, incubators, & aspiring entrepreneurs of both countries and provide them requisite resources for market entry & global expansion." The State Bank of India and Mahindra are mentoring the startup grand challenge "to channelize the entrepreneurial capacity between Indian and Korean Startups to work together and build solutions for the challenges facing the world, for example, Credit Rating, Predictive Analytics, Fraud Detection, Cyber Security, Primary/Secondary/Tertiary Healthcare."

Startups' Perspective on Small Business Financing

For the success of any new business, access to external finance and the ability to undertake profitable investment opportunities are especially important (Levine, 2005). Financing for small businesses, including startups, has been their Achilles' heel. Most of these startups rely initially on informal channels of funding, like family, friends, moneylenders, and self-funding. The formal channels of banks are not available to these new startups due to the requirements of a credit history/rating, the risk and viability of the business, and so on (Chavis *et al.*, 2011).

Soon after independence, the GOI provided mechanisms to support small-scale industries through initial funding and national schemes. At the level of state government, state financial corporations (SFCs) provided the small-scale sector with financial support. However, one of the greatest challenges in such financing was the "poor lending decision," creating "non-performing assets" (NPAs). Under the Startup India scheme, the GOI created the Fund of Funds under the SIDBI.

Table 3 deals with the number of startups which were provided financial assistance under the Fund of Funds scheme.

Table 3: Number of Startups Provided with Financial Assistance under the Fund of Funds (Year-Wise as on 13 June 2019)

Financial Year	2016–2017	2017–2018	2018–2019	2019–2020
No. of startups given financial assistance under the FFS	62	58	98	31

Source: PIB (2019a).

Private Funding

A robust private funding ecosystem is a *sine qua non* for a successful startup revolution. Startups in India, both tech and non-tech, face a dearth of funding beyond the Series B stage. The RBI, in its report, suggested, "A board that allows equities exchange of these SMEs can effectively help address this problem. It will also give the wider public an opportunity to participate in the dynamic Indian startup ecosystem. The Innovators Growth Platform (IGP) proposed by SEBI is a welcome development. Some modifications are required for the success of IGP. SEBI must relax the norms defining the Accredited Investors (AIs) who could participate. To create enough liquidity, participation of HNIs, Mutual Funds, FIIs, etc. must be encouraged. Most technology startups or high-growth startups are often loss-making, hence there should be no profitability requirement to list. SEBI should facilitate dual class share structure, which is very popular with tech startups across the world. Further, standards for internal governance of MSMEs may be developed that can help MSMEs identify current gaps and areas of improvement" (RBI, 2019).

CSR Funding for Incubators

The Companies Act 2013 (CA) requires companies beyond a threshold to spend at least 2% of their average net profits made during the three immediately preceding financial years in one or more of the areas specified in the Seventh Schedule of the Act (Section 135 of the CA). One of the areas in which such investment is possible is the contribution that specified institutes engaged in promoting scientific research make to incubators.

Table 4:   CSR Spending in the Area of Technology Incubators

Year	FY 2014–2015 (INR Cr.)	FY 2015–2016 (INR Cr.)	FY 2016–2017 (INR Cr.)	FY 2017–2018 (INR Cr.)
Spending in technology incubators	4.74	26.34	23.09	15.55
Overall CSR spending	10,065.93	14,517.37	14,329.78	13,623.62

Source: https://www.csr.gov.in/developmentlist.php.

Table 4 provides with the CSR spending made by the companies in the area of Technology Incubators

4. Role of State Governments

India works on the principle of cooperative federalism, which envisages that "national and state agencies undertake government functions jointly rather than exclusively. The nation and states would share power, without power being concentrated at any government level or in any agency" (Srikrishna, 2015). India is a large, heterogeneous, and complex nation, with multiple languages, religions, and ethnicities and over 1.30 billion people (Singh, 2007). The country has now evolved from having a few political partiesto 1,841 registered political parties (with 7 national, 49 state, and 1,785 unrecognized parties). In the initial years of independence, the relationship between the center and the states was stable due to a single party being in power both at the center and in the states. Over a period, the role of regional parties in subnational politics in several states increased, and they had a hold on the coalitions at the central level. The fiscal federalism in the country was not untouched by these developments and accordingly the fiscal relationship between the center and the states evolved by way of devising mechanisms and concessions to retain control (CUTS, 2011). The Constitution of India has an inbuilt mechanism to keep the economic unity of the country through provisions under Part XIII (Atiabari, 1961).

The Seventh Schedule of the Constitution of India provides three lists, specifically the Union List, State List, and Concurrent List, which people also refer to as List I, List II, and List III. While the Parliament of India has some supremacy in terms of having precedence in legislating laws in the concurrent list, it generally would not encroach on the items that the

Table 5: Startup India Recognition Heat Map

484 Districts out of about 732 Districts	29 States (All)	7 Union Territories out of 9
55% in Tier 1	27% in Tier 2	18% in Tier 3

Source: States Startup Ranking Report of 2018.

State List includes. Table 5 shows the penetration of startups across districts, states and union territories in India. Industries are normally under the purview of the state governments (Entry 24 of List II) subject to the industries that the Central Law declares to be expedient in the public interest, including the industries for the purposes of defense or for the prosecution of war (entries 7 and 52 of List I of the Seventh Schedule of the Constitution of India). Startups are not a particularly new idea for state governments, as the states of Andhra Pradesh, Kerala, Rajasthan, and Goa already had a startup policy before the GOI implemented the SAP in 2016. However, after the SAP, state governments started a huge push on startup initiatives, which is evident from the fact that 11 states adopted the policy immediately in 2016, four more did so in 2017, and three followed in 2018. Now, except the few union territories and northeastern states, all the states (25 in total) have their own policy to promote startups. However, in terms of the opening up of startups and the coverage of geographical areas, the following statistics are quite encouraging.

Startup Policy of State Governments

An analysis of the startup policies of the 25 state governments shows that they have developed their startup policies along the broad lines of the SAP; however, the incentives that they provide to the startup ecosystem vary. A comparison of the nodal agencies of these state governments indicates that the agencies for implementing the startup policy are in the hands of:

- Department of Industries — 8
- Department of MSMEs — 4
- Department of Information Technology (IT) — 9
- Special purpose vehicles, like the *Entrepreneurship Development and Innovation Institute* in Tamil Nadu — 4

While, as natural devolution, the states' MSME Department could have been the natural choice for a nodal agency, due to the perception that startups have more to do with information technology, in the majority of cases, the Department of Information Technology is the nodal agency. In many of the cases, the startup policy is part of the broader IT and e-commerce policy.

The startup policies of the states provide startups with a host of fiscal and non-fiscal benefits. Some of the major ones are the following:

- Self-certification in the case of some forms of statutory compliance and single-window clearance
- Interest subsidies on loans
- Tax holidays in terms of tax reimbursements
- Mentoring assistance
- Product development and marketing/commercialization assistance
- Availability of land at concession rates
- Subsidies on utilities like power
- Broadband and internet connection subsidies
- Seed funding and scaling-up funding
- Infrastructure availability, like co-working space
- Reimbursement of IPR (patent and trademark) application charges
- Encouragement for startup competitions
- Preference/promotion of startups in government procurement

States' Startup Ranking

In 2018, the DIPP conducted the first ever States' Startup Ranking Exercise, with the key objective "to encourage States and Union Territories to take proactive steps towards strengthening the Startup Ecosystems within their jurisdictions." The aim of this ranking was just like the World Bank's Ease of Doing Business Rankings, that is, "creating a healthy competition among states to further learn, share and adopt good practices." The government has also announced the Framework for Startup Ranking 2019 to evaluate progress made from 1 May 2018 to 30 June 2019. Table 6 provides the Ranking Framework pillars. One of the major components of this evaluation framework is the ease of financing startups. With an objective of infusing competitiveness (competitive federalism)

Table 6:   Startup Ranking Framework

Ranking Framework Overview Pillar#	Framework Pillar	Number of Action Points	Score
1	Startup policy and implementation	13	7
2	Incubation support	3	20
3	Seed funding support	2	15
4	Funding support — angel and venture	3	10
5	Simplified regulations	4	13
6	Easing public procurement	5	14
7	Awareness and outreach	8	11
Total		38	100

Source: States Startup Ranking Report of 2018.

among the state governments, the GOI launched a ranking framework in 2018 to determine the robustness of the startup ecosystem in the seven framework pillars and 38 action points, which are actually the reform areas in focus for promoting a conducive startup ecosystem (DIPP, 2018).

With an objective of promoting cross-learning and providing impetus for beginners, the government performed pairing for mentoring. A total of 30 states and UTs participated in this exercise. In line with their percentile-based grading, the government categorized states into the following six categories:

- Best Performer: 100th percentile (Gujarat).
- Top Performers: higher than the 85th and lower than the 100th percentile (Karnataka, Kerala, Odisha,[1] and Rajasthan).
- Leaders: higher than or equal to the 70th percentile and lower than or equal to the 85th percentile (Andhra Pradesh, Bihar, Chhattisgarh, Madhya Pradesh, and Telangana).
- Aspiring Leaders: higher than the 50th percentile and lower than the 70th percentile.

---

[1] In 2011, the Government of India approved the name change of the State of Orissa to Odisha. This document reflects this change. However, when reference is made to policies that predate the name change, the formal name Orissa is retained.

- Emerging States: Higher than the 25th percentile and lower than or equal to the 50th percentile.
- Beginners: Lower than or equal to the 25th percentile.

The ranking framework helped the states to take action and work on the key reform areas necessary for a facilitative startup ecosystem. There are several best practices of the states along the seven interventions that the ranking framework lists (StartupIndia 2019). The government has already announced the 2019 ranking framework and the process is underway for data collection at the startup portal. It has also announced the National Startup Awards 2020 for startups and ecosystem enablers (incubators and accelerators).

5. Startup Ecosystem Until 2019

The Startup Action Plan of the GOI has no doubt provided much-needed support and encouragement for entrepreneurship in India. The post-SAP data on startups with DPIIT recognition are very encouraging, making India the third-largest startup ecosystem in the world with close to 25,000 startups. Table 7 details the number of startups being recognized by DPIIT state-wise in states having a Startup Policy and Table 8 provides the details wherein there is no Startup Policy.

Table 7: State-Wise Number of Startups that the DPIIT has Recognized (as of 5 November 2019)

States with a Startup Policy		2016	2017	2018	2019*	Total
1	Andaman and Nicobar	0	1	2	5	8
2	Andhra Pradesh	4	103	162	140	409
3	Assam	10	35	68	57	170
4	Bihar	1	48	149	15	213
5	Chhattisgarh	11	57	121	143	332
6	Goa	2	20	44	32	98
7	Gujarat	29	298	452	514	1,293
8	Haryana	28	271	487	591	1,377
9	Himachal Pradesh	0	9	17	25	51
10	Jharkhand	2	35	88	80	205

Table 7:   (*Continued*)

States with a Startup Policy		2016	2017	2018	2019*	Total
11	Karnataka	67	886	1,213	1,374	3,540
12	Kerala	24	172	332	563	1091
13	Madhya Pradesh	7	107	297	272	683
14	Maharashtra	93	1,104	1,661	1,778	4,636
15	Manipur	0	4	7	4	15
16	Nagaland	1	4	2	2	9
17	Odisha[a]	4	115	168	142	429
18	Punjab	7	31	70	81	189
19	Rajasthan	14	140	246	300	700
20	Tamil Nadu	54	271	459	489	1,273
21	Telangana	20	328	511	492	1,351
22	Uttar Pradesh	29	413	791	709	1,942
23	Uttarakhand	4	45	69	84	202
24	West Bengal	8	181	275	255	719
		439	4,681	7,691	8,147	20,935

Note: [a] In 2011, the Government of India approved the name change of the State of Orissa to Odisha. This document reflects this change. However, when reference is made to policies that predate the name change, the formal name Orissa is retained.
Source: PIB (2019d).

Table 8:   State-Wise Number of Startups that the DPIIT has Recognized (as of 5 November 2019)

States/Union Territories without a Startup Policy		2016	2017	2018	2019*	Total
1	Chandigarh	9	22	27	32	90
2	Dadra and Nagar Haveli	0	3	0	2	5
3	Daman and Diu	0	1	0	1	2
4	Delhi	75	743	1,187	1,152	3,157
5	Meghalaya	0	0	2	6	8
6	Mizoram	0	0	2	1	3
7	Pondicherry	0	3	16	6	25
8	Sikkim	0	1	0	2	3
9	Tripura	0	0	4	5	9
		84	773	1,238	1,207	3,302

Source: PIB (2019d).

Major Sectors for Startups

The traditional perception is that startups operate in the area of information technology (primarily software development). However, the latest sector-wise data on startups show that they operate in more than 45 different sectors. The top 15 sectors in which startups operate in India are given in Table 9.

While IT services still lead, newer focus areas, like FinTech, the IOT, AI, aggrotech, and renewable energy, are encouraging. Realizing the potential of new areas like FinTech (technological solutions for providing financial services), one of the states in India (Maharashtra) has come up with a dedicated FinTech policy for startups with a vision of becoming a "global FinTech hub." Another example is the regulatory sandbox

Table 9:   Major Sectors for Startups

Sl. No.	Sector	2016	2017	2018	2019*	Total
1	IT Services	0	610	1,417	1,351	3,378
2	Healthcare and Life Sciences	0	424	768	808	2,000
3	Education	0	313	767	658	1,738
4	Food and Beverages	0	179	365	450	994
5	Professional and Commercial Services	0	190	388	400	978
6	Agriculture	0	174	319	427	920
7	Finance Technology (FinTech)	0	160	237	362	759
8	Green Technology	0	128	274	310	712
9	Technology Hardware	0	152	260	286	698
10	Renewable Energy	0	142	292	262	696
11	Enterprise Software	0	148	249	263	660
12	Internet of Things (IOT)	0	143	265	246	654
13	Retail	0	116	241	224	581
14	Artificial Intelligence (AI)	0	73	218	288	579
15	Construction	0	83	212	282	577
						17,519

Note: * As of 5 November 2019.
Source: PIB (2019d).

regulations that the Insurance Regulator in India implemented to facilitate FinTech innovations in the insurance sector.

Startup Culture

One of the major challenges for the government lies in creating a culture of entrepreneurship and developing confidence in the minds of the younger generation (Pereira, 2007). Looking at the numbers of new start-ups and initiatives at the level of schools and universities, the future in India looks positive; however, it will take more time to see the results of these initiatives. The Global Entrepreneurship Monitor (GEM) Report for India on entrepreneurial framework conditions ranks it higher on almost all its parameters, which include government support, internal market dynamics, and infrastructure. However, entrepreneurial and behavioral attitudes, like the motivational index, established business ownership rate, and so on, still require improvement (GEM, 2019). It is necessary to nurture the risk-taking appetite among youths so that they can venture into entrepreneurship, which has generally been associated with families with a business background.

Female Startup Founders

The phenomenon of female entrepreneurship is becoming increasingly global (Estrin and Mickiewicz, 2011). In India, women occupy about 30% of corporate senior management positions, which is notably higher than the global average (24%); however, women constitute only 13.76% of the total entrepreneurs, and the figure is even lower in the case of startups, about 10% (Colaco and Hans, 2018). Different state governments have devised incentives specifically to promote female entrepreneurship; for example, under MSMEs, Trade Related Entrepreneurship Assistance and Development (TREAD) provides women "with trade related training, information and counselling & grant of up to 30% of the total project cost." A dedicated online portal called *udyam sakhi* (entrepreneur friend) helps to provide women with information on entrepreneurship.

Bureaucratic Hassle

Irrespective of several measures to eliminate the bureaucratic hassle from the startup ecosystem, in a general review of writings/reviews on this subject, the perception of the ineffectiveness of bureaucracy has emerged as one of the prominent factors. While the situation has changed at the central level to a greater extent (StartupIndia, 2020), reforms in the complete hierarchy are still desirable. This is further complicated when different sets of governments at the state level become involved. Digitization and states' ranking framework have helped to bring some standardization; however, it is still a work in progress.

Funding Blues

Beating the "valley of death" has been a pertinent issue that startups have faced. The GOI has undertaken several initiatives in this regard by providing support through initial seed funding, incubation support, and various subsidies; however, this support has not been sufficient to bail out the startups. There is a need for startups to secure funding from private players (VCFs) and maybe even from the public at large (IPOs).

On the other hand, some authors have criticized the paternalistic and bureaucratic approach of the government in promoting small-scale industries, which leads to dependency. They have suggested that, when developing a self-reliant modern small-scale industry, it is important to make it free. How long can the protection last (Tendulkar and Bhavani, 1997)? Taking this argument forward, overreliance on and expectation of government support are not a good idea. The ecosystem has to generate the required trust from private investors, as private equity (PE) funding has proven to be a more stable source of equity funding (Pandit *et al.*, 2015).

Startup Failures

Studies have shown that 90% of startups fail within 3–5 years of commencing operation (Failory, 2020). However, during this research, it became apparent that there is a conspicuous absence of an official figure of closed startups and an analysis of lessons learnt on the Startup India portal. This may be because the SAP is just 4 years old and it is too early to judge the success/failure on the number of startups closed.

The "Stayzilla" Case — The founder of this travel startup in India entered into a wrangle with one of its creditors, which led to cases of fraud and so on. The issue became murkier to the extent that the robustness of the startup ecosystem came into question. Presently, the matter is still under liquidation proceedings. In such cases, preparing an exit strategy from the beginning, including pre-packaged insolvency, M&A, IPO, and so on, would be greatly useful (Chambers, 2019).

6. Conclusion and Policy Recommendations

A review of the Startup Action Plan of the GOI shows a positive impact on the number of startups, and it seems that the startup ecosystem has reached the early traction stage. One of the major requirements for this initiative to sustain momentum is the availability of funds so that the SAP is able to emerge from the "valley of death," a crucial period that requires acceleration and consistent efforts. There is a point at which one can state, "What entrepreneurs need, far more than the fine words or advice of politicians or academics, is the support, solace, and help of other entrepreneurs" (Broughton, 2012). There is a greater need for established businesses to handhold the startups and encourage them through mentorship, incubation, and financial support, crafting their role in the existing ecosystem of business. People should not perceive the startup revolution as a fad.

While the SAP does not have any fixed tenure as such, its performance in producing the desired results of creating an ecosystem of entrepreneurship that would drive "sustainable economic growth and generate large-scale employment opportunities" is subject to scrutiny from the Parliament through the elected representatives.

The RBI Committee on MSMEs deliberated on all the aspects relating to startups in India and found that "the major reason for migration of startups to other countries is better enabling environment such as tax concessions, well-developed infrastructure, ease of doing business, exit policy, etc. Hence, the Committee was of the view that financial incentives and excellent infrastructure facilities must be deployed to retain successful Indian startups and to lure the best talent from across the world to start businesses in India" (RBI, 2019).

There is a need to focus on developing a culture of entrepreneurship. The mindset of youths is still toward fixed-tenure employment rather than venturing out in startups. For a successful startup revolution, this attitude needs to change. Business failures should act as lessons for new entrepreneurs, and thus it is important to bring forward failure case studies of startups as a reference point to avoid known potholes.

The skewness of funding support toward IT- and software-focused startups requires diversion. There is a need to invite innovation in the areas of renewable energy, aggrotech, smart cities, health, water, and plastic waste management (Dhindaw and Kumar, 2019). The startup ecosystem also requires integration into the overall economic development perspective of the country (Jain, 2011). It cannot be a standalone policy. Whenever we discuss startups, we discuss them from the angle of startups themselves, but an analysis from the sectoral side concerning how small innovations can help a particular sector is necessary. One such analysis on how startups can ameliorate the conditions of Indian farmers has shown the way for other sectors (Anand and Raj, 2019).

It is good news that the startup ecosystem so far has performed well in accordance with the SAP. Rising numbers of soonicorns (startups that have the potential to become unicorns soon) and unicorns (startups with a value over a billion US dollars) in India are witnesses. A robust startup ecosystem will not only boost the economy but also contribute to the sustainable development goals (SDGs), specifically SDG 8 on decent work and economic growth. The recent announcement of the Government of India about the creation of the National Infrastructure Pipeline (NIP) to achieve the GDP of US$5 trillion by 2024–2025 raises further hope for the startup revolution. The hallmark of India's efforts in creating a startup ecosystem is the GOI's regular active interventions with the required policy and regulatory changes.

References

Anand, A. and S. Raj. 2019. Agritech Startups: The Ray of Hope in Indian Agriculture. MANAGE: Centre for Agricultural Extension Innovations,

Reforms, and Agripreneurship (CAEIRA). https://www.manage.gov.in/publications/discussion%20papers/MANAGE-Discussion%20Paper-10.pdf (accessed December 15, 2019).

Atiabari. 1961. *Atiabari Tea Co. Ltd. v. State of Assam* AIR 1961 SC 232.

Blank, S. 2013. Why the lean startup changes everything. *Harvard Business Review.* https://hbr.org/2013/05/why-the-lean-start-up-changes-everything?referral=00060 (accessed November 15, 2019).

Broughton, P. 2012. The start uprising: Eighteen months of the startup America partnership. *Ewing Marion Kauffman Foundation.* SSRN: https://ssrn.com/abstract=2186472 or http://dx.doi.org/10.2139/ssrn.2186472 (accessed December 12, 2019).

Burange, L.G. and S. Yamini. 2011. *A Review of India's Industrial Policy and Performance.* Working Paper, Department of Economics, University of Mumbai. https://www.researchgate.net/publication/280727114_A_Review_of_India's_Industrial_Policy_and_Performance (accessed November 30, 2019).

Chacko, E. 2007. From brain drain to brain gain: Reverse migration to Bangalore and Hyderabad: India's globalizing high tech cities. *GeoJournal*, 68(2/3): 131–40. www.jstor.org/stable/41148150.

Chambers, J.T. 2019. India is becoming an entrepreneurship model for the world. *Economic Times*, 1 January 2019. https://economictimes.indiatimes.com/smallbiz/startups/newsbuzz/india-is-becoming-an-entrepreneurship-model-for-the-world-john-chambers/articleshow/67332196.cms (accessed December 12, 2019).

Chavis, L., L. Klapper, and I. Love. 2011. The impact of the business environment on young firm financing. *World Bank Economic Review*, 25(3): 486–507. www.jstor.org/stable/41342486.

Colaco, V. and V. Basil Hans. 2018. Women entrepreneurship in India — changes and challenges. *Sahyadri Journal of Management*, 2(2). SSRN: https://ssrn.com/abstract=3319405.

Conti, A., J. Thursby, and M. Thursby. 2013. Patents as signals for startup financing. *Journal of Industrial Economics*, 61(3): 592–622. www.jstor.org/stable/43305837.

Consumer Unity and Trust Society (CUTS). 2011. Fiscal federalism in India call to revisit the debate, issues for parliamentarians. *CUTS International*, 1/2011. https://parfore.in/wp-content/themes/parfore/pdf/1-2011Fiscal_Federalism_in_India_Call_to_Revisit_the_Debate.pdf.

Department of Industrial Policy and Promotion (DIPP). 2018. States' startup ranking 2018. https://www.startupindia.gov.in/content/dam/invest-india/compendium/Startup%20India%20-%20National%20report_Final%20Version_web.pdf (accessed December 12, 2019).

Development Commissioner Ministry of Micro, Small and Medium Enterprise (DCMSME). 2018. Agenda Papers for 16th Meeting of National Board for Micro, Small & Medium Enterprises. https://www.dcmsme.gov.in/meetings/final-Agenda_16th_NBMSME.pdf (Accessed on September 15, 2020).

Dhindaw, J. and A. Kumar. 2019. How the government can play a role in spurring innovation and growing India's startup ecosystem. *CityFixLabs India.* https://yourstory.com/socialstory/2019/08/government-policy-innovation-indiatech-start-ups.attitude (Accessed on September 15, 2020).

Ester, P. 2017. Silicon valley: The DNA of an entrepreneurial region. In *Accelerators in Silicon Valley* (pp. 21–36). Amsterdam: Amsterdam University Press. doi:10.2307/j.ctt1zrvhk7.6.

Estrin, S. and T. Mickiewicz. 2011. Institutions and female entrepreneurship. *Small Business Economics,* 37(4): 397–415. www.jstor.org/stable/41486142.

Failory. 2020. The ultimate startup failure rate report. https://www.failory.com/blog/startup-failure-rate (accessed January 2, 2020).

GEM. 2019. *Global Entrepreneurship Monitor 2017–2018: India Report.* Ahmedabad: Entrepreneurship Development Institute India (EDII). https://www.gemconsortium.org/economy-profiles/india.

Green, R.A. 2014. Can 'Make in India' Make Jobs? The challenges of Manufacturing Growth and High-Quality Job Creation in India. James A. Baker III Institute for Public Policy of Rice University. https://www.bakerinstitute.org/media/files/files/9b2bf0a2/Econ-pub-MakeInIndia-121514.pdf (accessed November 24, 2019).

Hoselitz, B. 1952. Entrepreneurship and economic growth. *American Journal of Economics and Sociology,* 12(1): 97–110. www.jstor.org/stable/3484612.

Jain, V. 2011. Indian Entrepreneurship and the Challenges to India's Growth. https://iveybusinessjournal.com/publication/indian-entrepreneurship-and-the-challenges-to-indias-growth/ (accessed December 12, 2019).

Jang, J.J., J. Kim, and Y.-H. Cho. 2013. Change of industrial strategies and government-business relationship in India. *Journal of International and Area Studies,* 20(2): 101–115. www.jstor.org/stable/43107260 (accessed December 12, 2019).

Korreck, S. 2019. *The Indian Startup Ecosystem: Drivers, Challenges and Pillars of Support.* ORF Occasional Paper No. 210, September 2019. Delhi: Observer Research Foundation.

Kothari, V. 2016. *Taxmann's Guide to StartUps.* New Delhi: Taxmann Publications.

Levine, R. 2005. Finance and growth: Theory and evidence. In *Handbook of Economic Growth,* edited by Aghion P. and S. Durlauf. Amsterdam: Elsevier.

McGowan, E. 2017. From Early to Acquired: What Are the Stages of a Startup? https://www.startups.com/library/expert-advice/startup-stages (accessed December 12, 2019).

Medhora, P.B. 1965. Entrepreneurship in India. *Political Science Quarterly*, 80(4): 558–580.

Ministry of Skill Development and Entrepreneurship (MSDE). 2009. *National Skill Development Policy*. Government of India. https://www.msde.gov.in/assets/images/NationalSkillDevelopmentPolicyMar09.pdf.

Paltasingh, T. 2012. Entrepreneurship education & culture of enterprise: Relevance & policy issues. *Indian Journal of Industrial Relations*, 48(2): 233–246. www.jstor.org/stable/23509835.

Pandit, V., T. Tamhane, and R. Kapur. 2015. *Indian Private Equity: Route to Resurgence*. McKinsey & Company. https://www.mckinsey.com/business-functions/strategy-and-corporate-finance/our-insights/private-equity-and-indias-economic-development (accessed December 2019).

Pereira, A. 2007. Attitudes towards Entrepreneurship in Singapore: The Role of the State in Cultural Transition. *Asian Journal of Social Science*, 35(3): 321–39. www.jstor.org/stable/23654465.

PIB. 2016. Establishment of fund of funds for funding support to startups. Government of India, 22 June 2016. https://pib.gov.in/newsite/PrintRelease.aspx?relid=146400.

PIB. 2017. Credit guarantee fund for startups. Government of India, 26 July 2017. https://pib.gov.in/newsite/PrintRelease.aspx?relid=169037.

PIB. 2018. NITI Aayog Launches 'Pitch to MOVE.' Government of India, 14 August 2018. https://pib.gov.in/newsite/PrintRelease.aspx?relid=181877.

PIB. 2019a. Financial assistance to startups. Government of India, 21 June 2019. https://pib.gov.in/newsite/PrintRelease.aspx?relid=190561.

PIB. 2019b. Startup India scheme. Government of India, 28 June 2019. https://pib.gov.in/newsite/PrintRelease.aspx?relid=190914.

PIB. 2019c. Impact of startup India. Government of India, 3 July 2019. https://pib.gov.in/newsite/PrintRelease.aspx?relid=191151.

PIB. 2019d. Facilities for new startups. Government of India, 20 November 2019. https://pib.gov.in/PressReleasePage.aspx?PRID=1592372.

PIB. 2020. Central government notifies national startup advisory council. 21 January 2020. https://pib.gov.in/newsite/PrintRelease.aspx?relid=197539.

Press Information Bureau (PIB). 2015. Government Establishes NITI Aayog (National Institution for Transforming India) To Replace Planning Commission. Government of India. https://pib.gov.in/newsite/PrintRelease.aspx?relid=114276 (accessed January 1, 2015).

Ray, R. 1994. Entrepreneurship and Industry in India 1800–1947. Delhi: Oxford University Press.

Reddy, T. K. 2008. Problems and prospects of small scale industries in India. In *Man & Development*, 23–40. http://www.indiaenvironmentportal.org.in/files/Problems%20and%20prospects%20of%20small%20scale%20industry.pdf.

Redlich, F. 1948. The business leader in theory and reality. *American Journal of Economics and Sociology*, 8: 223–224.

Reserve Bank of India (RBI). 2019. Report of the Expert Committee on Micro, Small and Medium Enterprises. https://www.rbi.org.in/Scripts/PublicationReportDetails.aspx?UrlPage=&ID=924.

Shrivastava, A. and A. Garg. 2017. Private equity in India and Indian promoters' perspective: A primer. *Journal of Private Equity*, 20(3): 68–75. www.jstor.org/stable/44397525.

Singh, N. 2007. Fiscal Federalism and Decentralization in India. SSRN: https://ssrn.com/abstract=1282267.

Singh, V.K. 2010. MSME: 'Nursery for Entrepreneurship': A legal perspective. SSRN: https://ssrn.com/abstract=2973036 or http://dx.doi.org/10.2139/ssrn.2973036 (accessed December 2019).

Solanki, S. 2008. Sustainability of rural artisans. *Economic and Political Weekly*, 43(19): 24–27. www.jstor.org/stable/40277437.

Srikrishna, B.N. 2015. Foreword to the report 'cooperative federalism: From rhetoric to reality.' New Delhi: Vidhi Center for Legal Policy.

StartupIndia. 2016. Action Plan January 16, 2016. https://www.startupindia.gov.in/ (Accessed on September 15, 2020).

StartupIndia. 2019. Compendium of best practices. https://www.startupindia.gov.in/content/sih/en/compendium_of_good_practices.html (accessed December 25, 2019).

StartupIndia. 2020. Regulatory updates. https://www.startupindia.gov.in/content/sih/en/startupgov/regulatory_updates.html (accessed January 9, 2020).

Tendulkar, S. and T.A. Bhavani. 1997. Policy on modern small scale industries: A case of government failure. *Indian Economic Review*, 32(1): 39–64. www.jstor.org/stable/24010468.

Tripathi, D. 1971. Indian entrepreneurship in historical perspective — a re-interpretation. *Economic and Political Weekly*, 6(22): M59–M63.

Uddin, S. 1989. *Entrepreneurship Development in India*. Delhi: Mittal Publications.

Venkatapathy, R. 1989. Self Concept (Conative) in relation to first generation entrepreneurs and second generation entrepreneurs. *Indian Journal of Industrial Relations*, 24(3): 312–319. www.jstor.org/stable/27767052.

World Bank. 2020. Doing Business 2020: Comparing Business Regulation in 190 Economies: Economic Profile INDIA. https://www.doingbusiness.org/content/dam/doingBusiness/country/i/india/IND.pdf.

Part II

Schemes for Fostering Investments in Startups

Chapter 3

Measures to Enhance the Effectiveness of Startup Financing: Based on a Case Study of the Korea Credit Guarantee Fund

Jung-hwan Kim* and Yong-min Jeon[†]

*Director, Korea Credit Guarantee Fund
[†]Senior Deputy Director, Korea Credit Guarantee Fund

Abstract

Recently, the Republic of Korea has been focusing on vitalizing its startup ecosystem. In response, startup financing is also gaining importance. Therefore, this research aims to propose effective ways to support startup financing by exploring the cases of the startup financing programs managed by Korea Credit Guarantee Fund, hereinafter referred to as "KODIT". KODIT is managing diverse startup financing programs including Startup NEST, First Penguin guarantee, guarantee with investment option, and Innovative Icon guarantee. Through managing such startup financing programs, it has developed the following recommendations to improve the effectiveness of its startup financing programs. We expect the following recommendations will provide relevant policy implications to startup support institutions in diverse Asian countries, where the role of policy finance is extremely important. First, the clear setting of the target customers should take precedence in designing startup financing. Second, much effort should be taken to reinforce the expertise and capabilities of the staff who are dedicated to supporting startups. Third, it is necessary to manage startup financing based on the diagnosis of the issues of the startup ecosystem. Fourth, the evaluation on startups should be made based on future growth potential. Fifth, there should be phased support in link with the management performance of startups. Sixth, startup financing should be supported comprehensively together with customized non-finance solutions.

Keywords: SMEs, startup, Fintech, startup financing

1. Introduction

A startup is generally defined as "a new venture company having innovative technology and creative ideas" and "a company that is founded based on technology and grows rapidly". Recently, the Republic of Korea has been sparing no policy-related or institutional support to foster startups and to vitalize its startup ecosystem. It is because startups have emerged as the key alternative to create new jobs in the Korean economy where the jobless growth trend has become fixed. Moreover, as the Korean economic growth model that has relied on a trickle-down effect led by large companies reaches its limits, startups have begun to gain more importance from a national economic perspective as a new innovative growth engine for the Korean economy.

However, the Republic of Korea's startup ecosystem is confronted with many issues including a halting flow of the virtuous circle of "startup → investment → exit". To overcome such issues of the Korean startup ecosystem, joint efforts and diverse solutions are required by all stakeholders in startup ecosystem including founders, the government, public institutions, venture capital, colleges, large companies.

In particular, given that many studies have shown that the major obstacle that startups are faced with in R&D and commercialization is the securing of business funds, effective support for startup financing is one of the most important solutions required for the vitalization of the startup ecosystem. Until now, however, most of the research on startup financing has focused on investment. Therefore, this research aims to explore ways to improve the effectiveness of startup financing with a focus on credit guarantees, which is one of the major businesses of KODIT. We hope this research will provide policy implications to many Asian countries who seek to promote the continued growth of startups through startup financing.

2. Current Status of Startup Ecosystem

2.1 *Current Status of the Korean Startup Ecosystem*

The startup ecosystem refers to the series of processes or the overall environment of such processes where the virtuous cycles of "startup → growth or failure → retry" and "investment → exit or loss → re-investment" from an investment perspective are formed. In other words, the key axes of the startup ecosystem are "startups" and "investors".

Moreover, from a "startup" perspective, there are certainly more companies established because there are no other job options (necessity-motivated) than those established to pursue new business opportunities (opportunity-motivated) in the Korean startup ecosystem. Two studies, "2018 Research on the Current Status of Startups" (Ministry of SMEs and Startups of the Republic of Korea, Korea Institute of Startup & Entrepreneurship Development, 2019) and "Comparative Analysis of Startup and Venture Statistics of Major Advanced Countries" (Ministry of SMEs and Startups of the Republic of Korea, Korea Institute of Startup & Entrepreneurship Development, 2018), have shown that privately-owned companies account for 89.0% and incorporated companies account for 11% of the startups in the Republic of Korea. In terms of industries, wholesale and retail account for 26.5% of startups, accommodation and restaurants for 25.8%, manufacturing for 8.9%, and repair and other individual services for 7.8%, revealing that necessity-motivated industries excluding manufacturing account for a combined 60.1%. In conclusion, as opposed to "startups" that are established based on innovative technologies and ideas and pursue rapid growth, "necessity-motivated startups" account for the majority of startups in the Republic of Korea.

Table 1:   Current Status of the World's Major Cities' Startup Ecosystem

City	Startup Ecosystem Value (US$billion)	Funding Growth Index	Exit Growth Index	Early Stage Funding Per Startup (US$thousand)
Silicon Valley	312	3	7	700
Beijing	142	3	6	599
Singapore	25	3	3	202
Tokyo	14	3	1	336
Seoul	5	1	4	107

Source: Startup Genome, 2019

Next, from an "investor" perspective such as Altos Ventures and Korea Investor Partners, the investment market in the Korean startup ecosystem lacks the vitality of those in other major Asian countries as well as in advanced startup countries including the US, People's Republic of China, and Israel. According to "Global Startup Ecosystem Report 2019" (Startup Genome, 2019), which surveyed 54 cities around the world, the Funding Growth Index of Seoul stood at only 1 of 10 points, and the Exit Growth Index reached only 4 points. Seoul's "Value of Startup Ecosystem" that Startup Genome indicated in the same report stood at US$5 billion, which is much lower than other Asian cities including Beijing (US$142 billion), Singapore (US$25 billion), and Tokyo (US$14 billion), indicating that the Korean startup ecosystem ranks low in terms of global competitiveness.

2.2 Issues of the Korean Startup Ecosystem

2.2.1 *Regulatory environment that blocks the establishment and growth of startups*

For the startup ecosystem to be vitalized, it should be supported by a startup-friendly legal environment. However, the Republic of Korea is applying positive regulations based on its positive legal system, and this works as a major obstacle to the establishment and growth of startups that are newly emerging in the era of the 4th Industrial Revolution.

The regulatory barriers are disturbing the Korean startups from freely innovating their business models. According to research by IT-specialized law firm Tek & Law in 2017, 70% of the top 100 companies based on cumulative global investment cannot do business or have to change their business conditions in the Republic of Korea due to such regulatory barriers (Startup Korea, 2019).

2.2.2 *Unfavorable environment for re-challenge and retry*

To invigorate the startup ecosystem in the Republic of Korea, there needs to be an institutional and cultural environment where many founders can take on new challenges without fearing failure. However, due to the unfavorable environment in the Republic of Korea where it is difficult to recover from failure, the experience and knowledge obtained through the failure process are being lost, instead of being developed into new learning to face challenges.

The biggest difficulty in retrying after business failure is the repayment burden of loans that founders received in the process of operating their startups. There are many cases where startups secure funds through loans for business operation, and such loans remain as personal debts that founders need to repay in case the business fails, unlike equity investment. This works as an obstacle that impedes the growth of the new businesses.

2.2.3 *Immature venture capital investment market*

While the Republic of Korea's venture capital investment market has seen continued growth quantitatively, it still falls behind in comparison to advanced startup countries including the US. People's Republic of China, etc. Also, qualitatively, private funds' voluntary participation has yet to be vitalized as the investment market relies more heavily on the Fund of Funds from the government.

First, from a quantitative perspective, the investment volume of venture capital in Republic of Korea was KRW 1.3845 trillion (US$1,238 million, exchange rate can be referred to as KRW/US$1,118 as of the end of 2018) in 2013, and continued to grow to KRW 2.3803 trillion (US$2,129 million) in 2017. However, in comparison to the ratio of investment to GDP of advanced startup countries, which include the US and the People's Republic of China, Republic of Korea reveals that its ratio is only 0.14% whereas the ratio stands at 0.44% and 0.26% in the US and the People's Republic of China, respectively. This indicates that the investment market of the Republic of Korea is not proportional to the size of its economy.

Next, from a qualitative perspective, while the venture capital investment market of the Republic of Korea has grown relying on the government's Fund of Funds, funds from the private sector are not smoothly flowing into the investment market. The Government of the Republic of Korea has raised its "Fund of Funds" since 2005 and has expanded the venture capital investment market through matching the Fund of Funds to the funds established by venture capital. The Fund of Funds is evaluated to have substantially contributed to the expansion of Republic of Korea's investment market by attracting diverse LPs to venture capital funds with government finance shouldering part of the investment loss risks under the situation where it is difficult for venture capital to raise funds. However, as the share of the Fund of Funds in the Korean venture capital investment market continues to grow, there are side effects where the Fund of Funds reduces the amount of private funds flowing into the investment market. In other words, there is a continued vicious cycle of "investment fund raising based on the Fund of Funds → investment with focus on stability → low return → shortage of inflow of private funds → investment fund raising based on the Fund of Funds".

Table 2:   The Amount of Venture Capital Investment in the Republic of Korea

(Unit : ea, KRW billion)

Classification	2013	2014	2015	2016	2017
Investment Amount	1,384.5	1,639.3	2,085.8	2,150.3	2,380.3
No. of enterprises	755	901	1,045	1,191	1,266

Source: Ministry of SMEs & Startups, 2019.

Table 3: The Share of Venture Capital Investment to GDP of Each Country

Classification	2015 (%)	2016 (%)	2017 (%)
US	0.33	0.37	0.44
People's Republic of China	0.24	0.28	0.26
Republic of Korea	0.13	0.13	0.14

Source: Government of the Republic of Korea, 2017, 2018, 2019.

2.2.4 *Sluggish exit market*

The main reason why the Republic of Korea's venture capital investment market is not vitalized quantitatively or qualitatively is because the Korean exit market is not working smoothly. Capital flows to where it can maximize its return, which is how the market economy fundamentally works. In this regard, the lack of capital inflow into the Korean investment market is a manifestation of the reality where venture capital investment is not generating a high return.

The Republic of Korea's investment exit market shows a minimal share of M&A exit, and IPO's share is not big. As of 2016, the share of venture investment recovery types in Republic of Korea compared to overseas shows that the largest share is taken by "other types of recovery" including over-the-counter sales and repayment at 70%, while M&A accounts for 86% and 59%, much higher than IPO or over-the-counter sales, in the US and Europe, respectively. As such, while recovery through M&A is vitalized in advanced countries, venture investment in Republic of Korea is focused on the recovery method of over-the-counter sales of stock holdings or repayment to venture investors by companies, as it takes around 13 years to reach IPO from the establishment of a business and M&A is not vitalized. It is difficult to get a high return on investment as the over-the-counter sales method entails uncertainties in getting the right value due to the asymmetry of corporate information, and it is also hard to get a high return through investment in companies as the investment multiple is low in general. This works as a barrier blocking the establishment of the virtuous cycle of recovering investment funds and reinvesting.

Table 4:   The Share of Venture Investment Exit Types of Different Countries in 2016

Classification	IPO (%)	M&A (%)	Others (Over-the-counter sales and Repayment) (%)
Republic of Korea	27	3	70
US	9	86	5
Europe	13	59	28

Source: Lee, Hyuk-hee, 2018.

It's also a major reason for private investors in the Republic of Korea and abroad to invest in the Korean venture funds reluctantly.

2.3 *Policy Efforts to Vitalize the Korean Startup Ecosystem and Recent Changes*

The Government of the Republic of Korea has announced and systematically pursued diverse policies including its "Plan to Establish an Innovative Startup Ecosystem" in November 2017, "Plan for Private-Led Venture Ecosystem Innovation" in January 2018, and "Strategy to Spread the Second Venture Boom" in March 2019, based on the diagnosis of the issues facing the Korean startup ecosystem described above (Government of the Republic of Korea, 2017, 2018, 2019). As the Government of the Republic of Korea has systematically and consistently pursued its "private-led startup ecosystem vitalization" policy, there have been diverse positive changes in the Korean startup ecosystem as follows:

According to the adult population survey in "2018 Global Entrepreneurship Monitor" (Global Entrepreneurship Research Association, 2018), the Republic of Korea was found to have improved in 16 of the 17 total survey categories. In particular, the Republic of Korea jumped 12 spots from 49th with 47.2 points in 2017 to 37th with 53.0 points in 2018 in "entrepreneurship as a good career choice", and 7 spots from 20th with 22.8 points in 2017 to 13th with 31.0 points in 2018 in "entrepreneurial intentions". This shows that the social awareness on startups is changing positively.

Signs that the startup boom is reviving in the Republic of Korea can be found in the vitality of the venture capital investment market and exit

Table 5:   The Result of 2018 Global Entrepreneurship Monitor

Classification			2017 (A)	2018 (B)	Change (B-A)
Attitude towards startup	Startup as a good career choice	Point	47.2	53.0	5.8 ↑
Attitude for startup	Entrepreneurship as a good career choice	Rank	49	37	12 ↑
Attitude for startup	Startup Intentions	Points	22.8	31.0	8.2 ↑
Attitude for startup	Entrepreneurship Intentions	Rank	20	13	7 ↑
Motivation for startup	Opportunity-motivated startups	Points	64.2	67.1	2.9 ↑
Motivation for startup	Opportunity-type startups	Rank	8	4	4 ↑
Motivation for startup	Necessity-motivated startups	Points	22.0	21.0	1.0 ↓
Motivation for startup	Livelihood-type startups	Rank	23	27	4 ↓

Source: Global Entrepreneurship Research Association, 2018.

market. The Republic of Korea's venture capital investment amount has increased every year, reaching a record high of KRW 3,424.9 billion (US$3,063 million) in 2018, which is 43.9% higher than the KRW 2,380.3 billion (US$2,129 million) in 2017. There has also been an increase in investment exit. In 2018, investment exit reached KRW 2,678 billion (US$2,395 million), 49.1% higher than the KRW 1,796.5 billion (US$1,607 million) in 2017, and the ratio of investment exit value to investment principal recorded as 2.1 in 2018, demonstrating an improved investment return compared to the past.

The most notable recent change in the Korean startup ecosystem is the significant increase of unicorn companies. In the Republic of Korea, the number of unicorn companies was only two in 2014 and three in 2017, showing only a slight increase, but it increased substantially to nine as of August 2019, bringing the Republic of Korea to No. 6 globally.

Table 6: Investment Exits and Earning Multiple in Republic of Korea

(Unit : KRW billion, Multiple)

Classification	2014	2015	2016	2017	2018
Amount of Investment Exits	1,222.0	2,079.2	1,968.2	1,796.5	2,678.0
Earning Multiple	1.37	1.77	1.69	1.66	2.10

Source: Ministry of SMEs & Startups (2019).

Table 7: Current Status of Unicorn Companies in Different Country

(Unit : ea, %)

Classification	US	PRC	UK	India	Germany	Rep. of Korea	Others	Total
No. of Unicorn companies	194	96	20	19	10	9	45	393
Ratio	49.4	24.4	5.1	4.8	2.5	2.3	11.5	100

Source: https://www.cbinsights.com/ (Accessed on October 15, 2020).

As explored above, the Korean startup ecosystem is improving in a positive direction with several tangible recent achievements. Given this situation, the Korean startup ecosystem seems to have great potential to advance continuously, although it has a long way to go compared to advanced startup countries including the US and the People's Republic of China.

3. Management Direction of KODIT's Startup Financing Program

3.1 *Securing Effectiveness of Credit Guarantee as a Financing Tool for Startups*

Startups are characterized as high-return and high-risk as they generally have a high level of technology and innovativeness as well as a high possibility of business failure. Due to such characteristics, it is known that venture capital investment, which is in the form of direct financing, is a more appropriate way to finance startups than bank loans, which are in the form of indirect financing.

Table 8:   Comparison of Characteristics of Startups and Funding Institutions

Startup	Bank	Venture Capital
High-return & High-risk	Low-return & Low-risk	High-return & High-risk
Lack of experience	Evaluation on standard criterion	Evaluation on subjective judgement
Less accumulated assets	Request for collateral	Request for verification of future growth potential
Elongation of investment exit	Loan period: Short-term	Investment period: Long-term

Source: Song, Chi-Seung (2018).

Meanwhile, KODIT's "credit guarantees" are provided for SMEs in the form of a "loan" from banks. Therefore, it is natural to question the utility value that the "startup financing" of KODIT, which is based on "credit guarantee", can offer for startups for which financing through investment is appropriate. In response, KODIT has focused on securing usefulness as a financing tool by managing "startup financing" as follows.

First, KODIT startupprioritizes startups that are in the blind spots of the private investment market as its main support targets, as venture capital firms avoid investment in startups in the R&D stage or initial commercialization stage and so have a week foundation.

Second, KODIT's startup financing raises the possibilities for startups to attract investment from VC firms because from the perspective of venture capital firms, KODIT's startup financing can be a signal to gauge the confidence of founders in their business and business prospects.

Lastly, KODIT's startup financing is managed as long-term funding unlike bank loans. This is because KODIT's startup financing is more useful as a financing tool for startups in that it is patient capital that can offer continued support until startups grow to a certain level.

3.2 *Exemption of Founders' Personal Joint Surety*

KODIT used to require the personal joint surety of CEOs of the guaranteed companies when providing its credit guarantees for SMEs. Personal joint surety of the CEOs refers to the case where the CEOs personally bear the surety obligations jointly with the company before KODIT when KODIT repays the loans to banks on behalf of the company. This policy was intended to reduce the possibility of the company easily choosing business shut-down in a management crisis and to induce responsible management by the person in charge of company management. However, the personal joint surety of CEOs has been a major restraint to the vitalization of the startup ecosystem as it converts the liabilities of the company into CEOs' personal liabilities in the event of business failure, which makes it difficult to retry the business and undermines the willingness to start a business due to the fear of the high stakes of business failure.

In response, KODIT decided that building an entrepreneurial environment where many talented people try to start businesses and try again even after failure is a very important and urgent issue in vitalizing Republic of Korea's startup ecosystem, and has introduced and operated guarantees with the exemption of CEOs' personal joint surety. Therefore, all of KODIT's startup financing programs are based on the principle of exempting the personal joint surety of CEOs in providing guarantees.

3.3 *Expert Organization Dedicated to Startup Financing Programs*

As specialized programs considering the characteristics and growth stage of startups, KODIT's startup financing programs are differentiated from other credit guarantee programs in terms of support targets, screening methods, support methods, and support limits. Moreover, for the in-depth evaluation of the corporate value and future growth potential of startups, understanding of the overall startup ecosystem and expertise in diverse types of startups are required.

Therefore, KODIT's startup financing programs should be managed by an organization unit specialized in supporting startups. To this end, KODIT established "Startup Branches" in eight hub regions across the nation in 2017 and added two more branches to bring the total to ten branches in 2018. Specialists with expertise in screening, including accountants, tax accountants, and certified management consultants are assigned to the Startup Branches.

4. KODIT's Key Startup Financing Programs

4.1 *Startup NEST (New Expandability Startup Total Platform)*

4.1.1 *Background of introducing startup NEST*

The general startup financing program of KODIT had limits in raising the possibility of the success of startups with fund-centered support alone as there are many cases where startups fail due to diverse reasons including a lack of experience, a weak network, and shortage of funds. Moreover, startups pour considerable efforts and costs into exploring specialized support institutions in each area when they require external help due to diverse difficulties.

Based on the diagnosis of such issues, KODIT introduced Startup NEST, which is a "demand-oriented one-stop platform for convergence solutions". It was introduced in March 2017 to overcome such limits of piecemeal fund support and to ensure that startups can resolve a range of management difficulties without having to look for diverse specialized support institutions one by one.

4.1.2 *Major contents*

Startup NEST is a total platform providing both financial and non-financial support to help the growth of startups with expandability and future growth based on new business models. Startup NEST is managed in the four stages of "selection of targets → accelerating → financial support → growth support." KODIT is generally managing Startup NEST so that the support capabilities of private accelerators and specialized institutions are effectively delivered to startups.

First, in the target selection stage, KODIT publicly invites NEST company candidates within three years of their founding by targeting companies leading future new growth industries. It provides Pre-NEST training for candidates that pass the 1st-round screening based on their application submissions to upgrade their business models and business plans, then selects the final NEST companies through the 2nd-round presentation evaluation attended by experts from the Startup Branches of KODIT and accelerator companies.

Second, in the acceleration stage, KODIT assigns the selected NEST companies to accelerator companies taking into consideration business model type, industry, and location of operation, and the accelerator companies conduct the accelerating of NEST companies through collaboration with KODIT. KODIT monitors the overall accelerating processes, and at the end of the accelerating process, it holds the "Demo Day" to introduce the NEST companies to many venture capital firms to support their investment fundraising.

Third, in the financial support stage, KODIT provides customized guarantees taking into consideration the characteristics and types of the NEST companies. For example, KODIT is offering its "4.0 Startup Guarantee" to startups related to the 4th Industrial Revolution and "First Penguin Guarantee" to startups with great innovativeness and growth potential that need intensive support. Moreover, KODIT is either providing direct investment or inducing investment from venture capital firms by keeping continued connection of NEST startups with them.

Fourth, in the growth support stage, KODIT matches specialized institutions and NEST companies in each area to offer customized solutions so that NEST companies can effectively resolve diverse difficulties. KODIT matches NEST companies in need of market development, overseas market entry, technology advice, and marketing with specialized institutions in each area including large companies, Korea Trade-Investment Promotion Agency, Korea International Trade Association, the Institute of Engineering Research at Seoul National University, National Research Council of Science & Technology, and Korea Broadcast Advertising Corporation and monitors the overall support process to ensure the effective non-financial support of such specialized institutions.

KODIT is operating Startup NEST based on classes every half-year and from the 1st class in May 2017 through the 6th class in September 2019, 460 companies have been selected and systematically nurtured so that they can enter the full growth stage.

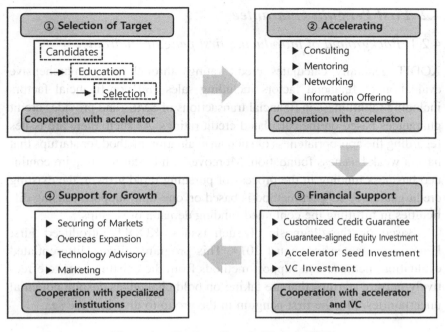

Figure 1: The Four Stages of Startup NEST

Table 9: Performance of Startup NEST Program

Class	No. of Applicant Enterprises	No. of Fnal Selected Enterprises	Competition Rate	Note
1st (May 2017)	124	40	3.1:1	− 3 accelerators
2nd (Sep. 2017)	218	60	3.6:1	− 5 accelerators
3rd (Apr. 2018)	533	80	6.7:1	− 7 accelerators
4th (Aug. 2018)	403	80	5.0:1	− 8 accelerators
5th (Apr. 2019)	792	100	7.9:1	− 9 accelerators
6th (Sep. 2019)	592	100	5.9:1	− 9 accelerators
Total	2,662	460	5.8:1	—

4.2 *First Penguin Guarantee*

4.2.1 *Background of introducing first penguin guarantee*

KODIT generally calculates credit ratings through the comprehensive evaluation of financial factors including sales and non-financial factors including faithfulness in financial transactions of SMEs and provides credit guarantees based on the calculated credit ratings. As such, there are issues regarding the appropriateness of such an evaluation method for startups that have a weak business foundation. Moreover, while startups require continued business funding in the process of pursuing rapid growth, the existing credit guarantee support method is based on one-time support, causing difficulties in fulfilling the continued funding demand of startups.

Based on the diagnosis of such issues, KODIT introduced First Penguin guarantee in August 2014. This program utilizes differentiated evaluation methods and support methods from the existing ones to effectively nurture startups that are taking on bold challenges despite potential uncertainties, like the first penguin in the group to dive into the sea.

4.2.2 *Major contents*

Under First Penguin guarantee, startups within five years of their founding with the potential to lead future industries through taking on challenges in new markets based on innovative technologies and creative ideas are selected as First Penguin companies and their credit line is set up to KRW 3 billion (US$2.7 million). Based on the evaluation results of management goal achievement, phased support is provided for three years.

As for the strength of First Penguin guarantee, one of its major advantages is that it provides sufficient funding required for the realization of growth potential for selected companies while also employing a strict selection process through the in-depth review of growth potential.

First, as for the selection process of First Penguin Companies, experts at the Startup Branches pre-screen First Penguin company candidates by inviting them to review committees of eight regional business headquarters across the country. The review committees thoroughly review CEOs' management capabilities, creativity, technological capabilities, and feasibility of business plans.

Second, as for the evaluation method of First Penguin guarantee, future growth potential based on a thorough estimation of sales in the next three years is evaluated. In the end, the key to the evaluation of future growth potential is the estimation of sales in the next three years because "continued increase of sales" is the most effective index to check the realization of the growth potential embedded in startups.

Third, as for the support method of First Penguin guarantee, First Penguin companies are given a credit line of up to KRW 3 billion (US$2.7 million) with half of the estimated sales in the next three years as the maximum limit. When setting the credit line, First Penguin companies establish their management goals based on the estimated sales that the company aims to achieve and the expected number of newly hired workforce in the following one, two, and three years from the date of setting the credit line. KODIT provides the credit guarantees of the 1st year when setting the credit line for First Penguin companies and offers phased guarantees for the 2nd and 3rd years based on the evaluation on the performance of management goal achievement.

Fourth, as for the evaluation of management goal achievement by First Penguin guarantee, experts at the Startup branches evaluate whether the management goals are achieved through a comprehensive evaluation of investment fundraising and technology development while also identifying the actual achievement of estimated sales and the number of expected newly hired workforce that First Penguin companies established under their management goals.

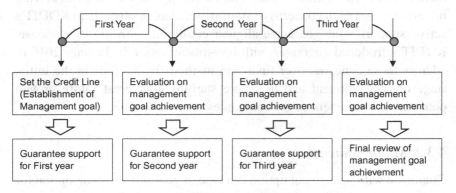

Figure 2: Support Method of First Penguin Guarantee

Table 10:   Performance of First Penguin Guarantee

(Unit : ea, KRW billion)

Classification	Jul. to Dec. 2014	2015	2016	2017	2018	Jan. to Sep. 2019	Total
No. of enterprises	51	108	150	118	105	74	606
New Guarantee	19.7	63.5	84.7	87.4	98.9	65.9	420.1

The status of First Penguin guarantee support shows that KODIT is selecting around 100 First Penguin Companies every year and has provided new credit guarantees of KRW 420.1 billion (US$376 million) for a total of 606 companies since its introduction in August 2014 through September 2019.

4.3 *Guarantee with Investment Option*

4.3.1 *Background of introducing guarantee with investment option*

KODIT has been providing guarantee-aligned equity investment for startups that received credit guarantees from January 2014 after establishing its legal foundation in August 2013 to resolve the blind spots of the private investment market. However, startups in the initial stage of establishment that have low capital and corporate value are reluctant to attract investment because the founders' share can be greatly reduced when receiving investment, and such concerns of startups stand as an obstacle to KODIT's active support with guarantee-aligned equity investment. In response, KODIT introduced guarantee with investment option in January 2016 to address these concerns over financing methods by startups in the initial stage of establishment and to secure startups with great future growth potential as investment target companies at an early date.

4.3.2 *Major contents*

Guarantee with investment option is a type of guarantee with an option for conversion to investment. More specifically regarding its structure,

KODIT first provides startups through guarantee with investment option. Then, if KODIT decides to convert the credit guarantee to an investment after a certain period of time, it can make an investment by terminating the guarantee through depositing the guaranteed loan amount in banks and subscribing to new stocks issued by the startups. If it decides not to convert the guarantee to an investment, the guarantee is maintained in the form of guaranteed loans.

Guarantee with investment option targets companies within seven years of their founding that meet the requirements for guarantee-aligned equity investment and offers support of up to KRW 1 billion (US$0.89 million). The investment option can be exercised for four years from one year after the guarantee was provided and the major strength of guarantee with investment option is that it offers startups the right to choose their financing methods.

The investment option is exercised when the company that was supported with guarantee with investment option attracts follow-up investment or when KODIT decides that future investment return is expected. When guarantee with investment option was first introduced, it was set up to calculate the exercise price (price per share) at the time of providing the credit guarantee. However, there was an issue with the exercise price tending to be calculated at a low price as the value of the company at the time of guarantee providing is generally calculated to be low. Such a low option exercise price set by KODIT then became the standard of corporate value when the startups attracted investment from venture capital firms, which

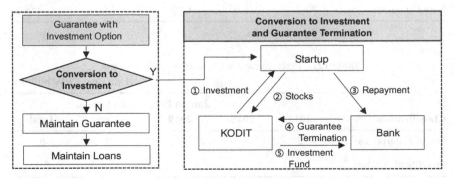

Figure 3:   Framework of Guarantee with Investment Option

ultimately was unfavorable for startups in the investment price negotiation process. In response, KODIT referred to Simple Agreement for Future Equity (SAFE), which is an investment method in Silicon Valley in the US, and overhauled its system in March 2019. Under this system, the exercise price of guarantee with investment option is decided at the time when the guarantee is converted to investment, not at the time when the guarantee is provided so that the exercise price is linked with the price evaluated at the venture capital investment.

As for the current status of guarantee with investment option support, KODIT has provided guarantee with investment option of KRW 158.8 billion (US$142 million) since its introduction in January 2016 through September 2019 to a total of 430 companies. Conversions to investment based on guarantee with investment option reached only KRW 2 billion (US$1.79 million) for two companies before the overhaul of the system in March 2019, but increased to KRW 5.3 billion (US$4.74 million) for six companies after the overhaul. It is expected that there will be more companies that convert guarantee with investment option to investment going forward.

Table 11:   Performance of Guarantee with Investment Option

(Unit : ea, KRW billion)

Classification	2016	2017	2018	Sep. 2019	Total
No. of Enterprises	92	84	158	96	430
New Guarantee	30.7	30.6	62.9	34.6	158.8

Table 12:   Performance of Conversion to Investment

(Unit : ea, KRW billion)

Classification	2017	2018	Jan. to Feb. 2019	Mar. to Sep. 2019	Total
No. of Enterprises	2	—	—	4	6
Investment Amount	2	—	—	3.3	5.3

4.4 *Innovative Icon Guarantee*

4.4.1 *Background of introducing innovative icon guarantee*

Private investment should be more vitalized to promote more unicorn companies as a driving force for generating new added value. However, the investment volume of Korean venture capital has yet to reach the level of advanced startup countries. The issue is that it is not easy to improve this situation in a short period of time because the major reason for such a passive investment environment is the sluggish exit market.

Based on the diagnosis of such issues and the operational experience of managing First Penguin guarantee, KODIT introduced Innovative Icon guarantee in May 2019 for startups with high growth potential to develop into unicorn companies by attracting large-scale private venture capital investment with KODIT's pump-primping startup financing support.

4.4.2 *Major contents*

Under Innovative Icon guarantee, startups within two to ten years of their founding with realization of sales at a certain level or with innovativeness and growth potential verified through investment by venture capital firms are selected and given a credit line of up to KRW 7 billion (US$6.26 million). Based on the results of management goal achievement, it provides guarantees in a phased manner up to six years.

Innovative Icon guarantee is similar to First Penguin guarantee in terms of its target company selection system, evaluation method based on the estimation of future sales, and support through setting a credit line. However, the main difference is that Innovative Icon Guarantee aims to nurture startups with a certain level of growth momentum into unicorn companies while First Penguin guarantee aims mainly to enhance corporate value through the realization of the growth potential of startups.

First, while First Penguin guarantee is exclusively managed by the Startup branches, Innovative Icon guarantee is exclusively managed by the Innovative Icon Support Team composed of the leading startup experts at KODIT.

Second, Innovative Icon guarantee invites candidates through both private venture capital recommendations and open invitation to expand interactions with private venture capital firms.

Third, the maximum support limit of Innovative Icon guarantee is set at KRW 7 billion (US$6.26 million), which is more than double that of First Penguin guarantee at KRW 3 billion (US$2.68 million), thus providing sufficient funding required for Innovative Icon companies to quickly grow into unicorn companies.

Fourth, the period of First Penguin guarantee's credit line is set at three years, while Innovative Icon guarantee sets the credit line and provides support for three years, and if it is decided that additional support is needed after these three years, there is an option to extend support for another three years.

Fifth, while First Penguin guarantee sets management goals based on sales estimation and the expected number of new hires, Innovative Icon guarantee sets management goals based on diverse indicators measuring growth potential including the number of new subscribers and repurchase ratio as well as sales and employment.

Lastly, Innovative Icon guarantee offers a higher level of non-financial solutions than that of First Penguin guarantee. The Innovative Icon Support Team intensively provides customized non-financial solutions to resolve diverse management pain points that Innovative Icon companies encounter in their growth process.

According to the Innovative Icon guarantee support plan, KODIT will select around 10 Innovative Icon companies every year from 2019 to

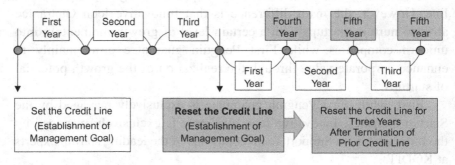

Figure 4:   Support Method of Innovative Icon Guarantee

nurture around 50 Innovative Icon companies over the next five years until 2023. It will then decide whether it will expand the number of companies to be selected through reviewing the results after the initial five years. KODIT selects Innovative Icon companies every half year based on a class system. It selected six companies for the 1st class of Innovative Icon companies in July 2019 and set credit lines of KRW 7 billion (US$6.26 million) each for five companies and KRW 5 billion (US$4.47 million) for one company.

5. KODIT's Startup Financing Program's Achievements and Next Steps

5.1 *Achievements of KODIT's Startup Financing Programs*

The specific details of the achievements of KODIT's startup financing programs are as follows. First, the programs are seeing tangible results as catalysts for increasing both the sales and number of employees of start-ups. First Penguin companies showed an average sales increase rate of 75.3% for three years from 2016 to 2018. When compared with the 3.2% of that of venture-certified companies, it is found that First Penguin

Table 13: Growth Rate in Sales and Employment of First Penguin Companies

Classification		First Penguin (%)	Venture Certificated (%)	Note
Growth rate in sales	2016	75.2	2.1	Average growth rate – First Penguin 75.3% – Venture certificated 3.2%
Growth rate in Sales	2017	82.9	4.3	Average growth rate – First Penguin 75.3% – Venture Certificated 3.2%
Growth rate in Sales	2018	67.9	—	Average growth rate – First Penguin 75.3% – Venture Certificated 3.2%
Growth rate in employment		32.3	4.3	—

guarantee is contributing substantially to the sales growth of First Penguin companies. Moreover, the rate of increase in the number of employees after one year of First Penguin guarantee support is 32.2%, which is much higher than the 4.3% of that of venture-certified companies.

Second, KODIT is evaluated to have substantially contributed to establishing an entrepreneurial environment where trying again after failure is easy through exempting the personal joint surety of CEOs in running startup financing programs. In the Republic of Korea, the typical mindset of those specialized in advanced technology with a stable occupation is one of great fear of entrepreneurial failure due to the personal joint surety of CEOs, thus making them more reluctant to start businesses. However, 60% of all startups that have received support from KODIT's startup financing programs are founded by CEOs who previously worked for large companies, are former research staff, or have a Master's degree or PhD.

Third, KODIT's startup financing program is assessed to be contributing to the vitalization of the private investment market through improving the possibility for startups to attract investment from private venture capital firms while also expanding the pool of investment targets for such firms. The current status of private investment fundraising by startups that have received support from KODIT's startup financing programs shows that as of September 2019, 28% of the 172 First Penguin companies have

Table 14:   Performance of Private Investment Attraction of First Penguin and NEST Companies

(Unit : ea, KRW billion)

Classification	First Penguin		NEST	
Classification	No. of Enterprises	Amount	No. of Enterprises	Amount
2015	7	9.1	"Before the system enforcement"	
2016	27	44.5		
2017	53	41.6	14	5.4
2018	67	93.6	50	20.7
Sep. 2019	52	157.2	4	1.7
Total	172	346.0	68	27.8

Table 15:   Default Rate of Startup Finance Program

Classification	First Penguin (%)	Startup NEST (%)	Guarantee with Investment Option (%)	Total Guarantee of KODIT (%)
2016	0.9	—[1]	0.0	3.9
2017	2.8	0.0	2.0	3.5
2018	6.0	0.0	2.5	3.5
Sep. 2019[2]	4.0	0.1	1.8	3.3

Notes: [1] Before the system enforcement.
[2] The default rate in Sep. 2019 is annualized.

raised KRW 346 billion (US$309 million) of private investment and 16% of the 68 Startup NEST companies have raised KRW 27.8 billion (US$24.9 million) of private investment.

Fourth, KODIT's startup financing programs are also seeing strong achievements in terms of risk management with a stable default rate. The default rate of First Penguin guarantee is 4.0% as of the end of September 2019, which is slightly higher than the overall default rate of KODIT at 3.3%, but not high enough to raise concerns. Impressively, Startup NEST's default rate is a mere 0.1%, with only one company experiencing default through September 2019. Guarantee with investment option is also being managed stably with its default rate standing at only 1.8%.

The main reason that KODIT's startup finance programs are able to maintain stable default rates will be discussed in further detail in the conclusion of the present report.

5.2 *Analysis of Success Factors of KODIT's Startup Financing Programs*

KODIT conducted in-depth interviews with accelerators and venture capital firms that are major players in the startup ecosystem as well as CEOs of startups who have received the support of the startup financing programs to analyze the success factors of the startup financing programs from an objective perspective.

The accelerators and venture capital firms that responded to interviews pointed out "select and concentrate strategy" as the major success factor of KODIT's startup financing programs. This strategy seems to be directly helpful to accelerators and venture capital firms that need to explore targets for seed investment or Series A investment in the market.

The second success factor that accelerators and venture capital firms indicated was that the Startup branches, which are expert organizations specialized in startup support, are fully in charge of the startup financing programs. The reason for this is that full cooperation with KODIT is now possible through the newly established Startup Branches, whereas there was no window of communication with KODIT for accelerators and venture capital firms before their establishment.

Next, the in-depth interviews with CEOs of startups that have received support revealed the following four factors as the success factors of KODIT's startup financing programs. First, the majority of CEOs who responded to the interview showed very high satisfaction with the startup financing programs' condition of exempting their personal joint surety. This is because the exemption of the personal joint surety allows startup CEOs to relieve their anxiety and fear over business failure and take on a challenge for the development and commercialization of new products and services.

Second, many startup CEOs highly evaluated the guarantee screening of KODIT's startup financing programs that focuses on future growth potential. Some startup CEOs expressed that they were impressed that KODIT is evaluating the future growth potential of startups more actively than venture capital firms unlike their impression that KODIT would be conservative in guarantee screening in the process of receiving startup financing support.

Third, CEOs of startups that have received support through First Penguin guarantee and Innovative Icon guarantee agree that phased guarantee support based on management achievement is a very appropriate method for startups that are pursuing continued growth.

Fourth, CEOs who have just started their businesses showed higher satisfaction with diverse non-financial support including accelerating, the securing of markets, and technical advice as well as with fund support through credit guarantees. CEOs of startups selected for Startup NEST pointed out the diverse customized support from many specialized support institutions as the main benefit of Startup NEST.

5.3 *Issues and Improvement Plans of Startup Financing Programs*

The issues and improvement plans of KODIT's startup financing programs are as follows:

First, while KODIT's financing programs help startups attract venture capital investment, a few startups seem to be attracting large amount of investments, which becomes problematic. In response, KODIT plans to introduce a private investment fundraising platform to more systematically carry out the investment fundraising support activities that the Startup branches have individually conducted to this point. This platform, operated both online and offline, will serve as a rendezvous point between startups and investors, enabling effective matching.

Second, there has been lack of continuous follow-up management of startups that receive support from its startup financing programs. Further, due to the lack of data about whether startups are growing continuously or are stagnant after receiving startup financing program, KODIT is experiencing difficulties in redesigning its startup financing programs plans. As such, KODIT plans to build an integrated growth management analysis system for the close performance management of startups that receive support from its startup financing programs. This system serves as a tool that can analyze "what kind of support was offered to which startup and how effective it was" from diverse perspectives and to operate the system in four stages: ① categorizing and registering startups based on individual company's characteristics, type, and growth stage, ② managing the details of diverse customized support, ③ entering growth impact data and monitoring, and ④ analyzing the growth patterns of startups with great growth impact.

6. Conclusion and Policy Proposals

The measures to improve the effectiveness of startup financing proposed in the following are the results of KODIT's painstaking efforts to more effectively manage startup financing. We hope these results will provide policy implications to startup support institutions in many Asian countries, and further, be utilized appropriately in such countries as suited to their respective realities.

6.1 *Startup Financing Design Based on the Setting of Clear Targets*

The top priority to consider for improving the effectiveness of startup financing is to set target customers clearly. This is because the clear setting of target customers should precede the designing of startup financing optimized to fulfill the needs of such targets and produce the tangible results in the continued growth of the startups.

KODIT's startup financing programs are categorizing the target customers for each program as follows and applying differentiated support methods based on the targets. First, Startup NEST is setting startups in their initial stages of establishment as its target customers that lack business experience and will support them in a comprehensive manner through accelerating, financial support, and growth support so that they can stably enter the growth track. Second, First Penguin guarantee is setting startups as its target customers that find it difficult to attract private investment as they are in the initial stages of commercialization but show very high growth potential. This program helps them improve their corporate value through the successful commercialization of their technologies and ideas with the phased support of sufficient funding based on credit line. Third, guarantee with investment option is setting startups as its target customers that are currently in the Death Valley but are highly likely to overcome it through first providing guarantee support and allowing the guarantee to be converted to investment. Fourth, Innovative Icon guarantee is setting startups as its target customers with growth momentum verified through overcoming the Death Valley and attracting a certain level of investment from private venture capital firms. This program offers focused support of much larger credit guarantees than that of First Penguin guarantee, thus helping startups quickly grow into unicorn companies.

Meanwhile, clearly defining a target client group is significant not only because it allows startup finance design to be optimized for target clients, but also in terms of startup finance risk management. KODIT's startup support experts select startups which closely match KODIT's target startup client through in-depth examination of entrepreneurial spirit, growth potential, and superiority of technology and ideas. This rigorous selection method has a positive impact on maintaining stable default rates in the startup finance program.

6.2 Strengthening the Expertise and Capabilities of Workforce Dedicated to Supporting Startups

To boost the effectiveness of startup finance, it is necessary to have dedicated startup support staff with the expertise and competencies to assess the innovative technologies and creative ideas that startups have. In affording effective support through startup finance, the question of how the innovativeness and creativity of a startup's technologies and ideas will be measured is inevitably raised. However, conventional quantitative and standardized measures are limited in their ability to assess their promise. This is to say that in measuring the innovative technologies and creative ideas of a startup, subjective and qualitative judgment to a certain extent on the part of the evaluator is unavoidable. Accordingly, dedicated startup support personnel with appropriate expertise and competencies are a basic and core requirement in providing effective support for startup finance.

To more effectively support its startup finance program, KODIT has established and is operating "startup branches," which are specialized bodies comprising workforce dedicated to supporting startups. At these startup branches, workforce dedicated to supporting startups engage in in-depth discussion to draw on "collective intelligence" in measuring the innovative technologies and creative ideas of startups. As necessary, technical advice is received from private venture capital funds, accelerators, and national research institutes to supplement the capacities of KODIT's dedicated workforce. This evaluation technique exercised by KODIT emphasizes subjective and qualitative judgment on the part of the evaluator, while effectively preventing errors in judgment by individual evaluators.

As explained above, the reason for KODIT's startup financing programs to be able to maintain their low default rates while reaping tangible results is that the dedicated startup support staff with extensive experience and expertise have exclusively managed the startup financing programs.

6.3 *Operating Startup Finance Based on the Diagnosis of Issues of Each Country's Startup Ecosystems*

Startup financing managed by policy financing institutions needs to be more effective not only by stimulating the growth of individual startups but also by contributing to the development of the country's startup ecosystem. Since it is difficult to expect this role from private stakeholders including venture capital firms pursuing private profit in reality, policy financing institutions pursuing public interests need to operate startup financing in a way that contributes to resolving the issues faced by the country's startup ecosystem.

KODIT operates startup financing under the principle of exempting the personal joint surety of founders to improve the "entrepreneurial environment where it is difficult to re-challenge and try again after business failure", which is one of the problems of the Korean startup ecosystem. This is evaluated as KODIT is making large contributions to improving the negative connotations of entrepreneurship found throughout society. In light of KODIT's experience, in order to improve the effectiveness of startup finance, it is necessary to operate startup finance as a means of resolving the problems of the domestic startup ecosystem.

Meanwhile, exempting individual entrepreneurs from joint and several guarantees may induce high moral hazard, including a tendency for entrepreneurs to easily abandon their businesses, or receive redundant funding from multiple directed finance institutions and use these funds recklessly. Accordingly, in the guarantee support phase, KODIT employs a responsible management evaluation system to closely examine the level of responsible management on the part of the entrepreneur prior to providing guarantee. Further, KODIT has implemented a system for sharing information on guarantee support afforded to individual startups with other policy financing institutions. This allows KODIT to track guarantee support provided by other policy financing institutions in real time. Through these means, when assessing guarantee ceilings for individual startups, guarantees provided by other policy financing institutions are deducted, preventing redundant or excessive policy funding.

6.4 *Evaluation Method Focusing on Future Growth Potential*

To effectively support startup financing, there should be reasonable and systematic tools to evaluate the future growth potential of startups. In this regard, the main issue is that it is difficult to apply a standardized and uniform method for evaluating the corporate value and future growth potential of startups. Even venture capital firms whose major work is to invest in startups have different evaluation methods from each other, which indicates that it is difficult to establish a standardized method for evaluating startups. Therefore, the evaluation of startups should be done from the perspective of "how reasonable and legitimate it is".

The key factor in the evaluation of the future growth potential of startups in KODIT's startup financing programs is the sales estimation of startups that is expected to be realized in the future. First Penguin guarantee and Innovative Icon guarantee are applying the sales estimation for three years as the criterion in deciding the limit of guarantee support based on the judgment that the sales estimation is a reasonable and legitimate criterion in evaluating future growth potential.

KODIT considers the sales estimation important because, first, it is possible to comprehensively evaluate other important factors on future growth potential through the sales estimation. In other words, it is because evaluation factors of future growth potential including the startup entrepreneurship, business capabilities, technological capabilities, market competition, and feasibility of and possibility to realize business plans are reflected in feasibility, size, and trend in changes of the sales estimation in the end. Second, sales is the clearest indicator of the value that a startup is providing to customers as the source of profit, which is the fundamental goal of business activities. The value of a startup is ultimately decided by the value provided to customers, and as this can be confirmed through sales, the value of a startup, i.e., its future growth potential, can be evaluated through the sales estimation.

Meanwhile, KODIT conducts evaluations to assess startups' risks. This evaluation system estimates startup's sales in next three years through big-data analytics in different stages of growth, sizes, and types of businesses, using these data to draw up future financial statements for the next three years. Based on its estimation, it quantifies startup's future growth potential into a score. As a risk assessment tool applicable to start-ups with lack of experience, KODIT utilizes the score of future management potential as a measure of startup's risks.

In conclusion, KODIT estimates startup's sales in next three years by a qualitative assessment with the expertise of the staff who are dedicated to supporting startups and calculates startup's future growth potential and risks through quantifying score of future management potential based on estimated sales.

6.5 *Phased Support Based on Management Achievement*

Startups need continued funding in the process of pursuing rapid growth. Therefore, financial support for startups is more effective when it is provided in a phased and continued manner in response to the funding demands of startups than when it takes the form of one-off support. What should be considered as critical in such phased financial support is how to secure the legitimacy of each phase of support. Continued support for funding without standards for each phase of support or without evaluation of whether the growth potential of startups is being realized, maintained, or even delayed can end up as "pouring water into a bottomless jar".

KODIT's First Penguin guarantee and Innovative Icon guarantee are operating credit lines for the phased guarantee support for startups. The credit line refers to the maximum guarantee limit for a certain period of time, and startups receive credit guarantees in a phased manner within the credit line amount. Moreover, First Penguin guarantee and Innovative Icon guarantee set management targets when setting the credit lines for startups and decide whether credit guarantees will be provided and how much credit guarantees will be provided in the next phase based on the level of management target achievement, i.e., management performance. In other words, the legitimacy of phased support is secured through the management performance by the startups.

Such a phased support method based on management achievement is advantageous as it is effective in raising corporate value through strengthening the motivation to achieve management targets by startups as well as reducing the risk exposure of startup financing programs through limiting guarantee support for startups experiencing delayed growth or regression. Risk management through suspending the guarantee support for startups that have failed to reach a certain level of management performance is one of the reasons that First Penguin guarantee has maintained a stable default rate.

6.6 *Combined Support of Financial and Non-financial Solutions*

For startups in the R&D stage or in the initial stages of establishment, not only business funding but also diverse non-financial solutions should be provided in parallel as these startups have a weaker business foundation. In other words, the concept of startup financing should be expanded to include the combined support of business funding and non-financial solutions instead of limiting its scope only to funding support. By expanding the concept this way, it is possible to improve the effectiveness of startup financing.

KODIT's Startup NEST is a one-stop platform of convergence solutions focusing on those startups receiving the combined support of financial and non-financial solutions. The major targets of Startup NEST are those startups that have just completed R&D and are attempting commercialization. At this stage, they are faced with diverse difficulties including the psychological burden that they need to be successful with R&D, questions over what the response to their business model will be in the market, and a lack of know-how in attracting venture capital investment. Startup NEST prioritizes support for accelerating and business funding so that startups can enter the full-fledged growth track while resolving such difficulties, and also supports the business stabilization and continued growth of startups through providing diverse non-financial solutions including technological advice, the securing of a market, entry into overseas markets, and investment fundraising.

Such combined support of financial and non-financial solutions not only contributes to the business stabilization of startups but also reduces the default rate of credit guarantees provided to startups, leading to effective risk management. Even considering the short history of Startup NEST, which was adopted in March 2017, the current default rate as of September 2019 stands at 0.1 percent, substantially lower than the 3.3 percent overall default rate for KODIT. The example of Startup NEST demonstrates that mixed financial and non-financial support supplements existing risk management methods such as establishing risk acceptance rate ceilings and conducting of post on-site audits, helping substantially to reduce default rates.

References

Asan Nanum Foundation, Startup Alliance, Google for Startups, Korea Startup Forum 2019. "2019 Startup Korea, pp. 11–12.

Global Entrepreneurship Research Association 2018. 2018 global entrepreneurship monitor.

Government of the Republic of Korea 2018. Measures for private-led innovation of venture ecosystem.

Government of the Republic of Korea 2019. Strategy to spread the 2nd venture boom.

Government of the Republic of Korea. 2017. Plan to establish innovative entrepreneurial ecosystem.

Hyundai Research Institute 2016. Current status and implications of startups in Korea and Abroad, p. 1.

Jeong, S.-h. 2017. Direction of vitalization of innovative startup. *The Institute For Democracy*, 2–5.

Korea Economic Research Institute 2017. Comparison and evaluation of korean and overseas venture capital and policy implications, p. 18.

Korea International Trade Association 2019. 2019 comparison of entrepreneurial ecosystem of Korea/China University Students, pp. 1–5.

Lee, H.-h. 2018. Current status and improvement direction of Korean startup ecosystem, Innovation and Technology Magazine, Issue of February 2018, pp. 20–25.

Ministry of SMEs and Startups of the Republic of Korea 2018. 2018 detailed research on venture companies' current status, p. 42.

Ministry of SMEs and Startups of the Republic of Korea 2019. 2018 venture investment trend.

Ministry of SMEs and Startups of the Republic of Korea 2019. Livelihood type startup decreased and opportunity-type startup Increased, press release.

Ministry of SMEs and Startups of the Republic of Korea 2019. Record-high venture investment in 2019 1st Half of KRW 1.9 Trillion, the 2nd Venture Boom on Track, press release.

Ministry of SMEs and Startups of the Republic of Korea, Korea Institute of Startup & Entrepreneurship Development 2019. "2018 research on current status of startups, pp. 48–49, 52.

Ministry of SMEs and Startups of the Republic of Korea, Korea Institute of Startup & Entrepreneurship Development 2018. Comparative analysis of startup and venture statistics of major advanced countries, p. 261.

Song, C.-S. 2018. Direction of developing venture fund ecosystem for innovation and growth of venture companies, pp. 12–17.

Startup Genome 2019. Global Startup Ecosystem Report 2019 https://www.cbinsights.com/ (Accessed on October 15, 2020).

Chapter 4

Techno-Economic Feasibility Study Methods in Startup Financing

M. Subramanian[*,‡] and Farhad Taghizadeh-Hesary[†,§]

Senior Consultant and Visiting Faculty, Bharathiar University, Coimbatore, India
†*Associate Professor of Economics, Social Science Research Institute, Tokai University, Hiratsuka, Kanagawa, Japan*
‡*musubra@gmail.com*
§*farhad@tsc.u-tokai.ac.jp*

Abstract

Startups play an important role in creating job opportunities and promoting economic stability, growth, and development. However, it is noted that most startups collapse within the first decade of operation, and those that continue to survive will remain small. The major cause of large-scale failure is primarily the difficulty in predicting the internal and external risk factors that influence the startups' potential success. The techno-economic feasibility study in startup financing is an effective method to safeguard against such risks preventing startup failures and the wastage of valuable investment resources. This study aims to explore the significance and the essence of the techno-economic feasibility study in stepping up the growth and advancement prospects of startups. The study findings promote useful insights into the value of techno-economic feasibility methods in startups by scholars, professionals, entrepreneurs, investors, banks, and financial institutions and provide some policy recommendations.

Keywords: Techno-economic feasibility study, startups, startups financing, entrepreneur

1. Introduction

An unprecedented number of new startups are launched every day as a result of rising new markets, open technology, venture capital, and private equity. Many startups such as WhatsApp, Facebook, LinkedIn, Dropbox, and Twitter, to name a few, have grown into very successful businesses. Despite a lot of flourishing tales, however, the vast majority of the startups collapse prematurely (Giardino, 2014). According to Yoshino and Taghizadeh-Hesary (2019), a large number of startups fail within their first ten years of operation and the majority of surviving small businesses do not grow and continue to remain small. An insignificant number of small businesses only show tremendous growth and high contribution to job creation.

Nobel (2011) noted that only 40% of startups survive the first five years, and only 25% of venture capital-funded startups are successful. The reasons for such a large number of startup failures include the volatile, unpredictable, and rapidly changing environment that compels the entre-preneurs to make quick decisions eventually leading to quick failures and the inability to learn the situation faster to identify a sustainable profit niche market (Giardino *et al.*, 2014).

Forecasting the potential and eventual success of a startup always depends on the internal and external factors which will have the most significant impact on the future performance and growth prospects of the startup. Among the various risk factors, only a few can be controlled, but it is not possible for the entrepreneur to eliminate some of the risks. Therefore, taking the valuable experience of professional experts in reducing the risks is generally advisable.

The promoter of the startups may have an idea about the product which he intends to produce. But, having an idea alone would not be enough to begin development. He has to take into account various other aspects of startup performance. Often, most promoters make investments and then find that there is a lack of demand for the product or that it is not fulfilling customer requirements. To minimize such risk of failure, the prospective investors have to clearly understand the various aspects of the project by consulting with the experts before committing the funds or securing loans from the financial institutions. This process is known as the Techno-Economic Feasibility Study (TEFS) method and the document showing the results is known as the business plan. The preparation of TEFS is neither difficult nor an expensive process. Nonetheless, it is necessary to consider all the essential aspects of the startups ensuring that the potential challenges are addressed.

TEFS is an investigation carried out to assess the financial feasibility and economic viability of a startup venture. Every startup has a possibility of success or failure. It is the responsibility of a prospective entrepreneur of the startup to thoroughly understand the business he is interested to start. The success or failure of the intended business could be determined based on the details of the information that are examined before the start of a particular venture.

The entrepreneur should know everything about the proposed enterprise, product, or service that he wants to provide and the best option for such an activity is a well-prepared TEFS. It should be carried out by the entrepreneur as a part of the planning stage which will reduce the level of risk by providing the required information.

All aspects of the startups such as the market, product, capital cost, credit facilities, manpower needs, technology requirements, etc. will be covered in the TEFS. The profitability aspect of the proposed startup can also be evaluated with the help of TEFS. Also, TEFS itself can be considered as the result of the investigation of all aspects of the startup. However, despite its importance, not all entrepreneurs carry out the TEFS method before planning the startup. It is because of the various issues such as the complexity and difficulty that are encountered in getting authentic, viable, and reliable information concerning the prospective startup venture.

Startups around the world are increasingly in need of properly prepared feasibility studies for taking sound investment decisions. In the past, too many investment projects did not produce the outputs for which they were originally designed or their actual construction costs exceeded those that had been envisaged. For this reason, many financial institutions and venture capitalists are increasingly dependent on well-prepared investment studies to prevent potential cost overruns later on, for the investors as well as for themselves.

A user manual provides the guidance required to plan a feasibility study report. Such a manual was first published in 1978 by UNIDO. Behrens and Hawranek (1991) later released the user manual which is considered of historical value for TEFS. The manual was originally developed to provide a guide for startups to enhance the quality of investment proposals and to help standardize industrial feasibility studies. UNIDO's user manual was found to be valuable and adopted by many universities, financial institutions, government ministries, banks, consulting firms as well as the investors. Besides, the manual includes the transition of technology, environmental impact evaluation, marketing, human resources, and fund mobilization. UNIDO released the Computer Model for Feasibility Analysis and Reporting (COMFAR III Expert) in 1994 and even now it is considered as a standard model for the industry.

The purpose of this chapter is to ascertain the importance of the TEFS method in enhancing the startup business' success, growth, and development. The main objectives of this study are to (i) explore the nature and types of information contained in a TEFS report; (ii) identify the problems and constraints of the TEFS method; (iii) assess the impact of TEFS methods in startups financing; (iv) compare the performance of startups that have used the TEFS method and those without it. This qualitative review chapter is descriptive and analytical. Two sample case studies from the healthcare service industry were adopted to demonstrate the application of TEFS methods in the funding of startups. The first case study shows the effectiveness of TEFS' effectiveness towards the startup venture's success, while the second case study reveals the failure of the startup due to the non-adaptation of TEFS.

2. Literature Review

An extensive review of literature has been performed focusing on the TEFS methods in startup financing. Business experts in the developing world continue to argue whether such a cumbersome, complex, and relatively expensive activity is necessary for business success. However, it is proved beyond apprehension that the TEFS method facilitates investigation of the anticipated potential outcome concerning the success or failure of a startup business.

A startup can be seen as a portfolio of different activities that all work towards simultaneously acquiring new customers, serving existing customers, improving the product, improving the marketing, improving the operations, and even making major decisions like when to pivot. All these activities must be balanced and this is the challenge that the startup entrepreneur faces. These challenges can be found in all the phases of a startup. Smaller startups sometimes struggle to support existing customers, while trying to innovate and grow (Ries, 2011).

Startups play an important role in the creation and growth of employment opportunities in a country. There won't be job growth in the US if there are no startups (Kane, 2010). In the US, the startup businesses contribute about 20% of the total job creation, whereas the high-growth businesses contribute about half the total job creation. (Haltiwanger *et al.*, 2013).

Giardino *et al.* (2014) stated that startups are newly created companies with little or no operating history facing high volatility in technologies and markets. In the US alone, 476,000 new businesses are established each month, accounting for about 20% of job creation (Fairlie, 2014a, 2014b). It is deplorable to note that out of the fifty startup proposals only one is considered a commercially viable proposition. TEFS for the startup is considered as an effective and efficient method of protection of wastage of additional investment or valuable resources (Bickerdyke *et al.*, 2000).

TEFS is a tool that helps an endeavor to realize its perspective. It is an endeavor to study a future project or an organization for the feasibility prospects. Also, a common feasibility design method has not been articulated by anyone so far (Claase, 2012). The framework of TEFS relating to the e-business type of startup is a vital step towards developing a thorough understanding of the startup entity itself, the startup business world, and to forecast the required direction to move to reach potential maximization (Bam, 2018).

TEFS can be considered as a process of defining what a startup is. Also, it is a process of examining the strategic issues to evaluate the start-ups and the chance of success. TEFS can be seen as the first stage of a product or service life cycle, to examine the viability of the project, product or service. TEFS analyzes the product or service by looking at the performance objectives that the startup expects to achieve as well as the cost–benefit analysis report (Overton, 2007).

TEFS and pilot studies have similar features. However, TEFS is different from a pilot study. TEFS attempts to answer the question whether something can be carried out, is it appropriate to proceed with it, and if so, how, etc. A pilot study also asks the same questions but incorporates a specific design feature and it is considered as a part of a future study conducted on a smaller scale. A research study was conducted to describe the difference between a pilot study and a TEFS, as well as the difference between the methods of both these studies (Lancaster *et al.*, 2010; Loannidis *et al.*, 2005).

TEFS can be used as a tool to make the right decisions when defining a business. A wrong decision in this step can lead to the failure of a startup. Only 50% of startups are still in business after the first 18 months and the percentage drops to 20 after 5 years. TEFS can also be conducted when acquiring an existing business, but this study only focused on the TEFS conducted before starting a new business (Hoagland and Williamson, 2000).

There are no guidelines, general standards, or even requirements on the TEFS design and TEFS can have more than one aim. The main aim of TEFS is to identify and make an assessment of future possibilities (Claase, 2012). The TEFS can be considered as an engineering method that provides both qualitative and quantitative aspects concerning the understanding of financial viability. Such an analysis is a combination of process modeling and engineering design along with economic evaluation (Gnansounou and Dauriat, 2010).

TEFS can find the time required to build a new system, whether it interferes with normal business operations, type and amount of resources required, etc. Also, it can provide contingency and mitigation plans. In the case of the overrun of the project, the company can get ready for such an eventuality by adopting the TEFS method. If a project takes too long a period for completion, it will end up in failure. It means that the TEFS methods for estimation of the period for developing a system within a specified duration involve using methods such as the payback period (Hoagland and Williamson, 2000).

The results of a case study conducted relating to the TEFS method of biomedical waste management in hospitals revealed that improper handling of biomedical waste treatment can lead to risks to healthcare communities, personnel, patients, and the associated environment. Different types of wastes, quantities, handling, and waste treatment/ disposal methods in different health-care systems were investigated. The recommendations of the study include the development of policies, plans, protocols, and healthcare professional training programs related to waste management and disposal (Lavanya, 2009).

In a similar case study, TEFS method was adopted to distinguish between a successful and a failed startup business venture. The characteristics of an entrepreneur and the factors concerning the firm leading to the failures in the technology startup ecosystem were assessed. Various factors such as the period for minimum viable product cycle, revenue realization, the promoter's age, and skill levels, along with their expertise, personality traits, attitude, and willingness, etc. largely differentiate the failed startups from successful ones. Based on the study, appropriate implications have been deduced to provide necessary assistance to potential investors in reducing the cost of startup failures (Ganesaraman, 2018).

Imam *et al.* (2019) presented a paper involving techno-economic feasibility evaluation for a grid-connected photovoltaic energy conversion system on the rooftop of a typical residential building in Saudi Arabia. Chauhan and Saini (2016) adopted TEFS method for the development of an Integrated Renewable Energy System (IRES) to meet the electrical and cooking energy demands of a cluster of the village hamlets of Chamoli district of Uttarakhand state in India. Their study attempted to identify the local availability and demand potential of renewable energy resources in the area. Xiongwen *et al.* (2016) utilized TEFS method in their study relating to the analysis of photovoltaic power generation for buildings in the context of the People's Republic of China.

Nandiyanto *et al.* (2019) conducted a TEFS to evaluate the feasibility of the production of a low-cost and portable Arduino-based spectrophotometer with white LED as a light source for analyzing solution concentration. The engineering result confirmed that the project was possible in the small-scale startup because all processing steps can be done using simple and commercially available equipment in the market. This TEFS was also completed with several basic theories for supporting the definition of spectrophotometer focused on in this study.

Bolaño *et al.* (2014) carried out a TEFS of Solar and Wind Based Irrigation Systems in Northern Colombia. They have adopted TEFS method to assess the pump irrigation systems based on solar and wind power considering the particular case of the local municipality in Northern Colombia. Morgan (2013) presented his thesis titled TEFS of Ammonia Plants Powered by Offshore wind which couples ammonia production with offshore wind power, a mature form of renewable energy that is poised for worldwide expansion in the near future.

However, the review of the literature reveals that there are no publicly available datasets or studies that could be looked into to clearly understand the general trends relating to the extent of use of TEFS methods in terms of evaluation of associated risks in startups' financing.

3. Theoretical Background

TEFS is a detailed analysis taking into account all relevant factors of a project including the technical, economic, legal, and scheduling aspects to determine the likelihood of successful completion of the project. However, in the absence of the relevant expertise, an experienced consultant who is well versed in the techno-economic and legal aspects of the startups should prepare a comprehensive TEFS that would provide guidance and assist the startups before the venture gains experience.

TEFS is different from a detailed project report (DPR) that takes into account the planning and design considerations of the project. A DPR is an appraisal report about the project and it is a blueprint of assessment for the eventual completion of the project. TEFS method is carried out when a startup or an existing project wants to know whether a project is possible under certain circumstances.

The TEFS method can be undertaken under different circumstances such as to ascertain whether a startup has enough funds for a project or to evaluate whether the product being developed will sell or assess if there are adequate skilled human resources available for the startup project. TEFS method can be considered effective only if it reveals the strengths and weaknesses before the planning stage of the business. By carrying out the TEFS beforehand, the startup can save money and valuable resources for the future by avoiding the non-feasible business project.

Feasibility studies can be classified based on the purpose. Some of the most common types of feasibility studies are shown in Table 1.

Table 1: Classification of Feasibility Studies

Type	Purpose/Function
Technical Feasibility Study	Assesses the technological resources, products machinery, and processes
Economic Feasibility Study	Performs cost–benefit analysis and evaluates financial resources requirement and mobilization of funds
Schedule Feasibility Study	Determines the capability of the project to complete or implementation of the project in time
Legal/Ethical Feasibility Study	Explores the legal implications and ethical considerations about the project
Resource Feasibility Study	Assesses the availability of all the resources and facilities requirements for the project
Operational Feasibility Study	Evaluates the capability to handle the challenges and to take advantage of the opportunities
Marketing Feasibility Study	Makes assessment of the product demand, life cycle sales estimates, and competition in the market
Real-Estate Feasibility Study	Evaluates the requirement of the land, location needs, and other facilities for the project
Cultural Feasibility Study	Assesses the impact of domestic culture and the local environmental implications on the project
Comprehensive Feasibility Study	Makes overall analysis relating to all aspects of the business including marketing, real estate, cultural, economic, and financial aspects

Source: Authors' compilation and Abou-Zeid *et al.* (2007).

The TEFS method can be used to assess both the technical feasibility and economic viability of a startup idea ensuring that the startup is technically feasible, and economically and legally justifiable. TEFS tells whether a startup is worthy of investing in or not. There could be several reasons for the non-worthiness of investment of a startup business and its not getting accepted for financing. Having resources above what is required might cost more than what the startup can earn back and it would lead to loss and eventually end in failure.

At the time of starting a new business, a lot of assumptions are required to be made to determine if it is worthwhile to pursue the idea. When an entrepreneur gets an idea or is approached with a business opportunity, the negative aspects are easily overlooked. The focus of a startup tends to be more on the positive aspects. TEFS helps the entrepreneur to make sure that a more practical approach is followed considering both the positive as well as the negative aspects of the startup venture. Before a startup can be started, the business objectives must be defined. This step is critical and can very easily be left out or underestimated. The startup venture's developmental process shown in Figure 1 illustrates the significance of TEFS and the importance of evaluating the start of a startup to explore its potential and growth prospects.

The idea or concept is the starting point of the TEFS. Before starting the TEFS, it is important to define the idea or conceptual elements. The format of TEFS can vary, but there must be a certain type of guidelines to support the study. There should be a structure for the TEFS and it should broadly cover the following aspects:

(i) A summary of the startup background and history covering the name and details of the promoter(s), the roles within the startup,

Figure 1: Startup Development Process

Source: Authors' depiction.

     product/service background, startup objective and basic strategy including geographical area, market niche and differentiation, startup location, the location of resources, and economic policies that are supporting the startup.

(ii)   A list of the raw materials and supplies which provide a description of the availability of raw materials, processed industrial materials, industrial components, factory and spare parts, and supplies for social and external needs, materials needed for supply requirements, i.e., a summary of the availability of critical material inputs.

(iii) A summary of the market analysis and the market concept summarizing all the market research including business environment, target market, target segmentation, the channel of distribution, competition, and life cycles list the annual data on demand, like quantities, prices, and supply, outline the marketing strategies for achieving the project objective, explain the marketing concept, make assumptions and calculate the revenue and elements of projected sales, and think about possible impacts on the supplies, location, environment, the production program, technology, etc.

(iv) A list of the location and the environment identifying the location of the startup, as well as the ecological and environmental impact, socio-economic policies, incentives, and constraints describe the significant cost relating to the location and site.

(v) A detailed explanation of the engineering and technology describe and justify technology selected focusing on the advantages and disadvantages as well as the life cycle, transfer of technology, training, risk control, cost, etc., outline the production program, and describe major engineering works.

(vi) A list of the organization and overhead costs which describe the basic management, organizational design and measures required, a list of the human resources describing all the social-economic environment and human resources availability, describing the training needed and recruitment process, indicating the skill requirement of the key persons and specifying the requirement of the total number of manpower and the cost involved.

(vii)   A project implementation schedule indicating the rate of the production startup and cost, and showing the duration of the production installation.

(viii) Financial analysis and investment assessment showing the total cost of the investment, a summary, and explanation of the different types of investment, the total cost of sold services or products, the financing of the project.

In the process of conducting the TEFS, a number of decisions are required to be made about several enduring characteristics of the startup. It shows several likely issues that will affect the decisions as well as some secondary issues that must also be considered.

TEFS can be used for any type of new startup venture and it does not depend on the type of business. It can be used to help in making the vital decision of proceeding with the startup after consideration of several business issues that can affect the startup venture. A good way to start the TEFS is to write down the aims and objectives that need to be achieved by the study. It is important to establish the extent of the study and state exactly what it intends to achieve. The long list of characteristics also emphasizes the importance of following a structured framework when conducting a TEFS, because otherwise many of these characteristics can easily be overlooked.

TEFS can be considered as a plan, a detailed written document prepared by the entrepreneur. It provides all information relating to the internal and external elements connected with the startup venture. TEFS is prepared by the entrepreneur after consultations with various sources that include professional consultants, legal experts, financial, technical, and marketing professionals, and engineers who could be useful in the preparation of different levels or steps in the plan. In some cases, the promoters would like to hire or join hands with another person offering equity partnership who could provide the required expertise in the preparation of the TEFS and become a key member of the management team to assist determine whether to hire a consultant or to make use of other resources.

TEFS can be an open book readily available for guidance to the entrepreneur, investors, banks, venture capital institutions, vendors, customers, advisors, and consultants. As the TEFS will be utilized by various institutions and individuals for different purposes, it is important that the study report takes into consideration the anticipated concerns and issues. In one way or the other, the plan must try to satisfy the needs of everyone. Most importantly, the entrepreneur should try to view his startup through the eyes of the customers and investors. The future projections should be made accordingly. If the entrepreneur is unable to prepare the information due to a lack of background or skills, outside professional sources can be approached.

4. Highlights of TEFS Methods

To prepare the TEFS, the entrepreneur needs to ask several questions such as if the idea is practicable or not, is there a good market for the proposed product, what is the nature of competition, what could be the possible market share, is the technology available locally or required to be imported, is the raw material locally available, what will be the capital requirement, can I provide the financial requirement for the project, what is the production process and what is the manpower skill level required, etc.

As the TEFS report is a complex technical cum financial document, it is better to take the services of a management consultant. An experienced TEFS writer collects all the required details including the market as well as the economic environment aspects. It is a preliminary study undertaken to determine the viability of the startup and documented for use by all concerned including the financial institution and venture capitalists.

TEFS document can be submitted for the startup financing approval. It will be used by the funding institution and venture capitalists to determine the likelihood of the startup's success. TEFS thoroughly investigates the techno-economic viability of a proposed startup compared to pre-specified evaluation criteria. Such criteria include a thorough understanding of the proposed product or service, industry, nature of the market, competition, and the financial requirements.

One of the basic features of a TEFS is that it should provide a thorough analysis of the business opportunity including a look at the possible roadblocks that may stand in the way of the startup's success. If the results of the TEFS are positive, then the entrepreneur can proceed to develop a business plan. If the results show negative prospects, then the startup should not be pursued.

The main functions of a TEFS report include an aid in startup planning, which involves an examination of all aspects of the intended business such as cost, sources of suppliers, technical data, and expected profit. Also, it offers basics and guidelines for the venture capitalists, investors, promoters, bankers, vendors of goods, and various government organizations for making their decisions on startup financing and other assistance. TEFS provides the stakeholders with varying degrees of evidence that the startup will be viable.

TEFS is essential for the startup as it compels the startup to base its ideas on proper reasoning and to assess whether or not those ideas are practicable and realistic. It also forces organizations to begin the formal evaluation, knowing what steps to take next. The entrepreneur and his management team have to thoroughly study the TEFS a number of times and should not hesitate to challenge the underlying assumptions of the study.

The evaluation process is based on the technical design of system requirements such as the costing of input, processes, output, programs, fields, and procedures. Such information can be supported with numerical data, trends, updating frequency, etc. to calculate if the new startup systems will perform well or not. It is important to understand the availability of technology with adequate knowledge of the production process. Answers to some of the questions have to be obtained to ensure the technical feasibility of the startup such as, is the technology as well as the machines readily available in the country? What infrastructure facilities are needed for the startup? etc. If these questions can be answered in the affirmative, then the startup is technically feasible. Technical feasibility includes both the hardware and software network capability.

The market, financial, and economic feasibility deals with cost–benefit analysis. The economic feasibility answers questions such as: Is the startup justified? Can the startup be completed within the budgeted cost limits? Which is the best return on investment alternatives? What is the best alternative financing arrangement among rent, lease, or purchase? There may be some difficulties in economic feasibility namely both the costs as well as the benefits can be hidden, intangible, and difficult to make estimates.

The economic feasibility analysis should eventually increase the revenue, reduce the cost, increase the investment requirements, and generate higher profits. The financial feasibility analysis is required to establish an investment commitment to the startup venture and demonstrate if the business plan is economically viable.

Some of the benefits of TEFS method include helping the entrepreneur as well as the financing institutions in investment decisions based on the technical feasibility and financial viability of the project. Also, it reveals the risks associated with the project and actions required for risk mitigation.

Despite the value and varying benefits of TEFS, entrepreneurs may often be under pressure to bypass the TEFS and proceed directly with the startup. Some members may push it hard to skip the TEFS providing lame reasons. Some people may feel that they know the startup is a successful idea and they don't need to conduct an expensive study just for the sake of demonstrating what's already known. Yet, these unfounded arguments do not deter the entrepreneur from introducing a suitable and practical TEFS.

In the modern world, though many newer technologies and business models are evolving, TEFS can still be used as an effective method of evaluation in the financing of startups. TEFS can determine the startup's potential and valuation. Besides, quality of management, startup's competitive edge, and regulatory risks involved can also be assessed through the use of TEFS methods.

Being innovative adds value to the startup promoter. An important aspect of entrepreneurship and 'creative destruction' is the development of new product/service categories. It is necessary to develop an appropriate strategy for market analysis and segmentation relating to a new product/service. Newer methodologies and key performance indicators (KPI) of the startups can be implemented while adopting the TEFS methods.

5. Application of TEFS Methods

Startup financing involves significant risks. Careful consideration of the various risk factors before seeking finance for the proposed startup venture is essential. The entrepreneur should try to identify the factors having a significant impact on the future performance of the startup. Most entrepreneurs do not carry out a full-fledged risk assessment before proceeding with the investment. This could be the reason for most startups failing within a few years of operation.

At the time of assessing the investment risks, it is important to consider various risk factors such as financial risk, product risk, teamwork risk, market risk, startup business valuation risk, operational risk, regulatory risk, reputational risk, physical risk, and cyber risk. It is important to analyze the level of technical risk and the financial viability, through a TEFS method based on which the financial institution or the lenders can consider the acceptability of the risk involved in the project and accord financing approval for the startup. The TEFS should cover the following aspects thoroughly:

(i)   First and foremost it is important to gather information about the project, promoters, financial strength, professional experience, business expertise, key personnel, etc.

(ii)   It is necessary to examine the product description, types and uses, applications, etc. In some cases, it may be observed that the product has limited use with fluctuating demand.

(iii) Study the current market scenario, both local and global, market forecast, demand/supply scenario, target market, barriers to entry, and competition analysis; these are important parameters and must never be ignored in a study.

(iv)   Availability of the industrial plot, connectivity, raw material availability, establishing labor and utilities, etc. The location of the startup project has to be preferably closer to either the raw material source location or the finished product market. In the case of an export-oriented product, the plant location can preferably be near the sea or airport.

(v) The startup project configuration and the plant and machinery selection have to be carefully scrutinized. The cost of the plant and equipment should be compared to protect against malpractices such as over-invoicing. The efficiency and the useful life of the machinery have to be evaluated and it should be of an acceptable standard.

(vi) There should be an adequate supply of stores and spare parts in case of an emergency to avoid loss of production. The estimates for building and civil works should be reasonable, duly certified by a qualified architect. The layout and design should have the local authorities' approval.

(vii) The manufacturing process should be well defined and documented. Proper teamwork and synergies should exist among various departments such as storage, production, maintenance, and finished products. The engineers and technical personnel should have adequate experience in the industry. All mandatory clearances connected with the startup business should be readily available to start production and shown in the report.

(viii) The competition analysis of other comparable manufacturers should be examined and commented upon. The pricing of the finished goods should be comparable to competitors.

(ix) The target market should be accessible with a wide distribution and retail network. It is necessary to have proper sales and marketing incentive policies.

(x) The startup project cost and the source of finance should be established. The promoter's contribution and the source should be verified through the bank statements and auditor certificates. The ratio of debt–equity should be within the industry benchmark standard.

(xi) The raw material cost, labor, and overheads should be comparable and at reasonable levels with the prevailing market standards. The finished product pricing assumptions should be reasonable to reach a conservative projected revenue.

(xii) The cost of consumables such as stores, spare parts, freight transportation, and other expenses and overheads have to be a minor percentage of the cost of the finished product.

(xiii) The projected financial statements including the details of income and expenditure over a sufficiently long period should be prepared. Given the inflation, market and economic development, there should be adequate growth potential in terms of revenue generation.

(xiv) The cash flow statement for the bank loan and financial indicators such as the internal rate of return, the payback period, the return on assets, the return on capital employed, etc. have to be computed and ensure that the indicators are well within the benchmark standard of the industry. These should also be stress tested for changes in the pricing of raw material and finished goods by say 5% (sensitivity analysis).

(xv) A strength, weakness, opportunity and threat (SWOT) analysis should be prepared and commented upon to understand the strengths and weaknesses of the proposed startup.

The startup project can be accepted as technically feasible and financially viable only after the satisfactory completion of the above analysis, and the TEFS report has to be submitted to the lenders for their scrutiny and approval of finance.

6. Startups Case Analysis

To illustrate the significance and the process of adopting TEFS methods in startups financing, two examples of case analyses have been undertaken based on the industry contexts and analyses performed accordingly. These two startups are selected from the healthcare sector from two different locations based on the author's direct involvement in the preparation of the TEFS in the startups' financing.

To meet the objectives of this chapter, it is considered appropriate to examine two industrial contextual case examples by contrast. Accordingly, a successful startup that opted for the TEFS method and a failed startup that ignored the TEFS in the financing process have been considered. These examples are chosen primarily for illustration of the importance and the impact of TEFS methods on startups' success regardless of other aspects such as the type, size industry, location, etc.

6.1 *Case Description*

Some highlights of both the startups are provided in Tables 2 and 3:

Table 2: Successful Startup

Item	Description
Startup Company	Bio-Medical Waste Management and Recycling Company (BMWTC)
Industry Location	Riyadh, Saudi Arabia
Product/Service	Medical waste treatment and recycling service. The various types of wastes that are generated in hospitals, laboratories, clinics, and diagnostic centers are classified as medical wastes. As these wastes can be harmful and hazardous to humans, proper disposal or recycling of the wastes is crucial and important for the society and environment
Market	A detailed market survey was conducted to evaluate the market potential, competitor activities, waste treatment pricing, and other relevant information. It was noted that there exists a huge market potential for waste treatment and the available facilities are not capable of meeting the demand requirements
Finance	Total estimated capital cost US$6,223,000 (Based on the TEFS detailed financial analysis)
TEFS	A professional consultant has prepared a full TEFS for this startup. Since the full report is very detailed and voluminous, the summary of the startup project is provided in Appendix (Table A–)
Sustainability & Growth	As per the TEFS, the projected sales, profitability, and the rate of return are attractive and there is a good scope for expansion and growth prospects as well
Final Results	Reaped the benefits of TEFS in terms of getting the finance from funding institutions and the startup is successful with expansion and growth prospects

Source: Authors' Compilation.

Table 3: Failed Startup

Item	Description
Startup Company	Medical Transcription Services Company (MTSC)
Industry Location	Coimbatore, India
Product/Service	Medical transcription services provided for independent practicing healthcare physicians and medical doctors working in hospitals and clinics abroad such as in the US
Market	Startup relied mostly on an off-the-cuff market estimate. There was no market survey. The investors were unaware of the customers, total market size, competition, and other requirements. In the absence of TEFS, market details were unknown
Finance	Roughly worked out capital cost US$1,150,000 (Based on experience and inquiries)
TEFS	TEFS was not conducted. However, an analysis was carried out after two years of operation
Sustainability & Growth	As there was no TEFS, projected sales, profitability, and rate of return and other projections have not been worked out and prospects and risks were unknown
Final Result	In the absence of a prior evaluation of the project, the startup has failed within the first two years of operation

Source: Author's Compilation.

6.2 *Comparison of Startups*

The characteristic features of the successful and failed startups are provided in Table 4:

6.3 *Startups Analysis and Findings*

A comparison of the two startups' case analysis brings some insight on the importance of TEFS methods in startups financing. The startups' case analysis very clearly distinguishes the successful startup from the failed startup. The findings from these two examples provide the importance of TEFS towards the success of a startup. Besides, some of the key lessons derived from the failed startup can be adapted appropriately for the success of startups by integrating a proper TEFS method in the starting stage of the startup.

Table 4: Successful and Failed Startups' Comparison

Item	Characteristics	Successful Startup (BMWTC)	Failed Startup (MTSC)
Startup	Small/Medium Enterprise	Medium Industry	Small Industry
Product/ Service	Service Industry	Medical Waste Treatment	Medical Transcription Service
Market	Market Size Estimates	Market survey conducted	Made some off-the-cuff calculations
	Demand Projections	Result of proper market study	Market Survey not carried out
Finance	Financial Analysis	Financial analysis/ estimates available	Financial Analysis not done
TEFS	Feasibility Study	Conducted	Not conducted
Startup Financing	Financial Institutions	Fully approved as requested	Approval based on false projections

Source: Author's Compilation.

The analysis of the failed startup case analysis reveals several reasons for the failure as follows:

(i) The promoter's lack of basic knowledge about the startup business of medical transcription services and the sources of getting job orders.

(ii) The market survey was not carried out and therefore information such as the market potential, competition, pricing for providing the medical transcription service, projected revenues, and other information relating to the market were not available.

(iii) The too noisy and unhygienic workplace location/venue of the facility was not conducive enough for carrying out the knowledge-based job of medical transcription services.

(iv) The startup had not recruited skilled transcribers for undertaking medical transcription activities. Also, the startup had not concentrated on the medical transcription training, which resulted in a lack of adequate professional knowledge and updated skills in the field.

(v) The cost of providing the medical transcription services, information about the pricing of the competitors, and other relevant information are not available. Most orders have ended up in negative results due to off-the-cuff cost calculation.

(vi)   In the absence of TEFS, the startup project could not get the required financing which resulted in high finance costs and the startup having to face severe financial constraints.

Overall, it is the lack of knowledge and insight into the startup that has resulted in the closure of the startup within a short period of two years. Specific knowledge and insight about the information pertaining to the startup venture could have been obtained if the entrepreneur had carried out a proper TEFS. A professional consultant could have helped to get all the relevant information by preparing the TEFS. It can, therefore, be concluded that the TEFS method could have saved the company from ending up in failure. Although conducting a TEFS might appear to be an unnecessary cost, eventually the necessity is felt only when there is a failure due to lack of knowledge and information as noticed in the case study of the failed startup.

However, it is noted from the startup case analysis that the successful startup has taken full advantage of the TEFS right from the concept to commercialization. TEFS has provided analysis on every aspect of the business and decision making was easy, effective, and the startup has reaped various benefits. Apart from embracing success, the startup has been chosen as the best green clean startup venture by providing the most efficient medical waste treatment and recycling services. Also, the startup could get local government support for providing eco-friendly services by fighting against the environmentally hazardous medical wastes.

It is, therefore, concluded that the success of the successful startup is mainly attributed to TEFS. It has provided much-needed strength and opportunity for the success of the startup. Also, apart from providing the requested finance, the funding institution and the venture capitalists offered to support the expansion of the startup in the second year of operation itself. It can, therefore, be concluded that the TEFS has contributed immensely to the sustainable development and growth of the successful startup.

7. Conclusion and Policy Recommendations

TEFS methods in the startups financing provide sufficient proof to the investors and the stakeholders on whether or not the startup project would be viable and worth investing in. Having strong initial awareness about the startup in the concept phase itself can have a beneficial impact on all the startup stakeholders. This chapter analyzed the TEFS' significance in evaluating the potential and enhancing the startup venture's growth and development. The study also revealed some of the reasons for the large-scale failures and key lessons to be learned when funding startups.

TEFS is certainly useful in startup financing because it makes it easier to improve the performance rate or to reduce the startups' failure rate. TEFS will provide valuable guidance to the potential emerging startups. In addition, TEFS allows the prospective entrepreneur or the promoters to take adequate precautions to reduce the risk for startup failures. The key lessons learned from the failed startups will help the ecosystem to ultimately mitigate the cost of failures.

Considering the significant contribution of TEFS to the success of the startups and recognizing the various benefits of the TEFS methods in startups financing, this study suggests that fully completed TEFS document be submitted by the startups as a mandatory requirement for the financing approval along with the application to the financial institutions and venture capitalists.

Also, the chapter proposes an interactive digital app user manual for TEFS instead of the current practice of preparing a list of questions that are required to be answered by the promoter of the startup. TEFS digital app user manual facilitates the startup promoter to complete the framework as well as startup development. The startup promoters would also be able to conveniently use the TEFS manual without the need to hire a qualified professional consultant.

In the present digital age, the entire process of TEFS can be implemented using the digital software platform. Data collection, preparation of technical, marketing, financial analysis calculations, and complete document preparation can be performed electronically, making the TEFS process much easier and faster, with more reliable information being shared with all concerned including the financial institutions and venture capitalists. Also, such electronic information processing in startups financing for TEFS will enable updating the changes and incorporating the modifications as and when necessary.

References

Abou-Zeid, A., A. Bushraa, and M. Ezzat. 2007. Overview of feasibility study procedures for public construction projects in Arab countries. *Journal of King Abdulaziz University-Engineering Sciences*, 18(1): 19–34.

Bam, H. 2018. A feasibility study framework for e-Business startups: A case study on sxuirrel. Retrieved from Stellenbosch University: https://scholar. sun.ac.za.

Behrens, W. and P.M. Hawranek. 1991. Manual for the preparation of Industrial Feasible Studies, United Nations Industrial Development Organization (UNIDO), Vienna.

Bickerdyke, I., Latimore, R., and Madge, A. (2000). Business Failure and Change. An Australian Perspective. Canberra: Productivity Commission Research Paper.

Bolaños, J.C., W.O. Orozco, and R. Bhandari. 2014. Techno-economic feasibility study of solar and wind based irrigation systems in Northern Colombia. *World Sustainability Forum- Conference Proceedings Paper*. Available via. http://www.sciforum.net/conference/wsf-4.

Chauhan, A. and R.P. Saini. 2016. Techno-economic feasibility study on Integrated renewable energy system for an isolated community of India. *Renewable and Sustainable Energy Reviews, Elsevier*, 59(C): 388–405.

Claase, M. 2012. Optimizing feasibility studies: Based on a Grounded Theory type comparison of feasibility design research. The University of Twente.

Fairlie, R.W. 2014a. Kauffman Index of Entrepreneurial Activity, Kauffman Foundation.

Fairlie, R.W. 2014b. State of Entrepreneurship Address, Kauffman Foundation.

Ganesaraman, K. 2018. Why do startups fail? A case study based empirical analysis in Bangalore. *Asian Journal of Innovation and Policy*, 7(1): 79–102.

Giardino, C., N. Paternoster, M. Unterkalmsteiner, T. Gorschek, and P. Abrahamsson. 2014. What do we know about software development in startups? *IEEE Software*, 31(5): 28–32 Available via https://www.researchgate. net/publication/265645676.

Gnansounou, E. and A. Dauriat. 2010. Techno-economic analysis of lignocellulosic ethanol a review. *Bio-resource Technology*, 101(13): 4980–4991.

Haltiwanger, J., R. Jarmin, and J. Miranda. 2013. Who Creates Jobs? Small vs Large vs. Young. *Review of Economics and Statistics*, 95(2): 347–361.

Hoagland, H., and L. Williamson. 2000. Feasibility studies. Kentucky: University of Kentucky.

Imam, A.A., Y.A. Al-Turki, and S.R. Kumar. 2019. Techno-economic feasibility assessment of grid-connected PV systems for residential buildings in Saudi Arabia — A case study. *Sustainability* 2020, *12*, 262. Available via https://www.mdpi.com/2071-1050/12/1/262.

Kane, T. 2010. The importance of startups in job creation and job destruction. Kansas: Kauffman foundation research series. The Kauffman Foundation.

Lancaster, G., M. Campbell, S. Eldridge, A. Farrin, M. Marchant, S. Muller, and G. Rait. 2010. Trials in primary care: Statistical issues in the design, conduct and evaluation of complex interventions. Statistics.

Lavanya, R. 2009. A case study of bio-medical waste management in hospitals. *Global Journal of Health Science*, 1(1): 82–88.

Loannidis, J.P., M.J. Campbell, C.L. Cooper, G.A. Lancaster, I. Nazareth, M. Petticrew, and G. Rait. 2005. Why most published research findings are false? *PLoS Medicine. Bio-Med Central*, 2(8): 124.

Morgan, E.R. 2013. Techno-economic feasibility study of ammonia plants powered by offshore wind. *Open Access Dissertations,* 697. Available via. https://doi.org/10.7275/11kt-3f59 https://scholarworks.umass.edu/open_access_dissertations/697.

Nandiyanto, A.B.D., R. Ragadhita, A.G. Abdullah, F. Triawan, G.K. Sunnardianto, and M. Aziz 2019. Techno-economic feasibility study of low-cost and portable home-made spectrophotometer for analyzing solution concentration. *Journal of Engineering Science and Technology*, 14(2), 599–609.

Nobel, C. 2011. Why Companies Fail — and How Their Founders Can Bounce Back, Harvard Business School.

Overton, R. 2007. Feasibility studies made simple. Martin Books.

Ries, E. 2011. The Lean Startup: How today's Entrepreneurs Use Continuous Innovation to Create.

Xiongwen, Z., L. Menyu, G. Yuanfei, and L. Guoiun. 2016. Techno-economic feasibility analysis of solar photovoltaic power generation for buildings. *Applied Thermal Engineering*, 108, 1362–1371. Available via ScienceDirect www.elsevier.com/locate/apthermeng.

Yoshino, N. and F. Taghizadeh-Hesary. 2019. Application of Distributed Ledger Technologies to Improve Funding in the Startup Ecosystem. In Nemoto, N. and Yoshino, N. FinTech for Asian SMEs. pp. 30–54. Tokyo, Japan: Asian Development Bank Institute.

Appendix

Table A: Techno-Economic Feasibility Study (TEFS)

Startup Summary

Startup Sponsors

Bio-Medical Waste Treatment Company (BMWTC) (the name changed for anonymity) is a licensed waste management startup company in Saudi Arabia with a strong bias for recycling medical waste. BMWTC has identified a suitable plot in Riyadh industrial area which is considered appropriate for the medical waste recycling plant and intend to erect necessary buildings on this site. BMWTC is in the waste management and recycling industry to contribute towards saving the earth and also to compete in the highly competitive waste management and recycling industry not only in the local market but also throughout the country. BMWTC will initially be involved in the collection and management of medical waste but will in the nearest future engage in the recycling of medical waste. The business goal is to become one of the leading medical waste management and recycling companies in the country and put all efforts to compete favorably with leaders in the industry.

Incineration is the only internationally recognized technology capable of dealing with all categories of medical wastes and many countries are now banning or restricting the use of autoclave technology for the treatment of medical waste in favor of incineration/thermal oxidation technology. The local Environmental Agency recently produced a guideline approving incineration as the only proper method for treating medical waste. According to the Government Mandate and various ministerial decrees all the medical waste must be properly treated and disposed of at the government approved specialized treatment facilities. BMWTC being the licensed medical waste treatment company; it is believed that such a mandate by the Government, the phenomenal growth in the medial facilities being witnessed in the country etc. will boost the demand for health care medical waste disposal services ensuring BMWTC's business growth prospects.

Marketing Highlights

BMWTC's medical waste treatment provides disposal services of hazardous medical waste for public and private health sectors in the country. BMWTC is providing its services by entering into an annual contract with all the health sectors and maintenance companies. The plant provides the following services to the Health Care Institutions:

(i) Collection of waste from the Clients' site.
(ii) Transportation of waste from Clients' site to Project's waste treatment facilities.
(iii) Treatment and disposal of medical waste at the project's facilities in compliance with all the applicable environmental regulations.
(iv) Consultation to clients for minimization/waste reduction at the source.

BMWTC's facility has a number of operational and environmental features as below:

(i) The reduction of waste volume in the initial treatment phase by 97%. The project is using a recycling system in which the ash resulting from processing will be treated and recycled. The ash is 3% of waste volume.
(ii) The thermal oxidation system will take all medical waste at elevated temperatures of $1800-2600^0$ F.
(iii) Control System is fully computerized and equipped with a continuous emission monitoring system that shuts off automatically in case of operational error.
(iv) The plant uses a power-saving system to reduce energy consumption, the gas fuel which is very clean and the recycling system saving a large amount of water.
(v) The project is designed to meet all local/international environmental conditions. United States-EPA approve the technology for the project.

The market size for medical waste treatment is estimated at around 37,000 tons and given the strong growth in the health sector and enforcement of Government mandate for compulsory disposal of medical wastes, the market size is expected to grow by around 6% per year over the next five years. However, as a conservative estimate, the study opted to take the growth rate as 3% p.a. BMWTC's facility is designed with a waste treatment of approximately 3,700 tons per year of medical waste treatment and disposal services at full capacity. The market share projections based on the market size reflects just around 5.4–9.1% of the total market size projected over the next 5 years.

Technical Highlights

Medical Wastes are collected from various hospitals and other wastes generation units and transported to BMWTC Plant in specialized refrigerated trucks. They are then sorted out stored as per the specific nature. The treatment process starts with the weighing of wastes and feeding to incinerators, where the burning takes place at high temperatures converting the waste to ashes. The ashes are then removed and transported to the landfill site.

With operation on three shifts and 325 working days per annum, BMWTC would be capable of incinerating 3,700 Tons of Biomedical wastes per year. The plant would be having a manning strength of 51 at full capacity operations. Electrical Power will be procured from the Electricity Board. The requirements of water shall be met by government water supply arrangements. The plant will not be facing any environmental concerns as the incineration process and subsequent processing of wastes is very carefully monitored at each stage. Ashes produced are being transported in special trucks to designated landfill sites. Regular emission test is arranged to ensure emission levels are kept well below the permissible limits set by applicable environmental regulations. Adequate arrangements have been made for Loss Prevention and Safety of the plant and personnel.

Core Process Machinery and equipment which includes Waste Incinerators and Scrubbing Systems will be procured from Anderson 2000 of the United States, who are the pioneers in waste incineration technology and have installations all over the world. Anderson 2000 shall provide all the necessary support required by BMWTC until the successful completion of the plant besides transferring technical know-how and technology to BMWTC.

Given the BMWTC management team's familiarity with environmental protection, given that most of the waste processing know-how is already built-in the machinery and equipment selected and given that the incineration technology for the Medical Wastes Treatment and Disposal is well established, no separate know-how transfer agreement would be required. Apart from providing the best technology, Anderson imparts training specifically for medical waste incineration and maintenance, quarterly technology update for all equipment, systems and staff members' visits to Andersen's facility in the United States to upgrade their skills and to discuss operations, performance, or other related subjects along with annual inspection by Andersen personnel of BMWTC facilities.

Financial Highlights

The capital cost of the startup is estimated to be US$6,223,000 as detailed in Table A.1:

Table A.1: Capital Cost of the Startup

Category	Amount (USD)		
	Year 0	Year 1	Total
Building and civil works	1,282,000		1,282,000
Machinery & equipment	2,900,000		2,900,000
Office Furniture & Equipment	61,000		61,000
Transport equipment/vehicles	586,000		586,000
Loss Prevention & Safety	Included in Building and Civil Works		
Pre-production & startup expenses	1,198,000		1,198,000
Working capital investment		148,000	148,000
Contingency	48,000		48,000
Total investment	**6.075,000**	**148,000**	**6,223,000**

Source: Author's compilation.

Table A.2:   Means of Financing

Source of Financing	%	Amount (USD)
Paid-in capital	25	1,556,000
Startup financing	48	3,021,000
Commercial financing	27	1,646,000
Total	**100.00%**	**6,223,000**

Source: Author's compilation.

Table A.3:   Financial Performance Indicators

Category	Year 1	Year 2	Year 3	Year 4	Year 5
Current ratio	28.6	50.3	7.4	7.1	6.9
Total Liabilities/ Net worth	1.4	1.2	0.8	0.6	0.4
Gross Margin/ Sales	−4.7%	27.5%	52.7%	52.7%	52.7%
Net Profit/Sales	−36.0%	5.5%	36.4%	36.4%	36.4%

Source: Author's compilation.

The proposed means of startup financing is as given in Table A.2:

The computations for various ratios/percentages of financial indicators are appended in Table A.3:

The financial study reveals that the Internal Rate of Return (IRR) of the project is expected to be around 14.5% establishing its financial viability. BMWTC startup is expected to generate sufficient cash flow that comfortably negotiates business risks and meets its financial obligations to lenders and other stakeholders. The study also indicates that the proposed project has a comfortable cushion that enables it to weather negative swings in key sales and cost drivers.

Chapter 5

Role of Soft Infrastructure in Fostering Startup Businesses During a Lack of Finance

Yeganeh Eghbalnia

Aalto University Executive Education Ltd, Helsinki, Finland

*Aalto University Executive, Education Ltd Mechelininkatu
3 C 00100 Helsinki, Finland
nannigia@gmail.com*

Abstract

In emerging and developing countries, the development of soft skills has been less emphasized. Attempts were made to get funding on the seed rounds by the founders, investors care the most to get the desired return on their investment, and employees are interested in securing their job compensation with minimum effort level. As a part of a firm's culture, there are essential soft factors which can establish a strong drive for succeeding and creating a high-commitment culture between founders, investors, employees, which can shape a vibrant culture of survival, growth, and success in a firm. The present study aimed to evaluate financial toughness, share option, networking, and performance management. In fact, the main hypothesis is whether startups with these attributes rely less on external funding or not. After collecting data from active startups in the Iranian startup ecosystem, no evidence was available regarding a strong association between the existence of these soft factors in the firm and the firm's survival/success rate.

Keywords: Soft infrastructure, startups, funding, survival

1. Introduction

1.1 *Background*

Technology driven companies like startups have been increasing in many advanced and developing countries. The annual growth rate of the number of people using social media was 135%, 32%, 14%, and 11% in Iran, Saudi Arabia, Morocco, and Egypt, respectively, while the worldwide annual growth rate is 13% (Göll and Zwiers, 2018). In addition, the government has attracted more attention to the formation of startup companies among the developing economies with a young population. In the Iranian economy, the service sector is considered as the largest contributor to employment, with 49% of total employment (Statistical Center of Iran, Summer, 2019). Over the past 10 years, the government supported startups and entrepreneurs to decrease unemployment and welcomed the expansion of the service sector through facilitating the formation of Small and Medium Enterprises (SMEs) in hospitality and fin-tech industries. The government granted 3G and 4G licenses to all mobile operators in September 2014 (Ministry of Information and Communications Technology of Iran, 2019). Further, 4.5G mobile technology is available nationwide and Iran has the highest number of internet users in the Middle East, which is responsible for almost 40% of internet use in the entire region (Ministry of Information and Communications Technology of Iran, 2019). Currently, 78% of rural areas have access to internet, all urban areas have internet coverage, and 55% of roads have 4G internet coverage (Ministry of Information and Communications Technology of Iran, 2019). In 2018, E-Government Development Index (EDGI) reached 0.6083 in Iran, among 17 countries which transitioned from middle- to high-EGDI level groups (United Nations, 2018). By 2020, the government planned to provide 80% of households with internet access (Ministry of Information and Communications Technology of Iran, 2019). Regarding the background of telecommunication infrastructure development in Iran, the startup ecosystem has been gradually developed during the same period and the digital economy is emerging, especially among the young and educated population. In mobile games, Iran has 23 million gamers with an average age of 21 years, and accounted for the second largest video game market in the Middle East after Turkey (Digital Games Research Center, 2017).

Successful local startups are well known in Iran and the number of these firms that managed to expand their operation in major large cities is expanding across the country (Financial Tribune, 2016). Digikala is the Iranian Amazon, Snapp and Tap30 are the Iranian Ubers, Sheypoor and Divar are the Iranian Craiglist. A local Iranian Instagram influencer earns US$2000 to promote a new service developed by a tech firm for the young and tech-savvy teenagers. The share of e-commerce in nominal GDP is estimated at 208,000 billion tomans, i.e., US$7 billion (at 30,000 tomans IRR/USD rate), which was 10% of GDP in 2018 (Digikala, 2019). Despite all these achievements, Iranian startups are at their infancy. For example, the share of online retail in the country remained a mere 1–2% compared to 4.7% in Turkey, 13.4% in the Republic of Korea, and 12.7% in Norway (Digikala, 2019). In addition, the COVID-19 pandemic increased the demand for online services and digitalization of the businesses substantially. Tech-based companies in Iran received higher demand and many local online shops have successfully managed this demand shift in the COVID-19 era. Understanding which soft infrastructure can contribute to the development of Iranian startups to survive and manage business cycles can help new founders and venture capital (VC) companies to optimize their management and business decisions. In addition, understanding which soft skills are working well in Iranian culture can help policy makers and managers to navigate the area in which they should increase their supervision and those in which they can be flexible and have less micromanagement. Due to scant academic studies over success factors of Iranian startups, the present study aimed to identify the essential soft skills for a startup to survive and become a successful firm in the Iranian startup ecosystem.

1.2 *Research Question and Methodology*

The present study seeks to see whether implementing tough financial management, offering share options, networking, and decision-making based on Key Performance Indicators (KPI) are considered as the key soft skills for the survival and success of Iranian startups. In the beginning of the operation, a majority of founders have lower sensitivity to financial metrics. This chapter aimed to analyze whether startups with tough financial measurement can be differentiated in terms of success compared to others with less monitoring attribute in accounting and book-keeping. Working in a startup company is substantially different from working in a corporate. Employees are asked to stay long hours to deliver projects within the deadline. They should be versatile, i.e., be able to work under pressure, and cope with specific challenges such as startup closure and job insecurity. Therefore, offering Employee Stock Ownership Plan (ESOP) and Employee Stock Purchase Plan (ESPP) may increase the sense of loyalty and commitment among the employees in a startup. Socially active founders are better at raising funds and marketing their products and services. The meaningful assumption is related to testing for success, especially in cultures like Iran, where connections and networking are the essences of business development. Agility in KPIs is related to seeing whether the business decisions are data-driven or not. I think this soft element is crucial in enhancing the culture of startups, which can help executives respond faster to the data originated from the market. While previous studies have focused on the key success factors in startups in advanced economies and highly competitive business environments, more research is required to research the critical factors found in developing and emerging economies especially those that are challenged by economic hardship and isolation. The present study measures the soft infrastructure development in the Iranian startups ecosystem over the past 5 years and analyzes if these factors have helped startups to fight back lack of capital. During the past 5 years, Iranian economy witnessed tremendous hardships through sanctions and it is noteworthy to analyze how the startups responded to ongoing economic pressure and increasing limitations in business conditions (e.g., sanction of mobile applications to Iranian users, etc.)

In this chapter, an online questionnaire was sent to 107 active founders and senior management of the top level of the Iranian startup ecosystem. The questionnaire included five questions with 4–5 categories. Nonparametric tests such as Spearman Chi-Square were used in SPSS software to see whether the soft elements can contribute to higher likelihood of survival/success of startups. Based on the results, developing the studied soft infrastructure in Iranian startups failed to increase the likelihood of survival and success. Thus, it is suggested that many other factors should be analyzed and evaluated with a higher number of observations.

The remainder of this study is as follows. Section 2 provides a review of the literature. Section 3 explains the method. Section 4 provides the empirical results. Finally, discussion and conclusion are elaborated in Section 5.

2. Literature Review

A large number of studies have focused on the success factors in startups to understand whether there is a standard framework to evaluate the exact factors behind the success, survival, or failure of startups. Some evaluated the determinants of startup performance and concluded that the successful performance is caused by various factors related to personality traits of founders and the size of funding. Khelil found that entrepreneurs' personality traits and their psychological motives for entrepreneurship are linked to the failure of startups (Khelil, 2016). Melissa *et al.* (2011) studied the importance of chance or misfortune and other soft elements such as pre-startup phase environment factors in enhancing the operation outcome of startups. In another study, Cantamessa *et al.* (2018) used SHELL method, as a well-known approach for describing the accident causes in the aviation sector, to analyze the startup failure patterns. The SHELL model coming from the aviation management system indicates the interactions between Software, Hardware, Environment, Liveware People, and Liveware Environment, and suggests that the human is rarely considered as the only cause of an accident. In fact, there are different factors interacting with the human operator and affecting performance. Using 214 startup post-mortem reports in multiple countries to assess the robustness of the finding, Cantamessa found that a typical failure pattern is related to the business development process. In addition, after consolidating the business model, entrepreneurs seem to focus directly on the sales or the product improvement and they are less concerned to design a reliable, measurable, and engineered business development phase. Headd challenged the belief that the rate of small business closure is high in the US. The study focused on businesses which opened from 1989 to 1992 by using government data sources like Business Information Tracking System (BITS) and Characteristics of Business Owners (CBO), and covered most industries in the US. Further, Headd reported that having ample capital, employees with good education, and the founders' motives to run their own business are considered as the leading factors for small businesses to remain open (Headd, 2000). Bates found the factors which play a significant role in firms to remain in business include the investment of the substantial amount of financial capital at the point of starting the business, competing in an open market place, and high level of owner education attainment (Bates, 1989). Blasi studied the effects of employee ownership, profit sharing, and stock options on workplace performance using General Social Surveys and National Bureau of Economic Research (NBER) surveys of over 40,000 employees in order to evaluate how revenue sharing influences turnover, absenteeism, loyalty, employee effort, and other outcomes affecting workplace performance. Blasi reported that share option plans have beneficial effects on all outcomes except for absenteeism. In addition, stock option plays a significant role on turnover, loyalty, and employee effort when it is combined with high-performance work policies, low levels of supervision, and fixed wages which are at or above the market level. Further, most employees reported that cash incentives, stock options, Employee Stock Ownership Plan (ESOP), and Employee Stock Purchase Plan (ESPP) can motivate them to work harder (Blasi *et al.*, 2008).

Lee examined the factors contributing to the success of startups in Hong Kong, China and found soft skills in managing the business and attracting financial support as important factors, along with Chinese market competitiveness and executive power of founders (Lee, 2018). Hong *et al.* (2018) found that a more competitive VC market increases the likelihood of a successful exit for startups with low-quality projects. In addition, the founder's characteristics such as management experience, industry experience, marketing skills, age, education, the parent having their own business, and external factors play a significant influence on the success of startups (Silva *et al.*, 2016).

Success rates in startups may be different in VC-backed firms compared to those with no VC involvement. The results of some empirical studies indicated faster growth, faster time-to-market including higher productivity, greater innovation, and successful exit in VC-backed firms (Bernstein *et al.*, 2016 and Chemmanur *et al.*, 2011). Gloor *et al.* (2020) scrutinized the relationship between the venture capital involvement and startup success by presenting a research framework based on the assumption that new ventures are likely to benefit from an active management of board members and venture capitalists by providing support in the areas of financial support, strategic support, managerial/operational support, and social legitimacy. Further, they were interested in testing how these supports influence the performance of new ventures. The results indicated that specific board composition and informal social networks by the board members can directly influence the startup performance. Startups with no venture capitalists on the board, and those with no board members on Twitter, can increase the ability for translating assets into sales. They found that previous investment support and interconnecting executives are not necessarily translated into the entrepreneur's ability to create value out of the available assets. Additionally, the more the startup employees share with members on the board, the higher the value that can be generated. Greenberg found trade-off between the benefits of going solo including a desire to keep control of the company and the costs associated with lack of connections to industry networks and the risk of growing at a slower pace (Greenberg and Mollick, 2018). In another study, by Gloor *et al.* (2018), it has been demonstrated that virtual network of founders is only as good as the real-world relationships by analyzing startups with founders\as members of a German business network site.

Roche *et al.* (2020) studied the role of differences in founders on new venture performance by using a novel dataset of 2998 founders creating 1723 innovative startups in biomedicine. Based on the results, academic and non-academic occupational backgrounds of founders have different impacts on startups. They found that academic founders have the advantage of comparative invention while non-academic counterparts have a comparative innovation advantage. Hence, academic startups are comparatively disadvantaged in bringing new technologies to the market. The findings suggest that startups created by academic founders stay longer in operation than startups initiated by non-academic ones to be cleared the exit market. Therefore, they can impose higher cost and risk compared to investments in startups with non-academic founders.

Hazudin *et al.* (2015) reported that it is more challenging for women founders to succeed in startup businesses without knowledge and skills compared to men. Furthermore, the successes of startups led by female entrepreneurs may be influenced by family needs and support, as well as the age of their children.

To summarize, key success factors in startups are personal traits and characteristics of the founders, business development process, mentorship, ample capital, VC competitive environment, open marketplace, providing share options to employees, and VCs' involvement. Most studies in the literature have focused on startups in advanced economies including US and Europe. Despite previous studies exploring the association between success rate and various factors, findings remain inconclusive and not up to date. Globally, under the COVID-19 environment, the trend of startups in social media have been increasing substantially in all countries and thus it has changed the startups' marketing channels drastically. Few studies have elaborated these new emerging soft infrastructures including social activities and their role in their success or survival. Moreover, the new emerging trends have received less attention of researchers for startups located in developing and emerging countries. In the present study, the selected factors are based on elements derived mostly from business culture attributes in Iran and it has attempted to understand how these factors have influenced the performance of startups over the past 5 years.

3. Methodology

3.1 *Participants*

The participants were selected from among the most active startup founders and senior managers in the Iranian startup ecosystem. Being active and have a running business over the past 3 years in Iran were considered as the key factors for selecting the firm. This filter seems necessary as the startup community is a small community, and some of firms had to close down or limit the business activity over the past few years. No other selection conditions such as revenue volume or ownership structure were considered. In order to collect data, 107 respondents were asked to fill questionnaire survey online in September 2019. The response rate was 98% and the questionnaire was designed categorically.

3.2 *Questionnaire Layout*

The present study aimed to understand the perception and mindset of founders in terms of business development and strategy. The main questions raised were: "What is the managers' perception over financial monitoring in their startups and how they implement it?", "Is there any difference in firm's spending pattern when the KPIs have drastic changes?", "How long does it take for a startup to go to the cost cutting phase?", "What founders think about revenue sharing with their employees?". The participants were asked if they are socially active and can promote their services in the social media or events. Tables 1 and 2 indicate the details of the questionnaire used in this chapter. Each respondent was only allowed to answer one of the categorical choices in each question.

Table 2 indicates the reasons why these questions are selected and how each question is assigned to each soft element. For example, a startup with 70% chance of survival under no funding option for more than 10 years is considered a successful startup.

Table 1: Questionnaire Format

Question	Choice 1	Choice 2	Choice 3	Choice 4	Choice 5
1 What is the probability of survival of your startup under current economic conditions given no new funding option will be available over the next 10 years?	Less than 20% chance of survival	Between 40 and 60% chance of survival	Between 60 and 70% chance of survival	Over 70% chance of survival	—
2 When did you start your operation when the financial and accounting system was set up?	Over 12 months since starting operation	Between 6 to 12 months since starting the operation	Between 2 to 4 months since starting operation	Less than 30 days since starting operation	—
3 Do you have ESOP in your startup?	Yes	No	—	—	—
4 Have you ever tried to be socially active in the startup community and is your startup somehow a well-known firm in the ecosystem?	Yes	No	—	—	—
5 Assume that you are monitoring your KPI in your startup and you see declining trend in your KPIs. In addition, you have tried all solutions to save your startup and no strategy was effective to improve the KPIs of your startup. How long does it take to decide to bootstrap your startup when you observe a declining trend in your KPIs?	Observing a declining trend in KPI over 12 months	Observing a declining trend in KPI over between 6 to 12 months	Observing a declining trend in KPI over between 4 to 6 months	Observing a declining trend in KPI over between 2 to 4 months	Observing a declining trend in KPI over less than 30 days

Table 2: Rational of Questions

Questions	Soft Infrastructure for Analysis
1. What is the probability of survival of your startup under current economic conditions assuming that no new funding option is available over the next 10 years?	Startup survival rate/ success rate
2. When was the financial and accounting system set up when you started your operation?	Financial toughness
3. Do you have ESOP in your startup?	Share option
4. Do you try to be socially active in the community and is your startup somehow a well-known firm in the ecosystem?	Networking & social activity
5. Assume that you are monitoring your KPI in your startup and you see a declining trend in your KPIs. In addition, you have tried all solutions to save your startup and no strategy was effective to improve the KPIs of your startup. How long does it take to decide to bootstrap your startup when you observe a declining trend in your KPIs?	Agility to downsize or expand the scope of business

4. Empirical Results

In this section, the descriptive statistics are presented, and the profiles of respondents' characteristics are studied. Then, the results are provided according to Spearman rank correlation test results.

4.1 *Descriptive Statistics*

Table 3 reports the characteristics of participants based on gender. The majority of startup founders are male (91%) and 9% are female.

Table 4 indicates the firms differentiated according to their types of operations. Around 34% are individual investors (19%) or institutional investors (15%).

4.2 *Descriptive Statistics (Survival Rate and Success Factors)*

4.2.1 *Survival rate*

Figure 1 displays the founders' views on their startups' survival under the condition that no further funding condition is available. The respondents

Table 3:   Gender Profile

Participants	Number	Percentage (%)
Male	10	9
Female	97	91
Total	107	100

Table 4:   Type of Activity

Participants	Number (%)
Game	1
Transport	1
Education	1
Movies	1
Clothing	1
Fin-tech	2
Shared Space	2
Insurance	2
Online Event	2
Financial	2
HR	2
Food Delivery	3
Retail Shops	4
Healthcare & Beauty	5
Government	5
Tourism	7
Marketing & Branding	8
Startup Studio & VC	15
Investor	19
Other	17
Total	100

are not generally in accordance with absolute success or failure, among which 51% expect their firms to survive under no further funding option. Around 18% give lower chance of survival and 31% see a low probability of survival.

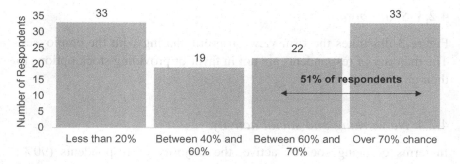

Figure 1: What is the Probability of Your Startup's Survival?

Source: Author Calculation.

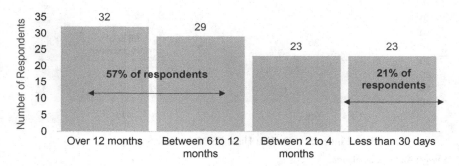

Figure 2: When was the Financial and Accounting System Set up After You Started Your Operation?

Source: Author Calculation.

4.2.2 *Financial toughness*

Figure 2 measures the firm view on the importance of financial system setup since starting the operation. The participants are not generally in favor of implementing tough measures in financial reporting and book-keeping system from the first day. Only 21% indicated that they will set up their financial system in the first month of their operation. Over 57% of firms implement financial system 6 months after the start of their operation.

4.2.3 *Share option*

Figure 3 illustrates the firm view on profit sharing with the employees. The majority of respondents are not in favor of providing stock options to their employees.

4.2.4 *Networking and social activity*

In terms of being socially active, the majority of respondents (90%) expressed that they try to attend events and increase networking activity in their schedule (Figure 4).

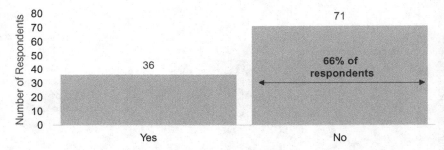

Figure 3:   Do You Have ESOP in Your Startup?

Source: Author Calculation.

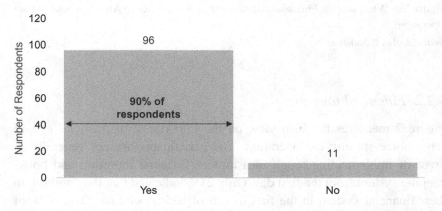

Figure 4:   Do You Try to be Active in Social Media and is Your Startup a Well-known Firm in the Ecosystem?

Source: Author Calculation.

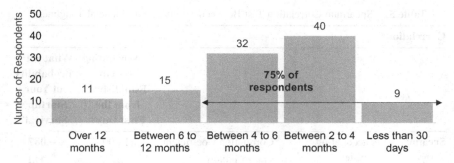

Figure 5:   When will You Decide to Bootstrap in the Case of Low KPI?

Source: Author Calculation.

4.2.5 *Agility to downsize*

The majority of respondents (75%) will start to downsize within less than 6 months if KPIs are lower than their expectations (Figure 5).

4.3 *Results of Spearman Rank-Order Correlation*

4.3.1 *Financial toughness*

The Spearman rank correlation test (Table 5) examines whether implementing tough financial measures in a startup increases the likelihood of the firm's survival/success. Based on the results, no relationship was observed between these two variables.

4.3.2 *Share option (ESOP)*

The results indicated no relationship between providing share options to employees and the survival or success of the firm (Table 6).

4.3.3 *Networking*

Based on the results, there is no relationship between more social activity of the founders and survival or success of the firm (Table 7).

Table 5:   Spearman Correlation Test Between Survival and Financial Toughness

Correlations

			Is Accounting System Established from the First Day?	What is the Probability of Your Startup's Survival?
Spearman's rho	Is accounting system established from the first day?	Correlation Coefficient	1.000	**−.087**
		Sig. (2-tailed)	—	**.374**
		N	107	107
	What is the probability of your startup's survival?	Correlation Coefficient	−.087	1.000
		Sig. (2-tailed)	.374	—
		N	107	107

Source: Author Calculation.

Table 6:   Spearman Correlation Test Between Survival and ESOP

Correlations

			Do You have ESOP in Your Startup?	What is the Probability of Your Startup's Survival?
Spearman's rho	Do you have ESOP in your startup?	Correlation Coefficient	1.000	**−.159**
		Sig. (2-tailed)	—	**.101**
		N	107	107
	What is the probability of your startup's survival?	Correlation Coefficient	−.159	1.000
		Sig. (2-tailed)	.101	—
		N	107	107

Source: Author Calculation.

Table 7: Spearman Correlation Test Between Survival and Social Activity

Correlations

			Are You a Well-known Startup?	**What is the Probability of Your Startup's Survival?**
Spearman's rho	Are you a well-known startup?	Correlation Coefficient	1.000	**.082**
		Sig. (2-tailed)	—	**.403**
		N	107	107
	What is the probability of your startup's survival?	Correlation Coefficient	.082	1.000
		Sig. (2-tailed)	.403	—
		N	107	107

Source: Author Calculation.

Table 8: Spearman Correlation Test Between Survival and Agility

Correlations

			When Will You Decide to Bootstrap in the Case of Low KPI?	**What is the Probability of Your Startup's Survival?**
Spearman's rho	When will you decide to bootstrap in the case of low KPI?	Correlation Coefficient	1.000	**.060**
		Sig. (2-tailed)	—	**.538**
		N	107	107
	What is the probability of your startup's survival?	Correlation Coefficient	.060	1.000
		Sig. (2-tailed)	.538	—
		N	107	107

Source: Author Calculation.

Table 9:   Results of Chi-squared Test for the Relationship Between the Variables

	Have startups with strict financial disciplines from the first day survived during dried up liquidity periods in Iran?	Have agile startups had a higher chance of survival compared to other startups?	Have startups with ESOP demonstrated higher resilience and survived during lack of fresh money?	Have startups with established business networks demonstrated higher resilience and survived during lack of fresh money?
Hypothesis testing				
Results of Association	Since the p-value is more than the selected significance level ($\alpha = 0.05$), the null hypothesis is accepted. In fact, there is no relationship between startup survival and tough financial system set up in the startup.	Since the p-value is more than the significance level ($\alpha = 0.05$), the null hypothesis is accepted. In other words, there is no relationship between startup survival and startup agility in KPI management.	Since the p-value is more than the significance level ($\alpha = 0.05$), the null hypothesis is rejected. In fact, there is no relationship between startup survival and providing ESOP to employees.	Since the p-value is more than the significance level ($\alpha = 0.05$), the null hypothesis is accepted. In other words, there is no relationship between startup survival and popularity of startups in the ecosystem.

Source: Author Calculation.

Table 10: Summary of the Results

	Tough Financial Measures	Agility	Share Option	Networking and Popularity
Probability of Survival	−0.087	0.060	−0.159	0.082
Result	Weak negative correlation	Weak positive correlation	Weak negative correlation	Weak positive correlation

Source: Author Calculation.

4.3.4 *Agility in KPI management*

As shown in Table 8, data-driven decision-making style (KPI management) of firms is not related to survival or success of startups. Our findings imply that agility may not be a significant success factor in the observed sample of startups.

Table 9 indicates a summary of the results and Table 10 interprets the probability statistics of the model.

Table 10 Spearman rank correlation test results for studying the relationship between the variables.

5. Discussion and Conclusion

The present study aimed to see whether the development of the selected soft infrastructures such as financial toughness, share options, networking, and KPI performance management (agility) can improve the chance of survival and success among Iranian tech firms. Based on the results (Table 10), no strong relationship was observed between the soft elements and the survival rate of startups. There was a weak negative relationship between tough financial measures and ESOP, while there was weak positive relationship between agility and networking. Some other factors might explain the success or failure causes of Iranian startups which can be elaborated with a wider range of samples in future studies.

The result of this study should be interpreted with caution and future study is necessary before generalizing the results to other contexts. There are some factors which may affect the performance of Iranian startups, as follows.

5.1 *Timing Factor*

Iran is a frontier market and has a government-based economy. Political factors may influence the businesses environment such as Iran's relationship with Western countries, neighboring economies, local government policy, liberal and expansionary vs. austerity and contractionary economic policy. For example, the business activity growth was significantly high after the Iran–Iraq war during 1988–1998, and the government attempted to rebuild the economy by expansionary policies such as providing low cost loans to households and facilities to refurnish the manufacturing sector. Between 2015 and 2017, with the signing of the Joint Comprehensive Plan Of Action (JPCOA) and reaching agreements with Western countries, many entrepreneurs and business owners were encouraged to invest in startups, while concerns on financial performance or providing share options to their employees were paid less attention. These businesses focused on gaining higher market share and increasing their brand awareness in Iran while ample capital was available. In addition, the international relationship was improved between Iran and other countries during 2014–2017. During this period, Foreign Direct Investment (FDI) in a number of manufacturing companies and startups started to grow from 0.4% of GDP in 2014 to 1.1% of GDP in 2017 (World Bank, 2020). This period was the formation period of successful startups in the country such as Digikala and Snapp. Today, Digikala is the largest online shopping market place and Snapp is the largest ride hailing application in Iran. These startups scaled up and expanded rapidly in large cities, and operation management was improved to respond to the growing number of customers. During this period, a number of Iranian talents abroad were encouraged to return to their home country and work in these new emerging startups.

Those startups that were founded after president Trump's election in 2016 had a different business strategy compared to the former group of founders. It is worth noting that the time of starting the operation in each startup was not considered in the present study. The results may be consistent when we deal with differentiated startups based on the time of starting their operation. During the past 2 years, when the funding option was limited and management was aware of this limitation from the first day, the behavior of management and investors tended to be significantly different from that of founders who started their operation between 2014 and 2016, when the Iranian economy hoped for higher growth of foreign capital. A mixture of both groups was considered in the present study.

The Bass Diffusion model on the adoption and diffusion of new technology products and services was developed by Frank M. Bass (Bass, 1969). His model is widely used in market analysis and demand forecasting for new technology products. The model is one of the best tools to explain and forecast the number of purchases for new consumer durable products. The results of this study failed to find evidence that Iranian startups have implemented financial toughness and being agile based on KPI results, which may be related to the fact that these startups focused their attention on introducing and growing their market in Iran as the Iranian consumers were adapting to digitized products and services. On the other hand, founders hoped to have enough financial resources, and ample capital will be provided over the next few years. These arguments should be further analyzed with a wider number of observations in Iranian startups.

The role of ample capital in helping Iranian startups to scale up their business was obvious. It is worth noting that the founders and investors have been less worried to implement tough financial measures during 2014–2017 due to the availability of ample capital and optimism toward the business environment. During this period, the founders concentrated on growth strategy such as setting up their presence, introducing their services, testing consumers' behavior, and increasing consumers' awareness in the market because the startups were newly introduced to the consumers. Therefore, it is possible that they are less concerned about the profitability of their business model at the beginning of their operation. As a result, soft elements such as tough financial controlling or being operationally agile in this period were less emphasized.

5.2 *VC Funds in Stock Market*

There is a substantial lack of cohesive aggregate data due to high fragmentation in startups and newly-emerged industries. Startups do not normally publish their financials and management practices (Swan, 2018). There are few successful startups with high scalability rate, and most of their owners are not interested in sharing their managerial strategies with other people. Hence, there is a lack of a substantial data on a diverse range of startups in countries like Iran.

It is suggested that authorities allow a higher number of venture capital funds to be listed in the stock market, and accordingly the startups are encouraged to be transparent and provide reports in a regular manner to attract the investments of VC funds. Currently, there are two venture funds listed in the stock market with a limited public knowledge or awareness about these funds. By increasing the number of venture capital funds in Iran, individual and institutional investors and media will start research on financial metrics and operation of startups. Financially transparent startups will get VCs and investment community attraction to invest in them. These venture capital funds have to do the due diligence of the startups' operation and cash-flow statements and interview the managers and founders. These funds are responsible for explaining to their unitholders why and how they have decided to invest in these particular startups and all these pieces of information will be accessible through online portals and available to the investors, similarly to normal listed equities. Managers of these funds should have annual general meetings and invite all to meet and ask their questions and report about their performance. Financial media are encouraged to interview and write reports about the performance of startups and the like.

In addition, helping startups to be listed in the stock market is recommended for facilitating the access of ample capital, making their operation track record public, and informing a large number of people in Iran about these companies. Financial media will be encouraged to interview these managers and founders, by which higher knowledge and level of data can be disclosed to the public. Currently, by an increasing interest to invest in Tehran Stock Exchange, each trading ticker has its own social media channel that all investors can join and share their opinions and financial data over that particular company. The same flow of public information about their operation, growth drivers, and challenges could be available if listing of startups will be facilitated by the policy makers.

The commercial law of Iran is outdated and requires companies to have a certain amount of capital and show records of three-year profitability. These requirements are very difficult to achieve for new startups. It is recommended that policy makers should amend the commercial law to allow startups to be listed in the stock market and increase the awareness on the financial records. Many startups are interested to be listed in the public market and, on the other hand, the investment community is also eager to invest in tech companies. The policy markers can find a safe channel to bring together investors and startups under capital market regulations.

References

Bass, F.M. 1969. A new product growth for model consumer durables. *Management Sciences*, 15(5).

Bates, T. 1989. *Entrepreneur Factor Inputs and Small Business Longevity.* University of Vermont, Economics. Working Papers 98-4 Center of Economic Studies, U.S. Census Bureau.

Bernstein, S., X., Giroud, X., and R.R. Townsend. 2016. The impact of venture capital monitoring. *The Journal of Finance*, 71, 1591–1622. doi:10.1111/jofi.12370.

Blank, S. and B. Dorf. 2012. *The Startup Owner's Manual: The Step-By-Step Guide for Building a Great Company.* Pescadero, California: K & S Ranch.

Blasi, J.R., R.B. Freeman, C. Mackin, and D.L. Kruse. 2008. Creating a Bigger Pie? The effects of employee ownership, Profit. *Nber.* New York: National Bureau of Economic Research.

Cantamessa, M., V. Gatteschi, G. Perboli, and M. Rosano. 2018. Startups' roads to failure. *Sustainability.* Retrieved from www.mdpi.com/journal/sustainability.

Ceausu, I., K. Marquardt, S.-J. Imer, and G. Elisa. 2017. Factors influencing performance within startup assistance organizations. *Proceedings of the International Conference on Business*, 11(1): 246–275:n:28. Sciendo.

Chemmanur, T.J., K. Krishnan, and D.K. Nandy. 2011. Efficieny in private firms? A look beneath the surface. *The Review of Financial Studies*, 24(12): 4037–4090. Retrieved from https://doi.org/10.1093/rfs/hhr096.

Cremades, A. 2019. The pros and cons of bootstrapping startups. *Forbes.* Retrieved from https://www.forbes.com/sites/alejandrocremades/2019/01/13/the-pros-and-cons-of-bootstrapping-startups/#1ce127273db5.

Digikala. 2019. *Semi-Annual Company Report.* Digikala. Retrieved from https://www.digikala.com/mag/wp-content/uploads/2019/12/report-1398-h1.pdf.

Digital Games Research Center. 2017. *Digital Games Market In Iran.* Retrieved from https://direc.ircg.ir/?p=1627&lang=en.

Dodge, Y. 2008. *The Concise Encyclopedia of Statistics.* Switzerland: Springer Science & Business Media.

Dowling, S. 2019. Middle east and north African startups gain traction, but challenges remain. Retrieved from https://news.crunchbase.com/news/middle-east-and-north-african-startups-gain-traction-but-challenges-remain/.

Financial Tribune. 2016. Retrieved from 60% growth in Iran online sales. https://financialtribune.com/articles/economy-sci-tech/50275/60-growth-in-iran-online-sales.

Forbes. 2017. The MENA startup scene lags behind Europe and the US, but it's growing fast. Retrieved from https://www.forbes.com/sites/suparnadutt/2017/11/20/the-mena-startup-scene-lags-behind-europe-and-the-us-but-its-growing-fast/#3047a7049c0e.

Gelderen, M., R. Thurik, and N. Bosma. 2005. Success and risk factors in the pre-startup phase. *Small Business Economics*, 24(4): 365–380.

Gloor, P.A., A.F. Colladen, F. Grippa, B.M. Hadley, and S. Woerner. 2020. The impact of social media presence and board member composition on new venture success: Evidences from VC-backed U.S. startups. *Technocolical Forecasting and Social Change*, 157.

Gloor, P.A., S. Woerner, K. Fischbach, and A.F. Colladon. 2018. Size does not matter — in the virtual world. Comparing online social networking behaviour with business success of entrepreneurs. *International Journal of Entrepreneurial Venturing*, 10(4).

Göll, E. and J. Zwiers. 2018. Technological trends in the mena region: The cases of digitalization and information and communications technology (Ict). MENARA Working Papers.

Greenberg, J. and E.R. Mollick. (2018). Solo survivors: Solo ventures versus founding teams. Retrieved from https://papers.ssrn.com/sol3/papers.cfm?abstract_id=3107898.

Gulati, R. and A. DeSantola. 2016. *Harvard Business Review.* Retrieved from Startups That Last, https://hbr.org/2016/03/start-ups-that-last.

Hazudin, S.F., M.A. Kader, N.H. Tarmuji, M. Ishak, and R. Ali. 2015. Discovering small business start up motives, success factors and barriers: A gender analysis. *Procedia Economics and Finance*, 436–443. doi:0.1016/S2212-5671(15)01218-6.

Headd, B. 2000. *Business Success: Factors Leading to Surviving and Closing Successfully.* Center of Economic Studies (CES), Washington.

Hong, S., K. Serfes, and V. Thiele. 2018. *Competition in the Venture Capital Market and the Success of Startup Companies: Theory and Evidence.* Drexel University, LeBow College of Business. School of Economics Working Paper Series.

Hunter, D., A. Saini, and T. Zaman. 2018. Picking winners: A data driven approach to evaluation the quality of startup companies. Papers 1706.04229. arXiv.org.

Khelil, N. 2016. The many faces of entrepreneurial failure: Insights from an empirical taxonomy. *Journal of Business Venturing,* 31(1): 72–94. doi:<10.1016/j.jbusvent.2015.08.001>. <halshs-01242692>.

Kim, B., H. Kim, and Y. Jeon. 2018. Critical success factors of a design startup business. *Sustainability, MDPI, Open Access Journal,* 10(9): 1–15.

Lasso, S.V., E.M. Mainardes, and F.Y. Motoki. (n.d.). Types of technological entrepreneurs: A study in a large emerging economy. *Journal of the Knowledge Economy,* 9(2): 378–401.

Lee, P.S. 2018. A Study of Startups in Hong Kong. *22nd Biennial Conference of the International Telecommunications Society: "Beyond the Boundaries Challenges for Business, Policy and Society".* Seoul, Republic of Korea: 190409, International Telecommunications Society (ITS).

Maclachlan, M. 2013. *Communicaid.* Retrieved from https://www.communicaid.com/cross-cultural-training/blog/red-tape-bureaucracy-and-its-influence-on-international-business/.

Mansoori, Y.T. Karlsson, and M. Lundqvist. 2019. The influence of the lean startup methodology on entrepreneur-coach. *Technovation.*

McHugh, M.L. 2013. The Chi-square test of independence. *Biochemia Medica,* 23(2): 143–149. doi:10.11613/bm.2013.018.

McKinsey & Company. 2018. Entrepreneurship in the Middle East and North Africa: How investors can support and enable growth. Retrieved from https://www.mckinsey.com/.

Melissa, S.C., E.S. Christopher, and P.D. Ryland. 2011. Misfortunes or mistakes?: Cultural sensemaking of entrepreneurial failure. *Journal of Business Venturing,* 26(1): 79–92.

Ministry of Information and Communications Technology of Iran. 2019. *Annual Performance Report.*

Popowska, M. and P. Nalepa. 2015. Lean startup as a new way of managing technology ventures illustrated by the example of welcome app, 2(19): 7–21. doi:10.7172/1733-9758.2015.19.1.

Robb, A.M. and R.W. Fairlie. 2008. Determinants of business success: An exami-
nation of asian-owned businesses in the United States. *CEPR Discussion
Papers*. Center of Economic Policy Research, Research School of Economics,
Australian National University.

Roche, M.P., A. Conti, and F.T. Rothaermel. 2020. Different founders, different
venture outcomes: A comparative analysis of academic and non-academic
startups. *Research Policy*, 49(10). Retrieved from https://doi.org/10.1016/j.
respol.2020.104062.

Saura, J.R., P. Palos-Sanchez, and A. Grilo. 2019. Detectingindicators for startup
business success: Sentiment analysis using text data mining. *Sustainability,
MDPI, Open Access Journal*, 11(3): 1–14.

Silva, D.S., A. Cerqueira, and E. Brandao. 2016. Portuguese startups: A success
prediction model. *(FEP Working Papers 581)*. Universidade do Porto,
Faculdade de Economia do Porto.

Statistical Center of Iran. 2019. *A Selection of Labour Force Survey Results:
Summer 1397*. Statistical Center of Iran.

Swan, C. 2018. *Scenearabia*. Retrieved from https://scenearabia.com/Money/
Challenges-MENA-Startups-Data-Pioneer-Magnitt-Philip-Bahoshy-Iraqi.

The Economist. 2018. *The Biggest Collapse In Private-Equity History will have
a Lasting Impact*. Retrieved from https://www.economist.com/finance-and-
economics/2019/05/18/the-biggest-collapse-in-private-equity-history-
will-have-a-lasting-impact.

The University of Texas at Austin. 2015. *Statistics Online Support (SOS)*. Retrieved
from   http://sites.utexas.edu/sos/guided/inferential/numeric/bivariate/
rankcor/.

United Nations. 2018. *E-Government Survey in Media*. Retrieved from https://
publicadministration.un.org/egovkb/en-us/Resources/E-Government-Survey-
in-Media/ID/1944/Iran-moves-up-in-UN-E-Government-Development-Index.

World Bank. 2020. *Foreign Direct Investment, Net Inflows (% of GDP) — Iran,
Islamic Rep.* Retrieved from https://data.worldbank.org/indicator/BX.KLT.
DINV.WD.GD.ZS?locations=IR.

World Bank Group. 2020. Retrieved from Doing Business 2020: https://open-
knowledge.worldbank.org/bitstream/handle/10986/32436/9781464814402.
pdf?sequence=24&isAllowed=y.

Chapter 6

Funding Tech Startups in Selected Asian Countries

Paul Vandenberg,*,§ Aimee Hampel-Milagrosa,†,¶ and
Matthias Helble‡,||

Senior Economist, Asian Development Bank,
†*Economist, Asian Development Bank,*
‡*Senior Economis, Asian Development Bank,*
§*pvandenberg@adb.org*
¶*ahampel@adb.org*
||*mhelble@adb.org*
(seconded to World Health Organization, May 2021)

Abstract

In many Asian countries, we observe a rapid expansion of technology-oriented startups. Governments hope that these startups will boost economic growth, create jobs, and foster sustainable development. However, transforming an innovative idea into a successful business is not easy and is constrained by limited access to funding. We analyze access to funding for tech startups in four sectors — greentech, agritech, edtech, and healthtech — that are linked directly to the Sustainable Development Goals. The chapter focuses on four countries, Cambodia, India, Thailand, and Viet Nam, and includes insights from interviews with startups, incubators, and other players. We find that tech startups rely on an array of funding sources and that venture capital is not a common source. In addition, greentech and agritech startups produce products that require long-term support through the design, testing, prototyping, and certification stages. Such "patient capital" is in short supply. On the positive side, enterprises in development-oriented sectors can seek funds from impact investors and international development (aid) agencies.

Keywords: Startups, enterprise funding, Asia

1. Introduction

Technology-oriented (or tech) startups play a vital role in transforming the traditional economy into a knowledge-based and digital economy through innovative activities. Tech startups are entrepreneurial ventures that deliver new, innovative, and scalable technology-based products and services to the market (Spender *et al.*, 2017). Tech startups are typically managed by the founders who came up with the idea for the innovation. The hallmark of startups is their creativity, which distinguishes them from other small and medium-sized enterprises (SMEs). Another distinctive feature is that startups are relatively young companies, typically less than five years old. Their short lifespan has important implications, particularly for finance and investment, the focus of this chapter. Without a long track record and offering a new and untested business idea, banks are often reluctant to provide funding. Yet, tech startups require considerable initial capital due to factors associated with testing new technologies or business models. In this context, it is important to note that startups develop within an ecosystem of agents, institutions, regulations, and other factors. Funding is a key part of that ecosystem and funds can be accessed through different channels. Startups are important for Asian economies because they introduce new technologies and economic models that drive innovation and improve efficiency. From 2013 to mid-2020, venture funding to Asian enterprises reached more than US$450 billion, involving over 35,000 individual investment deals (KPMG, 2020). The main objective of this chapter is to provide an analysis of access to finance and investment for tech startups in developing Asia, with specific reference to four countries, Cambodia, India, Thailand, and Viet Nam.

Table 1:   Four Tech Sectors and the Sustainable Development Goals (SDGs)

Sector	Innovations	SDGs
Clean/green tech	Sustainable energy (i.e., solar, wind) Tech for reducing, recycling, reusing Cleaning air and water discharge	6: Clean Water and Sanitation 7: Affordable and Clean Energy
Agritech	Tech solutions for smart farms Smart irrigation, crop monitoring Automation of farming practices Use of drones	2: Zero Hunger Target 2.3: "…double the agricultural productivity and the incomes of small-scale food producers…," through "technology" and other support
Edtech	In-school teaching solutions Attendance monitoring and administration After-school tutoring apps School, program, scholarship search Grading and feedback mechanisms	4: Quality Education
Healthtech	Tech for improved health treatment within hospitals and clinics For diagnosis, prescription, treatment, and monitoring outside of hospitals and clinics	3: Good Health and Well-Being

Source: Authors. For SDGs: https://sustainabledevelopment.un.org/?menu=1300.

Our analysis focuses on four sectors, namely greentech, agritech, edtech, and healthtech, as shown in Table 1. We have chosen these sectors because they not only make an important contribution to economic growth, but they also aid the achievement of the Sustainable Development Goals, or SDGs (ADB, 2019). Greentech startups, also known as cleantech, help reduce environmental damage, support climate change adaptation, and include solutions to reduce energy consumption and switch to renewable sources. Agritech startups use technology to improve farming methods for crop cultivation, animal husbandry, and produce processing, and contribute to creating what are known as "smart farms." Edtech startups employ technology in creative ways to improve teaching and learning, both within schools and through tutorials and other out-of-classroom activities. It can include digital solutions for improved school and school system management. Finally, healthtech offers technology innovation in the healthcare sector and can include the creation of new medical devices, innovative approaches to providing diagnosis (e.g., at distance through the internet) and treatment, as well as digital solutions for hospital and health system management.

We used a mixed-methods approach in researching this chapter. First, we conducted a review of documents and websites with information on policies, activities, and programs, and combined this with discussions with officials from government, academia, funding organizations (such as venture capital funds), incubators, and quasi-public bodies. Second, we conducted between 10 and 17 interviews with tech startups in each of the four countries. The startups interviewed were engaged in one of the four sectors of interest, except for Viet Nam, where all enterprises interviewed were from the agritech and healthtech sectors. Table A1 in the appendix lists the number of startups interviewed by sector and country. Most of the startups in our sample had been in operation for not more than five years.[1]

A researcher was engaged by the Asian Development Bank in each country to carry out a country study. The interviews were conducted one-on-one, except in India where small groups of entrepreneurs were organized. Researchers used a set of guiding questions, but deviated from those questions to explore interesting facets that arose in the course of the interview. This open-ended and nonstructured approach allowed the researchers to explore issues not considered at the outset. Key insights were gained from this approach, including: government not only providing policies and programs but being a major customer; side businesses and day job salaries as a funding source; the time needed for product certification; pitch competition prizes used for funding; and others. Furthermore, because the samples are small and not selected in a random manner, it would be misleading to gather and present quantitative results. Moreover, random sampling requires a sampling frame, which does not exist for startups in these four sectors in these countries. Instead, the insights gained from the interviews are embedded in the chapter, either in the

---

[1] The startups interviewed did not include all four sectors in every country. For example, the 11 enterprises interviewed in Viet Nam were from the agritech and healthtech sectors.

general analysis or as discrete examples from specific startups. The four country studies are contained in the list of references.[2]

The chapter adds to the current literature by providing an up-to-date overview of the tech startup scene in four Asian countries. We focus on development-oriented tech startups. Furthermore, we contribute to the literature by identifying various funding sources for tech startups and their usage in the four countries. Finally, we show that development-oriented tech startups have special funding needs and opportunities.

The chapter is structured into six sections. Following this introduction, we briefly set out the role of funding in the larger startup ecosystem. The third section then maps out the landscape of tech startups in the four countries. In the fourth section, we discuss the different sources of funding available for tech startups. We enrich the analysis here with examples gathered during the interviews. The fifth section shows how the funding needs of tech startups in the development field (greentech, agritech, edtech, and healthtech) differ from those of other tech startups. Our findings show that the development field holds specific risks, but also provides many new funding opportunities. The final section briefly concludes.

2. Ecosystem and the Role of Finance and Investment

Startups arise and develop within an ecosystem that consists of a range of actors, institutions, and relationships. A dense, interactive, and networked ecosystem will allow startups to flourish and it is such an ecosystem that governments in Asia's emerging economies, as elsewhere in the world, are building. Funding is a central component — it might be argued it is *the* central component, as inadequate funding will limit the potential of startups. The range of elements that are part of the ecosystem is vast. Figure 1 seeks to capture the full range. It includes incubators and accelerators, digital and hard infrastructure, and the human capital needed for invention and to master technology. Government policies and programs are key elements of the ecosystem (and support other aspects of the system, such as

---

[2] See Sopheara Ek (2019) for Cambodia, Sakdipon Juasrikul (2019) for Thailand, and Thinh Pham (2019) for Viet Nam. The report for India is to be completed in 2020.

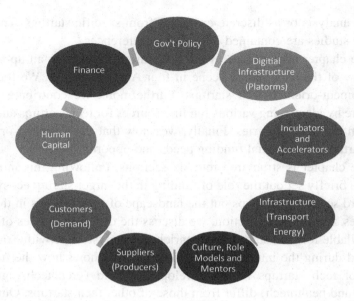

Figure 1:   Startup Ecosystem

Source: Authors. (Note to layout/typesetter: Write the word "Startups" in the middle of the circle, then delete this note.)

infrastructure, human capital, etc.). Startups operate within a cultural milieu that can encourage and reward (or constrain) entrepreneurship and includes role models and mentors. Finally, startups seek to create new products or services that create or fulfill demand and therefore the market for their output is important, as are markets (producers) that supply inputs and services to startups.

Nested within the broader startup ecosystem is a funding ecosystem (or subsystem) that comprises the various funding opportunities, options, and networks. Startups are closely associated with venture capital (VC), not only in Silicon Valley but in other innovation hubs throughout the world. VC is certainly important for startups. However, VC is one among many sources of funding and is certainly not the most frequently used source. Instead, it is often a hoped-for source after a product or service has been introduced to the market and capital is needed to scale up. This is

Table 2: Main Economic Indicators and Digital Access

	GDP (US$ billions)	GNI per Capita (US$)	Population (millions)	Individuals Using the Internet (% of population)		Mobile Cellular Subscriptions (per 100 people)	
	2018	2018	2018	2008	2018	2008	2018
Cambodia	25	1,230	16	0.5	40.0	30.5	119.5
Viet Nam	245	2,160	95	23.9	70.3	86.8	147.2
Thailand	505	5,950	66	18.2	56.8	92.9	180.2
India	2,726	1,800	1,332	4.4	34.5*	28.9	86.9

Note: *2017;

Sources: ADB for GDP per capita (Atlas method) and population. World Development Indicators, World Bank (2020) for other variables.

true for startups in developing Asia, but also for advanced countries such as the United States and the Republic of Korea (see Appendix).

3. Emergence of Startups in Four Countries

Startups have emerged as an important business model for countries throughout the world, and particularly in Asia. Getting a sense of their significance can be difficult as consistent lists of startups are often not available and seeking comparisons across countries may be difficult as national definitions differ.

The four countries in our study differ substantially in their economic and demographic size, as shown in Table 2. They provide for a range of experiences in developing Asia. India is a huge country with a deep and varied startup community, whereas Cambodia is much smaller, and startup activity is more nascent. Thailand and Viet Nam are in-between, middle-sized countries where startup development appears to be growing rapidly. We chose these four countries as they constitute an interesting set of countries with different characteristics. India has a population of 1.3 billion and generates an annual output of US$2.7 trillion. At the other end, Cambodia has 16 million people and a rapidly growing but still relatively small economy of US$25 billion. Three of the countries are classified as lower-middle income countries, while Thailand has reached the upper-middle stage with an annual income per capita of nearly US$6,000, more than twice as high as the next highest country. Internet use rose from less than 5% in Cambodia and India in 2008 to nearly or over 35% a decade later. The other two countries have internet usage rates of over 50% of the population, with Viet Nam as high as 70%. Mobile phone subscriptions exceed 100 for every 100 people (i.e., many people have more than one subscription), except India, which is at 87. Expanding internet access and mobile phone usage broadens the market for the many startups engaged in e-commerce, fintech, and digital marketplaces. However, digital access is important but less critical for the four sectors examined in this chapter.

India is a leader in startup development and has been for decades. While the idea of startups is of recent vintage, India developed a community of export-oriented software services and business process outsourcing (BPO) firms from the early 1980s — which were not called "startups" then but would be today. This first wave was followed by a second wave that emerged in the 2000s in which digital technology and the internet were adapted to develop smart solutions for the broader consumer market. A third wave has emerged in the past few years that is deep tech, focused on goods (as well as services), and is engaged in business-to-business (B2B) markets (Choudhury *et al.*, 2019). Through the three waves, the tech sector has been driven by an entrepreneurial culture, an elaborate system of engineering and related technical education, and the return of professionals from studying and working abroad.

India currently has an estimated 50,000 startups, of which about 8,900 might be considered tech startups (*Economic Times*, 2019a,b).[3] There are reportedly 19 unicorns, defined as startups with a value of US$1 billion or more. These include mostly fintech and e-commerce firms, but also BYJU'S, the world's largest edtech enterprise valued at over US$5 billion. India also boasts a vibrant venture capital and investment community

---

[3] Startups may establish and achieve scale but are not necessarily profitable. An end-of-decade review probably overstated the problem but nonetheless pinpointed a concern in noting that India's digitech startups "have built scale and totted up revenues, but none of them has yet found a path to profit" (Datta, 2019).

comprising local and foreign investors, including Walmart, which paid US$16 billion for a majority stake in India's successful e-commerce firm Flipkart.

In Viet Nam, tech startups started emerging as early as the 2000s, but it was only from about 2015 that the startup ecosystem was fully supported by good telecommunications (internet, 4G), and improvements in the country's levels of technology and education. The Ministry of Science and Technology is the lead agency involved in developing support programs and in organizing events for tech startups. A legal framework for startup investment has been established. The activity is heavily concentrated in Ha Noi and Ho Chi Minh City and is driven mainly by Viet Kieu, the generation of Vietnamese who studied abroad and then returned.

There may be 2,000 to 3,000 startups operating in the country, with a concentration in e-commerce, foodtech, fintech, media, logistics, and online travel (Topica Founder Institute, 2017). Aside from foodtech, agritech has not been a key sector for startup activity. Overall, new investments (deals) in startups by VC and related investors totaled US$291 million in 2017, with 85% of the funding coming from offshore venture capitalists. The government has recently committed to increasing capital inflows to the country to address funding difficulties for tech startups and VCs (VIR, 2019). Many startups use cryptocurrency and blockchain technologies, although the country has yet to craft a regulatory framework for those activities (Bathke, 2018).

In Thailand, the startup community emerged from the software-based SMEs that developed in the 2000s. The idea of startups, as a distinct segment of the SME community, emerged with two seminal events. The AIS Startup Weekend, organized by the large telecoms firm AIS in 2011, focused on digital innovation and was key to introducing the idea of startups to Thailand. The second event, Startup Thailand 2016, was organized by the government and marked the full development of, and effort toward, startups in the country. The government has seen innovation and advances in technology as a means to reignite growth and overcome the middle-income trap. Fostering startups is a means to meet that objective.

There were only three recorded funding deals for startups in 2012, but that figure rose to 90 in 2017. The number of venture capital funds has increased dramatically to over 100 and includes many corporate venture

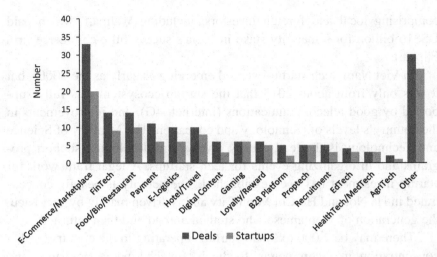

Figure 2:   Number of Deals and Startups by Sector, Thailand, 2011–2018

Note: The Other category includes: Crowdfunding, Insurance, MarTech, Ticket System, Construction, Enterprise Platform, Hardware, Retail, Car Sharing, Drone and Robotic, Messaging, Online Printing, Professional Service, Real Estate, and Social Media Analytics. Each of these sectors has four or fewer deals and startups.

Source: Techsauce (2019).

Table 3:   Active Tech Startups by Sector, Cambodia

Sectors	No. of Startups	Sectors	No. of Startups
Fintech	>50	Transportation	>10
Media and advertising	>40	Internet of things and hardware	>5
E-commerce and logistics	>30	Healthtech	>5
Development services	>30	Edtech	>5
Digital marketplaces	>20	Agritech	<5

Source: Kem *et al.* (2019).

capital (CVC) funds. The total number of startups may be over 1,000 and are concentrated in e-commerce and the digital marketplace, followed by fintech, food, payments, and e-logistics (Figure 2). As in other countries, there are relatively few startups in the four sectors that are the focus of this study, namely greentech, agritech, edtech, and healthtech.

Cambodia's startup sector is much less developed than those in the countries cited above. Yet there are some promising developments. The government is promoting the digital economy and Industry 4.0, and a vibrant startup scene is emerging. There is potential for startups given the size of the youth population and high GDP growth that averaged 7% between 2010 and 2018 (ADB, 2019). Cambodia has been described as possessing a "promising startup landscape,"[4] with many young people interested in starting a business. The number of tech startups has been increasing rapidly, albeit from a low base. Official figures are not available, however, there were estimated to be less than 50 startups in 2013 and this figure increased nearly sixfold to around 300 by 2018 (Ek, 2019). Nearly a third of all startups are engaged in two sectors: fintech, and media and advertising (Table 3). Other sectors include e-commerce, development services, and digital marketplaces. Only a few startups can be identified in the four sectors that are the focus of this study.

The digital transformation is happening rapidly in Cambodia, but many challenges remain. The country received the lowest rank among economies in East Asia and the Pacific on an index that measures the adoption of technology among government, business, and individuals (World Bank, 2018). Moreover, a low level of digital literacy constrains digital and technological adaption, which can constrain the market for tech startups that launch services on digital platforms. Less than a third of the population has basic digital skills, such as using a spreadsheet, while less than 3% can connect and install new devices (CDRI, 2019).

4. Funding Sources for Tech Startups

Tech startups tap various funding sources throughout their life cycles. Their access to specific types of funding may be easier or more relevant at specific stages of their business development. Table 4 sets out a list of funding sources that we encountered in our analysis of startups in the four countries.

---

[4] https://capitalcambodia.com/cambodias-tech-startup-ecosystem-at-a-glance/ (accessed on 19 November 2019).

Table 4: Funding Sources of Tech Startups

	Stage	Advantage	Risks/Limits	Usage*
Savings	Early	Availability; no screening by bank	Limited	Substantial
Family and Friends	Early	Availability; no screening by bank	Uncertainty about amount and repayment	Substantial
Salary from Other Job	Early	Continuous stream	Relatively small	Substantial
Prize Money	Early	Full fungibility	Relatively small amounts and hard to win	Limited
Company Revenues	Early-late	Possibly continuous stream	Revenues not invested in profitable business	Limited
Government Grants or Loans	Early	Full fungibility	Often small amounts	Limited
Angel Investor	Early	Access to potentially large pool of capital	Difficult to find	Very limited
Crowdfunding	Early-late	Relatively inexpensive	Uncertain response	Very limited
Banks	Early-late	Usually large amounts of capital available	Thorough screening; possibly onerous and restricted use of capital	Limited
Venture Capital	Early-late	Access to potentially large pool of capital	Participation in ownership	Very limited

Note: *Usage in four countries.
Source: Authors.

4.1 *Bootstrapping from Savings and Salaries*

The initial funding for most startups is contributed by the founders and their families and friends. This was apparent in the interviews we conducted with startups in the four countries. Initial startup activities include developing the idea, designing the product or service, conducting market research (to gauge demand), prototyping, and then testing the result in the market. These stages incur costs for materials, machinery, computing systems, access to plat-forms, testing activities, use of design and prototyping equipment, wages of employees, and the time of the founders. However, they do not generate revenue and need to be funded. The founders can use their savings and work full-time on the startup. For example, a Ha Noi-based agritech startup that develops smart fertilization systems began with three founders who worked from home and used their pooled savings as initial funding sources. The founders' savings were spent on product conceptualization and design.

Savings can be supplemented by funds provided by family and friends. In India, for example, data from a recent study by the Reserve Bank of India found that 43% of startups listed "family and friends" as the most frequently cited source. While this strategy helps a startup to advance quickly, the risk is that the savings are fully depleted before the startup starts generating any revenue.

Another option that was revealed by our interviews is that the found-ers initially work as salaried employees at other jobs and dedicate time to the startup during nonwork hours in the evening and on weekends.[5] Salary income in excess of personal and household expenditures can be invested in the startup. For example, an agritech startup in Cambodia was founded by two government employees and a student currently doing a PhD in Japan. The two employees worked on the startup in their spare time but also waited for the student cofounder to return to move the project for-ward. While this type of funding provides a continuous revenue stream (that allows the founders to support themselves), it limits the time that founders can spend on developing their startup. In certain sectors, being fast might be highly important.

4.2 *Pitching: Prize Money and Exposure to Investors*

The startup movement has given rise to the unique phenomenon of pitching competitions, in which startup entrepreneurs present or "pitch"

---

[5]For example, Phil Knight continued to work for an accounting firm after setting up and operating Blue Ribbon Sports, the sports shoe distribution company that he later trans-formed into Nike.

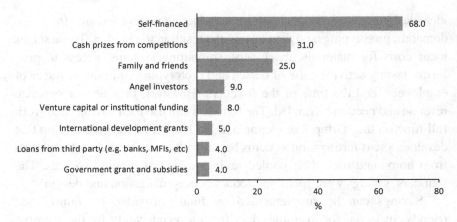

Figure 3:   Sources of Funds, % of Startups per Source, Cambodia, 2018

Notes: Startups could select multiple answers. MFIs = microfinance institutions.
Source: Kem *et al.* (2019).

their business idea to a group of judges and investors. The pitch competition can provide two sources of funds. One is prize money offered by the organizers and awarded by a set of judges for the best pitch(es). In Cambodia, for example, some pitch competitions offer US$5,000, which might seem like small change for a startup in Silicon Valley but provides important seed money for a startup in Cambodia and would be equivalent to the size of a small bank loan. The added benefit is that the funds do not need to be repaid and do not grant equity to an outsider. Prize money from competitions is cited by Cambodian startups as the second most common source of funding, after self-finance (Figure 3). The other source of funding that can arise from pitch competitions comes from investors who attend and identify potential firms for investment.

Pitching competitions are held in all four countries. For example, in Viet Nam they are well-established as part of regular fairs and networking events at provincial and national levels supported by the Ministry of Science and Technology (MOST). The largest and best-known event is the national Techfest organized annually by the National Agency for Technology Entrepreneurship and Commercialization Development

(NATEC) under MOST. Techfests are hosted by a different city each year and feature different themes. For example, the 2017 Techfest focused on connecting the local startup ecosystem, while the 2019 Techfest highlighted the development of startup hubs outside of Ha Noi and Ho Chi Minh City.

4.3 *Revenues from Separate Businesses*

Another strategy is to generate revenue from a separate business aside from the startup enterprise (or the key startup idea). This can be any type of business that uses the founders' expertise. We found interesting examples of this strategy among young engineering graduates from a college near Delhi in India. Several graduates set up businesses to provide design, testing, and other consulting services to local manufacturers. One graduate established a training college back in his home city to raise revenue. A startup in Ha Noi, which is developing a smart health app connecting doctors with patients, raises funds through a side business (also a tech startup) that provides e-receipt software for the local tax authorities. The stable stream of profits from the e-receipt software is reinvested into the development of the health app.

While operating these businesses, founders are refining their products, discussing partnerships with manufacturers, testing them in the market, or, in one case, moving a product through the long process of national product certification. A product can take several years to bring to market and funding is needed in the meantime not only to support product development but also the living expenses of the entrepreneur(s). This type of funding can not only help at the beginning, but also in the later development of the company. Having two or more businesses can help to better cope with sectoral downturns. In the best case, there might be synergies between business or technological spillovers.

4.4 *Grants and Government Credit*

Funding can sometimes be secured through grants from government agencies. These programs can vary by country. Sometimes they take the form of research grants, which support the R&D activities of the startup as it develops its product. Such grants support the technology side of development and are particularly important for startups engaged in product development, including in greentech and agritech activities, rather than in e-commerce and fintech. In addition to government sources, grants are also available from international cooperation (donor) agencies. It is difficult to know the full range of granting agencies and their funds, but we found evidence of this source in Cambodia. Indeed, survey results indicate that 5% of startups received "international development grants" and that it was a more common source of funding than loans from banks and other financial institutions (Figure 3). Such grants may be concentrated in specific sectors, particularly related to greentech, such as energy conservation, renewable energy, and climate change adaptation. Given the global climate change imperative, developed country governments have oriented a portion of their aid to climate change initiatives. Startups may not know about these opportunities and need to make a dedicated effort to search for funding from the global startup ecosystem.

Governments may also offer low-cost credit, although the eligibility may not be specific to startups and can include other SMEs. Indeed, programs by government financial institutions to support SMEs predate the startup concept in most countries. In Thailand, the SME Development Bank has been in operation since 2002, while the concept of startups gained general usage only from about 2016. The Small Industries Development Bank of India (SIDBI) has been providing credit since 1990, long before the recent era of startups. Despite the existence of these institutions, they do not necessarily provide a ready source of finance for startups. A study of 1,246 startups in India found that only 0.6% had borrowed from SIDBI. These banks can be conservative in their lending operations, providing credit to only more established businesses. They may require collateral that startups find difficult to provide and they may not be able to properly assess the risk of lending to untested startups.

However, governments are devising new facilities to fund startups. For example, the 2017 SME Law in Viet Nam provides for the creation of funds for preferential lending to "creative" SMEs (startups) and for credit guarantees. Elsewhere, the Small and Medium Enterprises Bank of Cambodia was established in 2019 and the following year an SME

Support Fund of US$50 million was created to provide funds to private financial institutions for on-lending to enterprises, including startups. In India, the government's Startup India program includes the creation of a "fund of funds" valued at Rs. 10,000 crores (US$1.4 billion) to provide funding over a four-year period to venture capital funds for investments in startups.

4.5 *Angel Investors*

Angel investors provide another potential source of funds for startups. Angels are normally high-wealth individuals and are often successful entrepreneurs themselves. This means that they may be more likely to provide "patient capital" that does not require a quick return and therefore can be suited to the long product development timespan for product (instead of service) activities in agritech and greentech. Angels provide funding by taking equity and therefore do require repayment, as does credit.

Angel investors are less visible than other forms of funding, having no physical presence, such as banks, and often having no "public" presence, such as government agencies or venture capital funds. Angels are most often found through personal connections and business networks or an appearance at a pitch competition. Because the existence of some angels remains below the radar, an accurate picture of their number and the flow of funds provided is hard to obtain. In some cases, angel investor associations have been formed.

The number of active angel investors in Thailand increased from two in 2012 to 35 in 2018 (Techsauce, 2019). Thailand has sought to encourage angel investment by providing a tax break. However, the deduction on personal income tax is applicable to an investment of not more than 100,000 baht (less than US$3,500). Angel investments are substantially higher than that and thus the fiscal incentive is not likely to have much impact on encouraging angel investment.

In Viet Nam, only an estimated 4% of investments in startups, by value, came from angel investors in 2016 (Topica Founder Institute, 2017). However, tech startups also refer to friends and family as angel investors, so the distinction between these two sources of investment is unclear in Viet Nam. For these family and friend angels, equity is not expected, and repayment of capital may or may not occur. Generally, the small number of angel investors operating in the country make it challenging for more investors to come in because of the low number of people with similar experiences that could provide guidance.

4.6 *Crowdfunding*

Crowdfunding is another potential funding source. Crowdfunding means that many people contribute relatively small amounts to fund an enterprise. People may have a special interest in supporting the startup. It could be a philanthropic motivation, to support local communities, or other reasons. Today, the internet offers the option to market new ideas at low cost to a large community of possible investors and to collect funds. New communication technologies also allow funders to be continuously updated on the progress and thereby open up the possibility of additional future funding. Some startups use crowdfunding to build up a customer base and repay their loans through products or services.

Crowdfunding was not mentioned as a funding source by the enterprises and key informants we interviewed in the four countries. It is not used in Cambodia as there are no crowdfunding firms registered with the Securities and Exchange Commission.[6] Only 2.2% of startups in India cite crowdfunding as a funding source. (It is also the least cited source of funding in the Republic of Korea and the United States. See Appendix Figures A1 and A2.)

4.7 *Bank Credit*

A side business also helps to secure bank credit. The business provides a cash flow that, channeled through a bank, provides a history of

---

[6]Cambodia has a regulation that prohibits each crowdfunding firm/platform from raising more than US$50,000 for a single transaction/campaign, with a maximum of four transactions allowed per year.

transactions. That history demonstrates a capacity to generate revenue and can be used to assess a business loan application. Getting the initial business loan can also be supported by a clean personal credit history. Securing and making timely payments on a car loan, for example, will help a business loan application. In India, for example, banks are quick to check a person's credit history on CRISIL, the main credit rating agency. We came across this strategy in our country case studies. Agritech and healthtech startups in Viet Nam have used banks for funding purposes despite the obvious difficulties young founders have in providing collateral.

4.8 *Venture Capital*

VC is the form of funding most directly associated with startups. In most countries, the mass of startup firms has grown in tandem with the expansion of venture capital. Because it is formally organized, it has a more public presence than angel investment and therefore is easier for startups to identify as a funding source.

Despite the interest in investing in new ventures, VC is often out of reach for early-start startups. Venture capitalists often need to see not just an idea but a developed product or service that is ready for market or is already being sold in the market. VC often provides an important spur to scale up. Venture capital funds can be solely domestically organized or involve an external element. While India has a large pool of venture capital and startups can be domestically funded (or funded by foreigners), in other countries, international venture capital (IVC) has an important presence. They often set up a local operation and search for promising startups to invest in.

An interesting finding from our research is that venture capital funds, notably foreign ones, feel uncomfortable with company regulation and legal processes in many developing Asian countries. As such, they often require startups to register in a country with a trusted legal framework. This is the case for Cambodia, Thailand, and Viet Nam, in which domestic startups are asked — or feel obliged — to register in Singapore. In addition, foreign startups operating in ASEAN countries also register in their home country or in another trusted high-income economy. For example, two prominent foreign startups that we interviewed in Cambodia had registered, respectively, in Australia (home country of the founders) and Hong Kong, China (Japanese founder). Startups may also register in, or indeed operate from, Singapore because that is where much of the region's venture capital is based, and therefore it is more likely that they will access funds if they are based there. Moed (2018) reports that one-third of Thai startups are registered in Singapore as a strategy to access VC.

CVC funds can also be an important source of funding. These are funds set up by large companies to invest in promising firms, normally in a sector related to their operations. In Viet Nam, large corporations have increased their interest in funding creative startups. For example, Vingroup, the country's largest conglomerate, announced the establishment of two startup investment funds: VinGroup Ventures is a venture capital fund with US$100 million and the VinTech Fund has US$86 million to both support and invest in innovative tech startups. Also, Startup Viet Partners now has a 100-billion dong (US$4.3 million) venture capital fund, which focuses on technology-based SMEs. At the 2019 Viet Nam Venture Summit, 18 foreign investment funds signed a commitment to invest US$425 million in startups over three years.

In Thailand, tech deals completed in 2017 and 2018 were valued at US$240 million in total, with the biggest deal valued at US$20 million and secured by Eko, a workplace communications platform (Itti, 2018). Completed deals in Viet Nam were valued at US$291 million in 2017 and were mostly in e-commerce, with 84% coming from offshore venture capitalists (Topica Founder Institute, 2017).

In Cambodia, the digital telecoms provider Smart has been particularly active as a source of corporate venture capital.[7] Total, the French petroleum and resources firm, has also been providing funding for startups. Cambodia has about 20 VC and private equity (PE) firms/funds in operation. Many of them provide both VC and PE.[8] They are mainly

---

[7] This is the firm owned by Smart Axiata, the Malaysian telecoms company, and is not to be confused with Smart Communications, the mobile service provider in the Philippines.
[8] Private equity takes a controlling equity stake, VC takes a minority stake.

interested in growth-stage businesses. Given the rise of startups in the country, some of the previously existing VC funds have diversified their targets in recent years to also invest in startups. Only a small number of VCs invest exclusively in one sector, because the total number of investment-ready startups is small and thus limiting to one sector restricts investment opportunities. Of the 20 investment firms/funds, about nine of them have been identified as targeting at least one of the four sectors that are the focus of our study (Ek, 2019). Since 2015, at least 25 startups have received investment funding, with 14 deals publicly disclosed in 2018 alone.

In Thailand, the number of venture capital investors, including CVCs, increased dramatically over a short period from only 1 to 108 between 2012 and 2018. The number of deals (investments) and the value have also risen substantially. There was only one recorded investment in a startup in 2011, valued at about US$1 million. However, between 2016 and 2018, there were between 31 and 35 deals annually with the aggregate value peaking at US$106 million in 2017 and an average that year of about US$3 million per investment.

4.9 *Incubators and Accelerators*

Incubators and accelerators can also play an important role in assisting the funding of startups. They serve as a platform where startups and funding partners can meet and get connected. In India, for example, one incubator we interviewed was regularly contacted by investors looking for promising startups for investment. Some incubators and accelerators also have their own funds that they invest in or lend to the startups they nurture. For example, 11.4% of startups surveyed in India indicated that they received funding from an incubator or accelerator (Figure 4). In Thailand, the number of accelerators increased from one to 13 between 2012 and 2018. In Viet Nam, around 50 incubators and accelerators were reported to be active in 2018, most of which were government led. However, we do not have a picture of how many of the incubators and accelerators provide funding in these two countries.

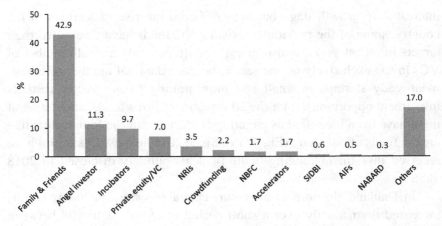

Figure 4:   Funding Sources for Startups, % of Enterprises Surveyed, India, 2019

Notes: Respondents could select multiple sources.
AIFs = Alternative Investment Funds, NABARD = National Bank for Agriculture and Rural Development, NBFCs = Nonbanking Financial Companies, NRIs = Nonresident Indians, SIDBI = Small Industries Development Bank of India, VC = Venture Capital.
Source: Reserve Bank of India (2019).

5. Constraints to Accessing Funding in the Four Sectors

We have focused on four specific sectors because of their potential development impact. However, there may be particular funding constraints for these sectors that do not affect more common tech startups engaged in e-commerce, marketplace, and fintech activities. Internet-based startups are seen as being at the core of the startups around the world because of the successes and the scale they have achieved. As such, investors may think it more plausible that new successful startups will emerge in those areas and be more willing to provide funding.

For the four sectors we have examined, the internet may be used or may provide partial support for the innovation, but in most cases the internet is not a key aspect of the firm's operations. Instead, these startups produce products. This is particularly true in cleantech and agritech, where startups develop such things as organic plant vaccines, pesticides and fertilizers, and mechanisms for reducing the energy needed to clean wastewater. As such, these products need to be developed, prototyped, refined, tested, and certified before they can be put on the market. Funding these efforts requires patience, which means providing "patient capital." VC investors may generally be less interested in waiting for many years before a product reaches the minimum viable product stage and starts to generate revenue. This point was made by Kerr, Nanda, Rhodes-Kropt (2014, p. 11), in which they argue that VC is particularly attractive to sectors that are "capital-efficient for both experimentation and subsequent scaling up," which characterizes digital technology or IT-based startups. Other sectors such as renewable energy "need to be proven at large scale to demonstrate technical feasibility" and they require traditional manufacturing plants. These investments in both experimentation and production take time and investors are often not that patient. We found this concern about long gestation and a lack of patient capital to be a constraint within agritech and cleantech in the countries that we studied. Furthermore, if the manufacturing capability is not available in-country, producers may need to be found abroad, which we found was the case with Cambodia.

That said, there are opportunities for tech startups in greentech and agritech due to the specific nature of their sectors. The first is that greentech/cleantech is a favored area for impact investors and donors seeking to support environmental management and climate change mitigation and adaption. As such, it is necessary for startups in these sectors to seek out funds with investors who want to invest for impact, rather than approaching traditional VC investors. One greentech startup (distributing energy load) was able to source considerable grant and equity funds by searching out these impact investors, including donors.[9]

The second opportunity arises from CVC, which would like to "go green." Large firms providing CVC may want to be part of new innovations that could help their firm be perceived as "green" or contributing to the SDGs. This might help the companies attract additional shareholders and build a customer base among people who are environmentally conscious.

---

[9] In fact, the startup contracted a researcher to search for funding sources. The startup's managers then reviewed the potential sources, drew up a shortlist, and submitted funding applications to the most promising ones.

In the health and education sectors, there are both similarities with and differences from the other two sectors. A major difference from the other two sectors, and other tech sectors more generally, is that the market can be largely public. This is true for edtech solutions that are used in public schools. It is also true of innovations in healthtech that involve hospitals and clinics. The healthtech innovations that involve products (medical devices) may have similar constraints to agritech and cleantech, but they might also have more stringent certification processes because they are related to personal health and would be used in hospitals. For tech startups in these sectors, cooperative relations with government agencies are crucial. The success of new products depends on government approval and the willingness of the government to engage the startup. This setup holds implications for funding. While other startups are subject to the dynamics of the market, these startups face a more dichotomic outcome: either they have no access to the market or they obtain access to a large market that they should quickly cover. In the latter case, they might face no or little competition from other providers and therefore offer interesting investment opportunities for venture capital investors or banks.

Another distinctive feature is that the education and health sectors are heavily regulated and typically not fully open to foreign competition. Providing goods and services for these sectors can thus have the advantage of being less exposed to foreign competition. At the same time, it might also limit the option to easily offer the products abroad. This might reduce the attractiveness of international venture capital, especially if the home market is small in size, such as in Cambodia.

Most tech startups are located in cities, where they have better access to talent, inputs, and funding. However, startups with a development focus might have a large customer base in rural areas. For example, agritech solutions are mostly developed for rural areas. Greentech startups often need to try out their solutions in areas where clean electricity is generated, typically rural areas. In terms of public health, there is a large gap between the provision of health services in cities and in rural areas. The fact that many development-oriented startups have a strong link to rural areas has implications for funding. First, the customer base in rural areas is less tech-savvy and poorer. Second, the startups face additional costs from being present in cities as well as in the countryside. This may have implications for the size of the market for agritech goods and services and profitability, which may deter investors.

6. Conclusion and Policy Recommendations

Asia is very much a part of the startup revolution that has swept the world over the last 15 years. Entrepreneurs with a knack for technology and the ability to conjure up good ideas for new services have been able to see their businesses grow to phenomenal levels. Most have been aided by the internet through which they have reached thousands and indeed millions of customer users. The rise of tech startups has occurred in parallel with the rapid expansion of two important elements of the startup ecosystem: incubators and venture capital.

Our review of tech startups in four sectors (agritech, cleantech, edtech, and healthtech) across four emerging Asian economies (Cambodia, India, Thailand, and Viet Nam) has drawn two main findings. First, there are a variety of opportunities to obtain funding aside from venture capital. Indeed, startups at their pre-market and market-entry stages are likely to rely on such sources as savings, money from family and friends, salaried employment, profits from side businesses, pitch competition prizes, and loans and grants from governments, donors, and other organizations. As they develop, funding may also come from angel investors. A small number will access venture capital and a much larger number will struggle, at least in the early stages, to gather less significant funding amounts from other sources.

The second main finding is that while the four focus sectors may be areas that support development objectives and are linked to the Sustainable Development Goals, there are far fewer tech startups in these sectors and they find it difficult to access funding. We can suggest some reasons why this might be the case. Partly, it may be that the business idea is a product, especially in greentech and agritech, that might require more patient capital as product development may take longer and be more costly than startups in other sectors. Similarly, it may be due to the perception that investments in these areas are more difficult, less easily scalable, and more similar to traditional products and services than are investments in e-commerce, digital marketplaces, and other internet-based firms. Investors may be looking for the next Amazon, Facebook, or Gojek and see — rightly or wrongly — less potential in more development-oriented sectors.

Each of the two key findings has policy implications. First, regarding the variety of funding sources, the government can encourage investment in tech startups from multiple sources — in addition to just venture capital. In particular, the government may ease the taxation of income (from employment, business profits, etc.) that is subsequently invested in tech startups. This can encourage angel investors, foundations, incubators, startup entrepreneurs holding day jobs, and others to invest. Second, startups in development-oriented sectors, such as agritech, cleantech, edutech and healthtech, may need targeted assistance because patient capital is scarce. Providing public sector venture capital is one option, but only if the government has the expertise to identify promising startups. Another option is to provide greater support to startups in identifying and applying to impact investors. Such investors — which include private domestic and foreign funders, bilateral and multilateral organizations, sovereign wealth funds — seek positive social and environmental outcomes, as well as a financial return.

References

Asian Development Bank (ADB). 2019. *ADB Ventures Facility (handout)*: Manila. https://www.adb.org/projects/52295-001/main.

Bathke, B. 2018. Returning Vietnamese are leaving their mark on Vietnam's burgeoning start-up scene. *Tech in Asia*. https://www.techinasia.com/vietnam-secret-super-weapons-startup-scene (accessed August 2019).

Born2Global Centre. 2019. *Korea Startup Index 2018*. Born2Global Centre, Republic of Korea. https://www.born2global.com/ (accessed January 2020).

Cambodia Development Research Institute (CDRI). 2019. Fostering an inclusive digital transformation in Cambodia: Briefing for Roundtable with Cambodia's Digital Economy Task Force, 4 November 2019. https://set.odi.org/wp-content/uploads/2019/10/Briefing-for-4-November-Roundtable-on-Digital-Economy-in-Cambodia.pdf (accessed November 2019).

Choudhury, S.P., S. Sharma, and S. Jain. 2019. Third waves: Tracking the evolution of India's startups. Knowledge at Wharton. November. https://knowledge.

wharton.upenn.edu/article/three-waves-tracking-evolution-indias-startups/ (accessed December 2019).

Datta, P. 2019. A roller-coaster ride. *India Today*, Special Issue, 23 December.

Ek, S. 2019. Mapping the Tech Startup Ecosystem in Cambodia. Final report for the Asian Development Bank. Manila.

Economic Times. 2019a. With 50,000 startups registered, India aims for as many more by 2024. (India). https://economictimes.indiatimes.com/small-biz/ startups/newsbuzz/with-50000-startups-registered-india-aims-for-as-many-more-by-2024/articleshow/71440117.cms (accessed January 2020).

Economic Times. 2019b. Over 1,300 startups added in 2019, over 8,900 tech startups now in India: NASSCOM. 5 November. India. https://economic-times.indiatimes.com/small-biz/startups/newsbuzz/over-1300-startups-added-in-2019-over-8900-tech-startups-in-india-now-nasscom/articleshow/ 71925791.cms.

Itti, V. 2018. Thailand Start-up Event 2018. Funding, exits and noteworthy events. *Medium*. https://medium.com/@vitavin/thailand-startup-2018-wrap-up-fundings-exits-noteworthy-events-ad8ae3efa40a (accessed August 2019).

Juasrikul, S. 2019. Financing and Growth of Tech Startups in Thailand. Final report for Asian Development Bank. Manila.

Kem, B., J. Sou, Z. Ng, and P. Chan. 2019. Startup Kingdom: Cambodia's Vibrant Tech Startup Ecosystem in 2018. Vol. 2. Phnom Penh, Cambodia. Mekong Strategic Partners and Raintree Development. https://www.raintreecambodia. com/research (accessed December 2019).

Kerr, W., R. Nanda, and M. Rhodes-Kropt. 2014. Entrepreneurship as experimentation. NBER Working Paper 20358. *National Bureau for Economic Research*. Cambridge, Mass.

KPMG. 2020. Venture Pulse Q2 2020, Global analysis of venture funding https:// assets.kpmg/content/dam/kpmg/xx/pdf/2020/07/venture-pulse-q2-2020-global.pdf (accessed September 2020).

Moed, J. 2018. A guide to Southeast Asia's thriving start-up ecosystem. *Forbes*. https://www.forbes.com/sites/jonathanmoed/2018/07/12/a-guide-to-south-east-asias-thriving-startup-ecosystem-heres-what-you-need-to-know/ #5d97a6346e18 (accessed August 2019).

Pham, T. 2019. Tech Startups in Viet Nam. Draft study report for Asian Development Bank. Manila.

Reserve Bank of India. 2019. Pilot Survey on Indian Startup Sector — Major Findings. https://www.rbi.org.in/scripts/PublicationReportDetails.aspx?ID=956.

Spender, J.C., V. Corvello, M. Grimaldi, and P. Rippa. 2017. Startups and open innovations: A review of literature. *European Journal of Innovation Management*, Vol. 20:1, pp. 4–30.

Techsauce. 2019. Thailand Tech Startup Ecosystem Report 2018 — Investor Guide. Techsauce, Thailand. https://techsauce.co/report/thailand-tech-startup-ecosystem-year-2018-th (accessed January 2020).

Topica Founder Institute. 2017. Vietnam Start-up Deals Insight 2017. https://www.slideshare.net/topicafounderinstitute/vietnam-startup-deals-insight-2017-87618940 (accessed August 2019).

Vietnam Investment Review (VIR). 2019. Minister promises to support startups at Vietnam Venture Summit. Issue: 10 June. https://www.vir.com.vn/minister-promises-to-support-startups-at-vietnam-venture-summit-68409.html (accessed March 2020).

World Bank. 2018. Benefitting from the Digital Economy Cambodia Policy Note. http://documents.worldbank.org/curated/en/100841543598854492/Benefiting-from-the-Digital-Economy-Cambodia-Policy-Note (accessed October 2019).

World Bank. 2020. World Development Indicators, database. https://databank.worldbank.org/source/world-development-indicators (accessed January 2020).

Appendix

Table A1:   Number of Incubators and Startups Interviewed (by country and sector)

	Cambodia	India	Thailand	Viet Nam
Agritech	6	5	3	5
Edtech	4	1	2	—
Greentech	4	1	2	—
Healthtech	3	4	4	5
Incubators	5	2	2	1

Source: Authors.

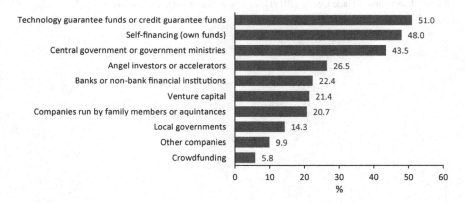

Figure A2:   Funding Sources for Startups, Republic of Korea, 2018 (% of enterprises indicating each source)

Note: Startups could select multiple sources. Local governments include Seoul Metropolitan Government and Gyeonggi Provincial Government.
Source: Born2Global Centre, Republic of Korea. https://www.born2global.com/Korea Startup Index 2018.

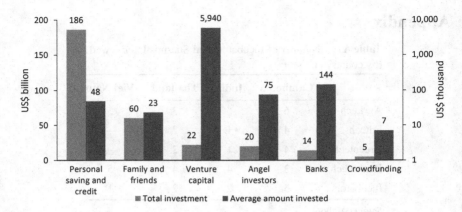

Figure A1:   Funding Sources for Startups in the United States, 2012

Note: Total investment is on the left axis. Average investment per startup is on the right axis.
Source: International Trade Centre (2019) based on data from Startup Funding.

Chapter 7

The Startup Environment and Funding Activity in India

Dharish David,*,§ Sasidaran Gopalan,†,¶ and
Suma Ramachandran‡,||

*Associate Faculty, Singapore Institute of Management - Global
Education (SIM-GE), Singapore
†Assistant Professor, Innovation in Government and Society
College of Business and Economics, Al Ain, UAE
‡Former Head of Content Strategy at YourStory Media, Bengaluru, India
§dharishd@zoho.com, david014@mymail.sim.edu.sg
¶sasi.gopalan@uaeu.ac.ae
||sumaramachandran@gmail.com

Abstract

India has the third-largest startup ecosystem in the world with an estimated
26,000 startups, 26 "unicorns" (startups valued at over US$1 billion), and
US$36 billion in consolidated investments over 2017–2019. The ecosystem has expanded rapidly, mainly through private investments including
seed, angel, venture capital, and private equity, along with technical support from incubators/accelerators, and public policy. On its part, the government has tried to create a conducive environment through its flagship
Startup India initiative. With India pushing towards a knowledge-based,

digital economy, the government is also attempting to deploy ICT infrastructure and provide policy support for enhanced e-governance, investments, and technology innovation through research and funding higher education to spur entrepreneurship and economic growth. Data suggest that the startup ecosystem is largely clustered in large (Tier 1) cities and states with financial depth, more so in IT-enabled sectors including e-commerce, transport, and finance. Despite the progress made so far, Indian startups face huge challenges, such as the unorganized and fragmented nature of consumer and business markets, lack of clear and transparent policy initiatives, lack of infrastructure and access to government incentives (e.g., tax breaks), lack of knowledge and exposure, and complexities in doing business. Increasing awareness of government initiatives and incentives, credit disbursement to priority sectors, promoting outreach and network benefits to Tier 2 and Tier 3 cities, as well as simplifying investment opportunities and taxation rules for foreign and domestic investors could improve opportunities for startups in India.

Keywords: Startups, India digital economy, small business, entrepreneurship, financial instruments, venture capital, government policy and regulation

1. Introduction

For decades, India has been known for its Information and Communication Technology (ICT) prowess, and more recently for its rapid economic development through digital transformation and innovation. Alongside its recent rapid economic development, it has become one of the largest startup ecosystems in the world. The Indian startup ecosystem has steadily evolved in the past few years through an increasing number of angel investors, venture capital (VC) funds, incubators and accelerators, as well as support from government initiatives such as Digital India, Startup India, and Smart Cities, which should amplify startup and investment activity across cities and new sectors. This growth in startup investments and the number of 'unicorns' comes in the wake of increasing spending power, mobile internet usage, access to new consumer markets, social media adoption, technological innovations, and favorable consumer demographics.

The current wave of startups began around 2004, when Silicon Valley Bank set up its first office in Bengaluru. By 2015, India had 10,000 start-ups, almost the same number as in the People's Republic of China (PRC) (Grant Thornton, Assocham India 2016). It also had eight "unicorns" — startups with a valuation of US$1 billion or more — across e-commerce marketplaces, transport and mobility, logistics and hyperdelivery, ad-tech, digital banking and finance, online aggregators, and analytics.

The period 2014–2015 is considered an inflection point for the Indian startup ecosystem with the emergence of six 'unicorns' in those 2 years. Since then, the Indian startup ecosystem has evolved steadily owing to several underlying factors.

For the past few years, India has been one of the fastest growing emerging economies in the world, with rising internet, smartphone, and financial services penetration. It is also poised to reap the demographic dividend of having 600 million citizens under the age of 25. Further, its growing middle class is characterized by rising disposable income and social media adoption. Together with changing, previously inaccessible consumer demographics, this makes India one of the largest markets in the world.

Particularly over the last five years, political will has greatly increased, with marked improvements in ease of doing business and government initiatives like Digital India pushing for faster digital transformation. Policies and regulatory infrastructure have created a more conducive environment for innovation, with adoption of digital technologies, considering mobile and data tariffs are one of the lowest in the world.

Moreover, an agglomeration effect is visible in Tier 1 cities, characterized by large clusters of startups, investors (angels/VCs), and supporting services and infrastructure, with spill-over effects from the presence of large listed and unlisted technology firms. Domestically too, there is a growing list of angel investors and a growing pool of experienced serial entrepreneurs who have contributed to the rapid increase in the number of startups that have been incorporated.

This growth has also upskilled the huge pool of technical and engineering graduates. Synergies are also being developed using industry–academic–government linkages with a spurt in the number of university and industry-led incubators and accelerators, and setting up of government-sponsored patent hubs.

Table 1:   Top VC* Investments in India (2019)

Company	Investors	Amount (US$M)
Udaan	Tencent, GGV Capital, Altimeter Capital, Hillhouse Capital, DST Global, Lightspeed Ventures, Others	586
Delhivery	SoftBank Corp, Carlyle, Fosun Group	413
FirstCry	SoftBank Corp	400
Ola Electric Mobility	SoftBank Corp	250
Grofers	SoftBank Corp, Tiger Global, Sequoia Capital India, KTB Ventures	220

Notes: *As of 24 December 2019, VC is defined as Seed to Series F investments in companies less than 10 years old (since registration);
PE investments are not included in this list.
Source: Venture Intelligence.

The value of private investments and the number of VC funds, both from India and globally, has also risen in the past few years. An interesting trend has emerged from the East, including Japan's SoftBank Group, which had invested over US$8 billion by the end of 2018, followed by the PRC's Tencent investment holding company, and Singapore's sovereign wealth funds, GIC and Temasek. With the Chinese startup market becoming overcrowded and overheated, and more mature markets like Japan and the Republic of Korea slow to build their startup ecosystems, India has become an attractive destination among emerging markets (Table 1).

Even as the startup ecosystem grew, exits and M&As were few and far between. That changed in 2018 when Walmart acquired a 77% stake in Indian e-commerce giant Flipkart for US$16 billion in the world's biggest e-commerce M&A deal. It reflected the scale and momentum at which startups in India had grown.

Despite its rapid expansion and vibrancy, India's startup ecosystem is far from mature. For a long time, Indian entrepreneurs did not focus on solving local problems or working with cutting-edge technologies. This reluctance can be partly attributed to the lack of bold venture funding, given the lack of investors with deep pockets, resolve, and patience. Further, changes in consumer behavior, low price points, long gestation periods, and cash burn, especially due to the diversity of stakeholders in a democratic and decentralized structure, did not allow for reforms to be rolled out at the same speed as in the PRC (Sharma and TN, 2018).

This study is an important contribution to the literature on Indian start-ups, not only providing a working definition of startups and funding options in the Indian context, but also by looking at the trends in investment by geography and industry, using both publicly available and proprietary data. Though startups get plenty of media coverage (market trends, funding data, etc.), this study seeks to understand the underlying reasons and policies that explain these trends, outlining relevant government policies and other initiatives that have led to this rapid growth. It also highlights the challenges and suggests potential policy interventions to overcome them.

We also extend the scope of the study to perform an empirical analysis using sub-national data to identify the determinants of startup investments. Our results underline the importance of many factors such as better infrastructure and higher labor productivity in generating positive effects on startup investments. The most significant finding comes from the strong, persistent, and positive effect produced by greater availability of bank credit on startup investments, which is also a loose proxy for sub-national financial depth.

As startups are early-stage, technology-based firms, it has been difficult for them to get bank-based funding. So, they have relied largely on private sources, including angel and seed investments, private equity, and venture capital for funding. Geographically, funding has been concentrated around Bengaluru, Delhi-NCR (National Capital Region), and Mumbai; the three cities account for 85% of the volume of investment over the last few years. IT and IT-enabled services (ITES) have taken the lion's share of funding, way ahead of banking, financial services and insurance (BFSI), healthcare, and logistics.

Interestingly, this trend has started shifting somewhat towards larger investments in B2C/consumer internet startups focused on e-commerce, transportation and mobility, healthtech, foodtech, fintech/payments, edtech, and even social media platforms in regional languages. Not surprisingly, the biggest chunk of funding goes to late-stage startups, where private investors are looking at these ventures scaling and turning profitable, hoping they will turn into the next 'unicorn' that will disrupt traditional markets with the ongoing digital transformation in the country. However, considering that India aims to become a US$5 trillion-dollar economy in the next few years, access to technology needs to be democratized along with scalable business models to create a positive socioeconomic impact for large sections of the population where affordability is a concern, especially in sectors like education, mobility, health, and agriculture.

Empirically, this study also suggests that when states invest more in R&D, startups benefit from better funding and access to technology and expertise. Similarly, improving subnational financial depth appears to be positively and significantly associated with higher startup investments, so increasing credit from banks and NBFCs and getting more startups to qualify for government programs is important.

This study suggests that though the government is actively promoting India as a startup-friendly nation, more can be done in raising the level of technical talent and investment in R&D, and strengthening the linkages among startups, corporates, academic institutions, and the government. With innovation and VC funding being concentrated in Tier 1 cities, IT-related sectors, and potential "unicorns", more outreach programs are required to expand funding access to smaller cities and towns where impact will be greater. This can be done by looking at alternate models of investment such as cooperatives and so-called "zebra" startups — firms that address social problems but are for-profit in sectors such as education, healthcare, and clean energy.

More open data regarding startups to understand investment trends and challenges will also help with analyzing and providing them with better credit options. With Indian startups being heavily criticized for only emulating successful global ideas, homegrown startups addressing local issues need more support. Indeed, they may even have the ability to be scaled and deployed in other countries that need low-cost solutions and business models.

2. India's Startup and Funding Opportunities

2.1 *Recent Trends in Investment in Indian Startups and Data Availability*

Between 2011 and 2015, investment values increased at a compound annual growth rate (CAGR) of over 75% and the number of deals at a CAGR of over 80%. Since then, VC investments have increased rapidly according to various estimates and peaked in 2019 (Figure 1).

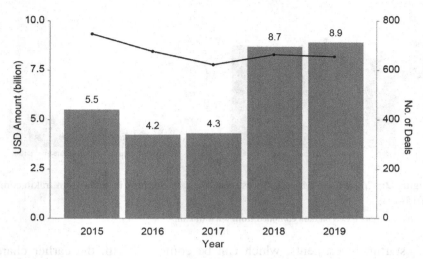

Figure 1:   VC* Investments into Startups in India, 2015–2019 ytd

Note: *VC is defined as Seed to Series F investments in companies less than 10 years old.
Source: Plotted by authors based on data from Venture Intelligence | As of 24 December 2019.

A challenge for obtaining data on startup funding is that they are mostly in the private realm; accessing investment data and corporate financials involves paying fees to firms like Venture Intelligence, Tracxn, etc. For this chapter, we have used two main sources tracking startup funding:

1. Proprietary data from Venture Intelligence (VI): a private firm launched in 2002 and considered a leading source of information and analysis on private company financials, transactions (private equity, venture capital, and M&A), and their valuations in India. VI provided only anonymized startup investment data that provided general trends, without any detailed/company-level data, as that would incur a fee.

2. Open-source data web-scraped from Trak.in: a business news and opinion site that also tracks investments in startups but with open-access data that is sourced publicly. This data was useful because it tracks detailed information but lacks clear definitions and classification. It required data-cleaning, but it was helpful for our empirical analysis, where, for example, we needed granular company-level investment data across various states. The following charts roughly show the difference and details in the data in terms of the value of

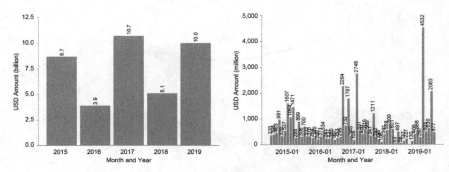

Figure 2: Yearly and Monthly Investment Data on Startups in India from trakin.com, 2015–2019

Source: Authors based on data compiled from www.trak.in.

startup investments, which can be compared with the earlier chart from VI (Figure 2).

2.2 Why India Can Be a Hub and Testing Ground for Innovation and Startups

By leveraging its strengths in human capital and ICT services, and transitioning to a digital and knowledge-based economy, India is fast becoming a breeding ground for innovation and startups. Knowledge economies use ICT, innovation and research, and higher education and specialized skills to create, disseminate, and apply knowledge for growth. According to the four indicators of the World Bank's Knowledge Economy Index, India ranked 109th out of 145 countries covered in 2012; however, the study has not been updated. India moved up five spots from 2018 to 2019 in the Global Innovation Index (GII) from 57th to 52nd place, among 129 countries across 80 indicators ranging from rates of intellectual property filing and mobile-application creation to spending on education, scientific and technical publications, as well as many other criteria.

This is promising, but challenges also exist in areas like developing low-cost technologies for price-sensitive customers, popularly known as "frugal innovation." Such low-ticket, low-tech solutions need to be implemented on a large scale to address underprivileged and underserved populations. Such swift technological advances provide startups in countries like India — unburdened by older, legacy technologies — with the ability to leapfrog and leverage mobiles to further the digital and mobile data transformation. Payments, banking, and associated services are also quickly moving towards mobiles. In fact, FinTech has been one of the most well-funded sectors over 2018–2019 (Rajan, 2019).

Despite having moved up 14 places in a year and ranking 63rd out of 190 nations in the Ease of Doing Business 2020 rankings, India still trails in areas such as enforcing contracts (163rd) and registering property (154th) (The World Bank Group, 2020). However, it is encouraging to know that the latest reforms are in the Doing Business areas of Starting a Business, Dealing with Construction Permits, Trading Across Borders, and Resolving Insolvency, among others.

The shift to a knowledge-based economic growth model is critical for India to reinvent its comparative advantages as labor- and capital-intensive manufacturing are fading. The fourth industrial revolution (Industry 4.0) presents a great opportunity for startups to disrupt and innovate by using technologies such as blockchain, the Internet of Things (IoT), artificial intelligence (AI), and machine learning (ML), among others. With the right backing and environment, startups can play a big role here, especially with a culture of research and innovation with respect for intellectual property rights, and flexible capital and labor markets (Figure 3).

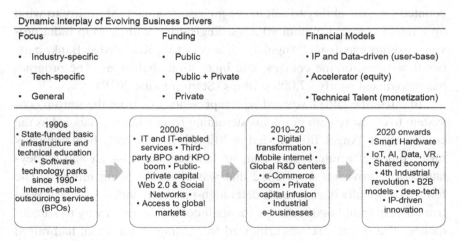

Dynamic Interplay of Evolving Business Drivers		
Focus	Funding	Financial Models
• Industry-specific	• Public	• IP and Data-driven (user-base)
• Tech-specific	• Public + Private	• Accelerator (equity)
• General	• Private	• Technical Talent (monetization)

Figure 3: Evolution of Innovation Ecosystems in India

Source: Adapted and modified by authors for the Indian case from: Sharma and Meyer (2019).

2.3 *Definition of Startups in the Indian Context*

Though there is no precise definition, the accepted characteristics of a "startup" span its age, scale of operations, and mode of funding. It is usually defined as a young company, a few years old, and yet to establish a steady stream of revenue. These firms have a small scale of operations, usually with a working prototype or paid pilot with the potential to grow and scale rapidly. They are initially funded by the founders' own private network of friends and family and actively seek additional funds to sustain themselves and become a viable business.

As an example, the GoI's Startup India program defines a "startup" as a company (PIB, 2017) that is:

1. Headquartered in India with not more than 10 years since incorporation or registration
2. Having an annual turnover of less than INR 1 billion (roughly US$14 million) (Startup India, 2019)

Following a revision in 2019, Startup India has updated its list of benefits (Startup India, 2019) to include income tax exemptions on capital gains and investments above fair market value, options for self-certification on various compliances, fast-tracking of patent applications at a discounted rate, the ability to sell to the government, and the ability to wind up a failed company within 90 days. Registering with Startup India provides exemptions from "Angel Tax", access to a Knowledge Bank, partnered services, online courses, and innovation challenges. The program has recognized nearly 27,000 startups (Startup India, 2019).

In 2019, the DPIIT worked with representatives from the startup ecosystem to do away with problems stemming from what was labeled as the controversial "Angel Tax" (levied at 30% when a privately held company raises funds at a rate higher than its fair valuation) — an anti-money-laundering provision since 2012 that was allegedly being misused. The law was originally introduced to deter high-net-worth individuals (HNWIs) from investing in bogus startups (or shell companies) as a way to launder money. The Angel Tax was criticized for stifling startups that had raised equity funding from unregistered foreign investors.

2.4 *Different Types of Funding for Startups in India from Early to Late Stage*

Funding for startups in India has followed the Anglo-Saxon model, which encourages entrepreneurial activity through investments from private and venture capital, as they are considered too risky by banking institutions. Venture capital (VC) and private equity (PE) are not regulated as in Europe. Fund-raising avenues extend from friends and family at the early stages, to seed/angel investors later, and finally VCs and PEs. Once the company is well established, it can then take on debt from banks, closed-end funds, and investment banks once they are ready to absorb late-stage investments, and edge towards listing an initial public offering (IPO) (Table 2).

Methods used elsewhere in the world have not been tried or are not applicable in India. For instance, in Japan and the US, equity crowdfunding has been a good option for startups. Pre-order crowdfunding allows customers to order products and startups to advertise their products produced on the internet and raise funds for their operations. This is legal in India, though not widely prevalent. Another way is to collect small amounts from individuals, as little as US$10–US$50 for a stake in the company called a "hometown investment trust" (HIT) fund to help riskier borrowers such as startups to get seed finance (Yoshino and Taghizadeh-Hesary, 2014). However, this method, known as "equity crowdfunding," has been deemed illegal in India by the country's financial regulator, the Securities and Exchange Board of India (SEBI) (Kaira, 2019).

Similarly, many Asian countries have money lenders that provide finance to MSMEs and startups. These lenders might essentially be loan sharks, who are not regulated and tend to charge high interest rates. While the MSME sector in India does count on such money lenders, early-stage startup funding is dominated by Seed/Angel investors, HNIs, some VC firms, and a growing list of FinTech lenders and nonbanking financial companies (NBFCs).

Besides Seed, VC, and PE funding, accelerators too have helped the startup ecosystem grow. The big trend in the past 3–5 years has been various corporate accelerator programs — a type of accelerator sponsored by a profitable company in a bid to discover and evaluate new technologies

Table 2:   Funding Available for Startups at Each Stage of Their Development

Funding Type (Avg US$ Value in India)	Startup Stage	Investor Type and Nature of Funds Raised
Angel funding (10K–1M)	Early/idea stage: seek funds for developing prototype of product/service	Individual/angel investors who provide mentorship to founders and early access to markets
Seed Funding (10K–1M)	Early/idea stage: test and develop the idea and require R&D funding (e.g., for patents)	Individual investors and VCs focused on seed funding to further support startup until it generates revenue
Pre-Series A (10K–1M)	Early stage: with some market traction looking for individual-bridge round	Bridge between individual and institutional investors focused on smaller cheques
Series A (1M–5M)	Early stage: demonstrated traction ready to expand operations and uses funds for capex, working capital, expansion	First round of institutional investors with existing individual investors and may include corporate venture arm of large corporations
Series B (3M upwards)	Early stage: established with demonstrated traction and needs to scale after demonstrating product–market fit	Second round led by institutional investors, can include existing individual investors, and venture capital funds
Series C, D (6M upwards)	Growth stage: established and successfully running at scale and poised to expand using funds for capex, organic, or acquisition growth	Institutional investors including large/late-stage VCs, Pes, hedge funds, and banks come in, buy out early investors, often with handsome returns
Series E, F, and beyond (15M upwards)	Growth stage: well established and successfully running at scale and maybe poised for IPO	Institutional investors including large/late-stage VCs, Pes, hedge funds, and banks fund further expansion or increase valuation before IPO

Source: Compiled by authors from various sources including startups.com and coporatefinanceinstitute.com. The Startups Team, 2019.

and solutions by providing grants, paid pilots, or joint go-to-market options.

Accelerator and incubation programs span the following formats:

1. **Corporate accelerator programs** by multinational companies (MNCs) such as Google and Microsoft, etc. and Indian groups such as Reliance, etc.
2. **Public–private partnerships (PPPs)** such as T-Hub, T-Labs, Startup Village, etc.
3. **Department of Science and Technology (DST)-approved technology business incubators** (TBIs), often in universities
4. **College/university-based incubators** in the nation's premier institutions such as IIMs and IITs
5. **Industry-led incubator/accelerator programs** such as NASSCOM 10,000 Startups
6. **Private accelerator programs**, often led by VCs, such as Axilor Ventures, Sequoia Capital's Surge, and others
7. **Government-sponsored programs** such as iStart Rajasthan and Kerala Startup Mission.

2.5 *Government Support through Startup India and Other Initiatives*

In 2012, India's market regulator SEBI had introduced new norms for Angel investors to be registered as AIFs as a new class of pooled-in investment vehicle for real estate, private equity (PE), and hedge funds. To prevent abuse of the regulation through money laundering, SEBI restricted investment by such funds to INR 5–50 million and only in companies incorporated in India not more than 3 years old, and with no family connections. By 2019, INR 17 billion had been invested in 254 startups through SEBI's AIFs and SIDBI committed a further INR 31 billion, as of July 2019, to 47 AIFs registered with SEBI (FE Online, 2019).

When the Startup India program was launched in January 2016, the GoI also announced a Fund of Funds for Startups (FFS) at the Small Industries Development Bank of India (SIDBI) with a corpus of INR 100 billion to be allocated to alternative investment funds (AIFs). In the

Table 3: Indian Government Initiatives to Create a Conducive Ecosystem for Emerging Businesses and Startups

Timeline	Government Program	Aims and Target
2009	Invest India	Creation of an investment promotion and facilitation agency
2009	IndiaStack and UiD	Digital push for cashless, paperless, consent-based scalable architecture to support Aadhaar — Universal Identification project
2013	SEBI's Alternative Investment Fund Regulations	New norms for angel investors, who provide funding to companies in their initial stages
2014	Make in India	Flagship initiative of the Government of India (GoI) aimed at making the country a "global design and manufacturing" destination
2015	Digital India	Flagship program of the GoI aimed at expanding e-governance to promote inclusive growth and transform India into a "digitally empowered society and knowledge economy"
2015	Skill India initiative	A vocational training and certification program aimed at giving 400 million youth the opportunity for a better livelihood by 2022
2016	Startup India Initiative	Flagship initiative of the GoI to catalyze the startup culture and build an ecosystem for innovation and entrepreneurship
2016	Startup India Online Portal	367,171 registered startups, 26,374 recognized startups, 221 I tax exemptions, and 264 were funded by SIDBI FFS (as of 31 December 2019)
2016	Atal Incubation Centres (AICs) under Atal Innovation Mission (AIM)	31 AICs have been funded with INR 1.4 billion (approximately US$20.39 million) and INR 576.8 million (US$8.12 million) disbursed
2016	SIDBI "Fund of Funds for Startups (FFS)"	INR 100 billion corpus (approximately US$1.4 billion) contributing to the Alternate Investment funds (AIFs) for investing in startups
2016	Bharat Interface for Money (BHIM) and United Payment Interface	Mobile payment app developed by the National Payments Corporation on the United Payments Interface to allow seamless and verified payments
2019	Technology Incubation and Development of Entrepreneurs (TIDE) 2.0	MeitY-sponsored program to promote socially relevant tech entrepreneurship through incubators engaged in supporting ICT startups using emerging technologies (IoT, AI, blockchain, etc.)

Source: Compiled by authors from multiple sources including DPIIT Annual Report 2018–2019, IVCA-EY, 2019; PIB 2019; PIB, 2020; NITI, 2019.

4 years since, this FFS has consistently fallen short of its targeted allocations, both in terms of direct investments in startups (only INR 6.02 billion across 142 startups) and in its allocation to AIFs (INR 226.5 million versus a targeted INR 33 billon) (Sen, 2019).

The government has also set up various other initiatives that tie into supporting startups and entrepreneurship (Table 3).

A look at the industry–academic–government linkages in patents, for example, shows that India is emerging as a patent hub, especially with newer government initiatives such as the Startup Hub at the Ministry of Electronics and Information Technology (MeitY), which helps strengthen 51 incubation hubs through fast-track patent clearances, with India known to have far fewer international patents filed vis-à-vis other countries like the Republic of Korea and Japan.

3. Trends in Private Equity and Venture Capital Investments in Startups

3.1 *From Seed to VC Activity in India: Number of Deals and Investments*

Early-stage investments contracted between 2015 and 2017 and which have been recovering since then have been presented (Figure 4). Between 2015 and 2017, Series A to C funding dominated investments, according to VI data, while 2018 saw late-stage funding (Series D+) peak. Industry experts attribute this reluctance to back early-stage ventures to a lack of exits for angel investors and cumbersome regulatory policies, particularly around taxation. The track record of angel investors getting an exit at Series A has not been very good in India, as exits have only been viable for established startups that have a growing and paying customer base, which usually happens at a later stage.

Not surprisingly, deals are fewer and yet larger in terms of value at later stages as investors are willing to put in more capital once the startup has achieved some commercial success and requires more resources to scale and expand. The size of investments per deal for YTD 2019 suggests that Series F and beyond (average: US$128 million) were greater,

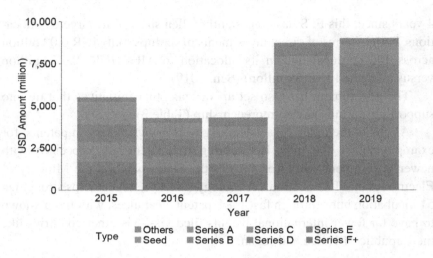

Figure 4: Types of Investments in Startups in India, 2017–2019 ytd

Note: Data for 2019 are as of 24 December 2019.
Source: Plotted by author based on data from Venture Intelligence.

followed by Series D (US$53 million) and Series E (US$52 million). Early-stage deals were naturally much smaller: Seed funding averaged US$1.12 million per deal, while Series A averaged US$5.12 million (Figure 5), but in spite of that, Series B and seed funding have cumulatively grown in the last 2 years.

VC investors continue to be bullish on Indian startups despite the larger macroeconomic slowdown. These investors are taking a long horizon view of up to 7 years of consumption-led growth through this period. A few significant exits have also created more liquidity for them to reinvest in the ecosystem.

Global VC and PE firms are investing heavily in India in search of the next "unicorn." The year 2019 saw the most VC inflows, with not only US-based and homegrown investors but Chinese investors betting bigger on Indian startups. Since 2018, Chinese VC investments have been the biggest trend in India's startup investments story, as they play catchup with their US counterparts. Tracxn (KrAsia Writers, 2019) reported that in 2018, Chinese VCs invested US$5.6 billion in India, more than what came from both the US and Japan.

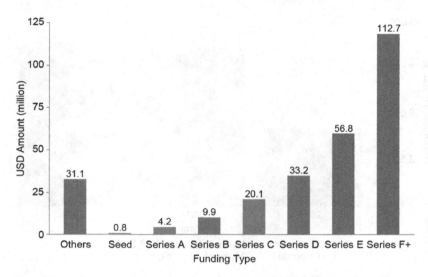

Figure 5: Average Deal Size by Funding Round in Indian Startups, 2015–2019 ytd

Note: Data for 2019 are as of 24 December 2019.
Source: Plotted by author based on data from Venture Intelligence.

3.2 *Geographic Distribution of Investments and Activity*

India's startup ecosystem remains concentrated in three clusters, Bengaluru, Delhi-NCR (National Capital Region), and Mumbai, which together accounted for 87% of total investment value and 84% of total investment volume in 2015. This ratio has not changed much since then; even in H1 of 2019, the three regions together accounted for about 85% of all the funding deals in Indian startups. Bengaluru particularly stands out as India's Silicon Valley owing to its legacy as an IT hub, receiving US$16.2 billion in funding across 1,244 deals between 2014 and September 2018 (Rajan, 2019). This concentration of startups in these three cities is extremely skewed as they host top-tier universities, and also serve as IT-enabled and financial hubs since the 1990s that attract a growing list of PE and VC firms.

After these Tier 1 metros, the largest startup clusters are in other Tier 1 cities: Chennai, Hyderabad, and Pune, though these cities trail the leaders significantly in terms of both value and investments. Together, the

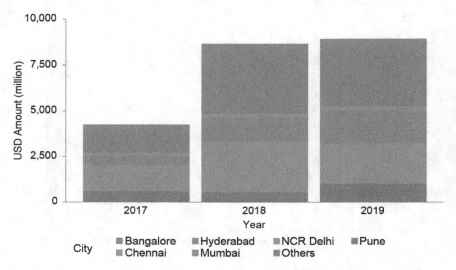

Figure 6:   VC* Investments in Indian Startups by City, 2017–2019 ytd

Note: Data for 2019 are as of 24 December 2019;
*As of 24 December 2019. VC is defined as Seed to Series F investments in companies less than 10 years old (since registration).
Source: Plotted by author based on data from Venture Intelligence.

six cities received almost all the VC funding in 2019 (Figure 6). While startup ecosystems are well established in Tier 1 cities, they are still nascent in smaller cities with some estimates suggesting that only 20% startups are based in Tier 2 and Tier 3 cities and they have raised only a small fraction of total funding (NASSCOM and Zinnov, 2019).

This highly skewed scenario is a great opportunity to develop the startup community in Tier 2, Tier 3, and smaller cities and among disadvantaged sections of the population. More support is needed to provide an opportunity to develop "zebra startups," i.e., young companies pursuing both profit and purpose, which are often started by women and other under-represented founders outside the traditional innovation clusters in smaller cities and towns.

The government too is taking initiatives to boost entrepreneurship in smaller cities through its Startup India Yatra, startup training, and a States' Startup ranking, among others (DPIIT, 2019). These initiatives will benefit from India's 100 Smart Cities Mission in providing infrastructure support like fast internet connections, uninterrupted power supply, transport connectivity, and favorable working conditions in terms of legal support, company laws, and regulations. Many states are in the process of developing their own state- and city-level startup ecosystems to capitalize on local talent and the lower costs in smaller cities.

3.3 *Sector and Emerging Subsegment Investments*

Looking at sector trends in startup investments, IT and IT-enabled services (ITES) topped investment value, followed by the banking and financial services industry (BFSI), healthcare, and logistics (Figure 7). Since 2018, more VC investments have also gone into tourism and transport.

Digital transformation and tech-enabled startups such as online aggregators have largely benefited from improving price discovery, removing middlemen, and reducing transaction costs for both producers and end consumers. Startups operating in the following traditional sectors that benefited from the digital transformation garnered more investments suggesting large market size and higher returns: B2C consumer technology

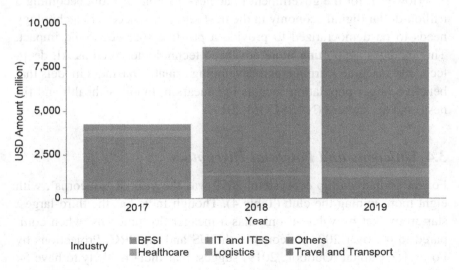

Figure 7: VC* Investments in Indian Startups by Industry, 2017–2019 ytd

Note: Data for 2019 are as of 24 December 2019.
Source: Plotted by author based on data from Venture Intelligence.

such as e-commerce, transportation and mobility, healthtech, foodtech, fintech/payments, and edtech. The trend has recently shifted to growth in edtech, mobility, social media and regional language content, and B2B e-commerce, among others.

Another recent trend has been in the boom of regional language-based social media and content sharing due to growing smartphone ownership and internet penetration through cheaper data plans, online payment integration, and better network connections in Tier 2 and Tier 3 cities. In 2009, there were only 54 million internet users, but this expanded tenfold to 530 million in 2018 (Kantar IMRB, 2019) with a larger rural population of Indian-language users going online with an annual spending power of US$300 billion (Jha, 2019). Further, the telecom war that ensued after a new entrant, Reliance Jio, entered the market in 2016, gave Indians the world's cheapest data plans at less than US$0.10 a GB, which nearly commoditized the internet and opened up an entire new user base. The Unified Payments Interface (UPI), a government-sponsored digital payment mechanism, has proved crucial for widespread adoption of online and mobile payments.

However, for the government to achieve its goal of India becoming a trillion-dollar digital economy in the next few years, access to technology needs to be democratized to provide a positive socioeconomic impact. This includes supporting more advanced technologies such as AI, deeptech, and machine learning, and developing scalable business models that benefit a larger population such as in education, mobility, health and fitness, and agriculture (NASSCOM 2019).

3.4 *Unicorns and Potential Disruptors*

For the Indian startup ecosystem, 2019 was the year of 'unicorns', with eight more joining the club (Table 4). Though India has the third-largest startup market by value, it only has a meager 26 'unicorns' when compared to the over 200+ unicorns in the US and the PRC. Projections by Fosun RZ Capital (Outlook, 2019) suggest that India is likely to have 54 tech unicorns by 2024. What started as a testing ground a decade ago for US-based VC firms such as Tiger Global and Sequoia Capital, who were

Table 4: India's "Unicorn" Club: Current Private Companies Valued at US$1 billion+

Startup	Valuation (in US$)	Year of Valuation	Industry and Vertical	Key Investors
*MuSigma	1.5 billion	2013	Analytics	Accel Partners, Sequoia Capital India, General Atlantic
InMobi	1 billion	2014	Mobile and telecommunications (ad-tech)	Kleiner Perkins Caufield and Byers, SoftBank Corp., Sherpalo Ventures
Snapdeal ↓	7 billion	2014	E-commerce and direct-to-consumer	SoftBankGroup, Blackrock, Alibaba Group
Ola Cabs	6.32 billion	2014	Auto and transportation	Accel Partners, SoftBank Group, Sequoia Capital
Zomato	2.18 billion	2015	Internet software and services	Sequoia Capital, VY Capital
One97 Communications (Paytm)	16 billion	2015	FinTech	Intel Capital, Sapphire Ventures, Alibaba Group
*Quikr ↓	1.6 billion	2015	Online classifieds	Matrix Partners, Omidyar Network India, Norwest, Kinnevik
Hike	1.40 billion	2016	Mobile and telecommunications	Foxconn, Tiger Global management, Tencent
*Shopclues ↓	1.1 billion	2016	E-commerce	Nexus Ventures, Helion Ventures, Beenos, Tiger Global, Kalaari Capital
ReNew Power	2 billion	2017	Other	Goldman Sachs, JERA, Asian Development Bank
BYJU'S	5.75 billion	2017	Edtech	Tencent Holdings, Lightspeed India Partners, Sequoia Capital India
Udaan	2.30 billion	2018	Supply chain, logistics, and delivery	DST Global, Lightspeed Venture Partners, Microsoft ScaleUp
Swiggy	3.30 billion	2018	Supply chain, logistics, and delivery	Accel India, SAIF Partners, Norwest Venture Partners

(Continued)

Table 4: (*Continued*)

Startup	Valuation (in US$)	Year of Valuation	Industry and Vertical	Key Investors
PolicyBazaar	1.50 billion	2018	FinTech	Info Edge, SoftBank Capital
OYO	10 billion	2018	Travel	SoftBank Group, Sequoia Capital India, LightSpeed India Partners
BillDesk	1.80 billion	2018	FinTech	Temasek Holdings, Visa, March Capital Partners
Freshworks	3.5 billion	2018	SaaS	Accel Partners, Tiger Global, Google, Sequoia Capital
Ola Electric Mobility	1 billion	2019	Auto and transportation	SoftBank Group, Tiger Global Management, Matrix Partners India
Delhivery	1.50 billion	2019	Supply chain, logistics, and delivery	Times Internet, Nexus Venture Partners, SoftBank Group
BigBasket	1 billion	2019	Supply chain, logistics, and delivery	Alibaba Group, Bessemer Venture Partners, Helion Venture Partners
Dream11	1 billion	2019	Internet software and services	Kaalari Capital, Tencent Holdings, Steadview Capital
Rivigo	1.07 billion	2019	Supply chain, logistics, and delivery	SAIF Partners India, Warburg Pincus, Trifecta Capital Advisors
Lenskart	1.50 billion	2019	E-commerce and direct-to-consumer	Chiratae Ventures, PremjiInvest, SoftBank
*Citius Tech	1.0 billion	2019	IT healthcare	General Atlantic, Baring Asia
*Icertis	1.0 billion	2019	Contract management	Eight Roads, B. Capital, PremjiInvest
*Druva	1.0 billion	2019	Data management	Westbridge, Nexus Venture Partners, Sequoia Capital India

Note: ↓ Indicates a "former" unicorn — a company that is no longer valued at US$1 billion or more.

* Venture Intelligence: (https://www.ventureintelligence.com/Indian-Unicorn-Tracker.php).

Source: CB Insights (https://www.cbinsights.com/research-unicorn-companies).

looking for the next big market after the US and the PRC, India has now emerged as one of the most promising destinations for investors from the PRC, the Republic of Korea, Japan, and the UAE.

4. Empirical Determinants of Startup Investments in India's Subnational Economies

In this section, we present a simple empirical examination of the possible determinants of startup investments in India's subnational economies. Documenting some stylized facts about the magnitude of startup investments in India demonstrates significant variation and clustering around specific subnational economies. Subsequently, we empirically attempt to identify the conditioning variables that could be instrumental in driving such investments. To do this, we assemble panel data at the subnational level dictated by the availability of data on startup investments and accordingly undertake a panel estimation.[1]

4.1 *Stylized Facts*

A snapshot of the geographical spread of startup investments across the country over the sample period of 2015–2018 is provided in Figure 8. A few salient trends emerge. First, in line with Bengaluru being one of the sought-after destinations for startups, the magnitude of investments channeled into the state of Karnataka is greater than in the rest of the country. Karnataka received startup investments[2] to the tune of US$13 billion — approximately half of the total startup investments in India during this period.

Other states that have seen notable startup investments include Maharashtra, followed by Haryana and New Delhi. While Maharashtra has received close to US$5 billion, Haryana (chiefly Gurgaon, which is part of the National Capital Region) and New Delhi have attracted about

---

[1] All data on startup investments are collected from a publicly available independent source, available at www.trak.in.

[2] Note that this overall figure captures startup funding and investments of all types including seed funding, venture capital, debt, and equity investment as well as Series A to H.

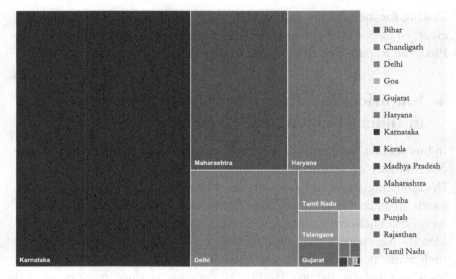

Figure 8:   Geographical Spread of Startup Investments 2015–2018

Note: ᵃ In 2011, the Government of India approved the name change of the State of Orissa to Odisha. This document reflects this change. However, when reference is made to policies that predate the name change, the formal name Orissa is retained;

States in gray denote negligible or no investments.

Source: Authors based on data compiled from www.trak.in.

US$3 billion each (Figure 8). It is worth noting that these four subnational economies have accounted for over 90% of startup investments in the entire country, highlighting the asymmetric nature of the investment distribution. Almost all 29 states in India have a Startup Policy and Program in place, of which Karnataka, Rajasthan, Maharashtra, Karnataka, Telangana, and Goa (to some extent) have some tangible track record.

Nevertheless, there are other states that are rapidly emerging as hot-spots for startup investments. Tamil Nadu, for instance, attracted close to US$0.7 billion, while Telangana (of which Hyderabad is the capital) and Gujarat each received about US$0.4 billion and US$0.3 billion, respectively, during the corresponding period.

Before we proceed with further empirical analysis, considering the variation in the values of startup investments, we apply a logarithmic transformation of the series to deal with extreme values of the distribution. We first show the mean value of startup investments by each state in

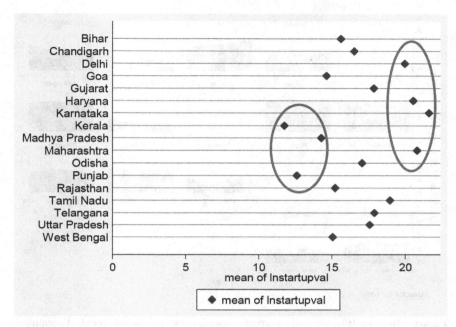

Figure 9: Average Value of Startup Investments (Log Transformed) across Subnational Economies

Note: [a] In 2011, the Government of India approved the name change of the State of Orissa to Odisha. This document reflects this change. However, when reference is made to policies that predate the name change, the formal name Orissa is retained.

Source: Authors based on data compiled from www.trak.in.

Figure 9, while the disaggregated time trends between 2015 and 2018 are plotted for each state. As Figure 8 shows, in line with what was stated earlier, the average investments of the top-four states are significantly higher than those of the rest of the states with active startup policies, while Madhya Pradesh, Punjab, and Kerala have received the lowest investments comparatively (on average).

Figure 9 highlights the trends in these investments across states over the period of analysis. Interestingly, Figure 10 unmasks the variations that average figures did not capture. While in totality, the broad trends in terms of magnitude of investments remain the same in the top four subnational economies, it appears as if startup investments in Delhi-NCR appear to have been on a gradual declining trend since 2015.

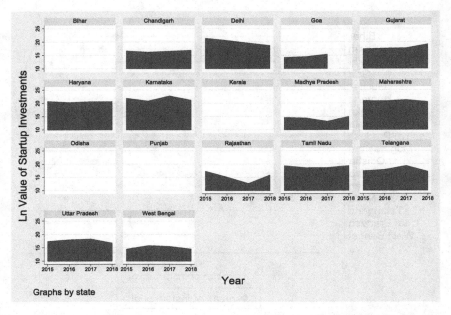

Figure 10: Distribution of Startup Investments by Subnational Economies (2015–2018)

Note: [a] In 2011, the Government of India approved the name change of the State of Orissa to Odisha. This document reflects this change. However, when reference is made to policies that predate the name change, the formal name Orissa is retained.

Source: Authors based on data compiled from www.trak.in.

While Karnataka has experienced some significant fluctuations since 2015, things have remained broadly consistent in Maharashtra and Haryana. It is notable that with the exceptions of Gujarat and Rajasthan, most other states for which data are available appear to be experiencing a slowdown in startup investments. While more analysis would be needed to identify whether such swings are merely cyclical or driven by structural characteristics of the subnational economies attracting such investments, it is worth noting that this period coincided with two large domestic shocks in the form of demonetization (November 2016) and the introduction of the Goods and Services Tax (GST) (July 2017).

To what extent are startup investments correlated with the influx of foreign direct investment (FDI) inflows into India's subnational

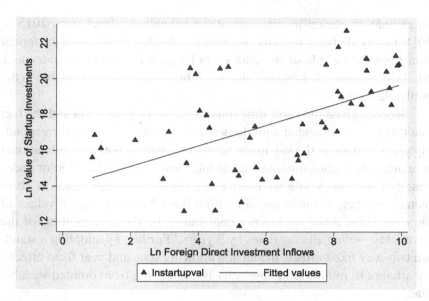

Figure 11: Relationship between Startup Investments and Subnational FDI Inflows

Source: Authors.

economies? We plot the correlations between the two variables graphically as shown in Figure 11. The scatterplot reveals an upward-tending relationship, although the fit does not appear to be quite tight. Given the conflated nature of startup investments and FDI flows into states (since it is not very clear whether startup investments overlap with the FDI data as the information on equity stakes is not systematically available) we do not include it as a regressor in the model.

To understand better the determinants of these startup investments and the extent to which distinct subnational characteristics influence the influx of such investments, we perform a more systematic empirical examination in what follows.

4.2 Determinants of Startup Investments

Before we proceed with the empirics, two caveats on the data and modeling strategy are in order. First, we assemble systematic data on the magnitude of startup investments at the subnational level from 2015 to 2018 purely dictated by data availability. While snapshots of historical data from the decade of the 2000s can be gathered for the country as a whole, no systematic breakdown at the subnational level is available in the public domain.

Second, given the short time dimension of the panel data and the fact that this period coincided with domestic policy shocks, using corresponding years of data on the key macroeconomic characteristics of subnational economies in a contemporaneous fashion leads to significant joint endogeneity concerns. While we cannot rule out endogeneity concerns completely, we can, as far as possible, limit these by using lagged values of the covariates. Since we are not constrained by data availability for the covariates, we lag all covariates by 3 years.[3] Further, by adopting a standard two-way fixed-effects model and allowing state and year fixed effects, we attempt to minimize endogeneity issues arising from omitted variable bias.[4]

Thus, we construct a panel dataset featuring 17 Indian subnational economies over the period 2015–2018.[5] The basic estimating equation is as follows (Eq. (1)):

$$y_{it} = \delta_i + \beta X_{it-3} + \rho_t + u_{it} \qquad (1)$$

y_{it} is the log-transformed value of startup investments in subnational economy (i) at time t;

X_{it} is the vector of determinants in subnational economy (i) at time t-3;

δ_i is subnational economy fixed effect;

ρ_t is time fixed effect;

u_{it} is the idiosyncratic error term.

---

[3] Our fundamental results are robust to the choice of different lags.

[4] Time fixed effects are included to ensure that we account for year-specific trends in our model.

[5] The choice of the time period and the sample of subnational economies were purely based on consistent availability of data for the value of startup investments (our focal dependent variable of interest).

The dependent variable in our empirics is the log-transformed value of startup investments in the respective subnational economy at a given point in time. Most estimating models, such as the one given in Eq. (1), tend to violate conditional mean independence, which is a prerequisite to obtain unbiased and consistent estimates. The specific source of violation of conditional mean independence typically arises from omitted variable bias. As has been well established in the literature, the unobserved effects model as given in Eq. (1) allows us to undertake a within transformation that in turn enables us to handle the unobserved heterogeneity bias resulting from estimating it, as long as the unobserved variables that could be potentially correlated with our regressors are time-invariant in nature. In such circumstances, we can reasonably argue that our fixed-effect model produces unbiased and robust estimates.

Furthermore, as noted earlier, the matrix of determinants of startup investments are based on available empirical literature. Empirical studies on determinants of startup rates at the subnational or regional level within a developing country context are limited (e.g., Naudé *et al.*, 2008 and references cited within), although there is a huge tangential empirical literature on determinants of entrepreneurship at the firm level (e.g., Audretsch and Keilbach, 2004; Acs *et al.*, 2007 for a discussion). We take a cue from this literature and estimate a parsimonious model that includes the following representative control variables at the subnational level:

- GSDP Per Capita Growth (+)
- Inflation (−)
- State Budget Deficit (−)
- Bank Credit (+)
- Infrastructure (+)
- Human Capital (+)
- Secondary Industry Value Added Per Worker (+)

Table A1 has the definitions and sources of the variables used.

On the one hand, we hypothesize that higher growth in the subnational economies, greater availability of bank credit, higher availability and coverage of hard infrastructure (like railways, roads, and telecommunications), as well as higher labor productivity and human capital should be positively associated with higher startup investments. On the other hand, a priori, we believe that a higher cost of living proxied by inflation and higher fiscal deficit of the states reflecting the government's fiscal responsibility should deter startup investments. As briefly mentioned earlier, all covariates are collected from publicly available data on Indian states from the Reserve Bank of India and they are lagged by three periods (different lag lengths were tried as a robustness check) to avoid simultaneity problems. The correlation matrix presented in Table 5 provides further evidence that there are no serious concerns over multicollinearity that we need to worry about before estimating our model.

Table 6 summarizes the empirical results. Columns 1 and 2 estimate the same regression as in Eq. (1) with and without year fixed effects, respectively. The magnitude and the direction of the coefficients are actually comparable across both the models. Most results are in accordance with the priors, but in terms of statistical and economic significance, there are a few notable observations.

First, focusing on the significant variables of interest, among the macro variables, fiscal deficit of the states carries the right negative sign and turns out to be the most consistent variable in terms of high statistical and economic significance. The results appear to imply that a higher fiscal deficit in subnational economies deters startup investments, in line with our priors.

Table 5:   Correlation Matrix

	GSDP PC Gr	Inflation	Budget Def	Bank Credit	Infra	Human Cap	Secondary VA
Startup value	1.00	–	–	–	–	–	–
GSDP PC Gr	0.02	1.00	–	–	–	–	–
Inflation	–0.11	0.13	1.00	–	–	–	–
Budget Def	0.11	–0.29	0.00	1.00	–	–	–
Bank Credit	0.54	–0.15	–0.04	0.20	1.00	–	–
Infra	0.09	–0.15	–0.10	0.33	0.02	1.00	–
Secondary VA	0.00	0.04	–0.07	0.13	–0.15	–0.21	1.00
Human Cap	0.19	0.07	–0.36	–0.01	–0.06	0.02	–0.16

Source: Authors' calculation.

Table 6: Determinants of Startup Investments: Fixed Effects Estimates

Dep Var: Ln Startup Investments	(1) Two-Way FE	(2) Without Year FE	(3) Competitiveness Index	(4) Dep Var: Ratio of Startup to Total Investments
GSDPPC Growth	0.506	0.473**		0.408**
	(0.330)	(0.226)		(0.164)
Inflation	−0.101	−0.019		−0.052
	(0.118)	(0.054)		(0.066)
Budget Deficit	−0.037**	−0.031**		−0.025**
	(0.016)	(0.014)		(0.011)
Bank Credit	1.439***	1.484***		1.770***
	(0.500)	(0.484)		(0.370)
Infrastructure	0.517*	0.477*		0.321*
	(0.299)	(0.282)		(0.173)
Secondary Value Added	1.739**	1.638**		2.599**
	(0.840)	(0.807)		(0.925)
Education	0.009	0.028		0.021
	(0.0633)	(0.0425)		(0.047)
Competitiveness Index			1.304***	
			(0.502)	
Observations	50	50	51	
Number of States	16	16	17	
State FE	Yes	Yes	Yes	Yes
Year FE	Yes	No	Yes	Yes

Notes: Robust standard errors clustered for states in parentheses; *** $p < 0.01$, ** $p < 0.05$, * $p < 0.1$.
Source: Authors' calculation

In a similar vein, higher labor productivity and better infrastructure enter the regression with the appropriate positive signs and statistically significant coefficients, suggesting that higher labor productivity and better infrastructure tend to attract higher startup investments.

Perhaps the most important finding emerging from the empirics is the role of bank credit. As one would expect, higher availability of bank credit, which can also be a loose proxy for subnational financial depth, appears to be positively and significantly associated with higher startup investments, underlining the importance of bank credit. This finding is also consistent with the prior empirical literature.

Other macroeconomic variables — growth in GDP per capita and inflation — turn out to be statistically insignificant, although both carry the appropriate signs. Note that GDP per capita growth turns statistically significant at the 5% level when we remove year fixed effects. The human capital variable proxied by secondary education also turns out to be statistically insignificant, though it carries the right sign.

The above empirical results also have significant policy implications, especially when it comes to the role of financial deepening in India's states. Admittedly, a longer panel dataset with an extended time period would offer more robust estimates, but we have made use of all publicly available data on startup investments at the subnational level.

In order to further verify the robustness of the significance of subnational determinants identified by our model, we attempt to make use of a comprehensive and holistic subnational index on competitiveness to check whether state competitiveness matters to startup investments. While it is seemingly obvious that state competitiveness would matter, it is much harder to empirically establish that, especially considering the definitional ambiguities inherent in defining competitiveness. We make use of a subnational competitiveness index available for India's states and union territories to check its potential explanatory power in our model.[6] It is useful to note that this index is a weighted average of 75 different indicators that subsume all the individual determinants we have used in estimating Eq. (1). Hence, we include a comprehensive index as a stand-alone regressor in addition to two-way fixed effects. The results are shown in Column 3 in Table 6. As expected, a 1% increase in the state competitive-

---

[6]Data for competitiveness index are taken from Tan *et al.* (2019).

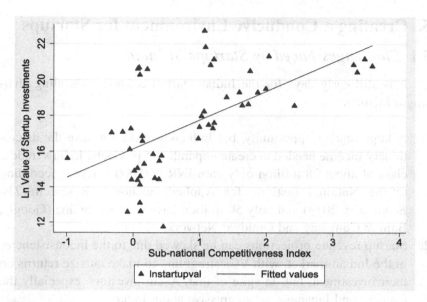

Figure 12: Relationship between Startup Investments and Subnational Competitiveness
Source: Authors.

ness index would result in a 1.3% increase in startup investment, which is an economically powerful result as well.

We also plot the nature of correlations between state-level competitiveness index and startup investments graphically. The scatterplot shown in Figure 12 does reveal an upward-tending relationship between the two variables of interest, and also appears to be a reasonably good fit. These add a measure of robustness to our results.

As our final robustness check, we rerun our regression using an alternative dependent variable. Instead of using absolute values of startup investments, we express it as a share of total investments in that subnational economy in each year. The results as summarized in Column 4 of Table 6 clearly show that the fundamental results established so far remain more or less robust to, and consistent with, the use of a different dependent variable, thereby highlighting the consistency of our empirical results.

5. Creating a Conducive Environment for Startups

5.1 *Challenges Faced by Startups in India*

It is still early days for the Indian startup ecosystem; scaling challenges include:

1. A large market opportunity, but Indians still do not have the discretionary income needed to create unparalleled products. India's middle class of about 78 million only earn INR 250,000 per year according to the National Institute for Applied Economic Research (*The Economist,* 2019) and only 50 million have shopped online (Google, Bain & Company and Omidyar Network, 2019).

2. Startup revenue projections can be skewed due to the inconsistencies in the Indian market, with VCs struggling to make outsize returns on their investment, but, in spite of that, Asian investors, especially the Chinese and Japanese, are aggressive about India.

3. Fund-raising still remains a challenge for Indian startups. While deal sizes of VC funding are significantly smaller than in Silicon Valley, considering India is an emerging economy, domestic lending rates are very high at 3× those of developed economies, incentivizing foreign funds to lend at cheaper rates.

4. Regulatory and taxation complexities affect startup profitability. Corporate tax rates are high, although reduced to 22% and 14% in 2019 from 33%. Terms for startups to qualify for government benefits are too stringent and the application process, cumbersome. Once revenues exceed INR 1 billion they are disqualified. This has led to a third of the entrepreneurs actively looking at relocating out of India to reduce compliance and tax burdens, according to a survey (LocalCircles, 2019).

5. Indian startups, like their global counterparts, struggle with a high failure rate with technology venture success rates at <5% worldwide. While incubators and accelerators have been most effective in supporting startups, the government will need to focus on simplifying regulation around registering companies, bankruptcy laws, and getting failed entrepreneurs back into the system.

6. Many Indian startups want to expand globally but face issues of credibility, except for software as a service (SaaS) players, and even such entrepreneurs cannot tap into a global market as they are often unaware of market opportunities.
7. India also struggles with a lack of innovation, lagging behind Japan, the PRC, and the Republic of Korea in international patents. One study cited lack of innovation as the most common reason for the high rate of failure (IBM Institute for Business Value and Oxford Economics, 2016).
8. A lack of skilled workforce, inadequate formal mentoring, and poor business ethics with over 70% of India's engineering graduates being considered "unemployable." New emerging industries such as deep-tech and deep-science startups that are technology based are hampered by the lack of specialized talent (PhDs, researchers, etc.).
9. Even though MeitY and the DST are forging institutionalized industry–academic–government linkages and collecting the data on Indian startups, a lot more work is needed in this space, in producing a conducive environment and providing much needed support for startups.

6. Conclusion and Policy Recommendations

India's startup policy initiatives and the rapidly growing investments and innovation in the sector already provide many lessons to other developing and emerging countries. Empirically, we have seen in this study that the increased competitiveness of states accounts for increased investments in startups within those states. This suggests that when states invest more in R&D, making it easier to file patents and develop tie-ups with universities and industry by expanding the incubator/accelerator ecosystem, startups benefit from better funding and access to technology and expertise.

Since 2016, policy initiatives have led to a more coordinated effort to support Indian startups: from making registrations easy online to providing tax benefits and streamlining patent clearances. Startup India, among other things, is also tasked with extending innovation and capacity development outreach beyond Tier 1 cities that have so far largely benefitted from an agglomeration effect. The Department of Science and Technology

(DST)-approved technology business incubators (TBIs), often in universities such as IITs and IIMs, strengthen existing linkages between startups, corporates, and academic institutions. These initiatives have also been taken further through integrated state-level startup platforms such as Startup Karnataka, Maharashtra State Innovation Society, and iStart Rajasthan.

The government is also trying to provide investment support through SIDBI's Fund of Funds and changing regulations to allow Alternate Investment funds (AIFs) to invest in startups. It has also been important to amend existing regulations, such as India's market regulator SEBI introduced new norms for allowing angel investors to be registered as AIFs as a new class of pooled-in investment vehicle for private equity (PE) and hedge funds. As empirical results show that improving subnational financial depth seems positively and significantly associated with higher startup investments, so increasing credit from banks and NBFCs and getting more startups to qualify for government programs is important.

Further, developing alternate models of investment such as cooperatives and "zebra" startups — firms that address social problems but are for-profit — will benefit startup policy. This will require more incubation support for first-time entrepreneurs to expand beyond overcrowded industry verticals such as e-commerce, fintech, ed-tech, and mobility, into social sectors such as education, healthcare, governance, sanitation, and alternate/clean energy in providing low-cost solutions.

India punches above its weight in terms of global innovation by improving its intellectual property, and investing in human capital and higher education, which is paying off through the commercialization and scaling of technology solutions through startups. But many Indian startups are known for emulating successful global ideas and applying them to the domestic context, so providing developing meta-level startups that address fundamental problems in India support is needed so that they can scale domestically and globally. While platforms such as Startup India have provided incentives, more protection from well-funded foreign competition and acquisitions for domestic corporates is still a challenge, requiring policies along the lines of support to infant industries.

References

Acs, Z., C. Armington, and T. Zhang. 2007. The determinants of new-firm survival across regional economies, Discussion Papers on Entrepreneurship, Growth and Public Policy no. 0407, *Max Planck Institute for Research into Economic Systems*.

Audretsch, D.B. and M. Keilbach. 2004. Entrepreneurship capital: Determinants and impact on regional economic performance. Discussion Paper 37/2004, *Max Planck Institute for Research into Economic Systems*.

DPIIT 2019. Annual report, government of India, ministry of commerce and industry, department for promotion of industry & internal trade (DPIIT). Retrieved from: https://dipp.gov.in/sites/default/files/annualReport_2018-19_E_0.pdf.

FE Online 2019. Rs. 1,700 crore poured into 254 startups by SEBI's alternative investment funds. FinancialExpress.com — Startup India | Published: July 24, 2019. Retrieved from: https://www.financialexpress.com/industry/sme/rs-1700-crore-poured-into-254-startups-by-sebis-alternative-investment-funds/1655107/.

Google, Bain & Company, and Omidyar Network 2019. Unlocking digital for Bharat — $50 billion opportunity. Published 9 August 2018. Retrieved from: https://www.omidyar.com/sites/default/files/Unlocking%20Digital%20For%20Bharat_Final.pdf.

Grant Thornton and Assocham India 2016. Startups India — An overview | Report released on 28 January 2016. Retrieved from: https://www.grantthornton.in/globalassets/1.-member-firms/india/assets/pdfs/grant_thornton-startups_report.pdf.

IBM Institute for Business Value and Oxford Economics 2016. Entrepreneurial India: How startups redefine India's economic growth. Published December 2019. Retrieved from: https://d1iydh3qrygeij.cloudfront.net/Media/Default/New%20release%20images%20and%20reports/Entrepreneurial%20India%20IBV%20mid%202016.pdf.

IVCA-EY 2019. Year-to-date PE/VC investments in India at a new all-time high of US$36.7 billion: IVCA-EY Report, Press release on 10 September 2019. Retrieved from: https://www.ey.com/en_in/news/2019/09/year-to-date-pe-vc-investments-in-india-at-new-all-time-high-of-us-dollar-36-7-billion-ivca-ey-report.

Jha, Lata for Mint 2019. Most of India's Digitally Monetizable Users Want Vernacular Content: Report. Livemint.com. Published 6 August 2019, 07:02

PM. Retrieved from: https://www.livemint.com/industry/media/most-of-indias-digitally-monetizable-users-want-vernacular-content-report-1565097932712.html.

Kaira, A. 2019. Crowdfunding in India, Invest India. 5 April 2019. https://www.investindia.gov.in/team-india-blogs/crowdfunding-india-0.

Kantar IMRB 2019. ICUBE Digital adoption & usage trends, 21st edition Highlights. https://imrbint.com/images/common/ICUBE%E2%84%A2_2019_Highlights.pdf.

KrAsia Writers 2019. A part of the third-largest startup ecosystem, Indian companies enjoy investors attention. KrAsia.com. Published 3 November 2019. Retrieved from: https://kr-asia.com/a-part-of-the-third-largest-startup-ecosystem-indian-companies-enjoy-investors-attention.

LocalCircles 2019. Indian startups struggling on multiple fronts going into 2019. https://www.localcircles.com/a/press/page/angel-tax-a-big-trouble#.XmWtlpMzbOQ.

NASSCOM 2018. Indian tech startup ecosystem 2018: Approaching escape velocity. Retrieved from: https://www.nasscom.in/ (Accessed on September 15, 2020).

NASSCOM and Zinnov 2019. Indian tech startup ecosystem: leading tech in the 20s. Edition 2019. Retrieved from: https://www.nasscom.in/knowledge-center/publications/indian-tech-start-ecosystem-leading-tech-20s.

Naudé, W., T. Gries, W. Wood, and A. Meintjies. 2008. Regional determinants of entrepreneurial start-ups in a developing country. *Entrepreneurship and Regional Development*, 20(2): 111–124.

NITI 2019. Guidelines for setting up of incubation centres under Atal Innovation Mission — 'Atal Incubation Centres'. Government of India NITI Aayog Atal Innovation Mission May 2016. https://niti.gov.in/writereaddata/files/Guidelines%20to%20setup%20AIC%20May%202016.pdf.

Outlook 2019. 54 tech unicorns expected in India by 2024. Outlook, The News Scroll. 1 August 2019. https://www.outlookindia.com/newsscroll/54-tech-unicorns-expected-in-india-by-2024-lead-correcting-headline/1587697.

PIB 2017. Start-Up: Definition changes. Press Information Bureau, Government of India, Ministry of Commerce & Industry, 25 May 2017 09:10 IST. Retrieved from: https://pib.gov.in/newsite/PrintRelease.aspx?relid=162140.

PIB 2019. Establishment of Atal Innovation Mission and Self-Employment and Talent Utilisation in NITI Aayog. Press Information Bureau, Government of India Cabinet. 24 February 2016. Retrieved from: https://pib.gov.in/newsite/PrintRelease.aspx?relid=136754.

PIB 2020. Features of Start Up India. Ministry of Commerce & Industry, Posted On: 11 March 2020 3:13PM by PIB Delhi. Retrieved from: https://pib.gov.in/PressReleseDetail.aspx?PRID=1605956.

Rajan, P. 2019. The startup ecosystem in India is scaling new heights. Here's why. Yourstory.com. Retrieved from: https://yourstory.com/2019/12/indian-startup-ecosystem-priyan-rajan-silicon-valley-bank?utm_pageloadtype=scroll.

Sen, A. 2019. Government looking at deploying larger funds for startups: Piyush Goyal. The Hindu Business Line 7 December 2019. Retrieved from: https://www.thehindubusinessline.com/economy/policy/govt-looking-at-deploying-larger-funds-for-startups-piyush-goyal/article30229659.ece.

Sharma, S. and T.N. Hari. 2018. The decade that was: How India's startup landscape has evolved," YS Journal 23 August 2018. Retrieved from: https://yourstory.com/journal/the-decade-that-was-india-part-1.

Sharma, S.K. and K.E. Meyer. 2019. Industrializing Innovation: The Next Revolution Springer Books, Springer, number 978-3-030-12430-4, October.

Startup India 2019. STARTUP INDIA KIT. October, 2019. Retrieved from: https://www.startupindia.gov.in/content/dam/invest-india/Templates/public/Startup%20India%20Kit_v5.pdf.

Tan, K., S. Gopalan, and J. Sharma. 2019. Impact of exchange rates on exports from India's sub-national economies: An empirical investigation. *South Asian Journal of Business Studies*, 8(2): 166–184.

The Economist 2019. India's missing middle class. Economist.com. Published on 11 January 2018. Retrieved from: https://www.economist.com/briefing/2018/01/11/indias-missing-middle-class.

The Startups Team 2019. The 5 types of startup funding. Published 12 April 2019. Retrieved from: https://www.startups.com/library/expert-advice/5-types-startup-funding.

The World Bank Group 2020. Doing Business 2020: Comparing Business Regulation in 190 Economies. Washington, DC. Retrieved from: http://documents.worldbank.org/curated/en/688761571934946384/pdf/Doing-Business-2020-Comparing-Business-Regulation-in-190-Economies.pdf.

Yoshino, N. and F. Taghizadeh-Hesary. 2014. Hometown investment trust funds: An analysis of credit risk. ADBI Working Paper 505. Tokyo: ADBI. https://www.adb.org/sites/default/files/publication/156360/adbi-wp505.pdf.

Appendix

Table A1:   Sources and Definitions of Control Variables Used in Empirical Analysis

Variable	Unit	Definition	Sources
Gross State Domestic Product per Capita (+)	Rupees Real Prices (Base Year, 2000)	Gross State Domestic Product per Capita is Gross State Domestic Product divided by population	GDP: http://mospi.nic.in/ Mospi_New/site/inner. aspx?status=3&menu_id=82
Inflation (Average of Rural and Industrial Laborers) (−)	%	Inflation is measured using all Indian CPI (Industrial Workers and Rural Laborers). The percentage change in this index over a period of time gives the amount of inflation over that specific period, i.e., the increase in prices of a representative basket of goods consumed. The inflation differential is given by state inflation subtracted from all Indian inflation for a given year	CPI (RL and IW): Ministry of Labor Bureau (Archive)
Human Capital: Student-Teacher Ratio (Secondary) (+)	Ratio	The average number of students per teacher in secondary educational institutions in a given year	www.indiastat.com
Infrastructure: Paved Road Length (+)	(km per 000 Sq. km)	Total surfaced and unsurfaced lengths of highways, urban roads, and project roads per 1,000 km of total land area of each state.	CMIE, States of India
Bank Credit (as a percentage of GSDP) (+)	10 Million Rupees, Real Prices (Base Year, 2000)	The bank credit in scheduled commercial banks, comprising term loans, cash credit, overdrafts, and bills purchased and discounted	RBI Handbook of Statistics on Indian States
Fiscal Deficit (−)	Percent of GSDP	Gross fiscal deficit expressed as a percentage of gross state domestic product	RBI Handbook of Statistics on Indian States
Secondary Industry, Value-Added per Worker	Rupees Per Person-Year (Real prices, 2000)	The net value added per employed worker in the secondary industry	RBI Handbook of Statistics on Indian States

Source: Authors' compilation.

https://doi.org/10.1142/9789811235825_0008

Chapter 8

Introduction of Entrepreneurship Development Fund for Startups and Small and Medium-sized Enterprises: Case of Kazakhstan

Keun Jung Lee

Professor of School of Business and Logistics
INHA University in Tashkent, Uzbekistan
leekj1000@gmail.com

Abstract

This chapter addresses the efficiency of financing mechanisms and tools of the state implemented in Kazakhstan through the national small and medium-sized enterprise (SME) development institute Entrepreneurship Development Fund (hereafter Damu). This study considers the data on Damu financing provided to SMEs during 2005–2019 and the relationship of this financing to the overall contribution of SMEs to the GDP of the country during this period. This chapter analyzes whether Damu's activities promoted the economic development of the country and whether Damu is overall financially efficient as an organization, how Damu has promoted startup businesses, and the factors by which microfinancing affects economic development in Kazakhstan. The results indicate that Damu has been successful, as shown by the number of SMEs financed and the number of jobs created, to reduce regional disparity in financing SMEs. The results also show that many small firms cannot grow into medium-sized enterprises in a competitive market, even with government support. Public financial institutions are recommended to help SMEs improve their management quality and to reduce information asymmetry between loan providers and clients so SMEs can grow with a long-term strategy in a competitive market.

Keywords: Entrepreneurship development fund, microfinance, SMEs, Kazakhstan

1. Introduction

Small and medium-sized enterprises (SMEs) are considered one of the main drivers of the development of a country's economy. The SME sector has excellent potential because it fosters flexibility in market economies and mobilizes labor, production, and financial resources. Small and medium entrepreneurship not only plays a social role by supporting the economic activity of a large share of the population but also ensures significant budget receipts. However, SMEs must meet various administrative, regulatory, and other organizational constraints that negatively affect their business processes, such as poor access to financial resources in the early stages of business development and underdevelopment of infrastructure for the SME sector.

Governments and state agencies that are responsible for promoting the development of the economy consistently believe that small and medium-sized businesses play a pivotal and decisive role in a country's economy and make local industries competitive in the global market (Jeppesen, 2005). To give appropriate support, governments need multiple measures for the establishment, development, and stabilization of the SME sector. Types and forms of government support can vary across countries. However, the main forms are subsidies; offering training, grants, and internships; promoting business incubators; holding exhibitions and regular activities; providing free consulting with specialists; and leasing of land or premises on preferential terms (World Bank, 2015).

This chapter focuses on the aspects of financing SMEs. The difficulties that SMEs have in accessing finance and the role of the Entrepreneurship Development Fund (Damu) in solving it in Kazakhstan.

Kazakhstan is one of richest countries in Central Asia due to its enormous reserves of oil and natural gas. Central Asia, the region east of the Caspian Sea, includes Uzbekistan, Kazakhstan, Tajikistan, Kyrgyz Republic, and Turkmenistan. After gaining independence in 1991 from the Soviet Union, Central Asian countries have followed divergent paths and are at different stages of development. Kazakhstan's economic dynamism represents more than 60% of the regional GDP (US$286.2 billion) for only 25% of the population in Central Asia (World Bank Data, 2019). Kazakhstan has achieved significant economic growth rates at 5.9% on average over the last 20 years. It is the highest-ranked country, at 28th place, for ease of doing business ranking in Central Asia (World Bank, 2019).

In the past two decades, Kazakhstan has become a major destination for foreign investment, mainly directed to resource-based industries. Between 2008 and 2017, the cumulative greenfield FDI in the country reached US$82 billion, which however was mainly driven by resource-based industries. Coal, oil, and gas represented 54% of the cumulative FDI inflow of the last decade and metals and minerals came close to 10%. Kazakhstan benefits from excess of natural resources, including coal (8th largest reserves), oil (10th largest proven reserves), iron (10th largest reserves), uranium (2nd largest reserves and the world's biggest production), and copper (4th biggest production) in the world (UNCDAD, 2018).

Therefore, the economy of Kazakhstan relies mainly on the oil sector, making it volatile due to oil price fluctuations. In resource-based economies like Kazakhstan's, diversification is very important in order to increase the resiliency of the economy. SMEs are a potential sector for diversifying the economy. The development of SMEs is one of the priorities of state policy in Kazakhstan. Successful state policies related to SMEs will broadly define the further economic and political development of the country. The Kazakhstani government created an entrepreneurship development fund called Damu, a joint stock company (JSC), to provide financial support to SMEs in Kazakhstan. The objective of this study is to analyze the efficiency of the Damu instruments to promote SMEs and startups in Kazakhstan. In addition, this research shows the effects of loans issued by commercial banks to small businesses facilitated by Damu from 2005 to 2019.

Despite the existence of various supporting mechanisms and programs, entrepreneurs widely use borrowing (financing loans), which is a traditional and essential financing instrument. However, the cost of financing through commercial finance institutions is relatively high due to different factors and risks which banks usually include in their loan rates, resulting in increased financial burden on the business. Other risk factors emphasized by banks are those associated with the difficulty of business and project assessment due to weak or poor prior financial history as well as more usual risks like the political situation and monetary and financial legislation. Nevertheless, commercial institutions are also involved in government programs and act as intermediaries in the distribution of funds using their competencies and requirements for business assessment.

Damu is a young organization compared to its counterparts in developed countries and has made significant contributions in a shorter time than other organizations to Kazakhstan's economic development. It is crucial to understand Damu's mechanism and whether it creates a favorable business environment as intended to support SMEs and startup business or whether Damu is just a waste of state resources and taxpayers' money.

This chapter is organized as follows. First, this study explores the role of public financial institutions such as Damu, microfinance institutions, and government agencies in promoting startups and SMEs in Kazakhstan. Next is a discussion of Damu's activities for economic development and how Damu promotes startup businesses. Third, this chapter analyzes the financial efficiency of Damu as a public financial institution in Kazakhstan.

The results show that Damu is efficient in developing Kazakhstan's SME sector and that the number of SMEs financed and the number of jobs created have grown, reducing regional disparity in financing SMEs. However, many small firms cannot grow into medium-sized enterprises in a competitive market, even with government support. Therefore, Damu may be the most efficient way to support SMEs in making a significant contribution to Kazakhstan's economic development. This study also recommends that credit loans in the Credit Guarantee System (CGS) for startups and SMEs should provide them with opportunities to increase management quality by themselves and promote small firms' growth into medium-sized firms. One solution to overcome this problem in Kazakhstan is to give SME entrepreneurs the confidence to develop a suitable long-term strategy in a competitive market by providing entrepreneurship development funds for startups and SMEs.

This chapter consists of five parts. The first part provides the introduction of this chapter and explains the background and objectives. The second part represents a literature review regarding the impact of SMEs' government support on economic development and credit loans for startups from public financial institutions. The third part reviews public financial institutions for startups and SMEs in Kazakhstan. The fourth part presents the data and methodology for analyzing SMEs' relationship with economic development, employment, and bank credit performance in Kazakhstan, as well as this study's results. The last part presents an overall review of the research, conclusions of this study, and discussion.

2. Literature Review

The advancement of SMEs and changes over time in amount of their contributions to GDP, yield composition, market shares, and region are typically thought to be identified with numerous variables, including the level of economic development and government support. Early studies on the role of SMEs and their pattern of development show that the manufacturing sector was dominated by artisans or craftsmen. Many of the artisans grew into larger sized and more modern establishments of industry, while smaller and more traditional units of production vanished (Hoselitz, 1959; Staley and Morse, 1965). Tambunan (2016) states,

> The use of economies of scale *with respect to* plant, management, marketing, and distribution (*depending on types of products and flexibility in production*); superior technical and management efficiency; better productive coordination and access to supporting infrastructure services and external finance; and concessionary finance along with investment incentives, tariff structures, and government subsidies are all powerful causes or incentives for firms to grow larger (p. 162).

Subsequently, early studies argue that the role of SMEs in economic development will decline and government support for SMEs will also decline steadily due to the possible preferred better performance of larger enterprises than small ones in industrialization (i.e., their shares in GDP, employment, sectoral output, and number of enterprises).

Modern theories emphasize the importance of subcontracting networks and the economic benefits of agglomeration and clustering for the development of SMEs in newly industrializing economies in East Asia like Taipei,China and the Republic of Korea and on the flexible specialization thesis based on many experiences from SMEs in west European countries (Berry and Mazumdar, 1991; Piore and Sabel, 1984; Levy, 1991; Doh and Kim, 2014; Tambunan, 2016). Piore and Sabel (1984) contended that SMEs situated in these areas have become the currently prevailing type of business. They describe these enterprises are as ventures with high- and multiskilled laborers, "flexible" hardware that typifies the most recent innovation, and venture *production for the global market*. Therefore, the share of SMEs per GDP would increase, although the assumed positive correlation will vary among countries due to differences in many internal factors, including level of economic development and economies scale.

Doh and Kim (2014) examined the impact of governmental support policies on the innovation of regional SMEs in the Republic of Korea and found that governmental support policies have positive relationships with the innovation, patents, and new design registrations of regional SMEs. They suggest that governmental financial aid is important for regional SME innovations and government support of SMEs promotes a strong social relationship in the advanced industrial business environment. The "Favorable to SME Policy" proposal, which the strategy supportive of SMEs advocates, contends that SMEs improve competition and entrepreneurship. Subsequently, they have advantages of economywide effectiveness, innovation, aggregate production, and social benefit (World Bank, 2020). Therefore, the government should support SMEs with *public services, infrastructure, government credit schemes, and training programs*.

However, the problem of government support to SMEs has been recognized, and many state, public, and private organizations are working to develop and promote alternative financing instruments as well as other supporting activities to sustain dynamic SME development. Especially in developing countries, authorities need an effective financial system that can provide financial resources to a broad range of companies.

The World Economic Forum (2016) reports new sources of capital and drivers of SMEs and explains their effects and importance for society. The capital sphere is affected by various factors, mainly regulations, changes in demand for capital, and technology. These factors differently affect each area of the SME industry; thus, for startups, the government lowers barriers, making it easier to get financing at different startup life stages. Crowdfunding and debt to mid-market businesses are regulated by government agencies, giving more flexibility to alternative investors to provide funds. SMEs comprise the most considerable portion of firms in almost all countries and contribute to two-thirds of total employment. SMEs also stimulate economic growth through contributions to innovation and productivity (ADB, 2014; OECD, 2018).

Despite all the theory on the importance of SME development, obtaining external financing for SMEs is a substantial barrier. This is partly because these firms seek small-scale lending given the size of their business, which cannot compensate banks for their monitoring and screening expenses. Lack of collateral, the need for longer maturities, and lack of information make the problem worse (OECD, 2014). Hence, despite the state's understanding of SMEs' importance and their continuous legislative support, most of the responsibility for financing SMEs still lies with commercial banks. This creates an impossible situation for those countries that have adopted the Basel Norms, which prevent banks from financing projects with high risk (Sen and Ghosh, 2005). In most countries, such banks are reluctant to finance small firms as they consider them to be risky.

Sen and Ghosh (2005) prescribed a few different ways for SMEs to receive credit from booked business banks. One of these ways is financing clusters. This is a method of financing a group of SMEs that allows individual SMEs to receive funding that otherwise would not be possible. Another way could be through relationship-lending in which the lender (i.e., a bank) bases its decision to finance on information gathered about the SME through a variety of contacts like members of the local community, suppliers, and customers, who can provide specific information about the owner of the business or overall about the business environment. Another recommendation is for the state to enable banks to finance SMEs by providing financial stimulation to the banks themselves.

Yoshino and Taghizadeh-Hesary (2015) found that SMEs represent a significant portion of the labor force and are influential in local economies. "Asian economies are characterized as having bank-dominated financial systems and underdeveloped capital markets, especially in terms of their investment for startup and venture companies. Therefore SMEs in good credit status could borrow more money from banks at lower interest rates because of their lower default risk, while SMEs in poor financial health would have to pay higher interest rates and have a lower borrowing ceiling" (p. 19). Hence, an efficient credit rating scheme that rates SMEs based on their financial health would help banks lend money to SMEs in a more rational way while at that same time reducing the risk to banks.

The Vienna Initiative Working Group (2014) reports the credit guarantee schemes for SME lending in Central, Eastern, and South-Eastern Europe in a transition economy as follows.

- Credit certifications should permit extending the universe of SMEs that can apply for funds, but credit guarantee systems ought to be set up to restrict the unfavorable choice of high-hazard borrowers and the ethical risk related with existing borrowers.
- The capacity of credit certifications to generously mitigate the requirement for guarantees (collateral) ought to be fortified through authoritative boundaries and estimates.
- Credit guarantee schemes should stop imposing exorbitant regulatory necessities and customers need to relax their criteria for qualification, as these regularly discourage lenders from utilizing credit ensures.

3. Public Financial Institutions for Startups and SMEs in Kazakhstan

This section introduces the role of Damu and government agencies in promoting startups and SMEs' finance in Kazakhstan.

Table 1: Criteria for Classifying Enterprises as SME Type

#	Sector	National Statistical Definition of SME	Kazakhstan: For State Support Purposes	
		Number of Employees	Number of Employees	Annual Turnover in Million *
1	Micro	<15	<15	<0.21
2	Small	<100	<100	<2.14
3	Medium	100–250	100–250	2.14–21.5
4	Large	>250	>250	>21.15

Note: *Average USD/KZT rate for 2018 is 344.71 tenge = US$1.
Source: Code of Republic of Kazakhstan (2015).

Criteria for assignment to certain sectors of SMEs are presented in Table 1. SMEs in Kazakhstan are defined as micro-businesses or as small, medium-sized, or large enterprises depending on their average number of employees and average annual income (Code of the Republic of Kazakhstan, 2015). Kapparov (2019) explains,

> The average annual number of employees consists of all employees, including employees of branches, representative offices, and other sepa-rate divisions of the subject, as well as the individual entrepreneur. The state support purpose defines the size of the firm: average number of employees and average annual income which is the sum of the total annual income for the last three years, divided by three. (p. 3).

3.1 *The Role of Damu for Startups and SMEs in Kazakhstan*

A case study of Kazakhstan will be presented to assess the importance of SMEs for Kazakhstan's economy and the role of Damu in contributing to economic growth. The development of a sustainable and competitive private sector is one of the priorities of the economic policy of the Republic of Kazakhstan (RK). The law "On private entrepreneurship" states that state support includes government regulation, infrastructure development, educational resources, financial support, and scientific information provision.

Over the course of more than 20 years, Damu has financed more than 16,000 entrepreneurs in a transition economy and facilitated consultation and training programs for more than 70,000 clients (Damu, 2014). Recipients of Damu funds created 26,000 jobs. In addition, supported enterprises produced 4 KZT trillion in sales of goods/services per year. Damu funds KZT 253 billion to enterprises per year. The mission of Damu is to facilitate quality SME development through comprehensive support that includes a wide range of financial instruments and capacity-building programs. Damu supported 31,000 projects and 1,506 KZT billion in loans through funding banks and microfinance organizations for further lending to businesses at a rate of 6%, guaranteed up to 85% of the loan amount of bank loans for 3,000 projects (104.3 billion KZT), and supported 9,700 projects through subsidizing interest rates of 7–10% for 1,811 billion KZT worth of loans. Damu also provided education programs for 3,300 startups and consulted with 257,000 entrepreneurs in training programs (Dame, 2017–2020).

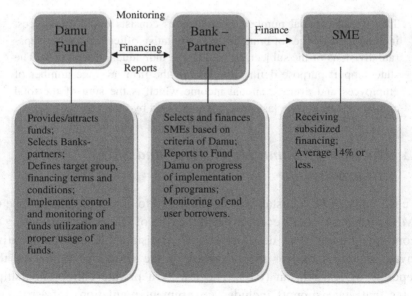

Figure 1: Overall Financing Mechanism of Damu

Source: Based on the information provided on the official website of Damu (www.damu.kz).

SME support tools implemented by Damu are unprecedented in the Commonwealth of Independent States (CIS) territory and can be compared with the SME development activities of agencies and corporations in developed countries. Damu's role includes the creation of a favorable business environment in which small businesses can flourish. Up until 2013, Damu's sole shareholder was the National Welfare Fund JSC "Samruk-Kazyna," and since 2013 it has been the National Management Holding JSC "Baiterek". Samruk-Kazyna (https://www.sk.kz/) has over 500 affiliates, while Baiterek (https://baiterek.gov.kz/en) has 10 affiliated companies (including Damu). Baiterek is responsible only for financial investment institutions in economic and financial market development, while Samruk-Kazyna covers all other economic activity sectors. The essence of "Samruk Kazyna" and "Baiterek" activities is to manage the country's assets in appropriate ways to guarantee the sustainability and growth of the economy through modernization and diversification. One of the main principles of Samruk-Kazyna and Baiterek is to safeguard the interests of the state, as the state is the sole shareholder of these two companies.

The functions of each institution are presented in Table 2.

Table 2: Main Functions of Samruk-Kazyna and Baiterek

Samruk-Kazyna's Functions	Baiterek's Functions
Development of sectors of the economy	Financial-investment support of the non-oil sector
Developing inter-regional economic relations	Attracting investments
Investments in prioritized sectors of the economy: oil & gas, power energy, metallurgy, chemistry, infrastructure	Supporting small and medium-sized businesses
Developing the energy sector of the economy, attracting investments	Building affordable homes
Technological support to the army	Promotion of export-orientation
Investment in the informational-communication system of Kazakhstan	Ensuring technological development
	Creating an infrastructure of private equity

Source: Samruk-Kazyna (http://www.sk.kz).

Damu's role is to implement the responsibility of the state in developing the SME sector in Kazakhstan. Up until 2001, Damu was the agent for accounting and control of the state budget under the program to support domestic producers of goods and was funded by credit lines provided by the European Bank of Reconstruction and Development and the Asian Development Bank.

The creation and growth of Damu mirror the concern of the government. Although the company was created in 1997, it could be argued that its real potential and importance have only been realized since the global financial crisis of 2007. This explains the changes in Damu's operations in 2007. Since 2010, Damu has become the financial operator of the large state program "Business Roadmap 2020" (hereafter — BR 2020). Damu's programs can be divided into four stages based on BR 2020:

1. Programs oriented toward increasing the volume and accessibility of SME funding through the conditional placement of funds in second-tier banks and leasing companies. The most popular programs are stabilization programs, Programs "Damu-Regions" and "Damu-Regions II", and special programs like financing SMEs in Zhanaozen for women entrepreneurs. Those programs are designed to diversify entrepreneurship and its industrial-innovative development.
2. It started to support medium entrepreneurs as well. Damu's financing mechanism was also amended significantly. Before 2007, Damu had provided financing to small entrepreneurs by direct financing, but in 2007 it was decided to conduct financing through experienced financial institutions with well-developed financial infrastructure, adequate risk management systems, adequate personnel to cover a large number of SMEs, and branches and operational offices in various regions and rural areas.
3. The state provides preferential loans to SMEs during periods of lack of liquidity in the market. Therefore, the interest rate target for SME loans is not higher than 19%. Funding from Damu has a market share of 8% of all loans for business purposes, up from 5% in 2014. Its share increases to 16% due to interest rate subsidizing and guaranteeing of loans in 2018 (Kapparov, 2019).

4. In its most recent stage, Damu planned a new initiative strategy for automation of services, financial supermarket, microfinancing, and training of startups and experienced entrepreneurs in 2016. Damu's services are automated by integrating its loan guarantee service with the EGOV.KZ portal to obtain guarantees more quickly by reducing the paperwork and increase transparency through online tracking of the application. A financial supermarket called "Digital Damu" is intended to include lending in a new economy through e-commerce, digital platforms and ecosystems, crowdfunding/crowd investing, Islamic financing instruments, and financing Public–Private Projects (PPPs). Microfinance will support lending to micro and small businesses through microfinance organizations funded by Damu and EBRD.

Damu provides funds to bank partners under specific financial programs and sets SME financing requirements. Banks independently select SMEs that satisfy these defined financial requirements because banks take all the risk in financing SMEs. If SMEs default, banks still have to repay the loan from Damu in full. Damu regularly monitors whether banks meet the requirements and whether eligible SMEs receive financing. Banks regularly send progress reports to Damu to ensure that state funds are used for their intended purposes and that there is no misuse of funds. Damu also reports regularly to the government.

This mechanism works well because of the mutual benefit for all partners involved in it. Damu uses infrastructural, technical, and staff advantages of commercial financial institutions to increase the availability of funds to SMEs. Banks' liquidity problems are also solved as it is hard for them to get cheap financing in the international financial market due to their low credit ratings. The interest rate at which they get financing from Damu ranges between 5 and 7%. Banks can add a margin to these funds and reinvest in SMEs at higher interest rates, but they cannot exceed the maximum interest rates for SMEs set by Damu, which ranges between 12 and 14%. SMEs benefit as they can get cheap Damu funds from almost any bank in Kazakhstan.

In summary, Damu is a financial development institution that implements a range of financial and non-financial programs, works with several banks and leasing companies, and gets its funds for funding small businesses from a range of sources.

3.2 Government Support Initiatives for Startups and SMEs in Kazakhstan

Innovation is an actively developing sector in Kazakhstan. There are many entrepreneurs with new ideas and projects in various spheres where innovation can be applied to solve different problems. In order to support and develop upcoming trends, the government developed some programs for supporting startups:

- DAMU funds provide collateral-free and low-rate loans. QazTech Ventures focuses on the development of the venture capital market and technology entrepreneurship. Grants will be handled by the Kazakhstan Institute for the Development of Industry (KIDI).
- SABY is a charity fund that provides the winner of an annual contest with a financial prize and the opportunity to attract investments.
- The young entrepreneurs club MOST is an informal resource of business angels and business incubators that provide financing to startups as well as consulting support to starting entrepreneurs.
- TECHGARDEN provides acceleration and incubation programs supported by grants, seed investments, and, if necessary, co-investment instruments as well as measures for developing entrepreneurs' competence. Priority spheres are intelligent industry, new materials, smart environment, energy and clean technologies, E-commerce, and media.

In addition to the abovementioned sources of support, networking technologies can be used for small startups. This type of financing is called crowdfunding. Citizens of Kazakhstan can use crowdfunding platforms like start-time.kz and attract individual investors to finance a project.

The relationship between the state and business in Kazakhstan is carried out through consultative bodies, state organs, and institutions of development created by the government's initiatives. The structural division of the Ministry of National Economy of the Republic of Kazakhstan that develops state policy in the sphere of development and support of entrepreneurship is the Entrepreneurship Promotion Department, which implements functions for financial, informational and analytics, material and technical support through specially created organizations and institutions of development that provide service support as follows:

- JSC Kazakh Invest different from "Development institutions that provide financial support to small and medium-sized businesses.
- Investment fund of Kazakhstan JSC realizes financial support by investing in equity of companies that process raw materials using modern and advanced technologies.
- The Damu Entrepreneurship Development Fund JSC assists the development of small and medium-sized businesses as well as microfinance organizations of Kazakhstan in the role of integrator and operator of financial and consulting services.
- The primary objective of "Kazyna Capital Management" JSC is financial support by participating in the equity of local and foreign investment funds and project companies.
- Agrarian Credit Corporation JSC finances producers of commodities through the network of credit cooperatives.
- KazAgroFinance JSC provides access for agricultural producers to financial resources and agricultural and technological equipment through leasing, and finances investment projects.
- Fund for Financial Support of Agriculture provides microfinancing services to farming communities and SMEs in rural areas by developing financial infrastructure in rural areas through microcredit organizations. The regional network has 14 divisions in various cities

4. Analysis and Findings

4.1 *Data and Methodology*

This study aims to understand whether Damu as a government support initiative to help startups and SMEs in Kazakhstan is providing a favorable business environment for SMEs where they can succeed. This analysis provides an overall understanding of the SME sector, such as how many SMEs are registered in Kazakhstan, the percentage of SMEs out of all businesses in Kazakhstan, and the dynamics of financing provided by the commercial banks in Kazakhstan during the period 2007–2019. Subsequently, this study considers the data on Damu's financing provided to SMEs during 2005–2019 and the relationship of this financing to the overall contribution of SMEs to the GDP of the country during this period. Finally, the calculation of the cost of the capital of Damu will be presented. Calculating the cost of capital is an essential indicator of the financial health of any company. As Damu is a state agency and most of its capital comes from the state, not only is it interesting to explore its tools for the support of SMEs and efficiency in promoting access to finance, but it is also crucial to analyze whether these programs are profitable for the company from a financial standpoint. Although Damu is a state agency, it is not considered to be a truly non-profit public sector company. Hence, its profitability is a crucial issue. The analysis results are based on statistical data from the official online portal of the Committee on Statistics of Kazakhstan.

4.2 *Analysis of the Current Situation of SMEs in Kazakhstan*

During the reviewed period, the number of registered SMEs increased on average by 7% annually, despite decreases in 2009 due to the global financial crisis (see Table 3). The number of registered and active SMEs in 2016 reflects a positive tendency of growth. In particular, starting in 2010, the SME sector continuously increased during the economy recovery. After the Kazakhstani currency (tenge) was devalued due to the oil price shock, the number of entrepreneurs and small businesses increased sharply: the total number of registered SMEs increased almost two-fold over the period 2005–2019. The number of active small and medium-sized businesses increased by 1.3 times as well. In real terms, the GDP of Kazakhstan showed stable growth from 2014 to 2018, growing 4.2% in 2014, decreasing 1.2% in 2015, and increasing 1.1% in 2016 and 2017.

Table 3: Number of Active and Registered SMEs in Kazakhstan (Thousand)

Year	Active SMEs	Registered SMEs	GDP (%)	Year	Active SMEs	Registered SMEs	GDP (%)
2005	507	743	10.5	2013	888	1536	16.7
2006	573	840	9.8	2014	927	1655	25.9
2007	643	938	10.7	2015	1,243	1481	24.9
2008	708	1026	16.7	2016	1,187	1501	26.8
2009	663	935	17.7	2017	1,145	1,540	26.8
2010	662	1197	20.6	2018	1,245	1,577	28.4
2011	846	1384	17.3	2019	1,329	1,625	28.5
2012	810	1400	17.1				

Source: Committee on Statistics of the Republic of Kazakhstan (2020).

In developed countries, the share of SME production is 50% of GDP or more. Criteria for allocating enterprises to categories of small or medium-sized businesses in different countries vary widely. Nevertheless, the contribution of SMEs to the Kazakhstani economy is still small. The modest contribution of SMEs to GDP raises flags given that the government has enacted an economic policy to diversify the economy and create a sustainable rate of economic growth by increasing the role of SMEs.

4.3 *Business Sectors and the Employment of SME in Kazakhstan*

There has been an annual increase in the employed population of Kazakhstan (see Table 4). More than 3 million people were employed in SMEs between 2005 and 2019, and the number of sole proprietors increased 1.4 times, while the number of farm sector employees decreased by 83%. The share of the employed population in Kazakhstan's SME sector is low compared with developed countries, around 27% compared to from 47% (Canada) to 75% (Japan). The contribution of Kazakhstan's SMEs to the Kazakhstani economy is to increase jobs. Small businesses increased their number of employees more than medium-sized businesses and farms from 2014 to 2019.

Table 4:   Number of Employees in SME Sector of Kazakhstan

Year	Small Business	Medium Business	Entrepreneurs	Farms	Total
2005	533,779	265,472	571,620	504,655	1,875,526
2006	557,884	267,074	622,668	504,262	1,951,888
2007	585,864	259,122	733,458	542,754	2,121,198
2008	464,622	397,607	828,963	461,768	2,152,960
2009	551,308	405,094	874,356	465,842	2,296,600
2010	746,240	748,240	710,559	425,541	2,630,580
2011	539,285	689,385	771,939	426,527	2,427,136
2012	500,591	675,486	831,425	375,836	2,383,338
2013	527,519	711,788	990,681	346,914	2,576,902
2014	849,015	516,520	1,136,050	309,377	2,810,962
2015	1,185,186	351,779	1,360,338	286,541	3,183,844
2016	1,249,270	352,954	1,288,167	276,401	3,166,792
2017	1,257,347	360,439	1,240,876	286,038	3,144,700
2018	1,307,469	364,601	1,315,162	280,525	3,267,757
2019	1,280,422	370,582	1,372,894	295,571	3,319,469

Source: Committee on Statistics of the Republic of Kazakhstan (2020).

The number of small businesses grew consistently from 2005 to 2014 and increased from 2014 to 2019 due to the impact of Damu and microfinance on the promotion of SMEs. Agribusiness also increased from 2014 to 2019 due to government support programs (e.g., KazAgroFinance JSC) even though the number of farm employees dropped from 2011 to 2019. However, the number of medium-sized enterprises decreased from 2014 to 2019. This result implicates that many small firms cannot grow to medium-sized enterprises in the competitive market even with government support. Table 5 provides more details.

4.4 *Bank Loans to SME Sector*

This study analyzed the relationship between the trends of bank loans given to SMEs and taxes received from SMEs using official data from the

Table 5: Structure of Active SMEs Sector by Forms

Year	Small Businesses	Medium-sized Businesses	Individual Entrepreneurs	Farms	Total
2005	50,612	2,541	297,234	156,978	507,365
2006	47,756	2,678	358,583	163,721	572,738
2007	55,865	2,476	415,709	169,326	643,376
2008	58,480	4,019	475,841	169,481	707,821
2009	60,601	4,160	428,420	170,193	663,374
2010	66,492	8,712	416,085	170,309	661,598
2011	64,457	9,028	589,640	182,986	846,111
2012	62,888	8,388	573,618	164,856	809,750
2013	61,076	8,312	660,262	158,583	888,233
2014	74,829	4,559	694,759	152,697	926,844
2015	175,679	2,897	882,849	181,154	1,242,579
2016	189,637	2,711	813,482	180,799	1,186,629
2017	208,742	2 618	747,107	187,527	1,145,994
2018	231,325	2 620	809,115	198,268	1,241,328
2019	254,415	2 480	860,712	212,214	1,329,821

Source: Statistics of the Republic of Kazakhstan (2020).

National Bank of Kazakhstan from 2005 to 2019. Table 6 shows a positive trend of the total volume of bank lending to SMEs, with an average growth of 20% and a total of 12.7 trillion tenge as of 2013. From 2013 to 2019, the number of loans for entrepreneurial purposes grew by 22%; as of 2019, there were about 37 trillion tenge in loans. The base interest rate for microfinance in 2019 is higher than in 2013. Especially the interest rates from banks increased sharply since 2015 (Table 6).

4.5 *Assessing the Financial Stability of Damu*

The return of rate on investment is calculated depending on the riskiness of the project. This reflects the fact that the cost of capital related to investment depends on the risk of that investment. Hence, the cost of capital depends mainly on the use of funds, not the source.

Table 6:   Bank Loans to SME Sector and Taxes Paid by the SMEs in Kazakhstan

Year	Taxes from Subjects of SME	Bank Loans to SME Sector	Microloan Interest Rate (%) Weighted Average Number		
			Base	Lend	Borrow
2005	15,479,633	470,164,000	7.74	13.75	3.05
2006	21,204,110	861,045,000	8.63	13.13	3.89
2007	43,497,233	1,505,487,000	9.71	13.57	5.05
2008	66,925,709	1,570,734,000	10.75	16.07	5.34
2009	107,735,786	1,708,189,000	8.35	15.21	4.71
2010	220,606,296	1,384,956,000	7.00	13.83	3.09
2011	194,606,939	1,341,385,000	7.41	11.88	2.83
2012	199,486,263	1,412,005,000	6.20	11.04	2.33
2013	71,993,807	1,283,440,000	5.50	10.55	3.73
2014	182,069,357	1,788,058,764	12.00	10.87	5.50
2015	277,618,551	2,060,454,516	17.00	15.65	11.47
2016	304,107,270	3,002,973,673	12.00	17.18	13.63
2017	196,615,000	3,932,300,000	9.25	13.69	8.69
2018	176,360,000	3,527,200,000	9.30	12.48	7.18
2019	186,655,000	3,733,100,000	9.15	12.03	7.20

Source: Statistics of the Republic of Kazakhstan (2020), National bank Kazakhstatn (2019–2020).

The weighted average cost of capital (WACC) is the cost of capital for a firm as a whole and can be interpreted as the required return on the firm (Ross *et al.*, 2008).

WACC is usually a mixture of returns that the company uses to compensate its creditors and shareholders and is based on capital structure. Capital structure refers to the way a firm finances its operations through loans, bond sales, preferred stock sales, and retention of earnings. Therefore, the cost of capital consists of the cost of debt and the cost of equity. WACC characterizes the opportunity cost of investing, the profitability level that a company can get when investing not in a new project but an existing one. The following formula calculates WACC:

$$WACC = kd * (1 - T) * \frac{D}{D + E} + Ke * \frac{E}{D + E}$$

where

Kd — market rate on debt capital used by the company, %;

T — income tax rate, %;

D — the amount of debt capital of the company;

E — the amount of equity capital of the company;

Ke — market (required) rate of return on equity of the company, %.

WACC is calculated by multiplying capital structure weights by the associated costs. Debt calculated the after-tax cost of Debt because the interest paid by any company is deductible for tax purposes, while compensation to shareholders is not. The main difficulty in calculating the WACC indicator is calculating the price of a unit of capital received from a particular source of funds. For some sources, it can be calculated quite easily and accurately (for example, the cost of a bank loan); for some other sources, it is quite difficult to do so, and exact calculations are impossible to implement. Nevertheless, even rough estimates of WACC are acceptable for analytical purposes and useful both for a comparative analysis of the effectiveness of advance payments to the organization, and to justify the investment policy of the organization.

As Damu is a national company, with the shareholder National Management Holding Baiterek owning 100% of its shares, Damu does not trade its shares on the stock equity market. Damu's capital structure is made up of equity provided by its shareholders and retained earnings combined with the government's funding in the form of debt to finance SMEs in Kazakhstan. Damu does not require the extra interest rate for its partner banks to be objectively defined under Damu's financial programs. As Brigham and Ehrhardt (2005) mentioned, book value can be used to estimate Damu's value stated in the balance sheet (1 January 2014). According to Kazakhstan's tax code, a single corporate tax rate of 20% is set for all companies. The book value of all debts is found to be 115,665 million KZT, while the book value of equity is 74,618 million KZT. The required rate of equity is 7.02%, and the required rate of debt is

Table 7: The Valuation of DAMU

	Variable	Damu's Interest Rate (A)	Base Interest Rate (B)
R_E	required rate of return of equity	7.02%	7.02%
R_D	required rate of return of debt	1.43%	3.73%
t_c	corporate tax rate	20%	20%
D	overall debt amount (million KZT)	115,665	115,665
E	overall equity amount (million KZT)	74,618	74,618
V	combined value of debt and equity	193,162	193,162

Source: National Bank Kazakhstan, 2019–2020.

1.43%. Considering the given D and E amount, we calculate the combined value of debt and equity, V = 115,665 + 74.618 = 193,162 million KZT (See Table 7).

The required rate of return of equity and debt was calculated by using historical data from STBs and Damu (Umiraliyeva, 2015). The interest rate for the cost of debt calculated both Damu's interest rate and the base interest rate in Kazakhstan's financial market to evaluate Damu's valuation.

To calculate the WACC, all financial programs of Damu were divided into two: those programs in which funds attracted from external parties (debt) are used to provide funds to banks and therefore to SMEs, and those programs that use Damu's own funds (equity) to finance SMEs through banks. The two types of programs and the historical interest rates are presented in Table 8.

The rate of return of borrowed funds for Damu is the average margin that Damu applied when refinancing the funds to banks. As Damu is obliged to return these funds to the external lenders upon the maturity date, the real rate of return it gets from these funds is equal to its margin. Hence, as R_d we take the average margin calculated at 1.43%. The rate at which Damu finances STBs is its required rate of return. This is what Damu gets from financing SMEs through second-tier banks (STBs). Therefore, R_E is taken as 7.02%. All these rates are approved by the Board of Directors and documented (Umiraliyeva, 2015). Taking these data, the

Table 8: Historical Data on Rates of Return of Damu's Financial Programs on Financing SMEs through STBs

		The Rate of Borrowing	Average Margin	Average Rate of
	Source of	for Damu	of Damu	Financing
Program	Financing	(%)	(%)	STBs (%)
Rate of Return for Funds Borrowed from External Parties				
Stabilization Program — 3	JSC "NWF Samruk-Kazyna"	5.50	1.48	6.98
Stabilization Program — 2	JSC "NWF Samruk-Kazyna"	6.50	1.00	7.50
ADB Investment Program	Asian Development Bank	4.99	1.50	6.49
Stabilization Program — 1	JSC "NWF Samruk-Kazyna"	7.00	2.10	9.10
Financial Leasing	Fund of Distressed Assets	1.00	2.50	3.50
Regional financing of SMEs in defined cities	Local executive bodies	1.00	1.49	2.49
Damu Regions 2	Local executive bodies	1.00	4.50	5.50
TOTAL		**5.69**	**1.43**	**7.09**
Rate of return for company's own funds				
Program Damu-Regions	Own funds	—	—	7.50
		—	—	8.28
Damu Regions 2	Own funds	—	—	5.50
Women Entrepreneurship	Own funds	—	—	8.00
Financing Microfinance Organizations	Own funds	—	—	8.00
Financial Leasing	Own funds	—	—	6.50
Financing SMEs in Zhanaozen (old program)	Own funds	—	—	5.48
SMEs in Small Cities	Own funds	—	—	7.50
Damu Koldau	Own funds	—	—	7.00
SMEs in Services sphere	Own funds	—	—	7.50
Damu Regions 3	Own funds	—	—	8.50
Financing SMEs in Zhanaozen (old program)	Own funds	—	—	5.50
Regional financing of SMEs in defined cities	Own funds	—	—	5.50
TOTAL:		—	—	**7.02**

Source: Damu (2014).

weighted average cost of capital of Damu can be calculated in historical data:

Damu's interest rate:

$$\text{WACC} = E/V * R_E + D/V * R_D * (1-t_c) = (74\ 618/193\ 162) * 7.02\%$$
$$+ (115\ 665/193\ 162) * 1.43\% * (1-0.2) = 3.40\%.$$

Base interest rate:

$$\text{WACC} = E/V * R_E + D/V * R_D * (1-t_c) = (74\ 618/193\ 162) * 7.02\%$$
$$+ (115\ 665/193\ 162) * 3.73\% * (1-0.2) = 6.25\%.$$

The overall return Damu should earn on its assets in order to maintain their value is 3.40–6.25%.

Table 8 shows that the average rate at which Damu financed STBs is 7%, which means that Damu maintains the value of its assets and receives considerable profit from these activities, with a profit of approximately 3.60% for its funds (3.40–7%). Damu makes about 49% profit to compensate its borrowers. This result shows that Damu effectively implements state programs for financing SMEs and is an efficient and sustainable company that is financially sound. This is an indicator of the company's financial health and demonstrates not only efficiency in implementing programs for financing SMEs but also the company's efficiency in operating its business.

5. Conclusion and Policy Implication

The Kazakhstani government understands that SMEs create the basis of the market economy. The findings of the overall research assessed the efficiency of Damu as an organization and as the agency of a state implementing a social mandate and explored the efficiency of its financial management. The comparative analysis of Kazakhstan's SME sector development highlighted the following: in developed industries, the share of the SME sector to GDP is approximately 50% overall, while in Kazakhstan it was only 28.4% in 2018. Overall, Damu is efficient in developing Kazakhstan's SME sector, and as it is a young organization compared to its counterparts in developed countries, a realization of its potential is yet to be expected in the future. Therefore, Damu may be the most efficient way for the government to support SMEs in making a significant contribution to Kazakhstan's economic development. As mentioned earlier, limited access to financial resources is a significant obstacle to the active development of small businesses. Well-timed and carefully implemented governmental stabilization programs can partially offset the negative impact of the oil price crisis on funding the SME sector. However, the solution to this problem requires a systematic approach and a set of interrelated measures aimed at reducing the SME sector risks and developing financial support institutions.

Targeted and practical support of private entrepreneurship is possible only with state support and united institutions that systematize the activities of existing and newly created structures and combine their opportunities.

The key factor in implementing government support to SMEs is providing entrepreneurs with affordable services to support business processes, such as maintenance of taxation and accounting, legal support, and other issues at all levels of the governmental policy.

Therefore, policy effectiveness of Damu and other public funds for supporting SMEs in Kazakhstan are given as follows:

First, it is necessary to strengthen analysts' capabilities. To this end, Damu should reinforce employee education and training. Damu has gradually increased the number of its branch offices in all regions so that the credit guarantee institution can directly handle the credit guarantee procedures to promote startup SMEs.

Secondly, the credit guarantee system (CGS) must improve its ability to manage credit risks systematically. Specifically, in terms of risk management for the non-profit loan, it is necessary to improve the auction system of collateral and streamline lawsuit procedures and governmental permission/approval procedures for investment.

Thirdly, Damu should consider offering a premium as an incentive to borrow so that SMEs can borrow at low rates.

Fourthly, the credit guarantee system (CGS) should make an effort to prevent conflicting interests between Damu, STBs, and clients in credit loans. Accordingly, Damu should support the use of credit guarantees by ensuring that loan officers/STBs are provided with the necessary incentives to roll out guaranteed loans. Damu should strengthen its internal IT systems and agreements with banks to monitor clients' moral hazard problems.

Finally, offering guaranteed loans to entrepreneurs should give them opportunities to engage in continuing education and promote the growth of small firms into medium-sized firms. One solution to overcome the difficulty of the growth of small firms into medium-sized firms in Kazakhstan is to give SME entrepreneurs the confidence to develop a suitable long-term strategy in a competitive market by providing entrepreneurship development funds for startups and SMEs.

References

Agrarian Credit Corporation JSC. Retrieved http://www.kazagro.kz/ (Accessed on September 07, 2020).

Asia Development Bank (ADB). 2014. Studies on enhancing financial accessibility for SMEs: Lessons from recent crises. Retrived http://www.adb.org/publications/adb-oecd-study-enhancing-financial-accessibility-SMEs-lessons-recent-crises.

Baiterek. Retrieved https://baiterek.gov.kz/en.

Berry, A. and D. Mazumdar. 1991. Small-scale industry in the Asian-Pacific region. *Asian-Pacific Economic Literature*, 5(2): 35–67.

Brigham, E.F. and M.C. Ehrhardt. 2005. *Financial Management: Theory and Practice*. 11th edition. South-Western, Thomson Corporation.

Code of the Republic of Kazakhstan. 2015. Retrieved http://adilet.zan.kz/eng/docs/K1500000375.

Damu. 2014. Annual report of the entrepreneurship development fund "Damu" JSC www.damu.kz.

Damu. 2017–2020. Official website of the entrepreneurship development fund "Damu" JSC www.damu.kz http://business.gov.kz/ (Accessed on September 07, 2020).

Doh S. and Kim.B. 2014, Government support for SME innovations in the regional industries: The case of government financial support program in South Korea, Research Policy, 43(9):1557–1569.

Entrepreneurship Development Fund "Damu" JSC. 2014. *The strategy of Development of JSC "Entrepreneurship Development Fund Damu for 2014–2023"*, 2–49.

Hoselitz, B.F. 1959. Small industry in underdeveloped countries. *Journal of Economic History*, 19(4): 600–618.

Investment fund of Kazakhstan JSC, https://www.ifk.kz/en/.

Jeppesen, S. 2005. Enhancing Competitiveness and Securing Equitable Development: Can Small, Micro, and Medium-Sized Enterprises (SMEs) Do the Trick? *Development in Practice*, 15(¾): 463–474.

KazAgroFinance JSC, https://www.kaf.kz/en/.

Kazakhstan Institute for the Development of Industry (KIDI), https://qazindustry.gov.kz/.

Kazyna Capital Management JSC, https://kcm-kazyna.kz/ (Accessed on September 07, 2020).

Kapparov, K. 2019. Leveraging SME finance through value Chains in Kazakhstan. *ADBI Working Paper Series No. 1021*.

Levy, B. 1991. Obstacles to developing small and medium-sized enterprises, an empirical assessment. *Policy, Research, and External Affairs Working Paper no. 588*, World Bank, Washington, D.C.

Lucia, C. 2015. *New Approaches to SME and Entrepreneurship Financing: Broadening the range of instruments*. https://www.oecd.org/cfe/smes/New-Approaches-SME-full-report.pdf.

Mambula, C. 2002. Perceptions of SME growth constraints in Nigeria. *Journal of Small Business Management*, 40(1): 58–65.

Meine Pieter van Dijk. 1995. Flexible specialisation, the new competition and industrial districts. *Small Business Economics*, (7): 15–27.

Morrison, J.B. and S. Ali. 2003. Small business growth: Intention, ability & opportunity. *Journal of Small Business Management*, 41(4): 417–425.

MOST, http://most.com.kz/.

National Bank Kazakhstan. 2019–2020. www.nationalbank.kz.

National Credit Regulator (NCR). 2011. *Literature Review on Small and Medium Enterprises' Access to Credit and Support in South Africa*. http://www.ncr.org.za (Accessed on September 07, 2020).

OECD. 2014. Studies on SMEs and Entrepreneurship Poland: Key Issues and Policies. OECD. http://oecd-library.org.

OECD. 2018. *Financing SMEs and Entrepreneurs 2018: An OECD Scoreboard*. Paris, France: OECD Publishing.

Piore, M.J. and C. Sabel. 1984. *The Second Industrial Divide*, New York: Basic Books.

Ross, S.A. *et al.*, 2008. *Corporate Finance Fundamentals: International Student Edition*. The McGrow-Hill Companies, Inc.

SABY, https://entrepreneur.saby.kz/.

Samruk-Kazyna, https://www.sk.kz/.

Sen, S. and S.K. Ghosh. 2005. Basel norms, Indian banking sector and impact on credit to SMEs and the poor. *Economic and Political Weekly*, 40(12): 1167–1180.

Soogwan, D. and B. Kim. 2014. Government support for SME innovations in the regional industries: The case of government financial support program in South Korea. *Research Policy*, 43(9): 1557–1569.

SouksavanhVixathep. 2014. *Entrepreneurship, Government Policy and Performance of SMEs in Laos*. http://www.research.kobe-u.ac.jp/gsics-publication/gwps/2014-28.pdf.

Staley, E. and M. Richard. 1965. Modern small industry in developing countries, New York: McGraw-Hill.

Statistics of the Republic of Kazakhstan (2020). https://stat.gov.kz

Tambunan, T. 2016. SME development, economic growth, and government intervention in a developing country: The Indonesian story. *Journal of International Entrepreneurship*, 6, 147–167.

TECHGARDEN, https://techgarden.kz/.

Turukpayeva, R.M. 2011. Condition and perspective of credit relations between small and medium businesses and second tier banks. *20 Years of Independence of the Republic of Kazakhstan in the Light of Formation of Civil Society*// http://articlekz.com/article/7473.

Umiraliyeva, A. 2015. *Analysis of Financing Small and Medium Enterprises in Business Environment of Kazakhstan*, MBA thesis, KIMEP University.

UNCDAD. 2018. https://unctadstat.unctad.org/countryprofile/generalprofile/en-gb/398/index.html.

Vienna Initiative. 2014, Credit Guarantee Schemes for SME lending in Central, Eastern and South-Eastern Europe, www.eib.org.

World Bank. 2015. Project appraisal document on a proposed loan in the amount of US$40 million to the Republic of Kazakhstan for a SME Competitiveness Project. http://documents.worldbank.org/curated/en/120501468253491149/pdf/PAD9560PAD0P14010Box385412B00OUO090.pdf.

World Bank. 2019. https://databank.worldbank.org/home.aspx.

World Bank. 2020. https://www.worldbank.org/en/topic/smefinance.

World Economic Forum. 2016. Alternative investments 2020, *The future of Capital for entrepreneurs and SMEs. Retrieved* http://www3.weforum.org/docs/WEF_AI_FUTURE.pdf.

Yoshino, N. and F. Taghizadeh-Hesary. 2015. Analysis of credit ratings for small and medium-sized enterprises: Evidence from Asia. *Asian Development Review*, 32(2): 18–37.

Part III

Solutions for Easing Small Businesses' Access to Finance

https://doi.org/10.1142/9789811235825_0009

Chapter 9

Credit Guarantee Scheme and Startup Businesses: Financial Pipelines and Successful Startups in South East Asia

Youngho Chang and Wai Mun Kock

*Singapore University of Social Sciences and
Ngee Ann Polytechnic, Singapore
yhchang@suss.edu.sg
KOCK_Wai_Mun@np.edu.sg*

Abstract

Disruption to the traditional businesses have highlighted the importance of startups to the economic well-being of a country. Numerous studies have shown that startups contribute positively to various economic indicators including job creation, economic growth, and improved productivity. Despite the obvious benefits successful startups can bring to the economy, they are not able to obtain sufficient funding persistently which is crucial for startups to grow. This persistent funding gap is often attributed to lack of collateral and asymmetric information on the viability of the products and startups. As a result, many startups could have stagnated as small and medium enterprises (SMEs). This is especially true in South East Asia. Credit guarantee schemes (CGS) could potentially reduce this funding gap to help startups grow. This chapter seeks to review the experiences of four very diverse CGS for comparative studies. These four CGS had contributed to the dynamic growth of the economies which were badly decimated in the Second World War. This chapter also takes stock of the existing CGS in various Southeast Asian countries and seeks to draw valuable lessons for policy implementation from the four CGS.

Keywords: Startup, financial pipeline, credit guarantee scheme

1. Introduction

Digital disruption to all sectors in the economy has suggested that new firms with new viable business solutions are required. Proliferation of various types of technologies such as data science, Artificial Intelligence (AI), Internet of Things (IOT), and Biometric technologies have profoundly impacted all the industries, giving rise to a new industry such as digital-only banks. Many startups were established to provide solutions to address the changing business needs. From a macro perspective, this leads to growing recognition of the contributions of the startups to the economic well-being of a country. Numerous studies have concluded that start-ups can contribute significantly to an economy's job creation (Haltiwanger *et al.*, 2013; Kane, 2010; PWC, 2013), economic growth (MTI, 2018), and/or improved productivity (PWC, 2013). Creating an ecosystem with a vibrant community of successful start-ups in an economy can eventually lift the level of living standards of a country and the well-being of the society. Consequently, governments of several countries including Singapore, Thailand, and Republic of Korea have set up agencies or departments dedicated to providing support for the startups. Startups are a starting point for small but competent Small and Medium Enterprises (SMEs). Nurturing small but competent SMEs should be a key objective of an economy that wishes to grow and ensure its people enjoy a reasonable standard of living. It is too easy to forget that just two decades ago Google was just a start-up. By end of 2019, Google had approximately 118,899 employees with a revenue of US$161,857 million (Alphabet

Annual Report, 2019). Unfortunately, many start-ups remain as SMEs as they lack sufficient funding to grow. In Southeast Asia, SMEs contribute to a sizeable proportion of a country's Gross Domestic Product (GDP) and provide more than half of the employment (ASEAN, 2018). Table 1 shows the structural contribution in terms of the GDP share and the employment ratio of Micro, Small, and Medium Enterprises (MSMEs) in 10 Southeast Asian countries.

Research from World Bank (2017) reported that most of the funds for investment or working capital for SMEs are sourced internally. Banks are the main source of external funding for startups and SMEs. Another survey conducted in United States on small businesses (Federal Reserve New York, 2017) stated that many owners, due to their fear of being heavily in debt, decided not to expand the companies. Collectively, this can represent huge opportunity cost for an economy. The impact of healthy start-ups and SMEs cannot be understated. Yet, despite their mass and significance in all Southeast Asian economies, they rely mainly on relationship banking and face severe difficulties in raising adequate funds that are needed to survive and transform entrepreneurship ideas into real businesses in order to be successful (Yoshino and Taghizadeh-Hesary, 2015). Even in

Table 1: Structural Contribution of MSMEs in Southeast Asia

Country	Share of GDP (%)	Share of Employment (%)	Data Year
Brunei	34.8	54.5	2015
Cambodia	Not available	71.7	2014
Indonesia	61.0	87.8	2016
Lao PDR	Not available	82.2	2014
Malaysia	36.5	65.3	2016
Myanmar	Not available	80.0	Estimate
Philippines	36.0	63.3	2016
Singapore	49.0	65.0	2017
Thailand	42.2	78.5	2016
Viet Nam	45.0	64.0	2015

Source: OECD/ERIA (2018).

developed economies, start-ups and SMEs are severely constraint by credit availability, especially start-ups (Federal Reserve New York, 2017). A survey conducted in United States on small business credit reported that 63% of the firms that were established up to 5 years experienced financing shortfalls when applying for loans compared to 52% reported for small business that were established up to 20 years and 40% for small businesses that were established for more than 20 years. The more severe funding gap experienced by younger firms exacerbate the reduction of job creation as the same survey also concluded that promising startups contribute most to employment gain (Federal Reserve Banks, 2019).

Deloitte (2015) reports that SMEs in Southeast Asian countries are generally under-served or unserved by the banks. Numerous studies have attempted to quantify the SME financing gap (IFC, Mckinsey, 2010; World Bank *et al.*, 2017). Despite differences in the methodology in quantifying the SME financing gap, the consensus is that the SME financing gap is staggering.

A key reason behind banks' tendency not to extend credit to startups and SMEs is asymmetric information where banks have effectively few measures to overcome the information disadvantage. Asymmetric information between borrower and the lender due to the opaque nature of startups and SMEs, where there are few verifiable records (de la Torre *et al.*, 2010; EC, 2006), lack of clarity on the ownership of assets between those owned by the business or owner (EC, 2006), hinder banks' ability to conduct credit assessment. The asymmetric information is more pronounced for startups as they have no credit history, and banks have less information on the innovative products and services (OECD, 2004). Cost inefficiency due to smaller loan size from startups and SMEs reduces incentives for banks (Boocock and Shariff, 2005). Lack of sufficient acceptable collateral also contributed to credit rationing by the banks (Deloitte, 2015; EC, 2006). Even if banks are willing to provide unsecured loan, borrowers are typically charged at a much higher rate (Federal Reserve New York, 2017). Regulatory reforms in the form of Basel Accord III implemented by the banks following the global financial crisis in 2008/2009 has compounded the credit rationing problem for startups and SMEs, especially in economies where the banking systems were not well capitalized (Yoshino and Taghizadeh-Hesary, 2019; Financial

Stability Board, 2019). Consequently, startup founders and SME owners are reliant on personal funds (Fed Reserve of New York, 2019; EU/OECD, 2014). As such, funding gaps for startups and SMEs persist (IFC, 2013; World Bank, SME Finance and IFC, 2017). A survey conducted by European Startup Monitor in 2018 showed that 77.8% of the startups in Europe were financed through savings (ESM, 2018).

Several financial pipelines such as credit guarantee, grants, soft loans, microcredit, crowdfunding, peer-to-peer lending, business angels, and venture capital are listed as tools that startups and SMEs can access for financing (EU/OECD, 2014). All pipelines, with the exception of credit guarantee, provide financing directly to the startups and SMEs. Credit guarantee's mechanism involves facilitating/enabling finance indirectly through its commitment to the source of funds. According to World Bank, "CGS provides third-party credit risk mitigation to lenders through the absorption of a portion of the lender's losses on the loans made to SMEs in case of default, typically in return for a fee." CGS effectively provide insurance to the lender which will reduce the lender's exposure in the case of default.

This chapter seeks to explore effectiveness of using credit guarantee to narrow financing gap to help start-ups survive and be successful. In Section Two, we explore how credit guarantee scheme (CGS) can alleviate startup and SMEs' credit constraint, and their contributions to various stakeholders and the economy. In Section Three, we showcase four different but well-established CGS across Europe and Asia as case studies for learning points and best practices. In Section Four, we review the CGS of selected Southeast Asian countries. In Section Five, we conclude the chapter with observations and recommendations.

2. Literature Review

Not all startups have the potential to contribute to a country's economy. In this chapter, we focus on those startups that, if they survive and grow, will be able to make an immense impact on the country's economy. Thus, we adopted European Startup Monitor (ESM)'s definition for startups. ESM defined startup as any firm that fulfills the three following criteria: 10 years or younger, feature innovative technologies or business models, and strive for significant employee and/or sales growth. We adopt this definition of startup as it most appropriately represents the type of new businesses that, once successful, can contribute to the nation economically such as in terms of employment growth and GDP.

Our definition of successful startups is not "hard coded" by a fixed target of number of innovative technologies developed or percentage of employee growth. We opined that there is no one-size-fits-all definition of success. We defined success as a process where a startup is one which survives, grows, and is capable of exporting its products or services to foreign markets. Our definition of a successful startup does not differentiate whether the startup produces the product offerings completely on its own, and thus sells directly to the consumers who are end-users, or is part of the global value chain in the production process.

Southeast Asia is a heterogeneous region where the stages of economic development among the countries are extremely varied. There are some countries that are relatively mature in economic development such as Singapore and Brunei, while many others are still in the stages of nascent development. Despite the heterogeneity, 10 Southeast Asian nations

Table 2:   Classification, GDP, and GDP per Capita of Southeast Asian Countries

Country	Classification by Income Level	2019 GDP (Current Million US$)	2019 GDP per Capita (US$)
Indonesia	Upper-middle income	1,119,190.78	4,135.57
Thailand	Upper-middle Income	543,649.98	7,808.19
Philippines	Lower-middle Income	376,795.51	3,485.08
Singapore	High Income	372,062.53	65,233.28
Malaysia	Upper-middle Income	364,701.52	11,414.84
Viet Nam	Lower-middle Income	261,921.24	2,715.28
Myanmar	Lower-middle Income	76,085.85	1,407.81
Cambodia	Lower-middle Income	27,089.39	1,643.12
Lao PDR	Lower-middle Income	18,173.84	2,534.90
Brunei Darussalam	High Income	13,469.42	31,086.75

Note: The youngest nation in Southeast Asia, Timor-Leste, is not included in this table.
Source: World Bank Open Data.

are members of a regional group — Association of South East Asian Nations (ASEAN). ASEAN has a population of 661.9 million in 2019 and a combined GDP of USD 3 billion (World Bank Open Data). The only country in Southeast Asia that is not a member of ASEAN is Timur-Leste.

In this chapter, we will scan the largest seven economies in Southeast Asia, collectively termed as SEA-7. They are Indonesia, Thailand, Singapore, Malaysia, Philippines, Viet Nam, and Myanmar. We believe that lessons learned from SEA-7 is largely representative of all Southeast Asian countries as the combined GDP of the largest seven economies account for 98% of the combined GDP of the 10 Southeast Asian countries.

In this comparative analysis, we have chosen four countries with successful CGS (Germany, Italy, Japan, and Republic of Korea) for comparison. All these economies are classified as High Income Economies by World Bank and had extensive experience in implementing credit guarantees in their domestic country with relatively broad outreach.

CGS can be broadly classified into four types: public CGS, corporate CGS, international CGS, and mutual CGS (OECD, 2010). A public CGS is typically owned by government and/or established by public policy. Funds for public CGS are mainly sourced from government with local financial institutions providing the rest. For example, the Republic of Korea's CGS operator was established under the provisions of a legislation — Korea Credit Guarantee Act (KODIT). Corporate CGS are typically owned by private companies. However, owing to their unique position where credit risk are concentrated in corporate CGS, typically CGS will be under some form of supervision. In Germany, the CGS are privately owned supervised credit institutions (KPMG, 2013). Mutual CGS typically operate as private and independent organizations that serve the members. To apply for credit guarantee with mutual CGS, the startup or SME must first apply to be a member (OECD, 2010). These type of CGS are typically funded by the members with support from the government. Germany's CGS was classified as corporate CGS, Italy's CGS operates under mutual CGS, while both Japan and Republic of Korea have public CGS.

Establishment of CGS, either full guarantee or partial guarantee, can help to close the funding gap between the amount that the banks would have lend and the socially optimum amount financing needed by the start-ups and SMEs. Several studies have suggested that credit guarantee schemes would provide the additional funding to the startups and SMEs that would otherwise be unavailable (Beck *et al.*, 2008; Boocock and Shariff, 2005). For the borrowers who had access but inadequate funding, the additional credit support provided by CGS improves startups and SMEs' loan (Beck *et al.*, 2008). Surveys have also shown that CGS is effective in increasing loan available to startups and SMEs (OECD, 2017). Implementation of CGS can also lower the interest cost paid by the borrowers (Beck *et al.*, 2008; D'Ignazio and Menon, 2012). Experience in Italy suggested that implementing CGS can effectively improve the long term viability of the SMEs (D'Ignzaio and Menon, 2019).

CGS's commitment can be regarded as a high quality collateral, subject to CGS operator's credit strength (AECM, 2010). We proposed that CGS's commitment is superior to most collaterals that borrowers posted with the banks. First, unlike other collaterals, CGS's guarantee value will not change with market conditions. Banks would not need to deploy staff to perform valuation of the collateral and to determine the proportion of haircut required. This cost savings from reduction of banking activities can mitigate the high operating cost. In addition, capital adequacy ratios for the banks guarantees may provide regulatory capital relief for banks. In jurisdictions that follow the Basel III rules, guarantees may be treated as unfunded credit protection. As such, guarantees may allow financial institutions to apply lower risk weights to the covered exposures, and thus to reduce the value of risk-weighted assets used in calculating the capital adequacy ratio (Chatzouz *et al.*, 2017).

Some CGS operators, due to the close relationships with startups and SMEs, have demonstrated superior knowledge and insights regarding the prospect of the borrower and the sector that the borrower is operating in. Consequently, CGS operators would be able to conduct a more accurate risk assessment on borrowers. This will help to bridge the information gap between the lending bank and borrower and facilitate credit access to the borrowers (AECM, 2010). Validity of this assertion largely depends on the approach that the CGS adopts. It is more valid if CGS operators adopt individual approach when offering credit guarantees instead of portfolio approach. Under individual approach, CGS operators provide guarantee to specific loans after conducting a risk assessment of the borrowers (World Bank, 2015). CGS operators may have established a relationship with the borrower during credit assessment, which will mitigate the effects of moral hazard. However, under portfolio approach, guarantees are offered by CGS operators to a pool of loans that the CGS operators have not accessed. Instead, CGS operators placed reliance on the lending banks (World Bank, 2015).

Studies have shown that CGS is an effective counter-cyclical tool (KPMG, 2013; EIB, 2014). Data collected by European Association of Guarantee Institutions (AECM) showed that the German Guarantee Banks had drastically increased working capital loans to SMEs during the global financial crisis and had contributed to maintaining more than 851,000 jobs across Europe (AECM, 2010).

CGS are also effective in achieving various economic objectives. A research using UK data showed that the CGS generated other benefits such as increase in employment, exports, improving existing product/services offering and introducing new product/service offerings (Cowling, 2010). Separate studies conducted in Japan also supported the effectiveness of a well-designed credit guarantee scheme (Ono *et al.*, 2010).

Numerous studies have shown that small businesses, including startups, have contributed positively towards job creation (Neumark *et al.*, 2008; Kane, 2010). This conclusion is largely in line with the observation of another study using US data that both small firms contributed disproportionately to employment and output once they survived past the first few years (Haltiwanger *et al.*, 2017). While these data are taken from US, the US experiences have shown that the aggregate impact on employment and output from all start-ups and SMEs will be considerable for the economy as a whole.

One major advantage CGS has over other startup and SMEs' support schemes is that it has less distortive effect on the market compared to other programs such as directed lending or discounted interest rate scheme. This is because the lending decision resides with the lending bank which is in the private sector and a profit-maximizing organization (Honohan, 2008). CGS merely provides support to both lenders and borrowers so that the lending decision in terms of the decision to lend and the amount to lend is potentially socially optimum.

Another advantage highlighted about CGS is the efficiency due to the effect of credit multiplier. The initial funds outlay by government would be lower relative to other expansionary fiscal policies such as directed financing programs (AECM, 2010; Chatzouz, 2017). This is especially attractive during times of severe fiscal strain generated by an economic recession. Governments may not have generated sufficient tax revenue to support the fiscal stimulus and are not able to increase tax rates without economic repercussion.

Despite the advantages, there are criticisms directed towards CGS. Several studies conducted on CGS have shown that CGS tends to attract relatively riskier startups and SMEs with poor creditworthiness and therefore attributed to higher default rates (Li, 1998; Boocock and Shariff, 2005). Concerns regarding asymmetric information on startups are more pronounced especially if lenders do not understand the viability of the start-up's product mix and the market it is serving. Persistent high default rates can hurt the sustainability of CGS in the long run. If the losses of CGS operator are ultimately bourne by the government, this may have an adverse impact on the country's fiscal well-being. To counter this problem, CGS operators should adopt risk-based pricing that penalizes risky startups and SMEs and incentivize borrowers to take concrete actions to manage risk to an acceptable level. And to encourage the borrowers to remain risk conscious after the dispensing of the loan, CGS operators should retain the right to adjust the guarantee fees to reflect CGS operator's risk exposure (World Bank, 2015). In addition, CGS should also adjust the guarantee fee according to the prevailing macroeconomic trends, such as raising the guarantee fee during a boom (Taghizadeh-Hesary *et al.*, 2020).

Another study (Gropp *et al.*, 2014) showed that banks' behavior will alter with CGS such that they are more likely to approve loans that are of poor credit risk if the loans are guaranteed. The payout to the bank is asymmetric — if the loan is honored, the lending bank receives all the interest payment net of guarantee fee; and if the borrower defaults, losses (depending on the coverage) will be bourne by the CGS operator. As such, CGS operators should only offer partial guarantees with a coverage ratio that is sufficiently large enough to induce the banks to lend but also to ensure that banks do retain sufficient risk to mitigate moral hazard. World

Bank (2015) recommends that the coverage should ideally be at least half of the loan amount and CGS operators should retain the right to adjust the coverage ratio depending on CGS operator's risk exposure.

3. Comparative Studies of Credit Guarantee Schemes of Various Countries

In terms of availability of CGS, countries in Southeast Asia are extremely diverse. In terms of income, Southeast Asia had countries designated as High Income (Singapore) and Lower-Middle Incomes (Lao PDR and Cambodia). As for CGS, there are countries with no CGS such as Brunei and Singapore, while there are some countries which have very established CGS such as Malaysia. Given the heterogeneity of Southeast Asia, we selected four countries for comparative analysis, namely Germany, Italy, Japan, and Republic (Rep.) of Korea. These four countries were very badly affected by the Second World War and had to rebuild their economies from scratch. For Rep. of Korea, apart from Second World War, there was another inter-Korean war in the 1950s which delayed the rebuilding efforts. However, the subsequent growth of the economies should provide valuable lessons for Southeast Asian countries.

These four countries were selected for diversity where CGS are either government owned or privately owned. The CGS operators in the Asian economies chosen for comparative analyses are owned ultimately by the government. That contrasted with the CGS operators in the economies chosen in Europe. In Germany, the CGS operators are regional guarantee banks with monopolistic markets in their respective states while the CGS operators in Italy are trade associations with much weaker market power. We believed that valuable lessons to support financing for startups can be learned from the CGS in all four countries. Table 3 summarizes the key features of the CGS in these four countries.

3.1 *Germany*

Germany traced the roots of its credit guarantee to early 1950s when Germans were rebuilding the country in the aftermath of the Second

Table 3:   Summary of the Key Characteristics of CGS in 4 Countries

	Germany	Italy	Japan	Rep. of Korea
Classification of country by Income	High Income	High Income	High Income	High Income
Inception of first CGS operator	1953	1950s	1937	1976
Types of CGS	Corporate	Mutual for Confidi/Public for IGF	Public	Public
Ownership of CGS operators	Private	Private for Confidi/Public for IGF	Public	Public
Re-insurance available for CGS operator	Counter-guarantee from state government and federal government	Counter-guarantee from IGF which is backed by government	Credit Insurance Scheme from JFC which is wholly by government	No
Individual Approach or Portfolio Approach when offering guarantees	Mainly individual	Mainly individual	Mainly individual	Mainly individual
Robust approach to credit risk assessment	Use Common Rating System with input from joint database	Use proprietary Rating Model	Use inputs from SME Credit Risk Database	Use KODIT Rating System for credit assessment and CVaR for credit risk quantification
CGS with specialized program for startups	Yes — such as "Startup Funding 80"	No — but start-ups are given flexibility in terms of the information that is required to be submitted for credit assessment	Yes — Business Assistance Plaza	Yes — "Startup NEST"

Source: Authors' compilation.

World War. Enormous amount of funds were required for the post-war reconstruction activities, but many SMEs were not able to obtain loans due to banks' demand for collateral. Consequently, guarantee societies were established to alleviate SMEs' access to credit by offering their commitment in lieu of a collateral to induce banks to lend (Valentin, 2014). These guarantee societies may have started to morph into guarantee banks offering CGS. As of 2019, there are 17 CGS operators offering credit guarantee to SMEs. Together with 15 SME-oriented investment companies, these 17 CGS operators formed the Association of German Guarantee Banks (Verband Deutscher Bürgschaftsbanken, VDB).

Every single federal state has a local CGS operator. The CGS operators in Germany are corporate CGS which function as private non-profit organizations supporting activities in the federal states they reside. For example, *Burgschaftsbank Baden-Wurttemberg GmbH* only provides guarantees to startups and SMEs residing or operating in the federal state of Baden-Wurttemberg, and would not be able to provide credit guarantees to startups and SMEs in neighboring federal state of Bayern. The capital of these CGS operators are sourced from their shareholders, which are mainly chambers of commerce, business federations of various sectors, banks, and insurance companies (*Verband Deutscher Bürgschaftsbanken, VDB*). The German CGS operators are not allowed to collect deposits and are governed by banking regulations (KPMG, 2011).

The guarantee coveraged underwritten by the CGS operators vary in the range of 50% to 80% depending on the programs. For example, *Burgschaftsbank Baden-Wurttemberg GmbH* has 20 different guarantee programs with some focused on startups, such as "Startup funding 80" which covers 80% of the loan or "Growth Financing" which covers 50% of the loan with varying guarantee fees determined by the risk classification. Some programs are targeted at specific industries such as agriculture or specific type of financing such as equipment financing (*Burgschaftsbank Baden-Wurttemberg GmbH*). Startups and SMEs are charged a flat processing fee of 1% of the approved guarantee and a guarantee commission that is determined by the risk classification ranging from 0.3% p.a. to 2.5% p.a based on outstanding balances.

CGS operators are reinsured by the Federal government and State government through counter-guarantee mechanism that will absorb a substantial proportion of the exposure at default. In the formal Western Germany states, the government will absorb 65% of the remaining exposure while in the formal Eastern Germany states, the government will take over 80% of the remaining exposure (Valentin, 2014). Suppose a startup in the state of Baden-Wurttemberg successfully obtained a loan of €100,000 from a lending bank with a guarantee coverage of 80%. The lending bank will be exposed to potential default loss of €20,000 as Burgschaftsbank Baden-Wurttemberg GmbH, the state CGS operator will guarantee €80,000. The counter-guarantee mechanism, which acts like credit insurance, will transfer 65% of the CGS's exposure to the Federal and the state government. This works out to be €52,000 worth of exposure at default to the government, effectively meaning that *Burgschaftsbank Baden-Wurttemberg GmbH's* exposure was €28,000 for a €100,000.

Germany's CGS operators developed a proprietary rating system, known as "Common Rating System", to help the CGS in assessment of the guarantee applications (Achtelik, 2011). The Common Rating System has three components including qualitative factors, quantitative measures, and macroeconomic elements which will be aggregated to form a total score to project the probability of default based on historical data captured in the database. The qualitative factors are derived from the assessments formed by CGS operator's assessors. Common assessments include firm specific information such as quality of management and projection of the market. Quantitative measures refer to the scoring based on the firm specific data such as financial data of the companies which had received guarantees for their loans. Macroeconomic elements cover sector specific information such as the outlook of the sector and the general macroeconomic performance.

Schmidt and van Elkan (2010) have attempted to quantify the impact of German guarantee banks on the economy in Germany during the global financial crisis by estimating the differences in terms of GDP, employment, and exports where CGS operators provided guarantees to start-ups and SMEs against a projected scenario where CGS were not present. They reported that CGS have positive impact on GDP, employment, and exports.

In conclusion, Germany's CGS operators are pure play companies that only offer sureties to facilitate financing within the ecosystem of support available for startups and SMEs. While addressing the market failure in the capital market for startups and SMEs, its non-participation in direct lending nor collecting deposits, diverse programs with varying levels of guarantee coverages, and risk-based approach towards pricing the guarantee fees resulted in minimal disruption of the financial markets.

3.2 *Italy*

Italy's credit guarantee systems first started in 1950s by entrepreneurs who were seeking ways to improve their access to financing from banks. Banks in Italy then were conservative and required collateral to justify the loan applications. These entrepreneurs started to organize themselves collectively into some form of trade associations in order to improve their market power before the banks. These trade associations were organized by sectors such as industry or agriculture. These trade organizations then slowly evolved into mutual credit guarantee schemes known as *Confidi* (OECD, 2014). To obtain guarantee *Confidi,* these startups or SMEs first apply to be members of the *Confidi.* Other members of the *Confidi,* typically in the same sector, will utilize their in-depth knowledge of the sector, close relationship with the borrowers, and better insights on the outlook of the sector, and appraise the feasibility of loan (OECD, 2014). As such, *Confidi* operates as mutual CGS. The strength of these *Confidi* was the information advantage these *Confidi* have over the lending banks and would be able to narrow down the extent of asymmetric information between the lending banks and the borrowers.

Italian *Confidi* plays an important role in facilitating credit access for startups and SMEs AECM (2018). reports that Italian's *Confidi* account for 39.64% and 27.24% of Europe's total outstanding guarantees in 2016 and 2017, respectively. Thus, any crisis on *Confidi* is able to post systemic risk within Italy and the economic impact may be felt in Italy and its biggest trading partners. Italian Guarantee Fund (IGF) provides counter-guarantees to *Confidi* and direct guarantees to the banks (Arcuri and Ielasi, 2019). For providing counter-guarantees to *Confidi,* it participates in risk sharing akin to re-insuring the *Confidi.* IGF, wholly owned by the Italian government, provides partial guarantees, capped at 80%, to the banks directly for startup and SME loans after the startups and SMEs' application are evaluated using a proprietary Rating Model for creditworthiness. The Rating Model requires information such as financial statements. Startups without financial statements are able to submit pro-forma financial statements instead. For certain innovative startups and certified incubators, applications may be received without a credit assessment (Guarantee Fund website).

D'Ignzaio and Menon (2012) have reported Italy's credit guarantee schemes have achieved the outcome of increasing funding available and lower financing cost for the startups. A further study by D'Ignzaio and Menon in 2019 also reported the improvement of long-term viability of SMEs that received support through credit guarantee (D'Ignzaio and Menon, 2019).

Italy's CGS market is big and fragmented. While *Confidi* are mutual CGS, IGF is a public CGS. As of 2016, there were 480 credit guarantees in Italy in which 108 of them were closed or liquidated and 12 of them did not offer guarantees (Bongiovanni and Rovera, 2018). IGF listed 140 affiliated *Confidi* which it provides counter guarantees to. With the exception of a few *Confidi* such as Italia Com-Fidi, most *Confidi* operate within their own region. The weakness of Italy's credit guarantee market was the instability where two of the three biggest *Confidi* (Eurofidi and Unionfidi) as of 2009 had failed. Despite this weakness, Italy's system of mutual CGS have narrowed the information gap between the borrower and CGS.

3.3 *Japan*

Japan has the world's oldest network of public credit guarantees and extensive experiences of utilizing CGS dating back to 1930s. There are 51 CGS operators in Japan organized geographically in which each prefecture and the cities of Nagoya, Yokohama, Kawasaki, and Gifu have a dedicated CGS operator. All CGS operators in Japan are public CGS and are governed under the legislation "Credit Guarantee Corporation Act". Japan's CGS is part of Japan's credit supplementation system which consists of CGS, which is administered by the 51 CGS operators, and credit insurance, which is operated by Japan Finance Corporation (JFC). Japan Finance Corporation, wholly owned by the Japanese government, established a credit insurance scheme that provides additional support to Japan's credit guarantee scheme. The complementary credit insurance scheme to CGS is similar to the reinsurance concept where insurance companies pool their risks together in order for individual insurance companies to mitigate their risks to improve their solvency.

In 2017, Japan's CGS collectively guaranteed close to 10% of all the loans made to SME (Website, Uesugi, RIETI, 2017) as compared to the Asian average of 2.7% (Abraham and Schmukler, 2017), which suggested that Japan's CGS has high utilization rate compared to their Asians peers. Japan has also enacted a legislation in 2017, commonly known as Credit Guarantee System Reform Act. The summary of the reform act includes amending the guarantee coverage ratio from full coverage to 80% and shifting from a flat guarantee fee structure to a floating, risk-based guarantee fee structure (Website and Yamori, 2017). Other items in this reform bill include the creation of a new credit guarantee facility with full coverage that will only be invoked under a specific set of conditions such as a major economic crisis, expanding a credit guarantee scheme for feasible startups and SMEs, and improved transparency and information sharing on all parts of the loan whether it is guaranteed or not guaranteed (Website, Uesugi, and RIETI, 2017).

Since the Japanese reform to introduce risk-based guarantee fee structure, the risk classification recorded in the SME Credit Risk database has become the reference for the determination of the guaranteed fee. One financial database, Credit Risk Database (CRD), develops scoring models for SMEs and holds the information in an anonymous form (Kuwahara *et al.*, 2015). CRD can help bridge the information gap in its work as, while it provides the privacy that many startups and SMEs appreciate, it provides the credit risk rating that CGS and banks require.

For loans made to startups and SMEs, the risk is shared among the lending bank, the CGS operator, and JFC (Yasushi, 2016). Suppose an SME defaults on a loan that is partially guaranteed by a CGS operator, the lending bank will be exposed to 20% of the loan at default. The remaining 80% will be absorbed by the CGS operator. Due to Japan's credit supplementation system involving JFC's credit insurance for the CGS operators, the CGS operator can claim insurance between 70% to 90% of the remaining liability depending on the credit insurance. Suppose the CGS operator claims 70% of the remaining liability with JFC, it will work out to be 56% of the loan amount. As such, the effective proportion of risk sharing ratio among lending bank, CGS operator, and JFC will be 20%, 24%, and 56%, respectively.

The biggest CGS operator in Japan is Credit Guarantee Corporation of Tokyo (CGCT). As of March 2018, CGCT reported that close to 40% of the SMEs operating in Tokyo Metropolitan utilized product offerings from CGCT. Following the reform in 2017, the guarantee coverage was reduced from full guarantee to a flat partial guarantee of 80% of the entire outstanding loan. Guarantee fee varies from 0.45% to 2.2%, dependent on risk classification. Adopting individual approach, CGCT appraises and grants all guarantee applications. The default rate for CGCT hovers around 2% (CGCT, annual report, 2018). The main criticism of lowering guarantee ratio of 80% to all lending institutions, regardless of the risk exposure, is moral hazard. This may incentivize banks to reduce the underwriting standards so that the banks are confident that they can recover their share of the loans. Consequently, banks with higher exposure to non-performing loans should receive lower coverage compared to safer lending institutions. This should help to improve sustainability of CGCT and reduce the potential fiscal stress of Japan.

CGCT supported startups through various channels. This includes offering discounted credit guarantee fees for startups, conducting courses related to startups and engaging startups in post-launch follow up (CGCT, annual report, 2017). CGCT's Business Assistance Plaza offers end-to-end support for start-up SMEs including advisory services and financing guarantee, etc.

In conclusion for the Japanese experience, Japanese CGS operates within credit supplementation system where it works in tandem with credit insurance scheme. The focus is to encourage banks to supply sufficient credit for startups through underwriting a substantial portion of the bank's loan to startups and SMEs. Japanese CGS operators will then transfer a substantial portion of their risks to JFCs. As a result, the Japanese government effectively provides the guarantee for all the loans with the different layers absorbing part of the risk. So as long as the Japanese government's creditworthiness continue to provide sufficient confidence, this programme will sustain. In recent years, Japan CGS operators have also started to offer programs to support entrepreneurs holistically in startups.

3.4 *Republic of Korea*

The Republic of Korea has an established CGS program and has been frequently invited by foreign countries to share its experience of creating CGS, such as Viet Nam and Kazakhstan. Like many public CGS, Republic of Korea's CGS are public CGS and are established under several legislations. Rep. of Korea's largest CGS operator, Korea Credit Guarantee Fund (KODIT), has been established under Korea Credit Guarantee Fund Act in 1976. Korea Technology Finance Corporation was established under the Korea Technology Credit Guarantee Fund Act in 1989 and specialized in facilitating the funding of technology startups. the Republic of Korea's CGS operators supervised by Financial Services Commission (FSC) are subjected to audit by the Board of Audit and Inspection of Korea.

KODIT is the most established CGS operator in Rep. of Korea. Until 1989, KODIT was the only CGS operator in the Rep. of Korea. Lee *et al.* (2018) reported KODIT's contribution to Rep. of Korea's GDP through observing a positive relationship between the volume of credit guarantees underwritten by KODIT and Rep. of Korea's GDP. They also reported that the Rep. of Korea, which had a credit guarantee volume equivalent to 5.3% of its GDP in 2014, had high outreach relative to Thailand and Indonesia for the entire period 2001 to 2014. Serving almost all sectors within the economy and with a relative high outreach of guarantee, KODIT has effectively concentrated bulk of the country's SMEs' credit risk onto itself. As such, risk management is one of the core focuses of KODIT.

KODIT has developed internal credit rating models for corporates (Kodit Rating System for Corporation) and start-ups (Kodit Rating System for Start-ups), for the purpose of loan approval and more robust risk management (KODIT, 2016). KRS is integral to the KODIT's credit risk management. Inputs from KRS will factor into its credit Value-at-Risk (VaR) system in measuring and monitoring its credit risk exposure. The credit risk management system seems to be functioning well as its default rate has been in the range of 4% to 5% since the global financial crisis in 2008/2009. KODIT credits the well-functioning of KRS to its emphasis on data quality, sufficiency, and accuracy (Lee *et al.*, 2018). Apart from credit risk, KODIT has also focused on liquidity risk and operational risk. Liquidity risk management relates to the budgeting of its cash flow and monitoring its outstanding guarantees in ensuring that its assets and liabilities are well-matched and well-placed to cope with exogenous adverse liquidity constraints. Operational risk relates to risk controls and other measures that staff in KODIT adhere to in keeping with KODIT's policies and processes when dispensing their responsibilities. To top it up, KODIT is also subjected to audit periodically. Thus, KODIT's risk management model is similar to the most commonly adopted "Three Lines of Defense" risk management framework among the banks.

KODIT, adopting an individual approach, provides partial guarantees for the loans with the coverage ratio in the range of 70% to 85% depending on the tenure and the risk classification of the company applying for the loan. The guarantee fee is a risk-based fee in the range of 0.5% to 3.0%, which reflects the credit risk of the enterprise applying for the loan. Apart from providing support to startups and SMEs, KODIT has also been mandated by legislation, "Act on Public–Private Partnership in Infrastructure" through Korea Infrastructure Credit Guarantee Fund (KICGF) to support private firms to obtain sufficient loans for infrastructure construction.

KODIT has established a platform, "Startup NEST (New Expandability Startup Total Platform)", that acts as both an incubator and accelerator for promising startups by providing both financial and non-financial support. "Startup NEST" support consists of 4 stages. The first stage involves a selection process whereby start-ups can apply to enroll in this program. Training will be provided during this stage and selection will be made by an evaluation committee. Selected start-ups will move into the second stage known as "accelerating", where consultancy services, mentoring, networking opportunities are provided. On completing the second stage, these start-ups will move into the third stage where financial support including credit guarantees, venture capital, and crowdfunding will be afforded to these start-ups. The last stage in "Startup NEST" aims to position these startup for growth by providing professional services including technology consulting, marketing support, and overseas expansion. It is also noted that KODIT purchases bonds issued by venture capitals as a way to indirectly support start-ups through these venture capitals.

Concluding Rep. of Korea's CGS experience is tantamount to concluding KODIT's experience. A key differentiating feature of KODIT is the emphasis on its risk management. While KODIT is principally funded by the Rep. of Korea's government, KODIT did not have a safety net for itself to transfer its risk away. In fact, KODIT manages its risk through a robust set of risk management activities. The way KODIT defines its risk boundaries, such as credit risk and operational risk, and its three lines of defense model, is reminiscent of a bank. Like banks, KODIT created proprietary credit risk rating mechanism and integrated that in its credit risk management process. Like many banks which use VaR in quantifying risk exposure, KODIT uses credit VaR to measure and monitor its credit exposure. For the support of start-ups, KODIT champions programs like "Start-up NEST" by providing holistic support directly or indirectly to develop high potential start-ups.

4. Overview of Southeast Asia

Start-ups and SMEs in Southeast Asia also faced constraints in raising funds from the banks (Deloitte, 2015; EY *et al.*, 2018). A study by the World Bank in 2017 attempted to quantify the financing gaps for Micro, Small, and Medium Enterprises (MSME) in the emerging economies (World Bank, SME Finance Forum, IFC, 2017). This study covered all of SEA-7 except for Singapore as Singapore is not classified as an emerging economy based on the income level classification. The methodology adopted by World Bank for the computation of MSME Finance Gap is to find the difference between potential demand for funds by MSME in each country and the existing supply of finance for MSME. In a separate study on Singapore, Chang and Rimaud (2018) observed that there are funds that are not supplied to SMEs. Going by the same reasoning from MSME Finance Gap, we can deduce that Singapore's SMEs also faced finance gaps.

Table 4: Financing Gap of SEA-7

Country	Income Level	MSME Finance Gap/GDP	Existence of CGS	Types of CGS
Indonesia	Upper-middle Income	19%	Yes	Public
Thailand	Upper-middle Income	10%	Yes	Public
Singapore	High Income	N.A	No	No
Malaysia	Upper-middle Income	7%	Yes	Public
Philippines	Lower-middle Income	76%	Yes	Public
Viet Nam	Lower-middle Income	12%	Yes	Public
Myanmar*	Lower-middle Income	21%	No	Public

Note: *Myanmar currently does not have a specialized credit guarantee scheme operator. Credit guarantee is currently offered by state-owned Myanma Insurance.
Source: World Bank, MSME Finance Gap report; authors' own compilation.

Table 4 shows the Finance Gap estimated by World Bank as a proportion of GDP for seven Southeast Asian countries.

Southeast Asia has a long history with credit guarantees. Apart from Singapore, the other 6 countries had CGS to support SME's access to financing. While Singapore does not have a dedicated CGS, Singapore government had several loan guarantee schemes to support trade finance and export. Indonesia and Malaysia have started utilizing CGS to support local SMEs since 1970s while Myanmar is in the midst of starting its own credit guarantee scheme. Credit guarantee scheme operators in Southeast Asia are all state-owned and have social objectives in addition to facilitating credit to SMEs. Despite Southeast Asia's long experience with credit guarantee, Lee reported that the CGS outreach has not been high with the exception of Thailand. In what follows, we will briefly explore the various CGS in the Southeast Asian countries.

4.1 *Indonesia*

SMEs, of which many are start-ups, contributed 61% of the GDP and 87.8% of the employment in 2016, in Indonesia (ASEAN, 2018). This indicates that the driving growth among start-ups and SMEs can greatly lift the country's economy. World Bank estimated the finance gap amounts to 19% of Indonesia's GDP, suggesting that inadequate access to financing or credit rationing for SMEs is still a major concern. CGS operators in Indonesia should more actively generate the awareness of credit guarantees. Indonesia was the first country to establish a credit guarantee scheme in South East Asia. Today, Indonesia has 2 tiers of credit guarantees — 2 CGS operators operate nationally (Jamkrindo and Askrido) and the other 18 regional CGS operators operate at a provincial level. The first CGS operator, Jamkrindo, was set up as a public CGS operator in 1970 to facilitate loans to SMEs from both banks and non-bank financial institutions. As a public CGS operator, it is wholly owned by government who provided all the initial capital and is regulated by the Ministry of State-Owned Enterprises. (OECD/ERIA, 2018) KPMG (2011) reported that Jamkrindo is one of the important CGS operators in the world as of December 2009. Like all CGS operators in Indonesia, Jamkrindo offers partial credit guarantee to the borrowing micro and SMEs who had limited quantity of collateral than the banks accepted. Jamkrindo does not have any specialized program for start-ups. While CGS operators such as Jamkrindo do not initiate programs to support start-ups, there are programs offered by various organizations such as the Ministry of Cooperative and SME Startup Incubator Program and the 1,000 Startups Movement.

The coverage ratios offered by Indonesia CGS operators differ from operator to operator, but the upper limit of the coverage ratios tends to be 75%. For Jamkrindo, the guarantee fee ranges from 0.5% to 1.5% depending on the risk assessed. One interesting observation on Jamkrindo's risk assessment is that it takes into account business continuity planning (BCP) when performing risk assessment. SMEs with a robust BCP will be given a favorable rating and thus enjoy either a higher coverage or lower guarantee fee (Jamkrindo). Given that Indonesia is frequently exposed to natural disasters such as earthquakes or volcanic eruptions, the differentiated interest rates or coverage will incentivize SMEs and the business owners to be aware of the risk to business, and thus effectively reducing the problem of moral hazard for Jamkrindo.

Alternative sources of financing are also gaining traction in Indonesia. There are FinTech companies involved in peer-to-peer lending, crowdfunding platforms, and microfinancing from several state-owned banks.

4.2 *Thailand*

Thailand's SMEs had contributed 42.2% of the country's GDP and accounted for 78.5% of employment in 2016 (ASEAN, 2018). For an economy where more than three-quarters of the employees generate less than half of the country's GDP, it suggests that more resources should be made available for SMEs to improve productivity, and for Thailand's economic performance to grow tremendously. Thailand, according to World Bank estimates, has one of the smallest finance gaps in South East Asia, an outcome that is largely aligned with Lee's observation that Thailand's CGS operator has a relatively high outreach (Lee, 2017). Thailand's CGS operator, Thai Credit Guarantee Corporation (TCG), was established by the Ministry of Finance in 1991 to alleviate the financing constraints faced by SMEs to help them acquire more loans from banks. TCG is a public CGS and is the only CGS operator in Thailand. It was established after Thailand enacted the "Small Industry Credit Guarantee Corporation Act". According to Lee, TCG has been relatively successful in reaching out to the SMEs. Although it is a public institution, the capital is provided by the government and various financial institutions. TCG also offers partial guarantee or up to 50% of guarantee portfolio where the guarantee limit of each borrower is capped at 40 million Baht (Panyanukul *et al.*, 2014). TCG practises mainly portfolio guarantee approach to drive CGS utilization. TCG relies on its partnering banks to assess the applicants. The guarantee fee of 1% to 2% varies according to the schemes taken by the borrower (TCG website).

TCG has specific schemes targeting start-ups and innovative technology entrepreneurs. These include giving preferential rates for the guarantee fee such as government absorbing the first year's guarantee fee. This works in tandem with other forms of support from Startup Thailand, which is a public organization that was established to foster innovative start-ups and the ecosystems (Startup Thailand website). TCG also has specific programs supporting SMEs in industry or projects that the government is keen to develop. In the cases of guarantees of the government targeted projects, government will absorb the first year's guarantee fee. Thus, TCG is also a policy tool used by Thailand government to support its national development strategy.

4.3 *Singapore*

In 2017, small firms in Singapore contributed to 49% of the country's GDP and accounted for 65% of the employees (ASEAN, 2018). Compared to other Southeast Asian countries, Singapore SMEs' performance was relatively respectable. While World Bank did not include Singapore in its exercise to quantify finance gap, Singapore's start-ups and SMEs do face constraints in financing even though Singapore has a developed banking system with sufficient liquidity (Chang and Rimaud, 2018). Singapore does not have a CGS operator. However, there are schemes that resemble credit guarantees provided by the Singapore government in partnership with the banks in the form of insurance. Enterprise Singapore, a government agency, has several insurance schemes for startups and SMEs. This includes Loan Insurance Scheme (LIS), which allows sharing of risk between lending banks and commercial insurance companies on loans made to SMEs, and Trade Credit Insurance Scheme (TCIS) which partially insures enterprises from loss from defaulting customers (Enterprise Singapore website n.d.). However, existing insurance schemes for startups and SMEs in Singapore are restrictive and may not have sufficient support for SMEs' growth.

Apart from loans from the banks, Singapore has a growing platform of FinTech companies that serve as alternative source of financing for startups and SMEs. There are crowdfunding platforms and peer-to-peer lending platforms that provide financial support as well.

The Singaporean government has been aggressive in providing support for start-ups. Enterprise Singapore has initiated a program — Startup Singapore — that provides both financial and non-financial support to entrepreneurs. This includes facilitating mentoring for the startup founders, establishing incubators and accelerators, creating a platform for investors such as venture capitalists.

4.4 *Malaysia*

Malaysia's SMEs, in 2016, have contributed to 65.3% of the country's GDP while accounting for 36.6% of the workforce (ASEAN, 2018), indicating potential for strong economic growth should capital be available for SMEs to boost their productivity. However, Malaysia's narrow finance gap (7% of its GDP) among SEA-7 according to World Bank may have cast a different picture. Interpreting World Bank's estimation, Malaysia's SMEs faced the least constraints on accessing credit among the emerging countries of Southeast Asia. Malaysia has quite a mature banking system and there are also numerous platforms for alternative financing such as microcredit, peer-to-peer lending, and crowdfunding. Isenberg (2010) reported that Malaysia's Ministry of Entrepreneur and Cooperative Development disbursed grants to 90% of the applicants in 2006, reflecting strong support from government. This suggests that Malaysia's SMEs require other types of support in addition to financial support in order to grow and be successful.

Malaysia had 1 CGS operator, Credit Guarantee Corporation Malaysia Berhad (CGCM), which facilitated credit to the country's SMEs by providing guarantees to overcome SMEs' difficulty of accessing credit. Established in 1972 by Malaysia's central bank (Bank Negara) and several financial institutions, CGCM is a public CGS. CGCM had evolved from a pure-play credit guarantee provider to an organization that provides other financial products such as direct financing (CGCM Annual Report). Lee (2017) classified CGCM's utilization rate as middle, which is lower compared to Japan, Rep. of Korea, and Thailand but higher than Philippines and Viet Nam. CGCM had started to embrace portfolio guarantee approach in partnership with selected commercial banks such as Malayan Banking Berhad, Affin Islamic Bank, and Standard Chartered Bank Malaysia. This is expected to improve the utilization rate in the following years. The guarantee coverage of CGCM ranges from 50% to 90% depending on the scheme applied.

Malaysia has comprehensive schemes for the startups. The government agency Malaysia Digital Economy Corporation (MDEC) set up to nurture Malaysia's startup ecosystem in technology related companies initiated programs like Malaysia Tech Entrepreneur Programme. Both financial and non-financial support can be sourced by tech startups in MDEC. CGCM does not have a specialized program to support startups.

4.5 *Philippines*

Philippines's SMEs have contributed to 63.3% of GDP and 36% of the workforce in 2016 (ASEAN, 2018). Among the SEA-7, Philippines has the biggest Finance Gap (76% of Philippines' GDP) according to World Bank's estimate and Lee (2017) also reported low utilization of CGS in Philippines. Combining all these statistics, this provides a prima facie case that making credit accessible to SMEs can have strong effect on Philippines's economic growth. There is a potential, huge untapped market for credit guarantees and Philippines CGS operators can do more to generate awareness of credit guarantees. Philippines have two major CGS operators — Small Business Corporation (SBC) and BSP Credit Surety Fund (CSF). SBC was formed in 2001 after its 2 predecessors, The Small Business Guarantee and Finance Corporation (SBGFC) and Guarantee Fund for Small and Medium Enterprises (GFSME), were merged due to a Presidential Executive Order (SBC website). Apart from offering guarantees for loan, SBC also provides microcredit for startup owners. The size of the loan is dependent on the scale of the business and the startup owners' capacity to repay the loan.

CSF was established by Philippines Central Bank under Credit Surety Fund Cooperative Act in 2015. Both CGS operators were public CGS and were established to help MSMEs to overcome the lack of collateral when applying for loans with credit institutions. One of the stated objectives of CSF is to drive more economic activities and generate employment opportunities in Philippines. Apart from providing guarantees for MSMEs, CSF also conducts training on finance, credit, and risk management (CSF Website). CSF offers partial guarantee of 80% of the loan and charges a guarantee fee not exceeding 5% depending on the CSF Cooperative policies.

The Philippines government also supports startups by the enactment and implementation of Innovation Startup Act and Youth Entrepreneurship Act as a means to institutionalize and mobilize support for startups. Department of Trade and Industry established a Startup Ecosystem Development Plan to provide a platform where startups and their supporting clusters are able to form a critical mass to create a sustainable network of startups.

4.6 *Viet Nam*

SMEs in Viet Nam accounted for 45% of Viet Nam's GDP and 64% of Viet Nam's workforce. Its MSME finance gap, according to World Bank estimate, is 12% of the GDP. Viet Nam's data suggest its situation is similar to neighboring Thailand where there is insufficient financing for SMEs to make investments to raise their productivity. Le and Anh (2019) have reported that lack of access to credit from the banks is the largest constraint to grow and success for Viet Nam's SMEs. Pham and Oleksandr (2016) attributed this to collateral requirement. Combining all these statistics and observations together, it is possible to build a case around the positive impact of highly utilized credit guarantee schemes that make credit accessible to a broader base of startups and SMEs by navigating past the collateral requirement.

Viet Nam has two different tiers of credit guarantees, with the Viet Nam Development Bank administering a credit guarantee nationwide and the remaining credit guarantees operating locally. Viet Nam Development Bank Credit Guarantee Fund, wholly owned by Viet Nam's government, is a public CGS. Among the factors to be considered by CGS operators on the coverage ratio, Le and Anh (2019) have noted that coverage ratio should be evaluated according to "feasibility and risk level of each enterprise, its investment project, and its production and business plan." Le and Anh (2019) have observed that Viet Nam's existing guarantee fees are between 0.5% to 1% per annum.

Like most countries in Southeast Asia, support for entrepreneurship is mainly geared towards the technology industry. Ministry of Science and Technology had launched an accelerator known as Vietnam Silicon Valley in which both financial support and non-financial support can be sourced. Examples of financial support would be the invitation to venture capital and angel finance to provide seed funding. Non-financial support includes logistics and education (Vietnam Silicon Valley website).

4.7 *Myanmar*

The World Bank estimated that Myanmar's MSME finance gap is 21% of Myanmar's GDP, suggesting that there is a lot of scope for improvement. Myanmar does not have a CGS operator to offer guarantee to startups and SMEs. Instead, Myanmar's credit guarantee is currently offered by Myanmar state-owned Myanma Insurance through partnerships with various banks, such as Myanmar Citizens Bank (MCB), CB Bank, Myanmar

Agri Development Bank (MADB), Myanma Economic Bank, and United Amara Bank (UAB) (GIZ, 2018). The coverage offered by the credit guarantee insurance is 60% (July 2018).

Myanmar's economy is still in the nascent stage of development. The focus of economic development is still attracting foreign investment and supporting local companies especially SMEs, which account for 80% of the employment (OECD/ERIA, 2018). Startup developments are mainly driven from the private sector. For example, SeedMyanmar, a program started by Vulpes Investment Manager provides seed funding. Private sector also leads efforts to create accelerator programs such as Phandeeyar Accelerator. The government is focused on SMEs, it enacted an SME Development Law in 2015.

Myanmar's local newspaper reported in July 2018 that Myanma Insurance is in the midst of preparing to establish a Credit Guarantee Corporation which will institutionalize the function of offering credit guarantees.

5. Conclusion and Policy Recommendations

Today's startups can be tomorrow's unicorns, only if the startups are allowed to grow. Southeast Asia, with a young population and huge internal market, has the potential to grow its own startups, especially the fast growing innovative sector. A joint study conducted by Google, Temasek and Bain forecasted that South East Asia's internet economy is going to grow from US$100 billion in 2019 to US$300 billion in 2025. Many governments are actively supporting startups with various incubators and acceleratos programs. However, lack of sufficient financing remains inadequately addressed. Policy makers should consider developing a credit guarantee scheme aimed at targeting innovative startups that can neither access sufficient bank loans nor attract equity financing.

Several insights can be drawn in the comparative studies.

Successful CGS also relied heavily on objective and quantitative measures of appraising credit risk exposure. Among the four highlighted CGS, all of them developed quantitative approach towards credit risk modeling. This could involve building a credit risk database to develop the basis for a credit risk rating system. CGS of Germany, Japan, and Republic of Korea had invested extensively in setting up a database whose information formed the basis for its credit risk assessment. Nevertheless, for innovative startups, this remains one of the most challenging obstacles for CGS and lending institutions to navigate as these startups have little data to allow modeling of their credit risk.

Successful CGS should always be able to appraise the risk exposure to the borrowers instead of relying on the lending institutions. The scope of appraisal should also include an appraisal on the viability of the startups' products and services offering mix. While Germany, Italy, Japan, and Rep. of Korea's CGS adopted individual approaches to assess each applicant, only Italy's mutual CGS confers the CGS information advantage. For example, if a FinTech company needs to raise funding in a relatively new technology that has almost no avenue of applications, a mutual CGS would be helpful as appraisers of the loans would probably be extensively involved in the financial technology industry. While the authors agree that such an approach will result in higher operating cost, technologies such as data science, Internet of Things (IoT), and artificial intelligence can help to mitigate the increased operating cost.

The success and sustainability of a CGS depends largely on the right mix of guarantee coverage ratio and the guarantee fee. A study using Iranian data shows that optimal guarantee coverage ratio is jointly determined by (i) government policies on non-performing loans and support for SMEs, (ii) prevailing macroeconomic indicators, and (iii) intrinsic behavior of the lending institutions (Yoshino and Taghizadeh-Hesary, 2019). The authors opined that administratively this could be difficult, but believe that better communication with stakeholders and greater reliance on statistical techniques would achieve that. With regards to guarantee fee, the fee differential across various risk classifications should be substantial enough to reduce moral hazard and encourage applicants to practice better decision-making in both risk governance and launching new products/services. All four CGS showcased in the comparative studies used risk-based approach for charging guarantee fees. In Japan's case, the financial support by JFC for the risk-sharing could have also incentivized the banks to come onboard the CGS program, thus benefitting more startups and SMEs.

The authors opined that establishing a CGS for innovative startups not only improves their odds of success, but also has spillover effects to bring immense benefits to the country. However, a successful CGS servicing these innovative startups requires a knowledge domain beyond the traditional financial services one. The authors believe that a successful CGS should be a partnership of government, banks, insurance companies, technology companies, trade associations (such as FinTech association), leading educational institutions, or even supranational organizations (such as OECD or ADB). Each will bring its own expertise to the CGS that will help the CGS address and navigate the challenges due to the inherent nature of startups, while directing the funding towards those with the highest probability of success.

References

Abraham, Facundo, Schmukler. Sergio L., 2017, Are Public Credit Guarantees Worth the Hype?, Work Bank Document, Retrieved from http://documents1. worldbank.org/curated/en/431261511201811430/pdf/Are-public-credit-guarantees-worth-the-hype.pdf

Achtelik, O. 2011. Guarantee systems in European Union countries — searching for the best model. The German Guarantee Banks. Warsaw.

AECM. 2010. Guarantees and the recovery: The impact of anti-crisis guarantee measures. Retrieved from https://aecm.eu/wp-content/uploads/2015/07/report-on-performance-of-anti-crisis-guarantee-measures1.pdf.

AECM. 2018. AECM members statistic overview. Retrieved from https://aecm. eu/wp-content/uploads/2018/06/Facts-and-Figures-2017-for-web.pdf.

Alphabet Inc. , 2020, Alphabet Inc. 2019. Annual Report. Retrieved from https://abc.xyz/investor/static/pdf/2019_alphabet_annual_report.pdf?cache=c3a4858

Arcuri, M. C., L. Gai, and F. Ielasi. 2019. Italian central guarantee fund: An analysis of the guaranteed SMEs' default risk. Retrieved from https://publications.waset.org/10010299/italian-central-guarantee-fund-an-analysis-of-the-guaranteed-smes-default-risk.

ASEAN. 2018. Boosting competitiveness and inclusive growth. Retrieved from https://asean.org/wp-content/uploads/2018/08/Report-ASEAN-SME-Policy-Index-2018.pdf.

ASEAN. 2018. SME policy index: ASEAN 2018: Boosting competitiveness and inclusive growth. Retrieved from https://asean.org/wp-content/uploads/2018/08/Report-ASEAN-SME-Policy-Index-2018.pdf.

ASEAN. 2019. Asean statistical leaflet 2019. Retrieved from https://www.aseanstats.org/wp-content/uploads/2019/11/ASEAN_Stats_Leaflet_2019.pdf.

Beck, T., L.F. Klapper, and J.C. Mendoza. 2008. The typology of partial credit guarantee funds around the world.

Bongiovanni, A. and C. Rovera. 2018. The determinants of the confidi delinquency rate . Retrieved from https://doi.org/10.5539/ijbm.v13n4p87.

Boocock, Grahame, Shariff, Mohd Noor Mohd., 2005. Measuring the effectiveness of credit guarantee schemes, International Small Business Journal.

CGC. 2018. CGC annual review website 2018. Retrieved from https://www.cgc.com.my (Accessed on September 01, 2020).

Chatzouz, M., A. Gereben, F. Lang, and W. Torfs. 2017. Credit guarantee schemes for SME lending in Western Europe. Retrieved from https://www01.eib.org/attachments/efs/economics_working_paper_2017_02_en.pdf.

Chang, Y. and Cedric Rimaud, 2019. "Small and Medium-sized Enterprises' Financing in Singapore," in *Unlocking SME Finance in Asia: Roles of Credit Rating and Credit Guarantee Scheme*, edited by Naoyuki Yoshino and Farhad Taghizadeh-Hesary, ADBI, OECD and Routledge, pp. 316–336.

Chau, T. 2018. Myanma Insurance to cover 60pc of CGI-backed loans. Retrieved from https://www.mmtimes.com/news/myanma-insurance-cover-60pc-cgi-backed-loans.html.

Cowling, M. 2010. Economic evaluation of the small firms loan guarantee scheme. Retrieved from https://www.employment-studies.co.uk/system/files/resources/files/bis10512.pdf.

Credit Guarantee Corporation of Tokyo. (n.d.). Annual report 2017. Retrieved from 2017: https://www.cgc-tokyo.or.jp/about/public/annualreport2017.pdf.

Credit Surety Fund . 2015. Credit surety fund cooperative act of 2015. Retrieved from https://www.bsp.gov.ph/ (Accessed on September 01, 2020).

Dang, L.N. and A.T. Chuc. 2019. Challenges in implementing the credit guarantee scheme for small and medium-sized enterprises: The case of Viet Nam. Retrieved from https://www.adb.org/sites/default/files/publication/496271/adbi-wp941.pdf.

de la Torre Augusto, Peria Maria Soledad Martinez, Schmukler Sergio L., 2010. Bank Involvement with SMEs: Beyond relationship lending, Journal of Banking & Finance

Deloitte. 2015. Digital banking for small and medium-sized enterprises. Improving access to finance for the underserved.

D'Ignazio, A. and C. Menon. 2012. The casual effect of credit guarantees for SMEs: Evidence from Italy. Retrieved from https://pdfs.semanticscholar.org /5fdd/42d383de6794b9fdd65bc59fe097a6f26e30.pdf.

D'Ignazio, A. and C. Menon, C. Causal Effect of Credit Guarantees for Small- and Medium-Sized Enterprises: Evidence from Italy, The Scandinavian Journal of Economics, 2018.

EBCI. 2014. Credit guarantee schemes for SME lending in central, eastern and south-Eastern Europe. Retrieved from https://www.eib.org/attachments/efs/ viwg_credit_guarantee_schemes_report_en.pdf.

Enterprise Singapore. (n.d.). Trade Credit Insurance Scheme (TCIS). Retrieved from https://www.enterprisesg.gov.sg/ (Accessed on September 01, 2020).

Ernst & Young, United Overseas Bank, Dun & Bradstreet, 2018. Asean SMEs: Are you Transforming for the Future, Retrieved from https://assets.ey.com/ content/dam/ey-sites/ey-com/en_sg/topics/financial-services/asean-smes-are-you-transforming-for-the-future.pdf?download

ESM, 2018, EU Startup Monitor 2018 Report, Retrieved from http://startupmonitor. eu/EU-Startup-Monitor-2018-Report-WEB.pdf (Accessed on September 01, 2020)

European Commission. 2006. Guarantees and mutual guarantees.

European Investment Bank, Credit Guarantee Schemes for SME Lending in Central, Eastern and South-Eastern Europe, 2014.

Falk, D. (n.d.). Economic impact of credit guarantees: The case of Germany. Retrieved from http://www.economistiassociati.com/files/Falk_Credit_ Guarantee_Funds_Germany_ENGLISH.pdf.

Federal Reserve Bank. 2017. Small business credit survey. Retrieved from https:// www.newyorkfed.org/medialibrary/media/smallbusiness/2016/SBCS-Report-EmployerFirms-2016.pdf.

Federal Reserve Bank of New York. 2017. Small business credit survey.

Federal Reserve Bank of New York. 2017. Small business credit survey. Retrieved from https://www.newyorkfed.org/medialibrary/media/smallbusiness/2016/ SBCS-Report-StartupFirms-2016.pdf.

Federal Reserve Banks. 2019. Small Business Credit Survey: 2019 Report on Employer Firms. Retrieved from https://www.smefinanceforum.org/sites/ deafault/files/blogs/SBCS-Employer-Firms-Report.pdf

Financial Stability Board. 2019. Evaluation of the effects of financial regulatory reforms on small and medium-sized enterprises (SME) financing. Retrieved from https://www.fsb.org/wp-content/uploads/P070619-1.pdf.

GIZ. 2018. Myanmar's banking sector in transition: Current status and challenges ahead. Retrieved from http://www.giz-banking-report-myanmar-2018.com/epaper/Myanmar_Banking_Report_2018.pdf.

Gropp, R., Gruendl, C., Guettler, A. 2014. The impact of public guarantees on bank risk taking: Evidence from a natural experiment. Review of Finance 18, 457–488.

Haltiwanger, John, Jarmin Ron S., Kulick Robert, Miranda Javier, 2014, High-Growth Young Firms: Contribution to Job, Output, and Productivity Growth, Retrieved from http://www.nber.org/system/files/chapters/c13492/c13492.pdf (Accessed on September 01, 2020)

Honohan, Patrick, 2008. Partial Credit Guarantees: Principles and Practice, Institute for International Integration Studies.

IFC, McKinsey & Co. 2010. Two trillion and counting. Assessing the credit gap for micro, small and medium-size enterprises in the developing world. Retrieved from http://documents.worldbank.org/curated/en/386141468331458415/pdf/713150WP0Box370rillion0and0counting.pdf.

IFC, 2013. MSME FINANCE GAP: Assessment of the Shortfalls and Opportunities in Financing Micro, Small and Medium Enterprises in Emerging Markets, Retrieved from https://www.ifc.org/wps/wcm/connect/03522e90-a13d-4a02-87cd-9ee9a297b311/121264-WP-PUBLIC-MSMEReportFINAL.pdf?MOD=AJPERES&CVID=m5SwAQA

Iichiro, U. 2017. Reforming Japan's credit guarantee program for small and medium-sized enterprises. Retrieved from https://www.rieti.go.jp/en/columns/a01_0478.html.

Isenberg, D.J. 2010. How to start an entrepreneurial revolution. Retrieved from https://institute.coop/sites/default/files/resources/Isenberg%20-%20How%20to%20Start%20an%20Entrepreneurial%20Revolution.pdf.

Jong Goo, L. 2017. Korean experience in credit guarantee scheme to enhance financial accessibility of MSMEs. Retrieved from https://www.unescap.org/sites/default/files/Panel%202-2.%20KODIT_Mr.%20Jong-goo%20Lee.pdf.

Kane, T. 2010. The importance of startups in job creation and job destruction. Retrieved from https://www.kauffman.org/wp-content/uploads/2019/12/firm_formation_importance_of_startups.pdf.

KPMG. 2011. Credit Access Guarantees: a Public Asset Between State and Market.

KPMG. 2013. Credit access guarantees: A public asset between State and Market. Retrieved from https://assets.kpmg/content/dam/kpmg/pdf/2013/06/KPMG-Credit-access-guarantees-public-asset-between-State-Market.pdf.

KSP. 2012. Credit guarantee and credit evaluation system for SME development in Kazakhstan. Retrieved from http://www.kcgf.co.kr/workingMgt/working_20161117133412.pdf.

Kuwahara, Satoshi, Naoyuki Yoshino, Megumi Sagara, and Farhad Taghizadeh-Hesary. 2019. "Establishment of the credit risk database: Concrete use to evaluate the creditworthiness of SMEs," ADBI Working Paper, No. 924.

Lee Jong Goo, 2017. Koran Experience in Credit Guarantee Scheme to Enhance Financial Accessibility of MSMEs, Retrieved from https://www.unescap.org/sites/default/files/Panel%202-2.%20KODIT_Mr.%20Jong-goo%20Lee.pdf

Lee Jongh-goo, Hong Sunyoung, Lee Taehyun, Wooinn Park, 2019. Unlocking SME Finance in Asia: Roles of Credit Rating and Credit Guarantee Schemes: The Korea Credit Guarantee Fund and its Contribution to the Economy, Rouledge

Le Ngoc Dang, Anh Tu Chuc, 2019. Challenges in Implementing the Credit Guarantee Scheme for Small and Medium- Sized Enterprises: The Case of Viet Nam, ADBI Working Paper Series, Retrieved from https://www.adb.org/sites/default/files/publication/496271/adbi-wp941.pdf

Li, W. 1998. Government loan, guarantee, and grant programs: An evaluation.

Loughborough University. 2005. Measuring the effectiveness of credit guarantee schemes: Evidence from Malaysia. Sage Publications.

Ministero Dello Sviluppo Economico. (n.d.). Portale rating per le imprese. Retrieved from https://www.fondidigaranzia.it/servizi-online-per-le-imprese/portale-rating-per-le-imprese/.

MTI. 2018. Economic survey of singapore second quarter 2018. Retrieved from https://www.mti.gov.sg/-/media/MTI/Resources/Economic-Survey-of-Singapore/2018/Economic-Survey-of-Singapore-Second-Quarter-2018/FA_2Q18.pdf.

Neumark, D., B. Wall, and J. Zhang. 2008. Do Small Businesses Create More Jobs? New evidence from the national establishment time series. Retrieved from https://www.nber.org/papers/w13818.

Nobuyoshi, Y. 2017. Fixing the misunderstanding about the proposed reform of the credit guarantee program. Retrieved from https://www.rieti.go.jp/en/papers/contribution/yamori-nobuyoshi/01.html.

OECD. 2004. Promoting entrepreneurship and innovative SMEs in a global economy: Towards a more responsible and inclusive globalisation. Istanbul.

OECD. 2017. Evaluating publicly supported credit guarantee programmes for SMEs. Retrieved from https://www.oecd.org/finance/Evaluating-Publicly-Supported-Credit-Guarantee-Programmes-for-SMEs.pdf.

OECD. (n.d.). Italy: Key issues and policies. Retrieved from http://dx.doi.org/10.1787/9789264213961-en.

OECD, European Union. 2010. Discussion paper on credit. Retrieved from https://www.oecd.org/global-relations/45324327.pdf.

OECD, European Union. 2014. Policy brief on access to business startup finance for inclusive entrepreneurship. Retrieved from https://www.oecd.org/cfe/leed/Finacing%20inclusive%20entrepreneurship%20policy%20brief%20EN.pdf.

OECD/ERIA. 2018. SME Policy Index: ASEAN 2018: Boosting Competitiveness and Inclusive Growth, SME Policy Index, OCED Publishing, Paris/ERIA, Jakarta, https://doi.org/10.1787/9789264305328-en.

Onishi, Y. 2016. Credit supplementation system in Japan. Retrieved from http://forochile.redegarantias.com/documentos/presentaciones/PANEL3_3.pdf.

Ono, A., I. Uesugi, and Y. Yasuda. 2010. Examining the effects of the emergency credit guarantee program on the availability of small business credit. Retrieved from https://pdfs.semanticscholar.org/1ae7/c7940dd3344b20c5d238aa7388d4719e99d9.pdf.

Panyanukul, S., W. Promboon, and W. Vorranikulkij. 2014. Role of government in improving SME access to financing: Credit guarantee schemes and the way forward. Retrieved from https://www.bot.or.th/Thai/MonetaryPolicy/ArticleAndResearch/SymposiumDocument/Paper3_SME2557.pdf.

Pham, T. and O. Talavera. 2018. Discrimination, social capital, and financial constraints: The case of Viet Nam. World Development.

PWC. 2013. The startup economy: How to support tech startups and accelerate Australian innovation. Retrieved from https://www.digitalpulse.pwc.com.au/wp-content/uploads/2013/04/PwC-Google-The-startup-economy-2013.pdf.

Schmidt, A.G. and M.v. Elkan. 2010. Macroeconomic benefits of German guarantee banks. Retrieved from https://aecm.eu/wp-content/uploads/2015/07/inmit-study-on-the-macroeconomic-benefits-of-the-german-guarantee-banks1.pdf.

Small Business Corporation. (n.d.). Small business corporation. Retrieved from https://brs.sbgfc.org.ph/ (Accessed on September 01, 2020).

Startup Thailand. (n.d.). About Us. Retrieved from https://startupthailand.org/ (Accessed on September 01, 2020).

Thai Credit Guarantee Corporation. (n.d.). Thai Credit Guarantee Corporation. Retrieved from https://www.tcg.or.th/customer_general_detail.php?customer_general_id=8.

The Institute of Internal Auditors. 2013. The Three Lines of Defence in Effective Risk Management and Control. Retrieved from https://na.theiia.org/standards-guidance/Public%20Documents/PP%20The%20Three%20Lines%20

of%20Defense%20in%20Effective%20Risk%20Management%20and%20
Control.pdf.

Taghizadeh-Hesary, F., N. Yoshino, L. Fukuda, and E. Rasoulinezhad. 2020. A
model for calculating optimal credit guarantee fee for small and medium-sized
enterprises, Economic Modelling, HYPERLINK "https://doi.org/10.1016/j.
econmod.2020.03.003" https://doi.org/10.1016/j.econmod.2020.03.003.

Tokyo Guarantee. 2018. *Annual report 2018*. Retrieved from https://www.cgc-
tokyo.or.jp/about/public/annualreport2018.pdf.

Uesugi, Iichiro, 2017. Reforming Japan's Credit Guarantee Program for Small
and Medium-sized Enterprises, Research Institute of Economy, Trade and
Industry (RIETI), Retrieved from https://www.rieti.go.jp/en/columns/
a01_0478.htm

Valentin, A. 2014. The impact of German guarantee banks on the access to
finance for SMEs. Retrieved from https://www.napier.ac.uk/ (Accessed on
September 01, 2020).

VDB. (n.d.). Association of German guarantee banks (Verband Deutscher
Bürgschaftsbanken). Retrieved from https://vdb-info.de/ (Accessed on
September 01, 2020).

Vietnam Silicon Valley. (n.d.). Vietnam silicon valley. Retrieved from http://www.
siliconvalley.com.vn/.

Wonhyuk, L. (n.d.). Korea's knowledge sharing program (KSP). Retrieved
from http://www.keia.org/sites/default/files/publications/koreas_knowledge_
sharing_program.pdf (Accessed on September 01, 2020).

World Bank. 2015. PRINCIPLES for public credit guarantee schemes for
SMEs. Retrieved from http://documents.worldbank.org/curated/en/
576961468197998372/pdf/101769-REVISED-ENGLISH-Principles-CGS-
for-SMEs.pdf.

World Bank. 2017. Are Public Credit Guarantees Worth the Hype? Retrieved
from http://documents.worldbank.org/curated/en/431261511201811430/pdf/
Are-public-credit-guarantees-worth-the-hype.pdf.

World Bank Open Data, https://data.worldbank.org/, assessed on 01 August 2020

World Bank, SME Finance Forum, IFC. 2017. MSME Finance Gap. Assessment
of the shortfalls and opportunities in financing micro, small and medium
enterprises in emerging markets. Retrieved from https://www.ifc.org/wps/
wcm/connect/03522e90-a13d-4a02-87cd-9ee9a297b311/121264-WP-PUB-
LIC-MSMEReportFINAL.pdf?MOD=AJPERES&CVID=m5SwAQA.

Yamori, Nobuyoshi, 2017. Fixing the Misunderstanding about the Proposed
Reform of the Credit Guarantee Program, Research Institute of Economy,

Trade and Industry (RIETI), Retrieved from https://www.rieti.go.jp/en/papers/contribution/yamori-nobuyoshi/01.html

Yasushi Onishi, 2016. Credit Supplemention System in Japan , Retrieved from http://forochile.redegarantias.com/documentos/presentaciones/PANEL3_3.pdf

Yoshino and Taghizadeh-Hesary 2015. Analysis of credit risk for small and medium-sized enterprises: Evidence from Asia. *Asian Development Review*, 32(2): 18–37.

Yoshino, N. and F. Taghizadeh-Hesary. 2019. Optimal credit guarantee ratio for small and medium-sized enterprises' financing: Evidence from Asia. *Economic Analysis and Policy*, 62: 342–356. doi: https://doi.org/10.1016/j.eap.2018.09.011.

https://doi.org/10.1142/9789811235825_0010

Chapter 10

Leveraging the Potential of Islamic Banking and Finance for Small Businesses

Mohamed Asmy Bin Mohd Thas Thaker[*,¶],
Hassanudin Bin Mohd Thas Thaker[†,|],
Anwar Bin Allah Pitchay[‡,**], Md Fouad Bin Amin[§,††],
and Ahmad Bin Khaliq[*,‡‡]

[*]*International Islamic University Malaysia Kuala Lumpur, Malaysia*
[†]*Sunway University, Malaysia Kuala Lumpur, Malaysia*
[‡]*Universiti Sains Malaysia Penang, Malaysia*
[§]*King Saud University, Riyadh, Saudi Arabia*
[¶]*asmy@iium.edu.my*
[|]*hassanudint@sunway.edu.my*
[**]*anwarap@usm.my*
[††]*fbinamin@ksu.edu.sa*
[‡‡]*ahmadkhaliq@iium.edu.my*

Abstract

Small businesses are considered one of the sources of innovation, productivity, and dynamism in many countries. Thus, to translate innovative ideas into sustainable businesses, access to capital becomes a part and parcel of the business lifecycle of small businesses. Despite their potential importance for economic development, small businesses are facing difficulties in attracting external finance at the early and middle stages of the entrepreneurial lifecycle in many countries, including developed and developing countries. Islamic banking and finance is a broad framework that has great potential for supporting development finance particularly related to small business, given their fundamental criteria emphasizing generating positive societal impact. The main objectives covered by this chapter are: (i) to identify and unpack innovative financing opportunities within Islamic banking and finance instruments such as Mudharabah (profit-sharing), Musharakah (profit–loss sharing), Murabahah (sale with cost plus profit margin, Ijarah [Islamic leasing]), and Salam (forward sale) as potential solutions for addressing small businesses' funding gaps; and (ii) to initiate the development of systematic principles for the utilization of Islamic banking and finance instruments in financing small businesses.

Keywords: Small businesses, financing, Islamic banking and finance, Malaysia, Indonesia

1. Introduction

Small businesses or micro-based businesses are considered one of the best potential platforms for innovation, productivity, and dynamism that support many economic sectors through employment creation, output expansion, export orientation, and income increases (Wong and Aspinwall, 2004). Furthermore, these businesses are also dominating various strategic business service subsectors, including services related to computer software and information processing, research and development, marketing, business organization, and human resource development (OECD, 2000). It is estimated that small businesses represent about 95% of the companies providing more than 65% of the jobs as well as more than 50% of the gross domestic product globally (World Trade Report, 2016). Hence, these businesses occupy a prominent position in the development agenda and essentially become a part of the overall national development strategy in most countries (Abdullah, 1999). Both developed and developing countries acknowledge the role of small businesses as the primary contributors to the growth and development of an economy.

Despite their potential importance for economic development, it is widely recognized that small businesses are facing difficulties in attracting external finance at the early and middle stages of the entrepreneurial life-cycle in many countries, including developed and developing countries. According to the World Bank Report (2015), small businesses in developing countries lack financial support to reach their optimal capacity. Existing empirical studies found that collateral condition, legal status, transaction cost, information and documentation, financial track record, nature and quality of business, and financing procedures and options are among the challenges of small businesses in accessing external financing (Hashim, 1999; Aris, 2006; Saleh and Ndubisi, 2006; Abdullah and Manan, 2010; SME Masterplan, 2012–2020; Thaker *et al.*, 2013; Thaker, 2015; Duasa and Thaker, 2016). In addition, lack of attraction and the uncertainty of cash flows are also becoming limitations for them in accessing external finance (Block *et al.*, 2018).

Islamic banking and finance industry is a broad framework that has great potential for supporting development finance particularly related to small businesses, given their fundamental criteria emphasizing generating positive societal impact. It has achieved remarkable success in terms of steady growth and product diversification across the world. According to a report by the Islamic Financial Services Board (2018), the industry has experienced a compound annual growth rate of 5.5% from 2018 and its total assets are projected to grow to US$3.5 trillion by 2024.[1] To be more specific, Islamic banking's total assets across the industry grew to US$2.52 trillion in 2018 from US$2.46 trillion previously.[2] The two most notable features of Islamic banking and finance that contribute to social and economic development via entrepreneurship are asset-backed financing and risk-sharing.

According to the policy paper jointly released by World Bank Group, Islamic Development Bank, and the G20 in 2015, the Islamic financial industry should be asset-based so that it can boost real economic activity that will be directing factors of production to the growth of financed assets

---

[1] https://themalaysianreserve.com/2020/01/13/global-islamic-finance-growth-slows-to-3-in-2018/ (Retrieved on September 29, 2020).

[2] https://themalaysianreserve.com/2020/01/13/global-islamic-finance-growth-slows-to-3-in-2018/ (Retrieved on September 29, 2020).

and eliminating the stigma of "financialization" of a particular economy (World Bank-IDB, 2015). Another key financial mechanism of the industry is that it is based on equity suitable for small businesses because the entrepreneurs can share profits and losses. This risk-sharing mode is a fundamental support for entrepreneurial development, particularly small business entrepreneurs relying on equity financing for their new ventures.

The financial products offered by Islamic financial institutions are subject to the teaching of Islam (the Shariah), which are governed by two primary sources — the Quran and the Sunnah of Prophet Muhammad (pbuh). According to the Shariah law, taking or giving interest are prohibited and it is the most important feature of Islamic banking. Therefore, most of the financing sources are developed based on profit sharing and fee-based financing which are in compliance with Shariah laws. This mode of financing has been applied in retail, private, and commercial banking for debt and capital market, insurance, asset management, structured and project financing, derivatives, etc. Distinguished from their conventional counterparts, all Islamic financial instruments in general must meet a number of criteria in order to be considered halal (acceptable). According to Komijani and Taghizadeh (2018), and as also cited in Moosavian (2007), the main features that distinguish Islamic banking and finance from conventional paradigms are as follows:

- Riba: Prohibit taking or giving interest rate
- Maysir: Involvement in gambling or speculative type of business and transaction are strictly prohibited
- Gharar: Uncertainty about the term of contract or the subject matters are prohibited
- Undesirable: Should not involve any type of businesses which deal with alcohol, gambling, etc.
- Real economy: Activities by sharing risks and rewards.

In Malaysia, a number of institutions participate in fostering financing accessibility, focusing on SMEs, include commercial banks, Islamic banks, merchant or investment banks, and development finance institutions (Bank Negara Malaysia, 2019). According to BNM, a total amount of RM2.17 billions of loans/financing disbursed was recorded by all the participant banks as of November 2019. Meanwhile, in the last 5 years, Indonesia's Shariah banks have seen their assets grow by 38% compared to 15% for conventional banks (Bank Indonesia). The sector is currently dominated by two leading players, namely Bank Mandiri Syariah and Bank Muamalat, which account for 50% of total Shariah financing between them (Global Business Guide-Indonesia, 2011).

Considering the importance of small businesses and the scope for Islamic financial services, the present research aims to achieve the following objectives:

 (i) to perform a landscape analysis of financing small businesses in selected Asian countries particularly Malaysia and Indonesia;
 (ii) to identify and unpack innovative financing opportunities within Islamic banking and finance instruments, such as Mudharabah (profit-sharing), Musharakah (profit–loss sharing), Murabahah (sale with cost plus profit margin, Ijarah [Islamic leasing]), and Salam (forward sale) as potential solutions for addressing small businesses' funding gaps; and
(iii) to initiate the development of systematic principles for the utilization of Islamic banking and finance instruments in financing small businesses.

There are two important contributions from these findings. Firstly, from a theoretical perspective, it contributes significantly in offering alternative techniques for SMEs in Malaysia and Indonesia which are rarely available in the existing literature. Further distinguished factor would be the incorporation of Islamic finance/banking products in the model make the model even more outstanding than the conventional models. Most of the past studies tend to focus on the conventional models instead of alternative models such as Islamic mode of financing. Given these facts, thus, this study will help to enrich and add value to the existing literature within the context. Secondly, from a managerial perspective, this study offers the following points: (i) an alternative model to mitigate financial accessing problem of small businesses, and (ii) flexible system and proper modus operandi of Islamic banking and finance products.

The implications from this study may benefit various stakeholders such as policy makers, governments, financial institutions, and investors.

2. Literature Review

2.1 *Issues of Financing Small Businesses*

The extant studies have shown that small businesses are facing the most common problem, which is financial challenges. In general, the majority of the studies have indicated the factors that prevent small businesses from accessing external financing are strict collateral requirements, high transaction costs, lack of response from financial institutions that consider the small business as a risky business, insufficient documents to support the loan application, and no financial track record.

Aris (2006) studied various challenges of external finance for small businesses in Malaysia, which are lack of collateral, insufficient documents to support loan applications, no financial track record, the nature of the business, and long loan processing time. These factors cause them to rely much more on internal financing rather than external financing.

Hassan (2015) described the various financial challenges of micro entrepreneurs in Malaysia and observed that most of the micro entrepreneurs experienced extreme financial difficulties in the initial stage of their businesses. They also found that the rigidity of the procedures for accessing financial programs also prevented the smooth success of the programs.

Subramaniam (2010) investigated the challenges faced by the youth in micro enterprises in Malaysia. Her results revealed that lack of access to external financing was a major factor that led them to rely more on internal financing.

In their study, Hassan *et al.* (2011) argued that most of the micro enterprises in Malaysia were restricted from accessing external financing because of lack of collateral and insufficient documents to support their loan applications. Indeed, the financial providers were reluctant to increase the initial loans due to the risk and uncertainty involved in the business.

Meza (2012) examined the financial barriers to financial assistance by micro enterprises in Malaysia and Cost Rica by conducting in-depth personal interviews with micro entrepreneurs. The author found that public banking institutions in both Malaysia and Costa Rica failed to provide sufficient financing without collateral needed to meet the financial requirement to run micro enterprises. As a result of this, micro entrepreneurs most of the time depended on their own or informal sources of financing.

Machmud and Huda (2011) explored the financial challenges of small businesses in Indonesia and they claimed a major challenge for their entrepreneurial development was the rising costs of business. The authors also identified three key causes of unsuccessful loan applications which were related to: (i) business plan; (ii) sales, revenue, and cash-flows; and (iii) credit history.

In his study, Tambunan (2011) critically examined the constraints of small businesses in Indonesia. By using secondary data of small businesses, the author pointed out that lack of financing is one of the top constraints, followed by lack of marketing, innovation, and skilled human capital resources.

Rahman (2010) discussed the financial constraints in Bangladesh among the small businesses. The author found that the high requirements for collateral and improper project planning also resulted in the lack of access to finance for small businesses in Bangladesh.

In his study, Das (2007) claimed that Indian small businesses have for decades continued to be hindered by constraints, particularly access to loan financing. The author pointed out that there were inadequate flows of funds, causing a specific bias against small loan portfolios that interrupted the normal flow of finance to small firms. The two most responsible factors — collateral condition and the lack of transparency — are identified as the main impediments to small businesses' receiving external financing.

In another study on Thailand, Punyasvatsut (2011) mentioned a number of obstacles related to financing that arose from both entrepreneurs and financial institutions. Regarding the financial institutions, SME entrepreneurs claimed to have inadequate information, insufficient advice from financial institutions, as well as complex and cumbersome loan application processes, whereas the entrepreneurs were observed to have constraints related to collateral, business experience, business plans, loan history, and transaction costs that prevented them from accessing finance.

Kyophilavong (2011) examined the financial constraints of small businesses in the Lao People's Democratic Republic and identified that all entrepreneurs of SMEs more or less experienced critical problems in accessing required finance at the early stages of their businesses. The author highlighted that majority of the entrepreneurs were dissatisfied with the existing terms and conditions of the financial institutions, and most of them had common complaints about the institutions' collateral conditions, lengthy and complex application processes, and insufficient information.

Ung and Hay (2010) focused on the various financial challenges faced by small businesses in Cambodia. They revealed that the small entrepreneurs were kept mostly out of the financing mechanism because of non-fulfillment of collateral conditions. Furthermore, the authors identified a few other negative factors responsible for financial inaccessibility, such as loan amount, interest rate, and repayment periods. It was suggested that unbiased lending principles of financial institutions can support the expansion of micro-sized firms in Cambodia.

Thanh *et al.* (2011) investigated the factors responsible for slow development of small businesses in Viet Nam, especially in the textiles and garment, electrical and electronics, and automotive components manufacturing industries. The authors found that capital inadequacy was one of the major obstacles to the development of small businesses. Similar to many other studies as outlined above, the authors also indicated a number of constraints related to accessing finance by the entrepreneurs of small businesses such as collateral, age of the enterprise, business experience, small size, and production networks.

Aldaba (2010) highlighted the difficulties faced by small businesses in accessing finance in the Philippines. The author surveyed a total of 97 firms in the textiles, garments, electrical and electronics, automotive, and food manufacturing industries. The author found that financial challenges were one of the most important ones that restricted the growth of small businesses. In most cases, small business entrepreneurs manage their startup capital by using internal sources, and the rest of the capital comes from the banks.

2.2 *The Role of Islamic Banking and Finance in Small Businesses' Financing*

Islamic banking and finance are widely known as banking systems focusing their operations and activities purely based on Shariah rules and regulations. Since 1960, the progression of Islamic banking and finance has been undeniably significant and continues to grow at peak levels and to compete against conventional counterparts who have been in existence for the last 420 years.

The spirit of an Islamic enterprise, however, distinguishes an Islamic bank from a conventional bank. Khan (1997) points out that different variants of conventional financial institutions (like mutual funds, Rental Equity Participation Trusts, etc.) appear very close to Islamic modes of financing, but this doesn't make these institutions Islamic. He asserts that Islamic banking has to relate its activities to faith if it has to distinguish itself from conventional financial institutions. Given this characteristic, it is imperative for Islamic banks to include social dimensions in their operations along with the normal banking practices. The question is how the social role of Islamic banks can be best exemplified in promoting small entrepreneurs.

One unique feature of Islamic banking and finance is the profit-and-loss scheme whereby all assets and liabilities are integrated, and with this arrangement, Islamic banking and finance are able to lend on a longer-term basis for projects or startup businesses that have higher or lower return characteristics. This will also promote economic well-being and growth. The most common types of financing used by Islamic banking and finance to support long-term businesses are Mudharabah (profit sharing) and Musharakah (joint venture). Existing literature highlighted that in view of the preference for profit/loss sharing scheme over other trading modes, Murabahah can also play a role as financing facility, given its permissibility. In addition, under the Murabahah scheme, the buy-and-sell financing, given equal instalments, is flexible, easier to understand, and simple to monitor (Suzuki and Uddin, 2016).

Kessler *et al.* (2007) mentioned that SMEs or startups encourage entrepreneurship and obviously will enhance economic expansion under the Islamic banking and finance setting. The products such as Murabahah,

Mudharabah, and Qardhul Hasan under IB seem to be most suited for startup businesses and other equivalent businesses. Interestingly, Qardhul Hasan, Murabahah, and Ijarah financing are flexible in usage and easy to implement in determining capital needs (Qardhul Hasan), equipment and assets (Murabahah), and leasing (Ijarah) for SMEs (World Bank-IDB, 2015; Dhumale and Sapcanin 1998). Thus, plenty of financial schemes can be suitable for startup businesses, but they are also subject to the risk profiles of those particular businesses. For example, in the case of SMEs, the study by Hussein *et al.* (2015) shows that 95% of all financing of SMEs in 2003 were approved based on Ijarah, Bay Bithaman Ajil, and Murabahah financing schemes.

Looking at the offering patterns of Islamic banking and finance facilities, startup businesses can utilize these facilities, which will be useful for accelerating their businesses. The availability of these types of financing for various businesses, including start-ups, have been recognized by various parties, such as policy makers in many countries, as it is consistent with Shariah principles. The Organization of Islamic Cooperation (OIC) emphasizes the importance of the development of SMEs and startup businesses via active usage of Islamic financial products linked to real economic activity. Thus, it allowed various businesses in member countries to tap into the rapidly growing pool of Shariah-compliant funds. Nevertheless, the General Council for Islamic Banks and Financial Institutions, together with the Islamic Development Bank (IDB), keep finding the best innovative ways of financing to further accelerate the growth of businesses worldwide and promote the role of Islamic finance, especially the social finance aspect.

2.3 *Principles and Characteristics of Islamic Banking and Finance*

Principles and practices of conventional banking and finance (based primarily on the Western worldview) may be inconsistent with the Islamic worldview, since the Islamic worldview is different from the Western one. The Islamic worldview is based on the Quran and Sunnah (practice of Prophet Muhammad [pbuh]). Besides, the philosophy of

Islamic banking is in accordance with the Shariah (Islamic law/ jurisprudence) (Haron and Nursofiza, 2009; Komijani and Taghizadeh, 2018), which states that Islamic banking and finance cannot deal in any transactions involving interest/riba (an increase stipulated or sought over the principal of a loan or debt). Further, they cannot deal in the transactions which have an element of Gharar (uncertainty) or Maisir (gambling) (Komijani and Taghizadeh, 2018) and in any transaction that has a subject matter that is invalid (prohibited in the eyes of Islam). Islamic banks focus on generating returns through investment tools that are Shariah-compliant as well. Operating within the sphere of Shariah, the operations of Islamic banking are based on sharing the risks that may arise through trading and investment activities using contracts of various Islamic modes of financing. The prohibition of a risk-free return and permission of trading, as enshrined in Verse 2:275 of the Quran, makes the financial activities asset-backed in an Islamic set-up, with the ability to cause "value addition" (Haron and Nursofiza, 2009). As a result, asset-based and equity-based contracts are promoted by Islamic finance as viable alternatives to conventional financing, which merely relies on an interest-based system. Besides, the philosophy of Islamic banking and finance emphasizes the ethical and social dimensions of financial transactions that enhance equity and fairness for general benefit of the society.

3. The Products of Islamic Banking and Finance for Small Businesses

The Islamic financing options for small businesses can be divided into two categories, namely (i) asset-based financing, and (ii) equity-based financing. These financing categories have been part and parcel of boosting the financial inclusion of small businesses and attracting prospective capital providers and sources. Asset-based financing instruments include Murabahah, Ijarah, Salam, Ar-Rahn, and Tawaruq. Meanwhile, equity-based financing instruments include Mudharabah, and Musharakah. Each of the instruments is illustrated graphically and explained briefly as follows.

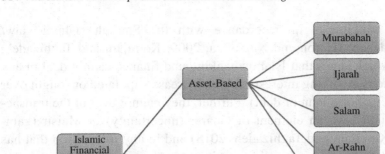

Figure 1:   Islamic Financial Products

Source: Author's illustration.

3.1 *Murabahah Financing*

Murabahah is one of the most-applied forms of Islamic financial contracts made between a financing institution and a client whereby the financier buys assets (usually at a lower price) specified and required by the client and then sells those assets (usually at a higher price) to a client; the profit margin is the difference between the buying and selling prices of the assets that are paid by the clients mostly on an installment basis. Among the benefits of this product are (i) a fixed rate of financing throughout the period of financing; (ii) the disclosure of the price and mark-up; (iii) its use for short-term financing; and (iv) getting rid of collateral requirements.

3.2 *Ijarah (Ijarah Muntahiya Bi Tamleek Financing)*

Ijarah Muntahia Bi Tamleek (IMBT) is a form of leasing contract. This is a special leasing contract whereby legal title of a leased asset is transferred to the lessee after the expiry of the leasing period. At the end, as a

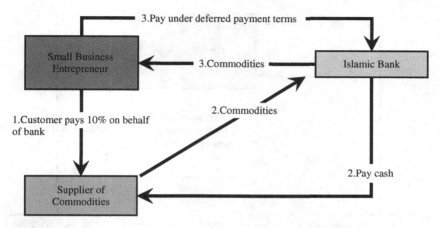

Figure 2: Modus Operandi of Murabahah Financing

Source: Author's illustration.

lessor, the financial institution or the bank hands over the ownership of the leased asset to the lessee, the client. The lesser here is entitled to claim all accumulated rental income, including the profit. The IMBT is adopted in several arrangements where the asset's ownership can be transferred, for example, the sale and transfer of the equity claim (from lessor to lessee).

3.3 *Salam (Parallel Salam Financing)*

Salam is another form of Islamic financial forward sale contract whereby the payment of the goods or commodities is paid in advance (present) (mostly agricultural goods) and the delivery takes place on the stipulated date (future). This kind of contact is beneficial for small agro-businesses that need working capital. Salam provides several benefits for small businesses: (i) provision of Shariah-compliant working capital, (ii) usefulness for short-term financing, and (iii) beneficial for the agricultural industry.

3.4 *Ar Rahn*

Ar-Rahnu is one type of short-term credit or loan (termed as Qardh in Arabic). The client will pledge gold or other valuable metals accepted as

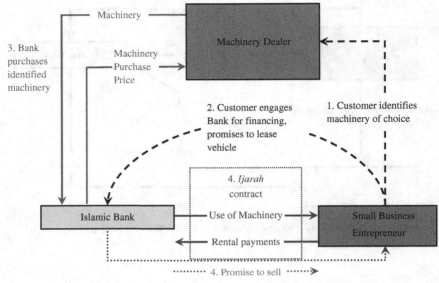

Figure 3:   Modus Operandi of Ijarah Muntahiya Bi Tamleek Financing

Source: Author's illustration.

security, which act as the collateral for the loan. This special kind of contract is based on the principle of Islamic law (Shariah) under savings with guarantee or safe-keeping (Rahn and Wadiah Yad Dhamanah). Ar Rahn provides benefits such as (i) no interest, (ii) short-term financing for small businesses, and (iii) surpluses to be returned after auction in the case of default.

3.5 *Tawarruq Financing (organized Tawarruq)*

Tawarruq is another Islamic financing mode in which a series of sales contracts are involved in the entire transaction process. Here, a client buys a commodity from a seller (on a deferred basis) and afterwards sells the commodity to a third party (not the original seller, and on a cash basis), to obtain liquidity. This instrument provides benefits in terms of (i) liquidity management, (ii) suitability for meeting the needs of small business' working capital, and (iii) no collateral requirement.

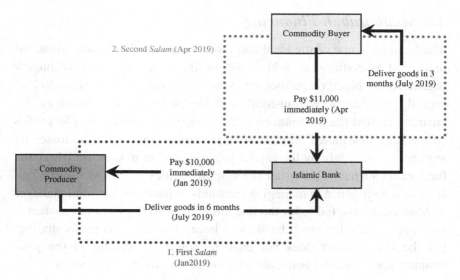

Figure 4: Modus Operandi of Salam (Parallel Salam Financing)

Source: Author's illustration.

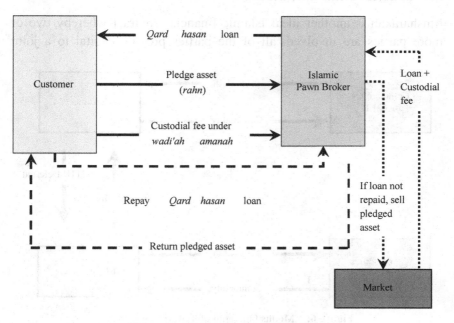

Figure 5: Modus Operandi of Ar Rahn

Source: Author's illustration.

3.6 *Mudharabah Financing*

Mudharabah is one of the ideal and most recommended Islamic financial modes of operations in which the business or project is managed/organized/run based on partnership. One party provides capital (called the capital provider or Rab-ul-Mal) and the second party manages the business (called the entrepreneur/fund manager or Mudarib). The profits (if any) are distributed based on the pre-agreed ratio, and the losses (if any) are borne solely by the capital provider except in the case where the fund manager has fulfilled all the responsibilities bestowed on him/her. If there is negligence in managing the funds or business, the fund manager or Mudarib is also liable for the loss amounts. The Mudharabah contact is very appropriate for small businesses because there is (i) profit sharing; (ii) the entrepreneur does not have to contribute capital to the joint venture; and (iii) there is the ability to negotiate the profit ratio.

3.7 *Musharakah Financing*

Musharakah is another ideal Islamic financial contract whereby two or more parties are involved, all of the parties provide capital to a joint

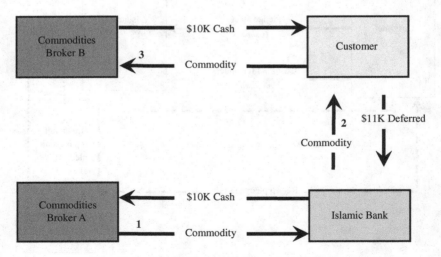

Figure 6:   Modus Operandi of Tawarruq Financing

Source: Author's illustration.

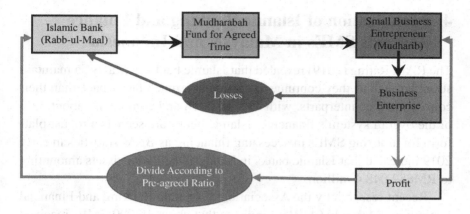

Figure 7: Modus Operandi of Mudharabah Financing

Source: Author's illustration.

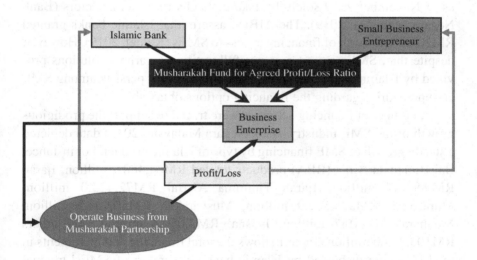

Figure 8: Modus Operandi of Musharakah Financing

Source: Author's illustration.

business or venture, they share the profits based on pre-agreed ratios, and losses (if any) are borne by all the parties proportionate to their capital contribution. The benefits of this particular instrument are (i) profit and loss sharing, and (ii) ability to receive the highest percentage of profits.

4. Mobilization of Islamic Banking and Finance Towards SMEs in Malaysia and Indonesia

The RAM Rating (2019) revealed that Islamic banks in Malaysia maintain strong growth as they continue to expand at a much faster pace than their conventional counterparts, with 11% in 2018 and comprising about 32% of the overall system's financing. Islamic banks are seen as a robust platform for assisting SMEs in accessing financing as BNM statistics in early 2019 indicated that Islamic banks in Malaysia held total assets amounting to RM682,048.4 million.

Recent research by the Association of Islamic Banking and Financial Institutions Malaysia (AIBIM) indicate that about 10,000 SMEs received more than 10 billion in funding (Kamel, 2019). A key indicator of the BNM reports is that RM4,716.2 million of total financing was disbursed as of November 2019 solely by Islamic banks for several sectors (Bank Negara Malaysia, 2019). The AIBIM asserts that Islamic banks granted RM20 billion worth of financing access to SMEs (Kamel, 2019). However, despite that, SMEs are seen as not fully utilizing various solutions provided by Islamic banks because a lack of awareness persists among SME entrepreneurs regarding the financing options obtainable.

A number of financing activities were traced to support the prodigious growth of the SME industry. Bank Negara Malaysia (2019) data depicted a steady growth of SME financing by type of Islamic product. For instance, Bai Bithaman Ajil's (BBA) products totaled RM64,488.9 million, Ijarah RM9,910.7 million, Ijarah Thumma Al-Bai RM72,423.0 million, Murabahah RM208,532.9 million, Musyarakah RM50,904.2 million, Mudharabah RM57 million, Istisna' RM2,059.8 million, and others RM103,284.0 million. Table 1 shows the total financing and increments in total financing disbursed by Islamic banks in support of SMEs' gradual advancement.

These financing products are found to be used for a number of productive purposes such as purchase of securities (RM316.2 million), purchase of transport vehicles (RM3,112.5 million), purchase of landed property (RM27,824.2 million), purchase of fixed assets other than land and buildings (RM1,189.1 million), personal uses, credit cards, purchase of consumer durable goods, and construction (RM6,280.8 million),

Table 1: Total Financing

Year	Total Financing (in RM million)	Increment in Percentage (%)
2014	335,385.1	–
2015	393,956.9	17.5
2016	436,708.4	10.9
2017	481,247.3	10.2
2018	511,660.5	6.3

mergers and acquisitions (RM22.8 million), working capital (RM38,019.5 million), and other purposes (RM3,820.0 million). Therefore, it is evident that a number of sectors are enormously aided through the financing facilities provided by Islamic banking and finance institutions to SMEs in Malaysia. For instance, the Bank Negara Malaysia (2019) reported these sectors included agriculture, mining and quarrying, manufacturing (including agro-based), electricity, gas and water supply, wholesale and retail trade, restaurants and hotels, transport, storage and communication, finance, insurance, real estate and business activities, education, health, household sector, and other sectors.

Meanwhile, Islamic banks in Indonesia were established in 1991 and pioneered by Bank Mualamat. According to Otoritas Jasa Keuangan (OJK) data on June 2018, there were 13 Shariah commercial banks, 21 Shariah business units, and 168 Shariah rural banks. The largest providers of Islamic microfinance in Indonesia are 150 Islamic rural banks (BPRS) and more than 3,000 BMTs (Baitul Maal wat Tamwils), a network of Islamic financial cooperatives. Bank Rakyat Indonesia Syariah (BRI Syariah) is an important player. It is a subsidiary of Indonesia's largest microfinance institution, Bank Rakyat Indonesia (BRI).

In the last five years, Indonesia's Shariah banks have seen assets grow by 38% compared to 15% for conventional banks (Bank Indonesia). The sector is currently dominated by two leading players, namely Bank Mandiri Syariah and Bank Muamalat, which account for 50% of total Shariah financing between them (Global Business Guide-Indonesia, 2011).

The development of Islamic banks in Indonesia started two decades ago, and the conventional banks still covered almost 70% of the industry at that time. However, the trend of subsidiaries and the promotion of rational behavior in this industry will trigger more Shariah-based banking in the near future.

In terms of the financing contracts, more than 80% of the financing at the full-fledged Islamic banks in the country is based on three contract types — Murabahah (54%), Musharakah (34%), and Mudharabah (6%), adhering more closely to the classical Islamic model of economics than possibly any other country.

Figure 9 shows that most of the financing of Islamic banks is for the household sector. The financial intermediaries are the best indicators of usage of Islamic financial products in the economic sectors. Thus, real usage of the microenterprises in Indonesia is still the lowest, and this may be influenced by various factors such as the scale of borrowing within the five economic sectors. Most of the time, the usage of SMEs is less

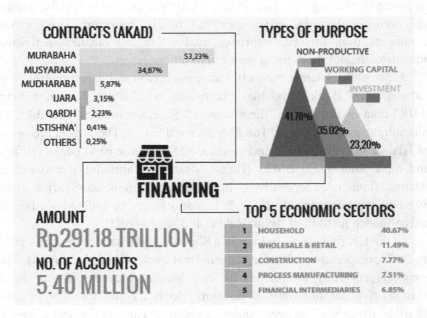

Figure 9:   Usage of Islamic Finance Product

Source: Global Business Guide-Indonesia, 2011.

compared to the above five sectors. In addition, these indicators also reveal that expansion and demand for Islamic finance products in Indonesia is significant in the top five economic sectors.

Indonesia appears to be a natural growing market for Shariah-compliant banking services, given the size of the Muslim majority population; however, the character of the market is starkly different from that of neighboring Malaysia or the Middle East. The majority of Indonesia's potential Islamic banking customers fall under the "rational market" as opposed to that of the "spiritual market." Islamic banking products are therefore pitted against their conventional counterparts and judged on their commercial merits as opposed to being chosen on the basis of faith.

5. Challenges of Implementation of Islamic Finance for Small Businesses

Some of the challenges involved in Islamic finance implementation for small businesses are as follows:

(i) Product Offerings
The Islamic financial products offered to small businesses are skewed more toward debt financing such as Murabahah. Although there are other products such as Musharakah, Mudharabah, and Ijarah, Murabahah is more suitable for specific financing purposes, and these products come with better profit and loss sharing. Thus, there is no diversity in offering different financial products to support small businesses' financial needs. There is a need to move towards equity-based financing instead of just relying on debt-based financing.

(ii) Regulatory Framework
One of the crucial challenges for Islamic finance, regardless of whether it is for small businesses or other platforms, is the lack of a regulatory framework for financial products. Looking at conventional financing, the regulation standards are more harmonized and standardized, which makes their products more marketable and easier to follow. In Islamic finance, the products are less standardized since there are no approved standards

per se for Islamic finance. Most of the Islamic finance products follow the conventional banking rules and regulations.

(ii) Transaction Costs and Non-movable Collateral

As far as Islamic finance for small business is concerned, the transaction costs and taxes involved are relatively higher compared to their conventional counterparts in financing. Possible reasons for this may be the Shariah verification processes and complicated taxation guidelines. Furthermore, small businesses generally facing the problem of non-movable collateral cause the Islamic banks to be reluctant to finance small businesses in general. Thus, a strong legal standard is needed in order to allow small businesses to utilize their movable tangible assets.

(iv) Knowledge and Information

The knowledge and availability of Islamic finance products for entrepreneurs, especially at the startup level, is still at a low level. This may be due to the limited number of Islamic finance products offered, and this industry is still at the beginning stage, compared to conventional banks. The Muslim majority countries such Malaysia, Indonesia, and others are moving toward full-fledged Islamic finance institutions, and this will lead to a better Islamic finance ecosystem.

(v) Smart Collaboration

Currently, the government and private sectors that offer Islamic finance products to small businesses are executing their roles individually. Smart collaboration such as shared capital, risk, training, and other responsibilities will attract more stakeholders, such as investors, to participate in the SMEs' investments as capital providers.

6. Conclusion, Policy Implications and Recommendations

To sum up, small businesses are playing a vital part in economies as they create employment and contribute to the national income. However, this sector faces many challenges, particularly in accessing financial services in many countries, including Malaysia and Indonesia. This research has compiled the findings of a number of empirical studies that can be viewed from the financier's as well as the entrepreneur's perspectives. It has been observed that the financier is quite reluctant to provide finance to the entrepreneurs of small businesses. The main causes for most of the loan applications of entrepreneurs to be denied are their early stage of business establishment and lack of proper business experience, no collateral security, higher transaction costs, improper business planning, small size of loans, limited or lower production networks, lower sales, revenue, and cash-flows, and bad credit history. On the other hand, the entrepreneurs of small businesses criticized the financiers because of their rigid terms and conditions of loan approval. In addition, there are many other objections regarding the financiers that are related to inadequate information, insufficient advice, collateral requirements, transaction costs, loan amounts, interest rate and repayment period, loan maturity, lending processes, etc. Apart from highlighting these financing challenges, this research also discussed the government policies and programs of small businesses in Malaysia and Indonesia for the development of the industry. As can be realized from the discussion, these programs do not fully satisfy the financial needs of the small businesses.

The SME sector has many challenges, and one of the most important ones is the lack of required financing either to start up or to expand the existing enterprises. In this chapter, we have presented a number of Islamic financial products such as Mudharabah, Musharakah, Murabaha, Ijarah, and Salam which can be adopted to meet the financial needs of the entrepreneurs. Among these products, there are some that are short-term in nature, i.e., Murabaha, which is particularly appropriate for financing day-to-day business activities and for satisfying the requirement of working capital, which has higher risks than some of the long-term products, i.e., Mudharabah, Musharakah, Ijarah, and Salam, which are most appropriate for the economic viability of the businesses. Ideally, Islamic financial institutions should be focusing more on non-borrowing and long-term Islamic products or contracts to finance the long-term projects. As a possible solution for those challenges, the present research presents a few innovative Islamic financing modes, i.e., Mudharabah, Musharakah, Murabahah, Ijarah, and Salam.

Islamic financial products can be better alternatives or substitutes for conventional financial contracts, but they are not complementary to each other. This is because of the underlying fundamental principle involved in Islamic financial contracts that is guided by Islamic law or Shariah. The key difference between these two financial systems is the practice of interest or riba, uncertainty (Gharar), gambling, and speculation, which are not accepted under any condition by the Islamic financial system. In addition, the current practice of conventional financing in most of the cases is not based on partnerships with profit-and-loss sharing principles.

In real situations, there are many uncertainties that make businesses either profitable or failures. An entrepreneur who starts a new enterprise can face many business uncertainties. The entrepreneur can share the risks of conducting business with an Islamic financial institution as the partner. In this case, the institution can create a risk-sharing investment account on its liability side based on Mudharabah or Musharakah, whereas on its assets side, there could be the underlying contract with various Islamic finance products. Along with this, Islamic financial institutions, including banks, can get necessary support from government and its policymakers to fruitfully use equity-based financing contracts to better serve the SME sector.

Small businesses were observed to positively cultivate the supportive culture between the local public and private sectors (McFarland and McConnell, 2013) in which these acts contribute to substantial innovation, productivity, and dynamism in many countries. In relation to findings from this study, number of policy implications could be derived in leveraging the Islamic banking and finance for small businesses. First, local government should initiate programs to provide greater flexible sources of capital with engagement of Islamic banking and finance industry. The equity-based contracts offered by Islamic banks such Mudharabah and Musharakah can be structured and applied to enable better loan terms on the basis of risk sharing between the small businesses entrepreneurs and Islamic banks. Second, the Islamic banking and finance practitioner should construct viable Islamic investment products to encourage takers among small business entrepreneurs. Innovation of products could further assist the new involvement and gain of productivity of the market players. Next, the entrepreneurs themselves need to enhance their skills and talents in developing their business ventures and at the same time forage for Shariah-compliant financial loan assistance.

The present research recommends that a successful implementation of the innovative Islamic financing mode of operations can not only mitigate the existing financial challenges of small businesses, but it can also bring solutions to varieties of problems faced by the financiers in financing small businesses. Further research can be conducted on the suitability of each of the financing modes in different contexts, i.e., the nature of project or business, type of sector (agriculture or industry), market condition, and infrastructural and technological capacity. It is also hoped that after the successful assessment of all the possible factors, selecting the most appropriate Islamic financial modes can elevate the small business sector not only in Malaysia and Indonesia but also in some other parts of the world and thus contribute to economic growth and social welfare.

References

Abdullah, M.A. 1999. The accessibility of the government-sponsored support program for small and medium-sized enterprises in penang. *Cities*, 16(2): 83–92.

Abdullah, M.A. and S.K.A. Manan. 2010. Adequacy of financial facilities for small-medium business: Empirical findings from Malaysia. *International Review of Business Research Papers*, 6(4): 535–548.

Aldaba, R. 2010. SMEs access to finance: Philippines. In *Small and Medium Enterprises (SMEs) Access to Finance in Selected East Asian Economies*, edited by C. Harvie, S. Oum, and D. Narjoko, 291–350. ERIA Research Project Report, No. 14. Jakarta: ERIA.

Aris, N.M. 2006. *SMEs: Building Blocks for Economic Growth*. National Statistics Conference, Department of Statistics, Kuala Lumpur, 4–5 September.

Bank Negara Malaysia. 2019. *Financial Inclusion Data for Malaysia. Key Statistics on SME Financing and Pembiayaan Mikro by Financial Institutions*. Kuala Lumpur, Malaysia: Bank Negara Malaysia.

Block, J.H., M.G. Colombo, D.J. Cumming, *et al.*, 2018. New players in entrepreneurial finance and why they are there. *Small Business Economics*, 50: 239–250.

Das, K. 2007. SMEs in India: Issues and possibilities in times of globalisation. *Asian SMEs and Globalization, ERIA Research Project Report*, 5: 69–97.

Duasa, J. and M.A.B.M.T. Thaker. 2016. A cash waqf investment model: An alternative model for financing micro-enterprises in Malaysia. *Journal of Islamic Monetary Economics and Finance*, 1(2): 161–188.

Dhumale, R. and A. Sapcanin. 1998. *An Application of Islamic Banking Principles to Microfinance*. World Bank.

Global Business Guide-Indonesia. 2011. Indonesia's Islamic Banking Sector. http://www.gbgindonesia.com/en/finance/article/2011/indonesia_s_islamic_banking_sector.php (accessed August 27, 2019).

Hassan, N.B., S.T.S. Chin, J.A. Yeow, and N.M. Rom. 2011. Financial constraints and opportunities of micro enterprise entrepreneurs: A theoretical framework. In *International Conference on Business and Economics Research*, 1, 2010.

Hassan, K. 2015. Entrepreneurship, Islamic finance and SME financing. Paper presented to the IFSB 7th Public Lecture on Financial Policy and Stability, Jakarta.

Hashim, M.K. 1999. A review of the role of SMEs in the manufacturing sector in Malaysia. *Malaysian Management Journal*, 1(2): 40–49.

Haron, S. and W.A. Nursofiza. 2009. *Islamic Finance Banking System*. McGraw-Hill Singapore-Professional.

Hussein, N., F. Noordin, and H. Taherdoost. 2015. The role of SMEs in economic development; case study of Malaysia. *International Journal of Academic Research in Management (IJARM)*, 4(3): 77–84.

Islamic Financial Services Board. 2018. Islamic financial services industry stability report. Kuala Lumpur, Malaysia.

Kamel, H. 2019. Islamic Banks Ready to Support SMEs. https://themalaysianreserve.com/2019/12/30/islamic-banks-ready-to-support-smes/ (accessed February 2, 2020).

Khan, M.F. 1997. Social dimensions of Islamic banks in theory and practice. *Islamic Research and Training Institute*, Islamic Development Bank, manuscript.

Kessler, E.H., M.A. Allocca, and N. Rahman. 2007. External knowledge accession and innovation speed in the small and medium-sized enterprise (SME). *Small Enterprise Research*, 15(1): 1–21.

Komijani, A. and F. Taghizadeh-Hesary. 2018. An overview of islamic banking and finance in Asia. ADBI Working Paper 853. Tokyo: Asian Development

Bank Institute. Available: https://www.adb.org/publications/overview-islamic-banking-and-finance-asia.

Kyophilavong, P. 2011. SMEs access to finance: Evidence from Laos. In *Small and Medium Enterprises (SMEs) Access to Finance in Selected East Asian Economies*, edited by C. Harvie, S. Oum, and D. Narjoko. ERIA Research Project 2010, No. 14. Jakarta: ERIA.

Machmud, Z. and A. Huda. 2011. SMEs' access to finance: An Indonesia case study. In *Small and Medium Enterprises (SMEs) Access to Finance in Selected East Asian Economies*, edited by C. Harvie, S. Oum, and D. Narjoko, 261–290. ERIA Research Project Report 2010–2014, Jakarta: ERIA.

McFarland, C. and J.K. McConnell. 2013. Small business growth during a recession: Local policy implications. *Economic Development Quarterly*, 27(2): 102–113.

Meza, V.S. 2012. Microfinancing access constraints in both Malaysia and Costa Rica: Case of the microenteprises sector. In *International Conference on Social Sciences & Humanities*.

Moosavian, S.A. 2007. Islamic Banking (in Farsi). Tehran: Monetary and Banking Research Institute.

OECD 2000. OECD Small and Medium Enterprise Outlook. OECD Publishing, France.

Pirvu, C., L. Giurca Vasilescu, and A. Mehedintu. 2008. Banking financing for romanian SMEs–challenges and opportunities. Working Paper, MPRA Paper No. 11788.

Punyasvatsut, T. 2011. SMEs access to finance in Thailand. In *Small and Medium Enterprises (SMEs) Access to Finance in Selected East Asian Economies*, edited by C. Harvie, S. Oum, and D. Narjoko. *ERIA Research Project* 2010, No. 14. Jakarta: ERIA.

RAM Rating. 2019. *Islamic Banks Still Anchoring Growth of Malaysian Banking Sector. Islamic Banking Insight 2019*. Kuala Lumpur, Malaysia: RAM Rating Services Berhad.

Rahman, K.A. 2010. Development of small and medium scale enterprise in Bangladesh: Prospects and constraints. Bangladesh Institute of Bank Management. http://papers.ssrn.com/sol3/papers.cfm?abstract_id=1583707 (accessed February 18, 2019).

Saleh, A.S. and N.O. Ndubisi. 2006. An evaluation of SME development in Malaysia. *International Review of Business Research Papers*, 2(1): 1–14.

SME Masterplan 2012–2020. *Catalysing Growth and Income.* Kuala Lumpur, Malaysia: National SME Development Council.

Subramaniam, T. 2010. Micro enterprise and employment creation among the youth in Malaysia. *Jati-Journal of Southeast Asian Studies*, 15: 151–166.

Suzuki, Y. and S. Uddin. 2016. Recent trends in Islamic banks' lending modes in Bangladesh: An evaluation. *Journal of Islamic Accounting and Business Research*, 7(1): 28–41.

Tambunan, T.T.H. 2011. Development of small and medium enterprises in a developing country: The Indonesian case. *Journal of Enterprising Communities: People and Places in the Global Economy*, 5(1): 68–82.

Thaker, M.A.M.T., M.O. Mohammed, J. Duasa, and M.A. Abdullah. 2013. An alternative model for financing micro enterprises in Malaysia. In *2nd International Symposium on Business and Social Sciences*, (pp. 7–9).

Thaker, M.A.B.M.T. 2015. *A Proposed Integrated Cash Waqf Micro Enterprise Investment (ICWME-I) Model for Mitigating the Financial and Human Capital Development Challenges of Micro Enterprises in Malaysia* (Doctoral dissertation, Kulliyyah of Economics and Management Sciences, International Islamic University Malaysia).

Thanh, V., Cuong, T. T., Dung, B., and Chieu, T. D. U. C. (2011). Small and medium enterprises access to finance in Vietnam. Small and Medium Enterprises (SMEs) Access to Finance in Selected East Asian Economies Jakarta: ERIA, 151–192.

Ung, L. and S. Hay. 2010. SMEs access to finance in Cambodia. Small and medium enterprises (SMEs) access to finance in selected east Asian economies. *ERIA Research Project Report*, 14: 83–116.

Wong, K.Y. and E. Aspinwall. 2004. Characterizing knowledge management in the small business environment. *Journal of Knowledge Management*, 8(3): 44–61.

World Bank-IDB. Annual Report. 2015. http://www.isdb.org/irj/portal/anonymous/idb_faq_ar (accessed August 27, 2017).

World Trade Report. 2016. Levelling the trading field for SMEs. *WTO, Geneva.*

Chapter 11

Improving Financial Accessibility of Small and Medium-sized Enterprises Through Fintech

Hyojin Im[*,†] and Taeho Yoon[*,‡]

*Korea Credit Guarantee Fund, Republic of Korea
†ihj@kodit.co.kr
‡kkandoli@kodit.co.kr

Abstract

With the remarkable advances in IT technologies, a range of financial services combining finance and technology have been developed in the financial sector, thereby leading to increased convenience for financial customers. However, small and medium-sized enterprises (SMEs), which have served as the foundation of the Republic of Korea and most Asia economies, have been marginalized from the benefits of these new technologies and continue to face difficulties in gaining access to finance. In this regards, our study will identify the difficulties which SMEs are facing in relation to financing and introduce cases to enhance the financial accessibility of SMEs through the convergence of financial services for SMEs and new financial technologies. This chapter examines financial technology (Fintech) that can satisfy such needs and attempts to resolve the financial exclusion of SMEs by establishing a new evaluation infrastructure that evaluates the current business activities of corporations by tapping into Big Data such as dynamic and non-financial alternative data that has otherwise been unused. In addition, we introduce a non-face-to-face finance service online platform which reduces SMEs' physical difficulties in accessing finance and enables 24-hour, 365-day financial service. We found that Big Data on SMEs' business activities and platform can improve the accessibility of SMEs to finance.

Keywords: SMEs, financial accessibility, FinTech, big data, dynamic management activities

1. Introduction

With the remarkable advances in IT technologies, various types of financial services combining finance and technology have been developed locally in the Republic of Korea and abroad. Moving away from traditional financial services centered on offline branch offices, a range of new financial services such as remittance, settlement, asset management and financing services by using Internet or mobile-based platforms, which offer greater customer accessibility, is emerging. In addition, Big Data, which derives meaningful information from seemingly valueless data, has been widely used in various fields such as loan assessment, anti-insurance fraud programs, and credit bureaus. By utilizing Big Data in credit evaluation, so-called thin file applicants with insufficient financial transaction history and credit profile are now able to take out loans, even at lower interest rates and reasonable financial costs. As such, those who have been financially marginalized have seen their financial accessibility greatly enhanced. Further, the advent of non-face-to-face financial services such as Internet-only banks makes financial services available anytime and anywhere, delivering customized services unrestricted by time and space.

It should be noted, however, that such new financial services utilizing new technologies are mostly available through personal banking, and that corporate banking has yet to fully take advantage of FinTech. While diverse FinTech products and alternative credit evaluation systems are available through personal banking, corporate credit evaluation is still conducted based on static and historic information such as financial statements, making it difficult for SMEs with a short history or small size to gain access to financing. Despite the various forms of financial support available to SMEs, they are still unable to utilize financial products and services appropriately because of their limited financial accessibility and thus cannot satisfy their financial needs (Gayeon Seo and Hyuncha Choe, 2019). Further, preceding research has focused on enhancing the financial accessibility of private individuals by utilizing various forms of FinTech, while only a few studies have been conducted to examine the corporate sector. Also, in terms of procedures of financing, having to visit financial institutions in person is one of the major inconveniences for SMEs that do not have sufficient manpower.

To resolve these limitations in the financial accessibility of SMEs, KODIT examined various types of FinTech in the financial market and sought ways to apply them to SME finance. As a result, we concluded that the use of Big Data and non-face-to-face channels may be the solution. This chapter is a novel study as it examines the usage of Big Data of SMEs in enhancing the accessibility and necessity of non-face-to-face channels. These findings can be used in overall applications of ICT technologies and FinTech to SME finance in developing Asia. In Section 2, we will identify the financing difficulties that SMEs are facing and KODIT's strategic directions to resolve such difficulties with new financial technologies. Sections 3, 4, and 5 will introduce specific cases pursuant to preceding research and strategic directions. Finally, in Section 6, we will present performance outcomes, future plans, and policy recommendations.

2. Methods to Enhance the Financial Accessibility of SMEs by Using FinTech

2.1 *Difficulties in Financial Accessibility of SMEs*

SMEs, which account for 99.9% of all companies and 89.9% of all employment in the Republic of Korea[1] (Ministry of SMEs and Startups), are undoubtedly the foundation of the Republic of Korea's economy. For the

---

[1] Of the total 3,737,465 businesses, 3,732,997 are SMEs, and of the total 17,294,316 employees, 15,527,605 are working at SMEs. (As of 2017).

economy to continue its growth and create new jobs, SMEs must maintain a stable business. The financing of SMEs is mostly indirect financing, or loans, from banks, rather than direct financings such as investment or the issuance of corporate bonds[2] (Financial Services Commission). Although the amount of bank loans to SMEs has continuously increased since the 1997 financial crisis in Asia, recording KR₩700 trillion (US$636.4 billion) as of August 2019, SMEs still experience financing difficulties. Banks' loans to SMEs can be classified into collateral loan and credit loan, and the former can be further classified into real estate mortgage loan and savings and deposit collateral loan. It should be noted that 49.2% of all lending for SMEs is in the form of real estate mortgage loans, suggesting that most loans are made against real estate rather than the creditworthiness of the borrower (Korea Federation of Small and Medium Businesses, 2018). A survey on SMEs that have been denied loans from banks revealed that the most frequent reason for loan denial was the lack of collateral (IBK Economic Research Institute, 2018). As such, it has been stated that collateral-focused lending practices make it difficult for SMEs to obtain funds.

Further, even in the case of credit loans for SMEs, credit evaluations are conducted mostly based on financial statements such as sales amounts, which also works as an impediment to SMEs obtaining funds (Korea Federation of Small and Medium Businesses, 2018). Due to the lack of comprehensiveness and credibility of the credit data of SMEs, loans to SMEs are made mostly through "lazy banking", based on static information and collateral, etc. (Sangyong Yun *et al.*, 2016). Financing can be even more difficult for startups, which mostly have few assets to be offered as collateral and for which the information asymmetry regarding repayment capacity is more serious. Due to such difficulties, SMEs are demanding that their creditworthiness be evaluated based on their current business activities and their future potential, rather than their past financial performances.

SMEs also experience difficulties in undergoing the procedures for financing (IBK Economic Research Institute, 2019, Korea Federation of

---

[2]According to the financing status of SMEs as of the end of 2018, the amount of indirect financing through banks is KR₩669.4 trillion (US$608.5 billion), while the amount of direct financing is a mere KR₩3.1 trillion (US$2.8 billion).

Small and Medium Businesses, 2018). According to many surveys, SMEs have stated that requirements for excessive documentary evidence and complicated loan procedures are impediments to smooth financing. As to the question of whether they are willing to utilize FinTech, 13.5% of the SMEs surveyed responded that they are willing to take out loans from Internet-only banks, highlighting the convenience of not having to visit an offline bank, increased accessibility via smartphones, and promptness of loan procedures. As indicated in the surveys, SMEs feel that the procedures for loans should be simplified and they are willing to use FinTech for convenient services.

2.2 *Current Status of FinTech in the World*

Recently, in the financial sector, innovative technologies such as artificial intelligence, Big Data, blockchain, crowdfunding, security, and Internet of Things (IoT) are being used, creating a new area of finance. Ernst & Young (2014) classified FinTech business models into "payment", "financial data & analytics", "financial software", and "platform".

First, "payment" is where a credit card or an account is registered with the payment service and payment is made either online or offline. Major payment platforms include Apple Pay, the People's Republic of China's WeChat Pay, and Alipay. Second, the 'financial data & analytics' aims at analyzing the vast amount of data of corporate customers and providing differentiated marketing and service in credit evaluation and insurance business. Companies that conduct credit evaluation based on algorithms for non-financial data such as social media activities, including the US's OnDeck and Lending Club, are among those that use such analysis. Third, 'financial software' is software for innovative financial services, such as robo advisor, which utilizes artificial intelligence. "Platform" is a system that enables financial transactions without a bank, and includes remittance, P2P, and crowdfunding. Blockchain is one of the most important and core algorithms in finance and security. Yoshino and Taghizadeh-Hesary (2019) suggest blockchain as a tool to enhance the existing community-based scheme of hometown investment trust (HIT) funds.

FinTech in the Republic of Korea was first utilized for remittance services. TOSS (Viva Republica, Inc.), a payment platform first introduced in 2015, recorded 13 million subscribers and accumulated remittances up to KR₩49 trillion (US$44.5 billion) as of the end of June 2019,[3] becoming Republic of Korea's first "Unicorn Company" as a FinTech startup.[4] Later, in 2017, FinTech became a greater part of financial consumers' lives with the launch of Internet-only banks. Kakao Bank rapidly expanded its subscriber base by using Kakao Talk, the biggest instant messaging app in the Republic of Korea, as its platform. Kakao Bank is now evolving into a comprehensive financial platform that offers various services including not only remittance and payment, but also asset management using artificial intelligence (AI), insurance, credit rating search, and membership services. The convergence of technology and finance, going beyond the stage of "destructive innovation", continues to develop to the extent that ICT companies are increasingly providing new financial services, a phenomenon illustrated by the emergence of the term "TechFin".[5]

As such, FinTech is offering new values to financial consumers while bringing changes to the existing financial industry. Jinbin Son *et al.* (2019) noted that FinTech can enhance transparency and expend financial inclusion through the elimination of information asymmetry, which finally results in enhancing the accessibility to and convenience of financial services. And its positive influences on the financial sectors are as follows.

2.3 *Methods to Enhance SMEs' Financial Accessibility by Using New Technologies*

Despite the emergence of innovative financial services combining technology and finance, it should be acknowledged that SMEs have been

---

[3] "TOSS recorded 30 million accumulated downloads and 13 million subscribers," Dong-a Daily News, 2019.

[4] KODIT, recognizing the growth potential of Viva Republica, provided financing to the company in 2015, when it was in its nascent stage, by offering a KR₩500 million (US$0.45 million).

[5] This refers to the phenomenon where technology companies, instead of financial companies, lead innovations in the financial sector.

Table 1: Positive Impacts of Innovations in FinTech on Financial Stability

Potential Advantages	Relationship with Financial Stability/Characteristics	Key Examples
Decentralization and Diversification	Dispersion of financial shocks in certain situations, lowering of entry barriers → Increase in the diversity of service providers	Use of Big Data for lending, automation of lending process, robo-advisor
Efficiency	Increase in cost and time efficiency, inducing of the establishment of stable business models by financial institutions	Robo-advisor, RegTech, crowdfunding
Transparency	Easing of information asymmetry, enhanced accuracy in risk evaluation	Lending, crowdfunding
Increased Access to Financial Services and Convenience	Increased financial inclusion of households and corporations, support for sustainable economic growth and diversification of risk exposure	Mobile banking, robo-advisor, InsureTech

Source: Considerations on the Status, Regulations, and Sustainability of the Domestic FinTech Industry (Jinbin *et al.*, 2019).

unable to utilize the benefits of these new technologies in the financial sector. This is because FinTech has been developed mostly in the area of personal banking rather than in corporate banking. We have sought ways to resolve this financial exclusion and to achieve inclusive finance[6] by utilizing new technologies in the financial sector that enable SMEs to access financial services more easily.

Various kinds of FinTech can be utilized for SME's financing. Sekyung Oh and Seokman Han (2016) argue that FinTech can offer new innovative financing methods in the areas of loan and credit risk evaluation for SMEs as new alternatives to existing SME financing. They also mention P2P loan, e-commerce finance, trade credit finance, and

---

[6]According to the Global Partnership for Financial Inclusion (GPFI) (2016), financial inclusion is where entities capable of economic activities can efficiently access the financial products and services provided by financial institutions, such as credit, savings, payment and settlement, insurance, and investment.

crowdfunding as FinTech areas that are applicable to SMEs. Haklim Dong and Kang Back (2016) also suggest crowdfunding as a new method of financing for startups. It should be noted, however, that P2P and crowdfunding may be limited in their abilities to enhance the low financial accessibility of SMEs as they are conducted mostly in small amounts and their market size is small[7] (KB Financial Group, 2019). Meanwhile, the World Economic Forum (WEF) (2015) reported that FinTech enables SMEs, which have been marginalized in the financial services market, to access the financial market in new ways by providing innovative methods for the evaluation of their credit risks. Concurring with the WEF report, a new credit evaluation infrastructure for facilitating financing by using FinTech, rather than direct financing methods such as P2P and crowdfunding, would be more suitable for enhancing the financial accessibility of SMEs. And, in terms of procedures, it is necessary to develop a process that enables financial access with less restrictions of time and space.

Based on such preceding research and surveys, we have established a new credit evaluation of SMEs through Big Data and at the same time non-face-to-face channels or platforms to improve physical accessibility of SMEs to finance. First, a new evaluation infrastructure to evaluate the dynamic business activities of companies by using Big Data such as quantitative data, qualitative data, non-financial data, and soft data of SMEs was necessary. In fact, Big Data has long been in existence, but has only received special attention recently because ICT has enabled the analysis of large-sized data, not practical in the past, thus making it possible to create new values. Data that has been ignored for being irrelevant to financing is now being used in the financial area thanks to the development of networks, devices, and AI, enabling financial companies to fine-tune their credit evaluation systems.[8] The financial industry, with its vast amounts of data and advanced analytic technologies, is one of the industries to which FinTech can be applied most easily. If credit evaluation is conducted based on dynamic Big Data that can demonstrate the current

---

[7] In August 2018, the amount of P2P loans to corporations stood at a mere KR₩2.8 billion (US$2.5 million).

[8] "Future of Banks 4th: AI Conducts Credit Evaluation by Identifying 70,000 Variables," Chosun Ilbo, 2017.

business activities of companies such as employment, telecommunications, and so on, the credit ratings of SMEs will more accurately correspond to their actual status, thereby enabling SMEs to obtain loans at a more reasonable cost.

The second method is to streamline the loan procedures by way of non-face-to-face platform satisfying the corporate need for simplified financing procedures. A non-face-to-face platform enhances SME's physical access to finance by facilitating online application, issuance of credit guarantee, and credit insurance without visiting an offline branch office.

3. Development of the Dynamic Business Activity Evaluation Model Based on Big Data

3.1 *Cases of Credit Evaluation Using Big Data and the Relevant Preceding Research*

3.1.1 *Cases of individual credit evaluation using big data*

Big Data-based credit evaluation is conducted mostly for credit evaluations on individuals. In addition to overdue payment information and financial history, which traditionally have been used as the criteria for individual credit evaluation, countries such as the US have conducted credit evaluations using non-financial and alternative data like payment histories of electric charges, gas charges, telecommunications charges, and monthly rents. Ethnic minorities, immigrants, and young people between the ages of 18 and 21 received loans at very high interest rates as they do not have credit scores as per the traditional methods, despite their repetitive and continued payments for monthly rents, electric charges, telephone charges, insurance, savings, and medical insurance. Against this backdrop, US commercial banks now calculate credit scores by collecting data on various types of payments which were traditionally not considered in credit evaluation (Youngjune Kwon *et al.*, 2011).

PRBC, a US developer of credit evaluation models based on alternative data, calculates credit scores known as PRBC Scores by collecting data such as use of online services and various other regular services with the consent of individuals who wish to receive credit evaluations.

Further, the Brookings Institution and the Political and Economic Research Council, based on the results of their credit evaluations on eight million individuals using information regarding their electricity, gas, and telecommunications use, found that the default rate for credit loans tended to decrease when the evaluation included non-financial data, and that such a tendency was more significant in the case of thin file applicants rather than thick file applicants (Sangyong Yun *et al.*, 2016).

The methods of credit evaluation are becoming more diverse, including qualitative data such as personality as well as reputation data on social media, the number of social media accounts, the length of use of each account, and the number of friends. The psychometric test method, conducted through questionnaires that have no set answers, identifies the characteristics of individuals such as their personality, tastes, habits, and preferences. Based on the test results an individual's character, repayment

Table 2:   Types of Alternative Data Collected by PRBC from Individuals

Classification	Details of Collected Data
Identification	Name, data of birth, driver's license no., address of residence, contact no.
Income	Job information, monthly income, other incomes, etc.
Savings and deposits	Name of bank, account no., account type (checking, installment savings, MMF, etc.), Internet access data
Credit card transactions	Credit card data, Internet access data
Utilities (telecom, electricity, water)	Name of providers, payment date, payment interval, Internet data
Housing	Information on ownership or lease (monthly payment amount, payment intervals, etc., for house mortgage loan)
Subscription	Name of provider, subscription no., payment date, payment interval
Social media	Name of social media in use, Internet access data

Source: Considerations on the Status, Regulations, and Sustainability of the Domestic FinTech Industry (Jinbin *et al.*, 2019).

will, business capability, and financial habits are evaluated and used for loan qualification review and post-management. Such a personality evaluation method, which is applicable to new customers with no credit history, is widely being used in emerging markets such as Latin America and Asia and underdeveloped countries in Africa that have insufficient quantitative data. Indeed, the related default rates are reported to have decreased from 50% to 17% (Sangyong Yun *et al.*, 2016).

In the Republic of Korea, research has continuously been conducted on individual credit evaluation using Big Data. Youngjune Kwon, Jaihyun Nam, and Minjeong Cho (2011) found that the number of default customers and the default rates decreased when non-financial data on electricity charges was additionally taken into account in evaluations of the individual credit status of thin file applicants. Jongyoon Kim, Wonjung Chang, and Gwangyong Gim (2019) developed the commerce scores model that reflects commercial transaction data, demonstrating that it is more accurate than other models that only use financial data.

Indeed, the number of FinTech companies that offer loans based on Big Data and analysis to the financially marginalized is increasing. For example, CrePASS Lending Solution provides loans to young people who have limited access to finance through alternative credit evaluations based on Big Data. The existing credit evaluation models used by the traditional financial institutions evaluate repayment capacity based on a banking history, often resulting in declining loans to young people who have no banking history. CrePASS Lending Solution, departing from the existing method of evaluation based solely on banking history and asset status,[9] has created new credit ratings collecting data from individuals' lifestyles such as the intervals of smartphone charging and OS updates, social media activities, and personality. And then the data is used to formulate an evaluation model by using machine-learning algorithms. This alternative evaluation model enables financing for those young people who previously could not obtain funds, while also offering reduced financing costs for lending by reducing 20% interest rates to 15% and 15% to 10% and the like. CrePASS Lending

---

[9] Private credit bureaus (CBs) in the Republic of Korea calculate individual credit ratings by using data such as repayment history, current debt level, period of credit transactions, and type of credit (number of credit transaction products and their ratio).

Solution, through this new evaluation model, has offered up to KR₩100 million (US$91 thousand) to young people at an interest rate of 5.5% per annum over the last 6 months (Chosun Ilbo, 2019).

3.1.2 *Literature review on SME evaluation using big data*

While individual credit evaluation based on Big Data is developing rapidly, the use of Big Data in corporate credit evaluation is still in its initial stage. The credit data of SMEs is insufficient both in terms of quantity and quality as the comprehensiveness and credibility of such credit data are considered low. Moreover, financial institutions are not as active in sharing positive information of SMEs such as financial status, contents of business, and future prospects as they are in sharing negative information such as overdue payment status (Kyungwon Lee and Changgyun Park, 2013). In particular, the lack of information on potential credit borrowers such as startups in their initial stage or companies with few assets further limits their access to the credit market. Gunhee Lee and Gilyeon Cho (2014) pointed out the existence of an information asymmetry resulting from the time gap between the occurrence of an event and the recognition of the information. And they argued that new methods should be made to supplement the static information from the past in order to prevent the adverse selection and moral hazard that may occur due to the information asymmetry. Heungjin Kwon (2018) also asserted that enhanced evaluation models, which can evaluate the business activities and growth potential of SMEs by using dynamic data such as commercial transactions and movable assets data and can supplement the insufficient financial information and other static data of SMEs, are necessary. Kyungwon Lee and Changgyun Park (2013) argued that evaluation based on financial statements is suitable for large-sized companies that regularly offer financial statements, but credit evaluation for SMEs, whose financial statements neither guarantee accuracy nor are offered regularly, requires the use of the latest dynamic data rather than static data of the past.

As such, there have been a number of studies on the necessity of using Big Data for evaluation of SMEs, but empirical research verifying the utility of Big Data in corporate credit evaluation has been limited to micro enterprises. These studies were mostly aimed at analyzing the financing needs of small merchants by using Big Data on business districts or at determining the insolvency of small merchants based on credit card sales information.[10] Although micro enterprises are also companies by definition, they are very small in size and the evaluation models are similar to those for individual credit evaluation. Therefore, the credit evaluation of micro enterprises is different from the Big Data-based credit evaluation reflecting the characteristics of SMEs.

3.2 *Dynamic Business Activity Evaluation Model Using Big Data*

In order to improve the financial accessibility of SMEs, we developed a new evaluation model that evaluates the business activities of SMEs by using Big Data. Through this new evaluation model, finance can be provided to companies with insufficient financial profile if such Big Data indicates that they are in active operation and have potential for future growth. This model was developed through the following process. First, various forms of alternative data of companies were collected. And then, the factors that are meaningful to the business activities of the companies were extracted using logistics regression analysis. Second, the evaluation model was developed based on the extracted factors. Lastly, suitability of the developed model was examined and its performance was compared with the results of traditional credit evaluation, which is focused on financial statements.

3.2.1 *Basic definitions and data structuring for model development*

We selected 1,078,364 companies that used credit guarantee services from 2012 to 2018. Since the purpose of the new model was to evaluate

---

[10]Previous studies conducted using Big Data in the credit evaluation of small merchants include "Research on Ways to Utilize Big Data for Expanding the Supply of Funds to micro enterprises," Juhee Lee and Haklim Dong (2018), "Research on the Roles of FinTechs in Facilitating the Medium Interest Rate Loan Market," Sangyong Yun and Mansu Kang (2017); "Micro enterprises Credit Evaluation Model Utilizing Credit Card Sales Information," Jongsik Yoon *et al.* (2007), etc.

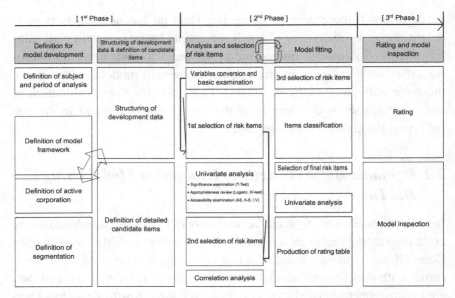

Figure 1: Development of the Dynamic Business Activity Evaluation Model

Source : KODIT, 2019

the current business activities of a company, we added the outcome of business activities as a target variable, in addition to bankruptcy and business closure, which have been used in traditional credit evaluation. Further, in order to maximize the forecasting capacity of the model, we segmented companies by external audit, into medium-sized companies, small-sized companies, and other companies[11] by their total asset amount.

And then, we also collected all available information which is considered meaningful in identifying the companies' business activities, from the KODIT database, other financial institutions, and public service providers such as telecommunications, electric companies, and so on. The collected data, mostly non-financial information, are created constantly or on a daily or monthly basis and can reflect changes in a company in a

---

[11] Details of the segmentation are as follows:

more timely manner than information created on a yearly basis such as financial statements. For instance, information on the use of electricity, gas, and telecommunications is meaningful because it is similar in nature to credit transactions in that a product or service is used first and then the cost is repaid regularly, and also because it shows the latest business activities of a company. Further, credit evaluation has traditionally been conducted focusing on negative data such as overdue payments, but now positive data is collected and analyzed as well in order to enhance the accuracy and credibility of the evaluation on business activities and to discover companies with great growth potential.

Also, after classifying the business activities of companies into employment, management, operation, and sales activities, we apportioned the selected data above to each classification of business activities and developed candidate items for each classification. For instance, national pension data indicates employment activities and management activities, and the rate of increase in the number of employees was selected as an item for evaluating employment activities, while total salaries and assets were selected as items that can demonstrate operation activities. In this way, a total of 2,520 candidate items were finalized in 14 data categories.

Table 3:   Types of Data in the Dynamic Business Activity Evaluation Model

Collection Interval	Types of Corporate Data
As necessary	Public disclosures, keywords in audit reports, news keywords, credit ratings of corporate bonds, number of searches for corporate information, industry trends
Daily	Patents, technology certifications, public tender information, approvals and permits, changes in real estate registration, changes in corporate registration, defaults in commercial transactions
Monthly	Subscriptions to national pension, telecommunications charges, granting of credit, representatives' CBs, R&D status, electricity and gas usage
Quarterly	Declarations of VAT
Yearly	Industry statistics, declarations of corporate tax, status of construction industry

Source: KODIT, 2019

Table 4:   Details of Analysis Items (partial examples)

Business Activity / Info Area	Employment Activities	Management Activities	Operation Activities	Sales Activities	...
National pension	Rate of increase in no. of employed persons	Total salaries/ assets			
Public tender			Number of biddings	Awarded contract price	
...					

Source: KODIT, 2019

3.2.2 *Items analysis and model fitting*

We statistically verified the relations between the collected data and the target variables of approximately 750,000 companies[12] in order to select the items that are most relevant to business activities. First, through mini-modeling, we converted candidate items into estimated target rates, based on which items were selected. Next, we conducted univariate analysis (T-test, Logistic test, K-S text, Concordant, AUROC) to select the first-stage relevant factors, and then conducted correlation analysis for each data area to find factors with strong correlations with other factors and incorporate them into a single most representative factor, based on which we selected the second-stage factors.

Next, we selected the third-stage factors through qualitative variables analysis[13] that verifies reasonable relationships with the target. Lastly, we conducted stepwise analysis, or multiple regression analysis through phased inputs, to confirm the final variables. Consequently, we selected

---

[12] We conducted a stratified sampling from the 1,078,364 companies that were the subjects of the analysis while ensuring that homogeneous groups were sampled according to bench-mark year, industry classification, and target in order to divide them into 754,864 development sets and 323,500 inspection sets.

[13] Chosen when the mini-modeling graph coincided with the pre-defined direction, or when the candidate item, qualitatively judged, had an implicit meaning.

34 detailed factors in seven data areas, namely national pension, representative's creditworthiness based on AI machine learning, Big Data on corporate telecommunications, reverse-direction VAT, public tender, and industrial statistics. Then, we added characteristics of corporations such as their business category and corporate history as dummy variables in order to produce a regression formula based on the logistics regression model and to develop a rating table for each segment. For instance, in the case of a medium-sized company eligible for a priority credit guarantee by KODIT,[14] the evaluation items selected in the final regression formula are as shown in Table 5.

3.2.3 *Measuring of activity grades and testing of model performance*

We finalized the modeling by classifying the business activity scores computed through the regression equation into four grades, namely good, average, cautionary, and risky. As a result of the performance tests of the models, AUROC and K-S turned out to be very good in all four segments.

We also found that the predictability of bankruptcy of a company was enhanced when the measuring was conducted in conjunction with the credit ratings as per the traditional evaluation methods and business activity grades. Research on the relationship between the business activity grade and the default rate surveying 132,117 companies with a credit rating found that the default rate of companies with a low credit rating but a high activity grade was low, whereas the default rate of those with a high credit rating but a low activity grade was high. Therefore, KODIT may provide guarantees to the companies with a "good" business activity grade even if they may have a low credit rating due to insufficient financial or banking information.

The dynamic business activity evaluation model is significant in that it has established a new evaluation infrastructure that enables companies with no financial transaction record to gain access to financing by utilizing meaningful dynamic data that has not been used in the current credit

---

[14] Article 3 of the Credit Guarantee Fund Act provides that the Fund shall provide preferential credit guarantees to SMEs.

Table 5: Evaluation Items for Business Activities of Medium-Sized Companies

Information Area	Evaluation Item
AI machine learning method Representative's CB	TIP score (information on capacity of repayment with income)
	PI score (detailed information on loans, credit pattern)
National pension	Time elapsed after subscription to national pension
	No. of national pension subscribers for latest (12) months/for current month
	Resignation rate for latest (09) months
Corporate telecommunications Big Data	Time elapsed after initial subscription date (for services in use)
	Total outstanding payments for latest (12) months/Total amount of bills for latest (12) months
	Total amount of settled payments for latest (12) months/ amount of settled payments for current month
VAT	Highest sales VAT on other companies & number of purchasers for latest (03) quarters
Credit granting	Total credit granted during the current month
Public tender	Average awarded price for latest (03) months
Period in industry	8 years or above or less than 8 years
Type of industry	Construction or manufacturing, retail, service

Source: KODIT, 2019

Table 6: Results of Performance Test on the Dynamic Management Activity Evaluation Model

(Unit: %)

Classification	External Audit	Medium-sized	Small-sized	Others
AUROC	79.4	73.9	78.6	77.3
K-S	46.6	37.2	47.0	45.2

Criteria: AUROC 75% or above: Excellent/65% or above: Good/Less than 65%: Average

K-S 40% or above: Excellent/30–40%: Good/20–30%: Average.

Source: KODIT, 2019

evaluation models. We discovered various kinds of new data which can explain well the activities of companies. The CEO's creditworthiness evaluated through the AI machine learning method is an individual credit

Credit Rating	Activity Grade			
	Good	Average	Caution	Risky
1				
2	Simplified assessment and active marketing for companies with a high credit rating and a high activity grade			
3				
4			Caution is needed in providing loans to companies with a good credit rating and a low activity grade	
5				
6				
7				
8				
9				
10	New loans may be provided to companies with a low credit rating and a good activity grade, or they may be exempted from post-management			
11				
12			Companies with a low credit rating and a low activity grade should be subject to intensive risk assessment	
13				
14				
15				
Total				

Figure 2: Default Rate Based on Credit Rating Combined with Activity Grade
Source : KODIT, 2019

evaluation that utilizes the rehabilitation application scores, which have not been used before. Also, national pension information enables the assessment of the quantity and the quality of employment by calculating the number of employees, their salaries, and the resignation rate at the end of every month using the national pension data provided by the National Pension Service through public APIs. Big Data on corporate telecommunications is an alternative data to short-term default data and covers a wide range of information including the number of telecommunications lines, amount of service used, and outstanding payments. It turned out that the data was highly explanatory of corporate activities in univariate analysis. The reverse-direction VAT data is used for tracking and identifying the sales activities of the companies even before the companies submit their documents, using the purchases and sales data of companies which have business relations with KODIT. It was also found that not only the information on awarded projects but also the information on the submission of bids for projects are indices that explain the business activities of a company.

3.3 *Development of Commercial Payment Index*

By combining the dynamic business activity model and the commercial transaction data accumulated in KODIT database, we developed a model to evaluate companies' payment capability in commercial transactions. Commercial transaction data are very useful in evaluating the credit risks of SMEs whose financial statements are hard to obtain or non-existent. Also, as payments for commercial transactions are usually made in 30 to 180 days credit period, they can be a better indicator of a company's current dynamic business activities than such static data as financial statements which are updated on a yearly basis and used in a traditional credit evaluation. Commercial transaction evaluation, combined with dynamic activity evaluation, enables a startup with a short history to have an opportunity to undergo credit evaluation. One of the most notable credit evaluation institutions that have indexed the capacity to make payment for commercial transactions is US's Dun & Bradstreet (D&B). D&B computes Paydex scores quantifying the credit of a company by utilizing commercial transaction data voluntarily provided by the company, such as the maximum amount of debts for commercial transactions for the latest 12 months, outstanding debts for commercial transactions, overdue amounts, sales conditions, and final sales times.

We developed a commercial payment index by utilizing Big Data on commercial transactions accumulated through the B2B E-Commerce Guarantees since 2001, as well as Big Data on accounts receivable collected from the E-Receivable Insurance Service.[15] B2B transaction data and E-Receivable Insurance Service transaction data have very high accuracy and comprehensiveness as they are based on the settlement of accounts receivable in commercial transactions occurring in marketplaces. Also, the index combines various forms of data that represent dynamic business activities, such as employment data and electricity data, in addition to commercial transaction data. The performance test of the model found that the default rate is low for companies whose credit rating was

---

[15] A type of receivables insurances, it enhances the transparency of transactions and enables the accumulation of accurate transaction data by requiring that commercial transactions be electronically registered in the marketplace.

low according to the traditional credit evaluation method but whose payment capacity was good. The commercial payment index made it possible to provide guarantees to companies with good transaction capacity and dynamic business activities, eliminating the blind spots related to the traditional evaluation method and enhancing the financial accessibility of companies that were financially excluded.

4. Establishment of a Non-face-to-face Service Platform

In addition to the development of a credit evaluation model using Big Data, we have established a non-face-to-face service platform in order to improve the corporations' physical accessibility to finance.

4.1 *Preceding Research and Cases Regarding Non-face-to-face Service Platforms*

Non-face-to-face financing with which one can use financial services anywhere and at any time (Hyundai Research Institute, 2017) has become commonplace in personal financing, from the opening of accounts to loan transactions. However, non-face-to-face finance service has not been common in corporate financing due to issues such as the verification of the real names of companies. However, as advances in information technology have enabled the online verification of identification, an increasing number of banks are starting to provide such non-face-to-face services. KB Kookmin Bank opens accounts for individual businesses and registers them for Internet banking without the submission of documents, and Shinhan Bank, for the first time among Korean banks, provides non-face-to-face loan services for corporates (Hankook Ilbo, 2019). As such services for corporate customers using non-face-to-face transaction processes are becoming more popular in the banking sector, companies are increasingly placing greater emphasis on the convenience of transactions than on interest rates when determining with which banks they will have financial transactions.

4.2 *Non-face-to-face Service Platform for SMEs*

A non-face-to-face service platform is meaningful in eliminating the difficulties of SMEs in visiting financial institutions. Using this platform, companies can apply for a credit guarantee and conclude a credit guarantee agreement without visiting a branch office.

In 2009, we first introduced this system for applications for guarantees and extensions of the guarantee period through the homepage, based on experience in operating the E-Commerce Guarantee system since 2001. This was a very innovative online financial service system at the time, but its usage was minimal due to the low awareness and use of Internet-based financial transactions (Ministry of Science and Technology). Ten years later, in 2019, we concluded that it was the appropriate time to re-introduce the system as the need for online financial services had increased and the speed and consistency of the system had been enhanced. In addition, according to a survey conducted on 986 guarantee customers to identify their needs related to non-face-to-face service processes, 95% of those surveyed responded that they were willing to use an online-only service process and that they would like to extend the guarantee period, conclude credit guarantee agreements, and submit documents online. The survey also indicated that websites are preferred to mobile platforms for the delivery of non-face-to-face services.[16]

Based on the customers' needs identified through the survey, we classified the non-face-to-face services into the three categories: the application for consulting including the consent to sharing information, the submission of documents necessary for evaluation, and the digital conclusion of terms. In particular, among these three service categories, the document submission system and the digital conclusion of terms were significantly improved, thus enhancing the financial accessibility of companies.

4.2.1 *Submission of documents through an online platform*

The essential aspect of a non-face-to-face service platform is its online document submission system. Traditionally, customers were required to

---

[16] 21.6% prefer mobile applications, while 78.4% prefer web pages.

have the necessary documents issued from the public offices and then submit them for credit evaluation. Due to these procedures, customers had to visit government agencies in person, and considerable costs for the storage of documents were also incurred. The main drawback, however, was that such hard copies only existed in paper format and were not added to the database. Against this backdrop, we, by using scraping technology,[17] set up a system through which customers can submit the necessary documents online without visiting public agencies. Once the customers press the relevant button, such as "submission of documents for new guarantee" or "submission of documents for extension of guarantee", on the KODIT non-face-to-face platform and verify their identification with the certificate digital public key, the system itself automatically visits the websites of government offices such as National Tax Service to have documents issued, which are then sent to KODIT and confirmed by employees in image files. This system allows customers to submit documents even when banks and government offices are closed during the evening or over the weekend, thereby greatly enhancing the financial accessibility of SMEs. In addition, the system reduces the possibility of mistakes that may occur in the process of document delivery and inputting data by hand, further enhancing the consistency and reliability of the information.

4.2.2 *Electronic conclusion of guarantee agreement through accredited digital signature*

Lastly, we introduced the accredited digital signature system as a method of concluding credit guarantee agreements to finalize transactions. The digital signature system is designed to provide legal effect to digital documents and digital signatures by verifying the signatories through an accredited certificate and obtaining signatures on digital forms. The

---

[17] A software technology that scrapes necessary information from the data displayed on Internet websites. As the legal issues involving the legitimacy of scraping technology have been resolved and its accuracy has been improved, it is now in active use in FinTech such as Internet banks and asset management.

Table 7: Documents that can be Submitted through the Online Document Submission System

Title of Document	Issuing Authority
Resident registration certificate	Ministry of Public Administration and Security
Business registration certificate, financial statements, VAT documents, evidence of tax payment	National Tax Service
Copy of real estate registration, corporation registration	Registration Office

Source: KODIT, 2019

Digital Signature Act recognizes a digital signature as having the same legal effect as a signature on a written document.[18] Further, the Supreme Court recognized the legal effect of digital signatures by ruling that "Unless specifically stated, digital signature is deemed to have been made by the executor of the digital document or his/her agent, and a legal act can be executed while the intentions expressed in the digital document are recognized as belonging to the executor, without an additional identification process such as a telephone call or an interview." A customer can conclude the guarantee agreement by putting the accredited digital signature on the essential documents such as the guarantee agreement form, the guarantee rollover form, and the consent to sharing of customer information with CBs, financial institutions, and the like.

In addition, we introduced the Time Stamp Authority (TSA) of the Korea Financial Telecommunications and Clearings Institute to verify the admissible evidence signed documents. The TSA shows that a signature was made at a certain time and has since not been modified, serving

---

[18] Digital Signature Act, Article 3 (Effect, Etc. of Digital Signature) (1) In cases where a signature, signature and seal or name and seal is, under other Acts and subordinate statutes, required to be affixed on a paper-based document or letter, it shall be deemed that such a requirement is satisfied if there is a certified digital signature affixed on an electronic document. (2) In cases where a certified digital signature is affixed on an electronic document, it shall be presumed that such a digital signature is the signature, signature and seal or name and seal of the signer of the electronic document concerned and that there has been no alteration in the contents of such a document since it was signed digitally.

as evidence of the timing of the creation of the digital document and preventing forgery or falsification.

As such, the non-face-to-face procedures on the platform allow customers to visit a branch office only one time or less and makes their access to credit guarantees easier.

5. New Products Combining Big Data and Non-face-to-face Platform

5.1 *Online-Exclusive Credit Guarantee Products*

In an attempt to enhance the financial accessibility of SMEs, we, based on the infrastructure explained above, have developed new financial products that combine the Big Data-based corporate evaluation system and the platform-based non-face-to-face financial services process.

The traditional procedures of credit guarantee are as follows: consultation to document receipt, credit research review including due diligence, the conclusion of credit guarantee agreement, and the issuance of the letter of guarantee. Customers used to be required to visit a branch office in person for the interview and the conclusion of credit guarantee agreement. In addition, the submission of various documents including financial statements was requisite for the credit evaluation of the applicant company. From the perspective of SMEs, such requirements incurred the loss of time for and the inconvenience of visiting a credit guarantee institute in person and preparing documents for submission. A survey on the customer satisfaction revealed that there is a growing need for speedy and simplified guarantee services, as many of the respondents indicated that they would like to submit their guarantee application online.[19] Moreover, the psychological burden, the fear of being rejected, and the sense of deprivation were the key factors that limited SMEs' accessibility to credit guarantee products.

---

[19] Percentage of demands for a fast and simple guarantee system as demonstrated in the customer satisfaction surveys: ('16) 14.5% → ('17) 14.7% → ('18) 18.1%.

To eliminate such issues, we introduced online-exclusive products using FinTech. Using the online platform, customers are able to apply for a guarantee more freely as they are relieved from the spatial and temporal limitations as well as the psychological burden regarding face-to-face consultation and the fear of being declined.

5.1.1 *Procedure of online-exclusive credit guarantee products*

SMEs that wish to make use of an online-only credit guarantee product can apply for that through the KODIT online platform. During the application procedure, the applicant is required to check the 10 items on a checklist.[20] When the applicant fails to pass the checklist procedure, she/he cannot use the online-exclusive credit guarantees. If negative answer is not checked on the checklist answer, and there are no problems in credit inquiry, the applicant is required to enter the guarantee amount and the name of the desired credit bank, after which the application procedures will be completed.

Once an SME applies for an online-only credit guarantee product through the platform, KODIT searches the total amount of debts of the single company and the CB grade of the CEO, upon receiving the consent to use personal information and the documents submitted by the company. KODIT then evaluates the company credit through indexing the dynamic business activities of the company by using Big Data such as commercial transactions, electricity use, and telecommunications use. If the resulting grade of the SME does not reach a certain level, the application will be rejected. If the grade is above a certain level, then KODIT will run a final check, using its inside and outside data, on whether the applicant has any default repayments for loans, unpaid taxes, or encumbrances on the places of business or residence. If no issues are found, a text message will be sent to the applicant company notifying the pre-approval of the credit guarantee.

When the pre-approval is completed, KODIT staff will visit the place of business of the company to interview the CEO and to check whether the company is in operation. If no issues are found in this process, KODIT

---

[20] Delay in tax payment, payment default for financial institutions, bankruptcy, etc.

will notify the applicant of final approval, and he/she shall then log on to the online platform to complete credit guarantee contract. Thereafter, the applicant shall remit the guarantee fee through the online banking and KODIT will send the electronic letter of credit guarantee to the creditor bank to finalize the credit guarantee procedure. Likewise, when the credit guarantees come to maturity, SMEs can extend the period of loan by using the non-face-to-face service and the Big Data-based evaluation without visiting a KODIT branch office.

Table 8: Comparison of Guarantee Issuance Procedures

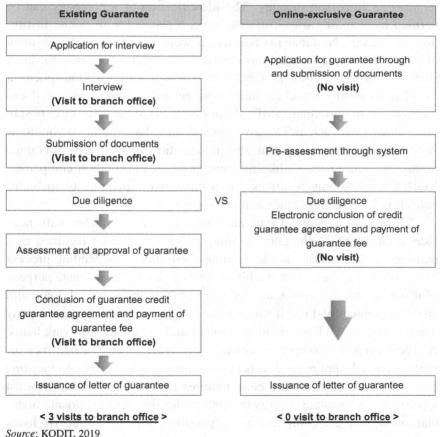

< **3 visits to branch office** >

< **0 visit to branch office** >

Source: KODIT, 2019

5.1.2 *Key issues regarding online-exclusive credit guarantee products*

Companies applying for the online-exclusive credit guarantee products can take advantage of the entire credit guarantee procedure completed online, from the application for the guarantee to the guarantee and the submission to the creditor bank, without visiting a KODIT branch. However, there are two issues to be considered.

First, even in the case of online-exclusive credit guarantee products, all processes are not conducted with non-face-to-face contact. The exception is the due diligence on a business place by KODIT staff, which requires an in-person meeting. The identification of a company can be verified by way of various official books registered with public institutions such as the National Tax Service, as well as the data on the payment of insurance premiums and transactions. However, it is not easy to verify such soft information as the CEO's entrepreneurship, the atmosphere at the place of business, and the labor-management relations through documents only. In particular, SMEs do not have the same level of exposure via online media such as TV news and social media as large corporations. As such, it is necessary that soft information on SMEs be obtained through on-site visits. Unlike private-run credit information companies, KODIT has 109 branch offices across the country, making it capable of collecting its own Big Data through on-site visits.

Second, even if credit guarantee procedure is conducted with non-face-to-face contact, the entire lending process cannot be regarded as a non-face-to-face service in the genuine sense unless the lending process by the bank is also conducted without direct contact. The ultimate purpose of using an online credit guarantee product is to obtain a bank loan with credit guarantees and use it for business purposes. Therefore, a company needs to use KODIT for credit guarantees and use a bank for bank loans. As such, even if a company receives a guarantee through a non-face-to-face process, the entire process is not considered as a non-face-to-face one if receiving the loan from a bank requires face-to-face contact. Against this backdrop, to create synergy through connection with the private financial market, we are going to make it possible for SMEs to receive loans and issue guarantees on our online platform through alliances with the non-face-to-face loan products of Internet-only banks. As a result, customers will complete the entire financial transaction process from obtaining a credit guarantee to receiving a loan through a single non-face-to-face channel.

5.2 Online-Exclusive Credit Insurance

5.2.1 Structure of credit insurance and difference from credit guarantee

Credit insurance[21] is designed for a company to receive compensations from KODIT if a company, after purchasing the insurance for the receivables arising from commercial transactions, suffers financial losses caused by purchaser's failure to make payment on the settlement date.

Credit insurance is different from credit guarantee in terms of work process. The creditors' risk on loans is alleviated through a credit evaluation of the guarantee applicants applying for credit guarantees, while the credit insurance applicants' (policy holders') risk can be alleviated through the evaluation of buyers who have obligation to pay the sales debt. In other words, in the case of credit guarantee, the applicant's cooperation in the submission of documents and evaluation is active because the target of the credit evaluation is the applicant company itself. However, in the case of credit insurance, the applicant (policy holder) and the subject of credit evaluation (buyer) are different entities, thus making it difficult to collect the information necessary for credit evaluation of buyer.

As a consequence, only the companies whose information is readily available can be the insured for applicants for credit insurance, while those companies on which KODIT does not have information cannot be accepted as the insured. As such, because of the difficulty in conducting the credit evaluation of the insured in a timely manner, applications for

---

[21] Credit insurance, along with credit guarantee, is one of the two key products designed to support SME financing, and it was provided to apprx. 1,500 companies in 2018 to the amount of apprx. KRW21 trillion (US$19.1 billion).

insurance were declined or the accurate calculation of loss ratio was not available.

5.2.2   *Expansion of commercial transaction safety net among corporations through online-exclusive credit insurance*

In order to overcome such limitations as explained above, to enhance the convenience of insurance applicants and improve the accessibility to insurance products, KODIT developed online platform insurance products combining a Big Data-based insurance assessment method and a non-face-to-face process. By conducting credit evaluations of buyers through calculations using KODIT-owned information and Big Data, timely and accurate credit evaluations are possible despite the limitations in collecting relevant data and documents. The accounts receivable arising in commercial transaction can be insured with evaluation of a wider range of buyers.

Furthermore, as in the case of credit guarantees discussed above, we introduced an online service process for credit insurance products in order that applicants can purchase accounts receivable insurance products without spatial and temporal limitations, which enhance the SMEs' financial accessibility. The existing insurance products required that the applicant visits a branch office in person for the interview, application, and receipt of the insurance terms and the insurance certificate. However, with the new online-based insurance products, all related procedures can be processed on the online platform.

To briefly explain the procedures, an SME that wishes to purchase credit insurance first needs to check in the online credit insurance platform whether the potential insured can be the target of credit insurance. Then, the applicant must enter information on whether the insurance terms and the explanation for critical conditions have been reviewed, the matters subject to notice, the status of accounts receivable, and the transactions between the applicant and the insured. Once these procedures are completed and the insurance fee is paid, the application for the insurance is completed in real time, followed by the online receipt of the insurance certificate and the insurance terms. As such, a policy holder (seller), having taken out the Receivable Insurance Service without spatial and temporal limitation, is protected against unexpected losses in case the buyer (purchaser) cannot settle the accounts receivable during the term of insurance policy because, in such a case, the policy holder can receive insurance compensations. This not only reduces the credit risk of the policy holder itself but at the same time alleviates the credit risks of the policy holder's business partners that offer credit to the policy holder, thereby producing positive effects.

We are now contemplating further developing such new online credit insurance products to establish a B2B market platform that enables safe credit transactions among companies. We aim to create a new credit market where companies can engage in credit transactions free of concerns by providing KODIT's Receivable Insurance Service in the existing B2B transaction market. By doing so, we expect to be able to support SMEs in their online sales activities, helping them explore new business partners and facilitating online sales based on credit transactions.

6. Conclusions and Policy Recommendations

6.1 *Conclusions*

The Big Data-based dynamic business activity evaluation model is significant in that it is the first attempt in the corporate financial sector to establish an evaluation infrastructure that enables companies with insufficient financial data or unsatisfactory financial performance to gain access to financing if they demonstrate active business activities. Thereby the model relieves SMEs' difficulties in financing caused by information asymmetry. Furthermore, the Big Data-based dynamic business activity evaluation and non-face-to-face platform are creating a virtuous circle coordinately and eliminating financial exclusion for SMEs. In other words, for the financial services processes available on non-face-to-face platforms, data is no longer collected through the existing offline analog method but through an online digital method. As a result, KODIT is now able to more systematically collect and utilize data on SMEs that use credit guarantees or credit insurance, both in terms of quantity and quality. The collected Big Data is then utilized for the evaluation of the dynamic business activities of a company in a timely manner.

And a non-face-to-face channel where credit guarantee and insurance services can be processed through an online platform reduces the physical difficulties in accessing public policy finance. Actually, the platform helped a lot of SMEs to get credit guarantee under COVID-19 without any contact or visit to KODIT branch offices.

6.2 *Policy Recommendations*

Through the two projects, we found two policy implications in successfully applying Big Data and non-face-to-face channels to SME financing. First, from the external perspective Big Data-based corporate evaluation requires that data collection be carried out systematically and specifically, and that SME data which is fragmented across many financial and public institutions be shared among these institutions. For instance, the utility of Big Data can be maximized when SMEs' electricity use status by KEPCO (Korea Electricity Power Corporation, Korean electricity provider) and the telecommunications line data and the utility charge payment history by telecommunications companies are shared and converged. This is also in line with the research conducted by Galino and Micco, who found that the sharing of credit data plays a positive role in small-sized companies' financing, thereby narrowing the funding gap between them and large-sized companies (Kyungwon Lee and Changgyun Park, 2013).

Second, from KODIT's perspective, the structures of main financial products such as credit guarantees and credit insurance should change in a way that dynamic Big Data is collected in real time. So far, in some cases we had collected data only in the phases of research or assessment for guarantees or insurance, and did not collect detailed data on company's use of funds or business activities after providing support for financing.[22] Now, however, our business structure can evolve in a way that various types of data and the traces of business activities created during SMEs' use of financing are continuously collected and analyzed even after financial support to SMEs.

---

[22] In some cases, information on the sales amounts and the financial statements was collected once a year when the guarantee was extended.

For these, the role of a corporate data bank is necessary. Unless the information asymmetry is resolved for SMEs in financial services, it will remain difficult for SMEs with insufficient information to procure a reasonable level of funds (Seoungje Seong, 2014). It needs to be acknowledged, however, that data collection and sharing have remained minimal in terms of high-quality information indicating the profitability and the potential of SMEs, soft information, information on commercial transactions, and information on movable assets. Against this backdrop, KODIT listened to opinions from its advisory organization which consisted of professors, former policy makers, startup CEOs, and so on. There were strong opinions that KODIT should focus on data regarding SMEs. In light of these considerations, KODIT developed a new plan and vision for a corporate data bank which collects, processes, and shares data on SMEs with the market participants to create higher value from data.

KODIT Data Bank can give benefits to all of the participants in the corporate finance market. For the government and nation, it can reduce the social costs to collect corporate information because KODIT as a policy institution collects and shares the data with the market participants as a public service. In terms of SMEs, the information asymmetry between SMEs and KODIT will be alleviated and accessibility to financing will be enhanced as SMEs provide their data to KODIT's commercial transaction database. Further, by processing the corporate data and providing it to financial institutions, the information asymmetry between SMEs and financial institutions would be eliminated and SMEs are ensured to receive proper financial support according to proper evaluation. In addition, a corporate data platform which KODIT is going to establish will enable SMEs to find new business partners and identify the credit status of such counterparts. We intend to set up a data environment encompassing SMEs, financial institutions, and credit information companies so as to maximize the network effect of information sharing and ensure that SMEs can enjoy the resulting benefits.

As we have discussed, the use of new technologies involving Big Data and non-face-to-face platform can enhance SMEs' financial accessibility thus realizing financial inclusion. We expect that the cases of KODIT will provide useful implications and insights to the financial policy institutions in formulating the policies for financial support for SMEs by utilizing FinTech.

References

Chosun Ilbo. 2017. Future of banks 4th: AI conducts credit evaluation by identifying 70,000 variables. (https://biz.chosun.com/site/data/html_dir/2017/03/21/2017032101045.html).

Chosun Ilbo. 2019. Providing loans to Young people having no credit information but potential. https://www.chosun.com/site/data/html_dir/2019/07/08/2019070801476.html.

Dong-a Daily News. 2019. TOSS recorded 30 million accumulated downloads and 13 million subscribers. http://www.donga.com/news/article/all/20190715/96491399/1.

Ernst & Young. 2014. Landscaping UK FinTech.

Financial Services Commission homepage www.fsc.go.kr.

Gayeon, S. and H. Choe. 2019. A study on consumers' financial exclusion: Focusing on financial products and channels of transaction. *Consumer Science Studies*, 30(2): 67–84.

GPFI homepage. 2016 www.gpfi.org.

Gunhee, L. and G. Cho. 2014. Historical perspectives for the sharing of business credit information. *Studies on Financial Information*, 3(2): 1–32.

Haklim, D. and K. Back. 2016. Equity financing for entrepreneurial ventures through crowdfunding platforms. *SME Studies*, 38(2): 67–85.

Hankook Ilbo. 2019. Banking sector moving to expand non-face-to-face services to corporate customers. (https://www.hankookilbo.com/News/Read/201909181609064744).

Heungjin Kwon 2018. Tasks for improving credit evaluation infrastructure for SMEs: Focusing on the use of dynamic data. *Weekly Briefing on Finance*, 27(8): 3–9.

Hyundai Research Institute. 2017. The fourth industrial revolution and the future of domestic industries.

IBK Economic Research Institute. 2018. 2017 research on the financial status of SMEs.

IBK Economic Research Institute. 2019. 2018 research on the financial status of SMEs.

Jinbin, S., D. Ryu, and C. Park. 2019. Korea's FinTech industry: Current status and suggestions for sustainable development. *Studies on Financial Engineering*, 18(2): 1–28.

Jongsik, Y., T. Roh, and Y. Kwon. 2007. Development of the credit evaluation model for small and micro business using credit card sales information. *SME Studies, Korean Association of Small Business Studies*, 29(2): 73–98.

Jongyoon, K., W. Chang, and G. Gim. 2019. Development of a personal credit scoring model (COMMERCE Score) Using on-line commerce data. *Journal of Information Technology and Architecture*, 16(1): 45–55.

Juhee, L. and H. Dong. 2018. Research on the application methods of big data within SME financing — Big data from Trading-area — . *Studies on Venture Business*, 13(3): 125–140.

KB Financial Group Business Research Institute. 2019. Intermediation of loan products with brilliant ideas: Changes in P2P financing.

Korea Federation of Small and Medium Businesses. 2018. Research on the status of use of financing services by SMEs and their difficulties in financing.

Kyungwon, L. and C. Park. 2013. Promoting production and sharing of SME credit information. *Studies on Financial Information*, 2(2): 1–28.

Ministry of Science and Technology, Comparison between the usage status of internet banking in 2009 and 2018.

Ministry of SMEs and Startups homepage www.mss.go.kr.

Sangyong, Y. and M. Kang. 2017. A study on the role of FinTech for activation of the medium-yield loan market. *Industry and Economy Studies*, 30(4): 1257–1274.

Sangyong, Y., M. Kang, and H. Lee. 2016. Is Non-Financial Data Important for Credit-rating of Micro-Enterprises? *Korean Management Consulting Review*, 16(2): 37–46.

Sekyung, O. and S. Han. 2016. FinTech and SME finance. The *Korean Finance Association Symposium*, 119–150.

Seoungje, S. 2014. The financial problems of small and medium-sized enterprises about legal aspects. *Studies on Economic Laws*, 13(3): 279–310.

World Economic Forum. 2015. The Future of FinTech: A paradigm shift in small business finance.

Yoshino, N. and F. Taghizaden-Hesary. 2019. Application of distributed ledger technologies to improve funding in the startup ecosystem. *Fintech for Asian SMEs*, ADBI.

Youngjune, K., J. Nam, and M. Cho. 2011. Economic effect of non-financial data sharing: The case of korean utility payment data. *Korea Economic Studies*, 29(2): 21–107.

Chapter 12

The New Role of Guarantee Institutions in the Fourth Industrial Revolution and Era of Inclusive Growth

ChulJu Kim*,‡, Yoonha Ham†,§, and Sangwon Cha†,¶

*Asian Development Bank Institute, Japan
†Director, Korea Credit Guarantee Fund, Republic of Korea
‡ckim2@adbi.org
§yhham@kodit.co.kr
¶chasw@kodit.co.kr

Abstract

Emergence of the Fourth Industrial Revolution, and the need for inclusive growth and other changes in the environment, require innovation in Republic of Korea's guarantee system. The Korea Credit Guarantee Fund, hereafter referred to as "KODIT", has provided credit guarantee services in a variety of industries and companies to achieve the dual policy goals of industrial development and market stabilization. It has also served as a market safety net in the event of national crisis, including the Asian Financial Crisis in 1997 and the Global Financial Crisis in 2008, helping the Korean economy quickly overcome them. Based on these experiences and results, KODIT is now seeking to vary its role in this rapidly-changing economic and technological environment, from merely providing guarantee services for small- and medium-sized enterprises (SMEs) to implementing innovation in the enterprise-wide business structure with a view to creating an innovative ecosystem, building data banks and platforms, and spreading social values. This chapter contains KODIT activities and performance in terms of its efforts to play a new part in this changing environment. We expect that the cases presented in this chapter will provide effective policy implications for the facilitation of SME financing in Asia, where public policy financing is relatively more important than in advanced countries, where venture capital investments are widely adopted and used.

Keywords: Korea credit guarantee fund (KODIT), small and medium-sized enterprises (SMEs), SME financing, credit guarantee

1. Changes in Economic Paradigm and Policy Environment

1.1 *Arrival of the Fourth Industrial Revolution*

The Fourth Industrial Revolution, primarily represented by hyper-connectivity and superintelligence,[1] is changing economic and industrial paradigms. The traditional three elements of production (land, capital, labor) are no longer as important as they once were, and production methods are undergoing significant changes as well. Cutting-edge information technology, such as AI (artificial intelligence), IoT (Internet of Things), cloud computing, Big Data, and mobile tech, are being combined with traditional industries or new technologies like robotics and biotechnology to connect all products and services through networks and realize "the intelligence of things". Through convergence of and hyper-connection between industries and between objects and people, we are seeing

---

[1] In the Fourth Industrial Revolution era, people and things are connected to the network so that data is constantly collected and accumulated (hyper-connection), while AI analyzes and utilizes this data (hyper-intelligence) to create added value (The Government of the Republic of Korea, 2017b).

"connected industry", while the traditional vertical industrial classification system is being reorganized into a horizontal system (The ROK
Government, 2017b).

As explained above, changes in the Fourth Industrial Revolution are
not simply limited to science and technology policies and ICT, but represent new paradigms of a scale to innovate all of society (Kang, 2018.). The
Korean society is also paying attention. Public interest in this concept has
grown noticeably since the beginning of the Jae-In Moon administration,
and, in July of 2017, the State Affairs Planning Advisory Committee put
forth "A Vibrant Innovation and Startup centered-Country that Leads the
Fourth Industrial Revolution" as one of the Republic of Korea's national
objectives, which reflects the intention to develop the Republic of Korea
into a leading country of new industries and jobs through scientific and
technological innovation, intelligence of all industries, institutional
reform, and innovation in education, the public sector, and eventually in
Korean society (State Affairs Planning Advisory Committee, 2017).

1.2 Changes in Policy Environment and Emergence of Inclusive Growth in the Republic of Korea

In the past, the rapid development of the Korean economy featured
exports-led by large corporations. Since the 1990s, however, the so-called
"trickle-down effect", a term describing the situation where an increase in
exports leads to increases in domestic employment and income, has
proven less effective and less successful than expected, meaning that the
increased income from increased exports does not boost domestic demand
(Oh *et al.*, 2018). Indeed, continued low growth and the "jobless growth"
have deepened social polarization and inequality in Korean society.

Against this backdrop, where growth-centered economic model is
showing its limitations, the Moon administration took office in May 2017.
The economic policies of Moon's administration can be summarized as
"inclusive growth" with the three pillars of income-led growth, innova-
tion-driven growth and a fairer economy. Inclusive growth differs from the
existing idea in that it focuses on growth through distribution, rather than
distribution after growth (Cheong Wadae, 2018). The concept of inclusive

growth has rather recently emerged, but the common view is largely from the perspective of fairness of distribution, a virtuous cycle of growth and distribution, and sharing of opportunities.[2] These values of inclusive growth have been spread primarily by the World Bank and are now actively discussed by the International Monetary Fund (IMF), Organization for Economic Co-operation and Development (OECD) and the World Economic Forum (WEF) today.

1.3 *Need for Innovation of Public Policy Financing Provider*

The guarantee system in the Republic of Korea has served critical roles in supporting the fast growth of economy. The recent series of changes in technology and the industrial environment, however, are increasing calls for innovation of the Republic of Korea's guarantee system. In this chapter, the direction of innovation for the Republic of Korea's guarantee system will be highlighted. In particular, we will discuss the new policy plans of KODIT, the largest credit guarantee institution in the Republic of Korea, in response to the rapidly-changing environment as represented by the Fourth Industrial Revolution and the trend towards inclusive growth. The reviews in this chapter will, we believe, provide effective policy suggestions mainly with a view to improving financial accessibility for SMEs through new role of credit guarantee system as public financing.

In the second section, we will introduce KODIT and discuss credit guarantee performance based on microscopic and macroscopic perspectives. The third section will elaborate on the series of changes KODIT is attempting to make, while the fourth section will address ways to cope

---

[2]More specifically, inclusive growth is defined as "a concept of understanding economic growth from the perspective of its trends and distributions" (IMF, 2014) or "growth that contributes to the improvement of equality", (IMF, 2017) or, from the perspective of the importance of opportunities, as "growth of sustainable output over a long period of time providing most of the workers with productive employment opportunities and reducing poverty in all economic sectors" (WEF, 2015) or "economic growth that provides opportunities for all members of the society and fairly distributes the outcomes of growth in both monetary and non-monetary terms" (OECD, 2015).

with the expansion of risk that will inevitably accompany such changes. In the final section, we will go over the remaining tasks for KODIT and make some suggestions as to the direction in which KODIT and other credit guarantee schemes in Asia should follow.

2. KODIT's Achievements and Results

2.1 *Overview*

KODIT is a special non-profit organization established in June of 1976 under the Korea Credit Guarantee Fund Act and, as of 2018, is the largest public credit guarantee institution in the Republic of Korea with a total outstanding guarantee amount of KR₩50.5 trillion (US$45.2 billion, exchange rate can be referred to KR₩/US$1,118 as of the end of 2018). KODIT provides credit guarantees, credit insurance, and guarantee-aligned equity investment services for a variety of industries and businesses with a view to achieving the dual policy objectives of industrial development and market stabilization. It has provided new credit guarantees and P-CBO (Primary Collateralized Bond Obligation) guarantees totaling KR₩11.3 trillion (US$10.2 billion) and KR₩500billion (US$447 million), respectively, and underwritten credit insurances and executed new investments totaling KR₩20.2 trillion (US$18.1 billion) and KR₩39.4 billion (US$35.2 million), respectively. In addition, KODIT has also served as a market safety net for national crises, including the Asian Financial Crisis in 1997 and the Global Financial Crisis in 2008, helping the Korean economy quickly overcome them.

2.2 *Microscopic Analysis of KODIT Activities and Results*

In this section, recent studies introducing the results of KODIT's activities[3] are presented. These studies were performed to verify the effectiveness of credit guarantees by ascertaining the objectives of KODIT's reported

---

[3] This analysis of microscopic and macroscopic results are a summary and edited version of "Analysis of the Results of Credit Guarantee and Thoughts on How KODIT Can

Table 1:   Status of Samples by Year

(Unit: No. of companies)

Classification	2013	2014	2015	2016	2017	Total
Newly-guaranteed	7,180	6,619	5,837	6,018	3,654	29,308
Non-guaranteed	38,207	49,420	51,638	56,079	22,371	217,715
Total	45,387	56,039	57,475	62,097	26,025	247,023

Source: https://www.kodit.co.kr/publicity/notice/notice130122.jsp (Lee,. *et al.*, 2018).

performance and results and identifying whether the purpose of its establishment as a public policy financing institution has been achieved. Analysis was conducted from both microscopic and macroscopic perspectives.

In the microscopic study, we compared the employment and financial results of newly-guaranteed companies with non-guaranteed companies.[4] For this comparison, we used employment and financial data and other characteristics of companies that participated in credit guarantee programs between 2012 and 2017, and selected companies — for whom the data necessary for our analysis were available — from KODIT's integrated database and Korea Enterprise Data.

First, the study used the integrated regression model to analyze employment and financial situation of the companies as a result of credit guarantees. Table 2 represents the results of the integrated regression analysis (pooled OLS) and shows the regression coefficient of the new guarantee dummy and the new guarantee amount, which are key verification variables in each analysis. Statistically significant positive values are observed in the analysis using various dependent variables that measure employment and financial performance, including employment growth rate, sales growth rate, and operating profit margin, which indicates that guarantee support has the effect of improving employment and financial

---

Increase Social Values", a research report by Yeong-Chan Lee, Sang-Jip Kwon, Jeong-Han Baek, and Gyeong-Min An (2018).

[4]A "newly-guaranteed company" is defined as a company without any outstanding guarantee amount as of the end of the preceding year, but with an outstanding guarantee amount as of the end of the current year.

Table 2: Effect of New Guarantees on Employment and Financial Performance (Integrated Regression Analysis)

Classification	t		t + 1		t + 2	
	Dummy	Amount	Dummy	Amount	Dummy	Amount
Employment growth rate	0.004	0.009	0.020***	0.051***	0.004	0.005
Sales growth rate	0.041**	0.023*	0.076***	0.012*	0.045*	0.001
Operating profit margin	0.001*	−0.05	0.006***	0.019**	−0.003*	0.008**
Return on assets	0.002	0.011	0.003***	0.015*	0.004*	0.015
Assets liability ratio	0.009***	0.035**	0.005***	0.058***	0.015***	0.033***
Current ratio	0.019	0.015	0.005*	0.008**	0.005**	0.003**
Asset turnover	−0.049*	−0.027	0.001*	0.017***	0.015	0.018**
Added value ratio	−0.005*	0.002	0.005*	0.003*	0.007	0.003*

Notes: *, **, *** refers to significance levels of 10%, 5%, and 1%, respectively.
Source: http://www.alio.go.kr/home.do (Accessed on October 15, 2020) (Lee *et al.*, 2018).

performance of guaranteed companies. This indication is most strongly pronounced in the "t + 1" period, which means that a certain time is required before the results of guarantee support are realized.

In this study, the microscopic results of guarantee support were re-verified by matching a non-guaranteed company with the most similar characteristics to those of a guaranteed company based on Propensity Score Matching (PSM) methodology. The results of analysis in Table 3 show generally positive ATTs between guaranteed and non-guaranteed companies, which indicates that the results of the guaranteed company are superior to those of the non-guaranteed company as well, based on PSM analysis. Although these results differ slightly from year to year, statistically significant positive values are observed throughout the full sample period. It can therefore be assumed that the credit guarantees produce results consistently, regardless of period. In particular, the fact that the number of full-time employees, which is a yardstick to measure

Table 3:   Analysis Results based on PSM Method

Classification	2013	2014	2015	2016	2017
No. of Employees	0.646***	0.591***	0.845***	0.859***	0.787***
Sales growth rate	0.037***	0.061***	0.055***	0.065***	0.070***
Operating Profit Margin	0.001	0.002	0.001	0.009***	0.004**
Return on assets	0.005	0.003	0.002	0.005	0.001
Assets liability ratio	0.002	0.002	0.006	0.004	0.012**
Current ratio	0.061***	0.004	0.100**	0.075*	0.204***
Asset turnover	0.021	−0.060***	0.016	−0.003	0.069*
Added value ratio	0	0.016***	0.002	0.006*	0.001

Notes: *, **, *** refers to significance levels of 10%, 5%, and 1%, respectively.
Source: http://www.alio.go.kr/home.do (Accessed on October 15, 2020) (Lee *et al.*, 2018).

employment performance, and the sales growth rate variable, which is used to measure profit growth, show significant positive values at around 1% gives rise to the assumption that credit guarantees contribute to the creation of jobs through the growth of company size.

To further support the analysis results of the effects of credit guarantees, we conducted a Difference-in-Difference (DID) analysis on the two groups with differences in the number of employees and financial results of the guaranteed and non-guaranteed companies being the dependent variables. The results are summarized in the following Table 4.[5]

Although the statistical significance decreased slightly from that of the integrated regression analysis, the results of DID analysis are consistent overall with the results of the above analyses, which confirms our assumption that new credit guarantees have a positive effect on business outcomes. While difference in employment growth rate between guaranteed and non-guaranteed companies was a little smaller than prior analyses, the values of the major verification variables are positive in all years and are statistically significant at around 1% in 2017, which also supports the conclusion that the provision of new credit guarantees contributes to

---

[5] We assumed a general trend that employment and financial performance, based on the time trend of a guaranteed and non-guaranteed company, are homogeneous.

Table 4: DID Estimation Results

Classification	2013	2014	2015	2016	2017
No. of Employees	0.013	0.016**	0.019*	0.038*	0.022***
Sales growth rate	0.031***	0.015**	0.015**	0.046***	0.019***
Operating Profit Margin	0.031	0.022*	0.032	0.025***	0.030***
Return on assets	0.014	0.035	0.018	−0.037	0.027**
Assets liability ratio	0.036	−0.059	−0.02	−0.054	−0.031
Current ratio	0.038*	−0.018*	0.035	0.105	0.052*
Asset turnover	−0.005	−0.002	−0.002	−0.006	−0.003
Added value ratio	0.005*	0.003	0.006*	0.001	0.01

Notes: *, **, *** refers to significance levels of 10%, 5%, and 1%, respectively.
Source: http://www.alio.go.kr/home.do (Accessed on October 15, 2020) (Lee *et al.*, 2018).

employment growth. As shown in the analysis results above, even after the control of sample selection bias through the PSM and DID methods as well as the integrated regression model, new credit guarantees generally have a positive effect on company employment and financial performance.

2.3 *Macroscopic Analysis of KODIT's Activities and Results*

For the macroscopic study, we selected a structural model of simultaneous equations and used domestic and international data to analyze the effect of credit guarantees on the national economy.

Estimation followed the general process of estimation of the individual behavioral equations → construction of a model and historical simulation (verification of predictability) → policy simulation (verification of stability) → estimation. Each of the explanatory variables used in estimation of the individual behavioral equations was constructed in a way to ensure that the results of the estimate are in agreement with the theory, and the model was constructed as a simultaneous equations model to ensure that individual behavioral equations interact with one another. Accordingly, the endogenous and exogenous variables of the model were defined and the values of the endogenous variables estimated using the Gauss–Siedel Method.

The analysis results of the macroeconomic effects of credit guarantees using the above estimation model are as follows. First, when the credit guarantees increased by KR₩1 trillion (US$0.9 billion), approximately KR₩308.2 billion (US$275.7 million) in added value was created in the entire economy from a long-term perspective. Each increase of KR₩100 million (US$89.4 thousand) in credit guarantees also equaled an increase of 0.4 persons in employment. Considering the employment maintenance effect amounts to 0.41 persons for each KR₩100 million (US$89.4 thousand) in guarantee support in a study by Noh *et al.* (2015), the total employment effect of a KR₩100 million (US$89.4 thousand) increase in the amount of guarantees can be estimated at 0.81 persons. In terms of financial additionality, the multiplier of M3 (total monetary aggregates) of credit guarantees was 3.08 in the short term and converged to 2.72 in the long term. Lastly, regarding tax revenue, an increase of KR₩100 million (US$89.4 thousand) in credit guarantees was estimated to increase tax revenue by approx. KR₩293.2 billion (US$262.3 million). In light of these findings, it is easy for us to conclude that increasing credit guarantees creates added value through supply of funds and expansion of investment and contributes significantly to the national economy by expanding employment and increasing tax revenue.

3. Change in KODIT's Role to Adapt to Changes in Environment

For over 40 years, KODIT has supported the financing of companies and worked towards stable growth of the national economy since its establishment in 1976. As mentioned above, the Korean economy is now faced with inclusive growth and the Fourth Industrial Revolution. Moving beyond its present role, which is the provision of guarantees for SMEs, KODIT is innovating its business structure to create an innovative ecosystem, build databanks and platforms, and spread social values. In this chapter, we will provide an introduction to KODIT's efforts and achievements in this area.

Table 5: KODIT's Changes and Major Tasks

(1) Creating an Innovative Ecosystem for SMEs and Startups	• Expanding support for innovative startups • Focusing support on future industries • Promoting direct financing
(2) Operating Databanks and Platforms based on Big Data	• Building databanks • Introducing a "Commercial payment index" • Launching a "Startup Planet" platform
(3) Spreading Social Values for Inclusive Growth	• Promoting the social economy • Strengthening job-oriented credit guarantee support • Providing new opportunities for failed companies
(4) Innovating Public Services through Adoption of Technological Advances	• Expanding untact (non-face-to-face) services • Going paperless

Source: https://www.kodit.co.kr/support/cust_plza/info_opn/info_opn_monthly.jsp (KODIT).

3.1 *Creating an Innovative Ecosystem for SMEs and Startups*

Today, the competitiveness of a country depends on how many companies with innovative ideas or technology can be discovered and developed. The United States, Germany, and many other advanced nations are focusing their efforts and resources on future industries and innovative new companies because they acknowledge that what they can achieve will shape their future. An innovative ecosystem that can support a company's smooth start and growth is essential. KODIT is focusing on creating an innovative ecosystem centered on SMEs and startups by providing various forms of financial and non-financial support and is committed to playing a unique part in expanding future growth engines for the Korean economy.

3.1.1 *Expanding support for innovative startups — quantitative expansion, qualitative results*

The direction of KODIT in this regard is clear — it aims to gradually increase the total amount of support, systematize its support system, and increase the quality of its support. For starters, KODIT plans to increase the amount of new credit guarantees for innovative startups on a step-by-step basis from approximately KRW420 billion (US$376 million) in 2018 to around KRW520 billion (US$465 million) in 2023.

KODIT also plans to ease its criteria for startup eligibility and embrace more innovative startups. Table 6 shows how companies are categorized to determine eligibility. KODIT will closely monitors new trends and changes, such as those included in the Fourth Industrial Revolution and the Eight Core Leading Industries designated by the government, to ensure that no business area is left out from innovative startup support.[6] In addition, it will lower the bar in terms of years in business to remain eligible from the current 3–5 years to 7 years after establishment to provide support for more companies to achieve stable growth.

Efforts to systematize its support programs more focus on the integration of the existing innovative startup support systems and their systematization by growth stage. A "Startup Support by Growth Stage" program is planned to provide support customized to the characteristics of individual companies, representatives, and businesses.

In addition to its effort to quantitatively expand its support, KODIT is also committed to improving the qualitative results of companies. The "Innovative Startup Selection and Development Program" is a follow-up support system that aims to help First Penguins[7] grow into unicorns.[8] The program will be implemented by selecting first penguins with a high potential for innovation and growth, and then 50 strong-but-small companies capable of growing into a valuation of over KRW100 billion (US$89.4 million) for special support. Also, 25 innovative startup

---

[6]The eight Core Leading Industries are smart factories, smart farms, Fintech, new renewable energy, smart cities, drones, future automobiles, and bio-health. ("Strategic Investment Direction for Innovation Growth" published by the concerned ministries, administrations, and agencies, August 2018)

[7]This refers to startups that take on present uncertainties and the challenge of pioneering into new markets with their ideas and knowledge, as the first penguin that jumps into the ocean takes the greatest risk.

[8]A unicorn company refers to a privately-held startup company valued at over US$1 billion within 10 years after establishment, coined in 2013 to represent the statistical difficulty of achieving such valuation before even going public.

Table 6:   Current Eligibility Criteria for Innovative Startup Support

Category	Examples
First Penguin companies	Highly competitive startups in manufacturing, new growth engine areas, or promising service areas
4.0 Startups	Companies with a history of 3 years or less and engaged in development of any of the 11 leading technologies of the Fourth Industrial Revolution
2030 Startups	Companies with a history of 3 years or less and engaged in technology, culture, content, software and mobile communications, etc.
Campus Startups	Companies classified as Promising Startups with a history of 5 years or less and mainly comprising professors, students, or other persons in academia
Spin-off Startups	Companies classified as Promising Startups with a history of 3 years or less and spun off from large corporations or research institutes
Job Creation Startups	Companies with a history of 3 years or less and engaged in new growth service areas or local specialty areas

Source: https://www.kodit.co.kr/work/crdt_guar/crdt_guar/crdt_gd/new_gd/fundpro01.jsp (KODIT).

companies will be selected as unicorns and receive focused support designed to develop them into global companies, which will include not only an increase in guarantee limit, but also priority support for investment and P-CBO guarantees, and support in conjunction with other specialized institutions.

3.1.2 *Focusing support on future new industries — encouraging the scale-up of innovative companies*

KODIT plans to introduce a special support system for companies that develop technology or provide services related to the Fourth Industrial Revolution or produce related products for all growth stages of a company, from R&D to commercialization to mass production, on the condition of success in the previous stage. This program, called "Future New Industry-Focused Support Program", originates from the Small Business Innovation Research (SBIR) program of the US Small Business

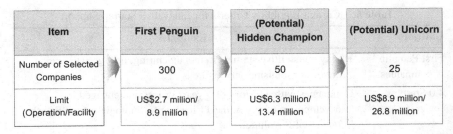

Item	First Penguin	(Potential) Hidden Champion	(Potential) Unicorn
Number of Selected Companies	300	50	25
Limit (Operation/Facility	US$2.7 million/ 8.9 million	US$6.3 million/ 13.4 million	US$8.9 million/ 26.8 million

Figure 1:   Support Program for Innovative Startups by Growth Stage

Note: "(Potential) Hidden champions" companies are those with potential to achieve a valuation of KR₩100 billion (US$89.4 million) or more, while "(Potential) Unicorn" companies are those with potential to achieve a valuation of KR₩1 trillion (US$0.9 billion) or more.

Source: https://www.kodit.co.kr/work/crdt_guar/crdt_guar/crdt_gd/new_gd/fundpro01.jsp (KODIT).

Administration combined with KODIT's startup platform and support system.[9] Companies selected for this program will be eligible for an increase in guarantee limit and for a screening process customized to each business stage, while companies considered in "Death Valley"[10] will be eligible for additional financial support based on the results of screening by the consultative group.

In 2017, KODIT launched "Startup NEST (New Expandability Startup Total platform)", a program designed to select promising startups and potential entrepreneurs in the areas of innovative growth and support them until they are ready for independent growth. Through this program, KODIT provided credit guarantees worth KR₩96 billion (US$86 million) and invested a total of KR₩6.5 billion (US$5.8 million) in 360 companies up to the first half of 2019, and also succeeded in attracting investment amounting to KR₩21 billion (US$18.8 million) from private

---

[9]The SBIR (Small Business Innovation Research) program is a US federal support program introduced in accordance with the Small Business Innovation Development Act of 1982. It is a large-scale program in which 11 government departments and agencies provide support valued at an aggregate amount of US$3 billion per annum. Specifically, this program sets three stages and an objective for each stage, and provides financial support in three installments, having effects similar to those of the staged financing in venture capital.

[10]This refers to a period during which a new company, even after R&D success, is first faced with the risk of bankruptcy due to a failure to attract funding.

venture capital companies. On the other hand, the Innovative Icon 50 Project, launched in 2019, is a program that helps innovative startups grow into unicorn companies able to lead the national economy. An innovative company that has just passed Death Valley but is still taking its first steps requires quick and bold financing to move to the next stage. The purpose of the Innovative Icon 50 Project is to provide sufficient funding, up to KR₩7 billion (US$6.3 million), and other various forms of customized non-financial support to a selected group of such innovative companies. KODIT selected six companies for this program in July 2019 and plans to select a total of 50 companies by 2023. These companies will receive financial and related service support, such as through introduction of new investors and customers, as well as consulting services, which will help them grow into global unicorns.

3.1.3 *Promoting direct financing — serving as private investment facilitator*

KODIT is strengthening its role not only in the indirect financing market, where SMEs obtain financing from financial institutions, but also in the direct financing market to facilitate private investment. As part of this effort, KODIT plans to diversify the methods and targets of its P-CBO guarantees and increase policy-directed investment with a view to promoting private investment. The first step is to expand the scope of its existing P-CBO guarantees. KODIT plans to increase the percentage of prioritized customers, including hidden champions, in the total amount of P-CBO guarantees provided on a phased basis, and will launch new credit guarantees to offer more diversified P-CBO guarantee options, including "Securitization for Mutual Growth of Large Corporations and SMEs", in which large corporations would purchase subordinated debt or share risk by contributing securitization funds, and "Securitization for Project Financing", in which future cash flows would be treated as collateral.

An expansion of policy investment to facilitate private investment is also planned. Internally, the related procedures and processes will be streamlined for more expeditious provision of investment and financing

Classification	Yr2019	Yr2020	Yr2021	Yr2022	Yr2023
Prioritized Customer	25.0%	30.0% (+5%p)	35.0% (+5%p)	37.5% (+2.5%p)	40.0% (+2.5%p)
General SMEs	75.0%	70.0% (Δ5%p)	65.0% (Δ5%p)	30.0% (Δ2.5%p)	30.0% (Δ2.5%p)

Figure 2: P-CBO Guarantee Portfolio for the Next Five Years (Draft)

Note: Prioritized customer groups: Mid-sized companies, potential mid-sized companies, hidden champions with growth potential.

Source: https://www.kodit.co.kr/support/cust_plza/info_opn/info_opn_monthly.jsp (KODIT).

convergence programs. In the case of guarantee-aligned equity investment,[11] the currently separate inquiry and screening processes for investment and guarantees will be integrated so that credit guarantee and guarantee-aligned equity investment may be offered as a single package to certain innovative startup companies, such as First Penguins and those selected for Startup NEST. As for the guarantee with investment option,[12] the application process for innovative startups will be simplified and the bar for application will also be lowered.

3.2 *Managing Databank and Platform Based on Big Data*

KODIT seeks to contribute to spreading the value of data by expanding the credit information market centered on personal information through the sharing of corporate data. Its aim is to change and diversify the current corporate data, mostly consisting of personal, fixed, and static forms of data into a form that is more business-focused, flexible, and dynamic. This kind of data is generally difficult to collect and measure, but KODIT already has access to Big Data from over 210,000 companies collected by its 109 branch offices nationwide. This data is also considered very reliable as it includes not only publicly disclosed corporate data but also

---

[11] This is a system to purchase securities issued by companies in connection with credit guarantees to support the company's financing and improve its financial structure.

[12] A financial instrument combining both investment and financing in which a guarantee is issued and a conversion option attached, which can be exercised according to the business performance of the company.

actual field survey results. KODIT is taking advantage of such Big Data to position itself as the hub for the corporate data market.

3.2.1 *Building databank — collecting and providing differentiated data*

In general, quantitative information from SMEs, such as their financial information, tends to be less reliable than that from large corporations, and there is very limited access to information reliable enough for financial institutions. Such information asymmetry disturbs high growth potential SMEs in their obtaining funds. Databank will basically perform the public role of relieving such information asymmetry by providing raw data produced by KODIT to the private sector, including the Credit Bureau. As a balanced sharing of roles with the private sector will be most important for such a databank, KODIT is focusing its efforts on creating a virtuous circle that benefits all participants, including DBs, banks, and companies, in pursuing the databank building project.

Databank is expected to bring about various changes to KODIT both internally and externally. First of all, the convergence between existing credit investigation and screening capabilities and external data will enable a more accurate and precise assessment and diversify assessment methods. Follow-up management practices based on dynamic data can directly contribute to the reduction of risk. For example, data related to production, sales, and personnel management (e.g., electricity, communications, and water usage data, and the four mandatory insurances) can be analyzed and then used to select abnormal companies for closer monitoring. Development of new products using Big Data will also be easier. The databank will make it possible for KODIT staff to approve the application for credit guarantees right after they conduct a non-face-to-face simplified screening using Big Data. Databank can be used to improve customer service processes as well. For example, early warning alarms can be provided to credit insurance policyholders to prevent exposure to additional risk, and the customer relations management process can be reformed so that it is based on data, which will make it easier to provide services more customized to individual customers.

3.2.2 *Commercial payment index — utilizing commercial big data*

KODIT is planning to develop a Commercial payment index (similar to PAYDEX[13]) as one of the means to utilize databanks. It is being conceived as a system in which KODIT would provide B2B commercial transaction data to CBs in the private sector, who would then combine it with other underlying data that it owns, such as on credit card transactions and telecom bill payments, to create an index. This index will provide a simplified way to evaluate a company's future risk levels and trading limits. KODIT expects this will lead to transparent commercial transactions between businesses and replace the current complex face-to-face procedures required for loans and investments from financial institutions and government bids and certifications.

3.2.3 *Innovating startup platform "startup planet" — a data hub for innovative startups*

KODIT will also actively use its Big Data to support innovative startup companies. An online platform to be called "Startup Planet" is one way this will be done. KODIT envisages the platform as a space where every participant in the innovative startup ecosystem can easily find the information it needs and communicate, interact, and cooperate with other participants. The underlying system will be designed to enable the realization of all services related to starting a business within the platform, including the building of a Big Data ecosystem, information exchange, networking, financing, and investment matching. The ultimate goal is to make the platform a center for networking, where every institution and innovative startup in every sector can communicate and cooperate with each other.

The primary role of Startup Planet will be to reduce information asymmetry in the ecosystem, as it will be a data hub that collects, verifies,

---

[13] PAYDEX is a score first developed by the US company Dun & Bradstreet and is based on collected commercial transaction and payment data as a way of overcoming the limitations of credit ratings based on past financial scores. PAYDEX provides a variety of information, including total extended credit, based on payment behavior data for trade payables.

and provides information on innovative startup companies. The accumulated Big Data can be used to search for and recommend qualified innovative startups as well as provide investment-matching services for private investors. In addition, being an online platform with startup specialized institutions, policy institutions, accelerators, and venture capital companies, Startup Planet will enable more efficient management of joint development programs such as Startup NEST. Startup Planet will be launched at the end of March, 2020.

3.3 *Spreading Social Values for Inclusive Growth*

Over the past decades, the Republic of Korea's economy has grown rapidly and relentlessly. In 2017, its per-capita GNI (gross national income) exceeded US$30,000, and the nation became the seventh to join the "30–50 Club",[14] which is seen as a group of advanced countries. The Republic of Korea's per-capita GNI has increased nearly 500 times since 1953, and the nation has become the world's 12th largest economy and 6th largest in terms of exports. However, concerns are growing that the Korean economy now faces significant challenges. The "trickle-down effect", which thus far has guided the government's actions towards economic development, does not seem to work anymore, resulting in intensifying polarization and increasing income concentration.[15] The limits of structural low growth have been imposed upon the Republic of Korea. Its actual and potential GDP growth has continued to decline. Low growth, polarization, and employment insecurity have become the greatest threats to the Korean economy.

To overcome such obstacles, the government has presented "inclusive growth" as a new development model for the Republic of Korea. The spread of social values is essential for the Korean government to realize the people-centered and job creation-oriented inclusive growth model. Social values can be defined as those values that can contribute to the

---

[14] Used to describe countries whose per-capita GNI passes US$30,000 and whose populations pass 50 million. Republic of Korea's entry follows that of Japan, the United States, the UK, Germany, France, and Italy.

[15] Republic of Korea's income concentration is known to have increased most rapidly among OECD member states in the 20 years between 1996 and 2016.

public interest and community development in all areas, including society, economy, environment, and culture (The ROK Government, 2018a). A global movement to realize and spread these social values already exists, seeking to overcome the structural problems of the economy and achieve sustainable growth.[16] KODIT has created an environment in which social values are regarded as essential principles in managing its organizations and is putting a variety of plans in action to spread those principles.

3.3.1 *Promoting the social economy — serving as a pipeline for Republic of Korea's social finance*

Governments around the world are paying attention to the concept of the social economy as it is known to create quality jobs and relieve social polarization. In the European countries and other advanced ones, the social economy serves as an important axis of the economy and complements both the public sector and the market economy. Indeed, the social economy is a key factor in inclusive growth as it can provide solutions to many economic and social problems while improving market economy efficiency. The Government of the Republic of Korea is also taking it seriously (The ROK Government, 2017a; 2018b).

As financial support for social enterprises has increased, so has the need for an evaluation system reflecting their characteristics. Traditional evaluation systems based on financial performance cannot properly reflect the social values created by social enterprises. There is also a problem of subjectivity as social values are difficult to quantify for assessment. To resolve these and other problems, KODIT began developing a new evaluation system for social enterprises in August of 2018, which was one of the joint missions of the Social Finance Council.[17]

---

[16] Examples include the EU's CSR Procurement Guidelines, Germany's Restriction of Competition Law, the UK's Social Value Act, the US' SDGs (Sustainable Development Goals), and ISO26000.

[17] The Social Finance Council was established in April 2018 to promote cooperation among institutions concerned with social finance and has 17 member institutions, including KODIT, the Korean SMEs and Startups Agency and Credit Union.

Table 7:   KODIT's Plan to Provide Financial Support for Social Enterprises

(Unit: US$million)

Classification	yr2018		yr2019	yr2020	yr2021	yr2022	Total
	Plan	Result					
General Guarantee Provision	80.5	96.3	80.5	80.5	80.5	80.5	402.5

Source: https://www.kodit.co.kr/support/cust_plza/info_opn/info_opn_monthly.jsp (KODIT).

As KODIT had in mind the potential to develop into a web-based platform capable of being shared with other institutions in developing this evaluation system, it invited various institutions and stakeholders to participate from the early development stage to improve reliability and universality. KODIT's objective was to create a virtuous circle in which evaluation data is accumulated by various participants, with such accumulated data contributing to sophistication of the evaluation model. Developed in this way, the system can be used not only in evaluating individual companies but also in joint screening and support of urban regeneration, social housing supply, and other social and economic projects through cooperation with local governments.

3.3.2 *Strengthening jobs creation-centered credit guarantee support — adopting assessment for job creation capability*

In November 2018, KODIT implemented the Job Creation Capability Assessment System designed to provide preferential benefit to businesses where there is great ability to create jobs. This system assesses job creation potential and maintenance capability of companies, dividing them into groups based on assessment outcomes, and applies differentiated guarantee limits, approval decision by authority (who makes final approval decision on guarantee provision), and screening methods for each group. Under this assessment system, companies able to create jobs can receive more incentives even if their credit rating is somewhat low. More credit guarantees are also more easily and more promptly available to such companies than previously. Currently, the job creation capability assessment system applies only to those companies classified into the "New Growth Engine Industry" and "Promising Services", but it will

Table 8:   Job Creation Capability Assessment Items

Category		Assessment Items
Quantitative Index	Job Creation	▪ Number of full-time employees, increase in full-time employees (number), employment growth rate, growth potential (growth of sales and total assets)
	Job Maintenance	▪ Profitability (operating profit margin), future growth potential, employment maintenance rate, turnover rate
Qualitative Index	Job Quality	▪ Average monthly wage, duration of business, average length of service, percentage of full-time employees, balance between work and family, welfare benefits

Source: https://www.kodit.co.kr/work/crdt_guar/crdt_guar/crdt_gd/new_gd/fundpro01.jsp (KODIT).

apply to all companies and industries in the long run. KODIT expects that the new job creation capability assessment system will contribute to both quantitative increase and qualitative growth in jobs.

3.3.3 *Helping SMEs re-challenge and retry — creating an environment where failure becomes an asset*

The "SME Value-up Program" implemented by KODIT in May of 2019 provides relief to SMEs facing temporary financial difficulties. The purpose of the program is to help SMEs with growth potential avoid financial insolvency and recover from financial failure. Companies eligible for this program can save on guarantee fees and interest expenses on loans through an agreement with a creditor bank and quickly receive new financing for normalization of their business. In addition, consulting services provided by external consultants will allow for systematic management consultations, establishment and implementation of management improvement plans, and regaining market competitiveness.

KODIT's plan is to provide KR₩15 billion (US$13.4 million) in financial support to 60 companies in 2019 and KR₩200 billion (US$179 million) in financial support to a total of 520 companies by 2023 under the SME Value-up Program. KODIT expects that many businesses in the support "blind spot" but with high growth potential and social contributions will benefit.

Table 9: SME Value-up Program Overview

Details of Support	Required Procedures
• Free specialized consulting services (Worth KR₩4 million – 10 million: US$3.6 k – 8.9 k)	• Preparation of a business improvement plan * Sales, financial structure, self-help efforts, etc.
• Provision of new credit guarantees and rollover of the full amount of an existing guarantee	• Contract of a special agreement for implementation of a business improvement plan
• Discounted guarantee fee rate (max. 1.0%) • Discounted credit insurance premium (10%discount)	• Submission of a plan to use funds and a report on their use

*Total program duration is 4 years (3 years + 1 year (extension)).
Source: https://www.kodit.co.kr/work/crdt_guar/crdt_guar/support/support01.jsp (KODIT).

Table 10: SME Value-up Program Overview

Item	Guarantee for Restarting Businesses	Guarantee for Re-challenging Businesses	Guarantee for Businesses Discharged from Bankruptcy
Subject	Multiple Debtors	Debtor to KODIT alone	Persons discharged from debts publicly and privately
Method	Joint guarantee by institutions	KODIT's own support program	KODIT's own guarantee program
Support Provided (No. of companies, amount)	Yr 2017 (108, KR₩ 3.7 billion – US$3.3 million) Yr 2018 (135, KR₩5.6 billion – US$5.0 million)	Yr 2017 (114, KR₩ 10.4 billion – US$9.3 million) Yr 2018 (136, KR₩13.4 billion – US$12.0 million)	Yr 2017 (19, KR₩2.5 billion – US$2.2 million) Yr 2018 (54, KR₩ 5.9 billion – US$5.3 million)

Source: https://www.kodit.co.kr/work/crdt_guar/crdt_guar/support/support01.jsp (KODIT).

KODIT operates this "Trying Again after Failure Program" to create an environment where "Unfortunate Failure with Intention of Re-challenge" is accepted and forgiven and bold debt adjustment and easily-accessible new financing support is provided. This program will select targets in comprehensive consideration of entrepreneurship (including avoiding moral hazard) and the possibility of overcoming the failure and business competitiveness, with support focused on relieving burdens resulting from failure. It helps selected companies recover and restart through both financial and non-financial support, including debt adjustment, sufficient financing, and management consulting.

3.4 *Innovating Technology-based Public Services*

KODIT is committed to improving the quality of its public services, as well as productivity and work efficiency through the convergence of innovative technology and business. What follows are a few examples of these changes.

3.4.1 *Non-face-to-face services — expanding non-visit business processes*

KODIT also implements a credit insurance service that compensates for losses incurred when a company fails to collect its receivables. To take out a credit insurance policy, in general, a person representing the company must visit a KODIT branch office and the company applying for subscription must pass KODIT screening. To make the process simpler and more accessible, an "Online Credit Insurance" was introduced in January 2019. All customers need to do is enter their information on KODIT's website, after which the system will automatically conduct a non-face-to-face screening.

The credit guarantee service, which accounts for the biggest portion of KODIT's business, is adopting the non-face-to-face process as well. As a guarantee is usually issued for a term of one year, a customer who wishes to continue to use a guarantee for a longer period needs to visit a KODIT branch office to extend the term. However, from July 2019, all privately-owned companies are allowed to extend the maturity of their credit guarantees through a telephone screening process (recording required), without a visit. This change has had the dual effect of improving customer convenience and relieving the KODIT employee workload. KODIT is now considering expanding the non-visit rollover policy to incorporated companies and providing other access options, such as via the web or mobile. Such changes are expected to provide customers the ability to extend the maturity of their guarantees more easily and conveniently and allow them to manage their funds in a more planned manner.

The "One-Point Management Clinic" is KODIT's non-face-to-face online-based consulting service for businesses. When a customer registers an inquiry on KODIT's consulting platform, professional consultants for the relevant field send an answer by email, and KODIT pays a fee to the professional consultant whose answer is selected. This way, customers can receive quick and quality answers to simple questions without wasting time and money.

3.4.2 *Paperless KODIT — The goal of zero paper environment*

KODIT is going paperless through automation and digitization of its processes and procedures required to be completed by customers. "Simplification of required documents and procedures" has been one of the top agenda items in annual customer satisfaction surveys for some years.[18] In fact, KODIT has been working to minimize the number of documents for a long time. In 2001, KODIT set out to digitize its forms and documents, including, but not limited to, the application form for letters of guarantees, and financial transaction certificates, under agreements with financial institutions, and began to collect real estate and commercial registry information in electronic form in 2002. In 2003, KODIT established a system for submitting corporate financial information online, and in 2006, it became the first financial institution to collect various forms of administrative information from customers online in connection with the

---

[18] In the customer satisfaction survey for the second half of 2018, customer complaints and suggestions were made most for the "expansion of guarantee support (20.1%)" followed by the "simplification of required documents and procedures (14.5%)" and by "lessening of the burden, such as the guarantee fee (14.5%)".

government's administrative information network. Customer-submitted data and materials have continued to be replaced by electronic forms, and recent technological advances are expected to simplify even more the methods and procedures for data collection. At present, most required documents are collected by KODIT employees after informed customer consent. In the future, however, KODIT's computer systems will be linked to those of other institutions and companies so that such documents can be collected automatically. Only those documents that cannot be automatically collected for unavoidable reasons will be collected electronically by KODIT employees, meaning that most customers will not have to submit any paper documents at all.

KODIT will implement a system that enables direct online transmission of such collected documents to electronic files without having to print them on paper. To be more specific, KODIT plans to create a work environment where e-books are automatically generated upon collection of data according to the order of standardization, with the electronic files stored in the cloud for viewing at any time, wherever you are. This change will greatly improve customer convenience while significantly reducing the costly space for storage of paper documents. In addition, KODIT's current audits, which require visits to branch offices and review of paper documents, will be replaced by online audits, which will undoubtedly contribute to improving audit efficiency and accuracy.

4. KODIT's Efforts to Manage Enterprise Risk

As reviewed above, KODIT is undergoing significant changes. It is worth noting that the Government of the Republic of Korea recently decided to abolish the joint surety requirement for new credit guarantees to create a business environment for startups. Although such a change is basically desirable, it is expected to significantly affect the business environment of guarantee institutions and their exposure to credit risk. KODIT may also be exposed to more risk. In this section, we will look into how KODIT is responding to the possibility of increased risk exposure following such environmental changes.

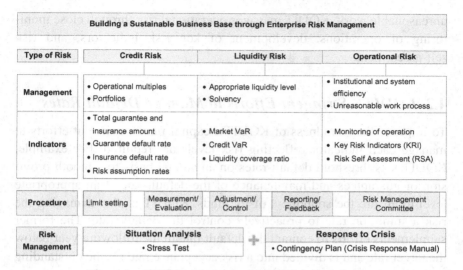

Figure 3: KODIT's Enterprise Risk Management System

Source: KODIT's Annual Report, https://www.kodit.co.kr (KODIT, 2019a. The annual report 2018.).

4.1 *Proactive and Enterprise Risk Management based on Systems*

KODIT divides risks into credit risks, liquidity risks, and operational risks, and runs an Enterprise Risk Management (ERM) system to maximize its ability to respond to crises.

Credit risk is related to operational multiples and credit guarantee portfolios. Indicators such as the total guarantee and insurance amounts, guarantee default rate, insurance default rate, and risk acceptance rate[19] are set to manage credit risk. Liquidity risk is related to the appropriate level of liquidity and solvency and managed by indicators such as Market VaR (Value at Risk), Credit VaR, and liquidity coverage ratio.[20] Operational risk is attributable to the efficiency of institutions and systems as well as

---

[19] An indicator of potential default rate, calculated by weighted averaging of default probability by credit rating by guarantee amount.

[20] The ratio of income (contributions, guarantee fees, collection of reimbursements, liquidity) to cover expenditures (subrogation, administrative expenses) over the next year.

unreasonable work. KODIT manages operational risk through close monitoring of operations, development of key risk indicators, and risk self-assessment.

4.2 *KODIT's Stringent Efforts to Manage Default Rates*

To improve the soundness of KODIT's capital funds, stringent efforts to manage each indicator reflecting risk levels are required. For example, KODIT sets threshold default rates on an annual basis for smooth provision of guarantees and maintenance of the default rate at an appropriate level to ensure the soundness of its funds. KODIT is also managing the risk assumption rate to proactively control the default rate. The former supplements efforts to contain the default rate in the following year below the target rate and is divided into a risk acceptance rate for the outstanding credit guarantees and a risk acceptance rate for new credit guarantees. Such threshold rates and target rates are managed in a variety of ways. For example, Table 11 shows the simultaneous management of both causes

Table 11:   KODIT's Various Means of Managing Default Rate

Category	Description	Effect
Portfolio Management	• Analysis of outstanding amounts and default rates by segment	• Alleviation of concentration risk
Default Management	• Efforts to eliminate default causes	• Reduction of defaults, rehabilitation of companies
Assessment of guarantee soundness	• Evaluation of individual tendency of treating guarantees	• Securing the soundness of new guarantees
Risk Agreement	• Assessment of the impact of a risk when introducing or changing a system	• Proactive control of systems
Default Analysis	• Analysis of trends and causes for default within 6 months from the date of provision or default of large amount of guarantees	• Development of ideas to reduce defaults

Source: KODIT's Annual Report, https://www.kodit.co.kr (KODIT 2019a. The annual report 2018.).

and quality level of defaults by controlling various factors, including concentration by segment, cause of default, individual tendency regarding guarantees, and introduction of new systems.

Despite the increase in credit guarantees provided to relatively risky areas, including startups and social enterprises, and repeal of the joint surety on guarantees, KODIT's stringent target-rate-setting and various management efforts have proven effective. As a result, its guarantee default rate as of the end of June 2019 remains at around 3.6%. This rate is the lowest in the past 20 years and all the more remarkable given the worsening internal and external economic situations.

4.3 *Management of Operational Multiple*

From an economic perspective, the operating multiple is an indicator to measure the additional guarantee capacity at present, and KODIT's determination of the proper operational multiple and actual management thereof is an important issue in the SME funds market. Article 25 of the Credit Guarantee Fund Act provides that the operational multiple shall not exceed 20 times. This is a statutory rule and, as such, must be abided by KODIT. The 20-times ceiling, however, is for exceptional situations rather than normal, and KODIT set and managed the operational multiple at 12.5 times in 2019, which was up from the previous year's 11.8 times as a result of the government's policy to increase the supply of guarantees towards revitalizing the economy and supporting innovative growth.[21] The operational multiple of 12.5 times is based on the Bank for International Settlements (BIS) minimum capital requirement and is the operational multiple when the percentage of the underlying assets is 8% of the outstanding credit guarantees. This is close to the highest multiple KODIT would set in normal circumstances (KODIT, 2019b).

---

[21] The operating multiple of 12.5 times is the multiple for general guarantees. The operating multiple is 9 times for SPC guarantees and 7.3 times for industrial support guarantees (these three types of guarantees will be collectively referred to as "aggregate guarantees").

4.4 *Management and Optimization of Risk Assessment and Management System*

KODIT intends to thoroughly manage risk from the credit rating stage by developing and operating its own system for evaluation and measurement of risk. For measurement of the credit risk of individual companies, it developed and continues to upgrade a credit rating system customized for evaluation of SMEs.

KODIT was the first in the Republic of Korea to develop a Corporate Credit Rating System (CCRS) in 2001 and introduced a Startup Business Scoring System (SBSS) in 2007. An Automatic Rating System (ARS) KODIT introduced in 2009 greatly simplified its credit check and screening process. In 2013, a Credit Insurance Rating System (CIRS) was added and is used for credit insurance. In January of 2018, KODIT conducted an overhaul of its credit rating system with the purpose of strengthening support for startups and improving its capabilities of

Table 12: Risk Assessment and Management System

Category		Function	Application
Proactive Risk Management	Credit rating system	• Determination of credit rating based on default probability (15 ratings: KR1 – 15) • Current system introduced in January 2018	• Credit assessment of startups (7 years or less since startup) • Credit assessment of general companies (more than 7 years beyond startup) • Credit insurance assessment
	Future growth potential assessment system	• Valuation of corporate assets, technology and intellectual properties (10 ratings) for guarantee support focused on growth potential	• Firm valuation (FV1 – 10) • Technology property valuation (TR1 – 10) • Intellectual property valuation (GR1 – 10)
Post Risk Management	Management default data	• Analysis of data related to defaults for early detection of default signs	• Default risk alarm system • Credit information change provision system

Source: KODIT's Annual Report, https://www.kodit.co.kr (KODIT).

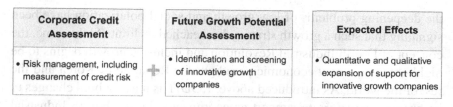

Corporate Credit Assessment		Future Growth Potential Assessment		Expected Effects
• Risk management, including measurement of credit risk	+	• Identification and screening of innovative growth companies		• Quantitative and qualitative expansion of support for innovative growth companies

Figure 4:   Utilization Plans for New Future Growth Potential Assessment System

Source: KODIT's Annual Report, https://www.kodit.co.kr.

identifying defaults. This revised system finally became more precise with recent default trend information and the latest assessment techniques added to each credit rating system (CCRS, SBSS, and CIRS). After the application of a new credit rating system named KODIT Rating System (KRS), the names of each sub-model were changed to KRW-C (for general companies), KRS-S (for startups), and KRS-I (for insurance), respectively.

Another evaluation system, the Future Growth Potential Assessment System, is a tool for evaluating the future value of a company. Its purpose is to identify and evaluate growth factors that lead to potential future performance. In late 2019, a new Future Growth Potential Assessment System was introduced with advanced assessment of innovative growth factors such as technology, Ips, business models and content, and improved future value predictability and model utilization. This system is expected to contribute to expansion of the guarantee support for technology-based and knowledge-based startups.

5. New Future of Public Policy Financing and Its Challenges

5.1 *Current Challenges of KODIT*

The Republic of Korea experienced rapid economic growth from the early 1970s to the late 1990s, when it suffered the Asian Financial Crisis, which significantly changed the structure of the Korean economy. During the period of rapid growth, Republic of Korea achieved fast economic growth by imitating the advanced technology of developed countries, but recently the deepening problems of low growth and social polarization have been signaling that such a growth strategy has reached its limit. At this time, the concept of Fourth Industrial Revolution and inclusive growth begins to be highlighted as a new economic paradigm for Republic of Korea and the rest of the world. As introduced above, KODIT is making bold changes to its business structure to support areas impacted by the Fourth Industrial Revolution and inclusive growth as one of the pillars of Republic of Korea's policy-directed financing. In addition to its existing role of providing guarantee support for SMEs, KODIT is expanding into the creation of an innovative ecosystem, as SMEs business environment and a source databank of digital corporate information, and taking the lead in spreading social values. The direction of such change is clear — restoring the public nature of credit guarantees and shifting the economic paradigm towards innovative growth.

KODIT's internal environment, however, is not very conducive for such change. It has insufficient authority to expand its original areas of business, which restrains its autonomous operation. In fact, every KODIT activity, including those related to budgeting, personnel management, organizational structure, and business operations, are strictly governed by the Credit Guarantee Fund Act and the Act on the Management of Public Institutions and other relevant laws as well as government directives. Also, as multiple government ministries and agencies have authority to control KODIT management, supervision, and budget, this might put its management efficiency at risk.[22] Its system to quickly reflect the needs of the market, collaborate with other organizations, and initiate new projects needs further development. Such limitations inevitably weaken KODIT's ability to respond to rapid environmental changes because, in order for it to plan and initiate a new project, complex procedures are required such as obtaining approvals from various competent government agencies and the National Assembly or even amending the law. KODIT is not, however, passively accepting such limits as inherent to a policy financial institution.

---

[22] The Financial Services Commission has the authority to approve and supervise KODIT's business plans and implementations, the Ministry of Economy and Finance has the authority to approve the budget and evaluates business performances, while the Ministry of SMEs and Startups manages government contributions to KODIT.

Whenever it deems necessary, it collects data and opinions necessary to justify a new project and actively works to persuade the government to sufficiently reflect the new project in government policy.

KODIT's current business structure, still centered on the credit guarantee for bank loans, is also a limitation. Although it has developed various new financial products and programs to support startup companies and innovative SMEs, they have never gone beyond the business area of credit guarantee for bank loans. Innovative new convergence financing programs, such as the guarantee-aligned equity investment program and guarantee with investment option program, have yet to show satisfactory results due to institutional and legal limits.[23] It is encouraging, however, that with the first penguin support program and Startup NEST, KODIT is successfully enhancing its prestige and boosting its image to one of being an institution dedicated to providing support to startups.

As shown above, KODIT is expanding support for high-risk sectors such as startups and social enterprises which often have difficulty receiving support in the private sector due to high information asymmetry. This suggests that while KODIT is certainly a public institution that should pursue the public interest, it is also a financial institution that needs to properly manage its risks. Although KODIT is a policy financial institution that provides financial services on behalf of the government, which are difficult for the private sector to provide due to the risk to profitability, if it does not manage its risks properly, defaults on guarantees will increase and become a huge burden on government finances. Hence, the effort to find a proper balance between public interest and profitability. Of course, KODIT has 40 years' experience with managing its funds stably and providing credit rating services for SMEs. There is a saying that "risk management involves risk", which means that risk management comes with a cost, and there is no complete and perfect "risk management" regardless of how much effort and money is invested. In this rapidly-changing financial and economic environment, what we need is the attitude of constant preparedness for any possibility, however small.

---

[23] In 2018 alone, KODIT provided guarantee-linked investments totaling KR₩39.4 billion (US$35.2 million) to 61 companies, and totaling KR₩69.2 billion (US$61.9 million) to 158 companies.

5.2 SMEs and the Future of Public Policy Financing

Ever since Schumpeter (1934) argued the importance of innovation, scholars around the world have studied the ideal conditions for innovation to occur. Among other issues, adequate supply of funding has been discussed by scholars for a long time. Schumpeter argued that funding is a necessary condition for corporate innovation, and that providing credit is the most fundamental role of the banking system (Lee, 2015). A company cannot grow unless it is provided with an appropriate amount of funding. A company that does not grow does not create jobs or provide income or tax revenue. In practice, companies are having difficulty procuring the funding they need for innovation. Where financing from the capital market is the principal means of financing, such as in the US or the UK, companies use their surplus funds or borrow from a third party such as a venture capital company rather than banks. On the other hand, in Germany and France, where bank-oriented loans are widely used, banks take the place of venture capitals. In such cases, banks can obtain information and reduce monitoring costs by taking advantage of their close relationship with companies.

According to the "credit rationing" theory (Stiglitz and Weiss, 1981), even when the market is in equilibrium, banks tend to present strict conditions on loans due to information asymmetry, making it harder for low rated companies and SMEs to take out loans or be eligible for low interest rates. In short, when there is excess demand for funds, credit allocation causes less funding to be supplied than the amount of funds that achieve a balance in the lending market due to information asymmetry between the fund provider and consumer (Rhee, 2018). As a result, SMEs are left more vulnerable to financial risks. If the market suffers an external shock or lenders otherwise become more risk-averse, the supply of funds from venture capitals and banks can be significantly reduced.

SMEs and, in particular, the recently increasing number of joint venture companies and startups face greater uncertainty and information asymmetry due to their untested technology and feasibility. As such, they are at a disadvantage when it comes to resource allocation in the private sector. For SMEs that do not have access to the financial market or have weak negotiating hands because of the nonexistence of or a lower credit rating and are thus exposed to the risk of unfavorable financial conditions, the government needs to provide policy support to ensure their access to funds and to the financial market (Lee, 2018).

Public policy financing institutions, such as KODIT, are especially useful for companies that have difficulty obtaining financing from the private sector. The role of public policy financing is essential for the Fourth Industrial Revolution and inclusive growth as they are based on startup and SME innovation. While various forms of policy backing are important to promote technological innovation, it is financial support that is vital. While government intervention in the market can be justified in the event of a market failure due to information asymmetry, there are mixed opinions as to the efficiency of such intervention. From this perspective, the desirable role of the government is to create a framework to facilitate proper functioning of the market so that autonomous financial support in the private sector becomes possible and is encouraged.

KODIT puts great emphasis on such basic principles. Particularly, it is increasing support for startups and social enterprises having difficulty obtaining private funding, and is focusing on creation of infrastructure to eliminate information asymmetry in SME banking through data utilization and openness. These efforts require the participation and cooperation of the private sector. KODIT exists to efficiently provide funding to SMEs while minimizing conflict with the private sector. We hope that the cases and practices of KODIT presented in this chapter will help improve SME access to financing in Asia and with achieving the overarching goals of supporting innovating SMEs and finding new growth engines.

References

Cheong WaDae. 2018. The Collection of Speeches of President Jae-In Moon, Vol. 1.

Kang, B.-J. 2018. Tasks of administrative service innovation in the fourth industrial revolution era. *The Journal of Policy Development*, 18(1): 159–193.

KODIT 2019a. The annual report for 2018.

KODIT 2019b. The basic plan for risk management for 2019.

Lee, I.-H. 2015. Korea's financial policy to support technological innovation and the venture capital industry. KIF Working Paper 15-09, Korea Institute of Finance.

Lee, Y.-C. and J.-H. Baek. 2018. The calculation of operating multiples for credit guarantee. The Industry-Academia Cooperation Group of the Gyeongju Campus of Dongguk University.

Lee, Y.-C., S.-J. Kwon, J.-H. Baek, and G.-M. An. 2018. An analysis of results of credit guarantees and ideas for increasing KODIT's social value. The Industry-Academia Cooperation Group of the Gyeongju Campus of Dongguk University.

Noh, Y.-H., C.-S. Song, and S.-C. Hong. 2015. An analysis of the results of credit guarantees and establishment of a proper reflux system. The Korean Association of Small Business Studies.

Oh J.-S., S.-W. Hong, and D.-Y. Kang. 2018. Reduced impact of Export on Korea's Economic Growth, Export multiplier approach. The review of social & economic studies 56. Korean association for political economy.

Rhee, C.-O. 2018. Systemic risk, SMEs' government-supported financing for inclusive growth and the limit of monetary policy. *Asia Pacific Journal of Small Business*, 40(4): 95–116.

State Affairs Planning Advisory Committee. 2017. The five-year plan for state affairs management of the moon administration. *National Challenge Reporting Assembly* (July 2017).

Stiglitz, J.E. and A. Weiss. 1981. Credit rationing in markets with imperfect information. *The American Economic Review*, 393–410.

The ROK Government. 2017a. A plan for promotion of the social economy. *The 3rd Presidential Committee on Jobs* (October 2017).

The ROK Government. 2017b. A strategy for building hyper-connected intelligent network for the fourth industrial revolution. *The Fourth Industrial Revolution Committee* (December 2017).

The ROK Government 2018a. The comprehensive implementation plan for government innovation. *The First Government Innovation Strategy Meeting* (March 2018).

The ROK Government. 2018b. A plan for promotion of the social economy. *State Affairs Current Issue Inspection and Adjustment Meeting* (February 2018).

Printed in the United States
by Baker & Taylor Publisher Services

Printed in the United States
by Baker & Taylor Publisher Services